Loveless Volume 6
Created by Yun Kouga

Translation - Ray Yoshimoto
English Adaptation - Christine Boylan
Retouch and Lettering - Star Print Brokers
Production Artist - Vicente Rivera, Jr. & Michael Paolilli
Graphic Designer - Monalisa De Asis

Editor - Lillian Diaz-Przybyl
Digital Imaging Manager - Chris Buford
Pre-Production Supervisor - Erika Terriquez
Art Director - Anne Marie Horne
Production Manager - Elisabeth Brizzi
Managing Editor - Vy Nguyen
VP of Production - Ron Klamert
Editor-in-Chief - Rob Tokar
Publisher - Mike Kiley
President and C.O.O. - John Parker
C.E.O. and Chief Creative Officer - Stuart Levy

A **TOKYOPOP** Manga

TOKYOPOP Inc.
5900 Wilshire Blvd. Suite 2000
Los Angeles, CA 90036

E-mail: info@TOKYOPOP.com
Come visit us online at www.TOKYOPOP.com

ISBN: 978-1-59816-864-8
First TOKYOPOP printing: August 2007
10 9 8 7 6
Printed in the USA

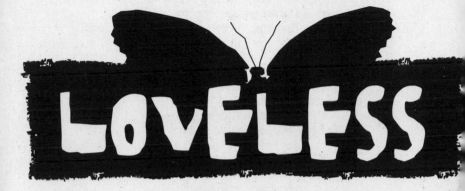

Volume 6

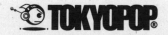

HAMBURG // LONDON // LOS ANGELES // TOKYO

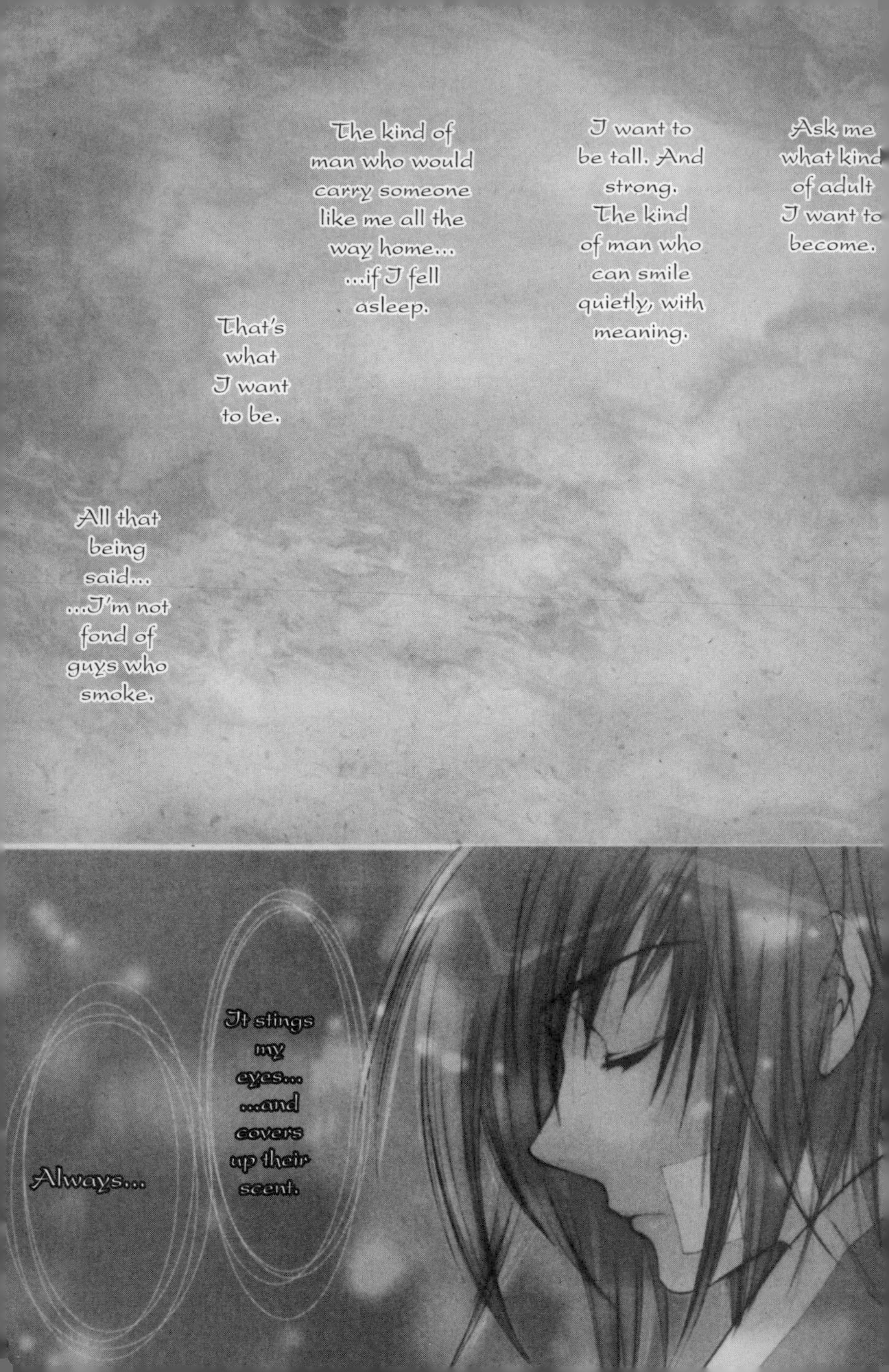
Ask me what kind of adult I want to become.
I want to be tall. And strong. The kind of man who can smile quietly, with meaning.
The kind of man who would carry someone like me all the way home... ...if I fell asleep.
That's what I want to be.
All that being said... ...I'm not fond of guys who smoke.
It stings my eyes... ...and covers up their scent.
Always...

The Birth Chapters
Chapter 1

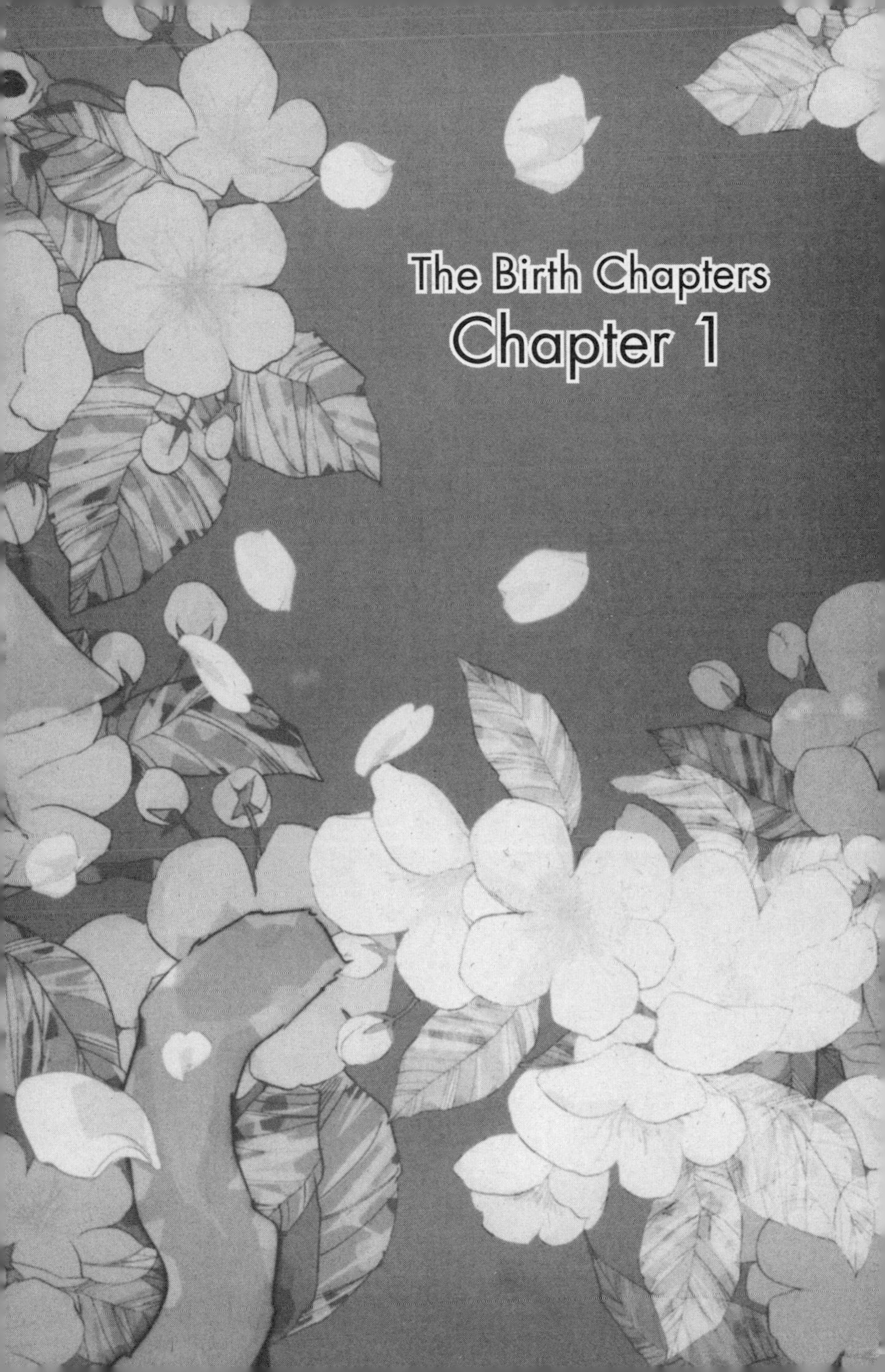

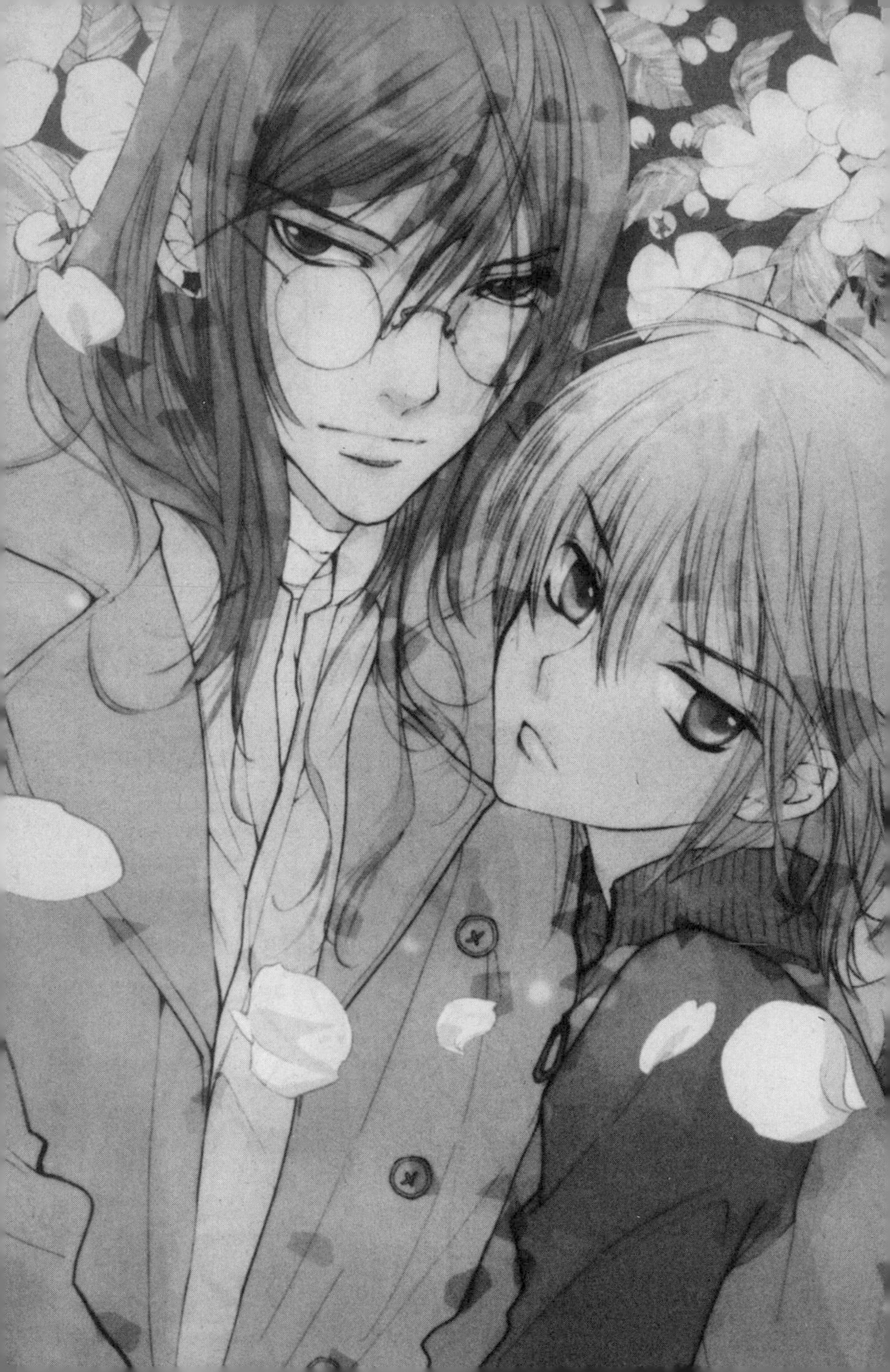

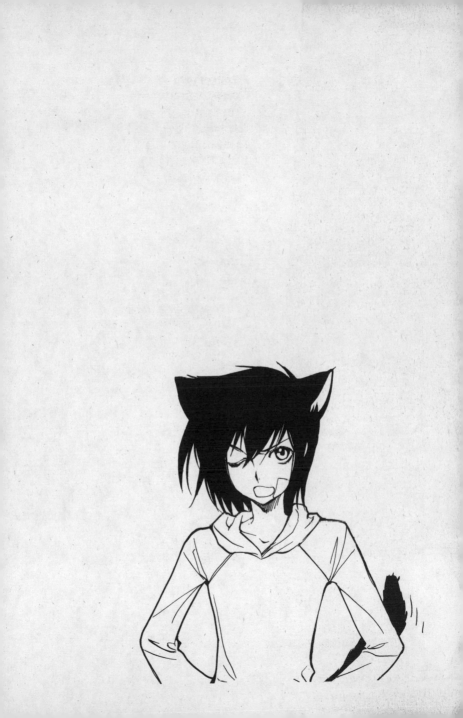

Protect with
words unable
to protect.
Tear such things
as these apart...
Touch them with
bare hands...

All else then
fades and only
the truth will
reach you.

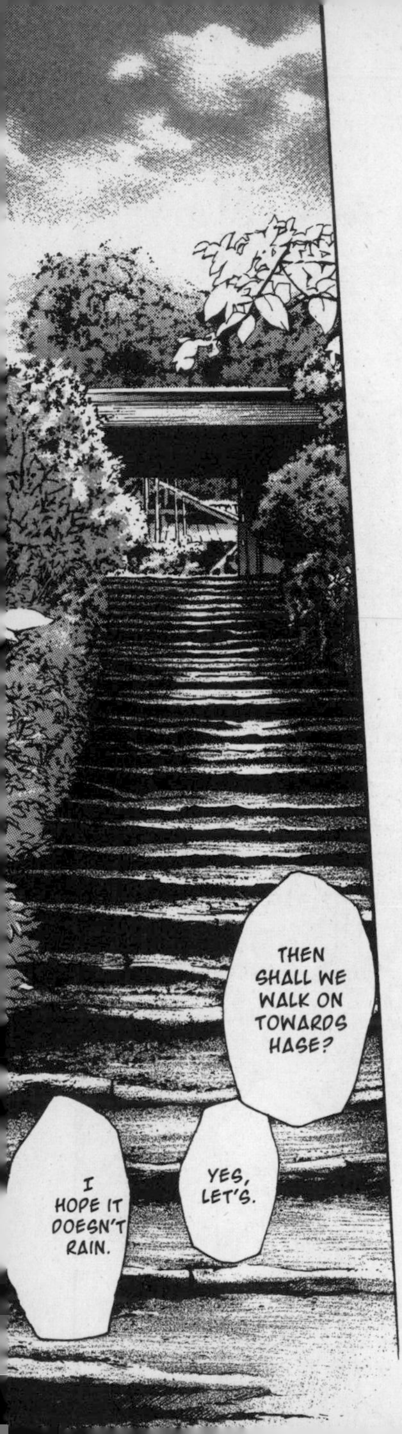
THEN SHALL WE WALK ON TOWARDS HASE?
YES, LET'S.
I HOPE IT DOESN'T RAIN.

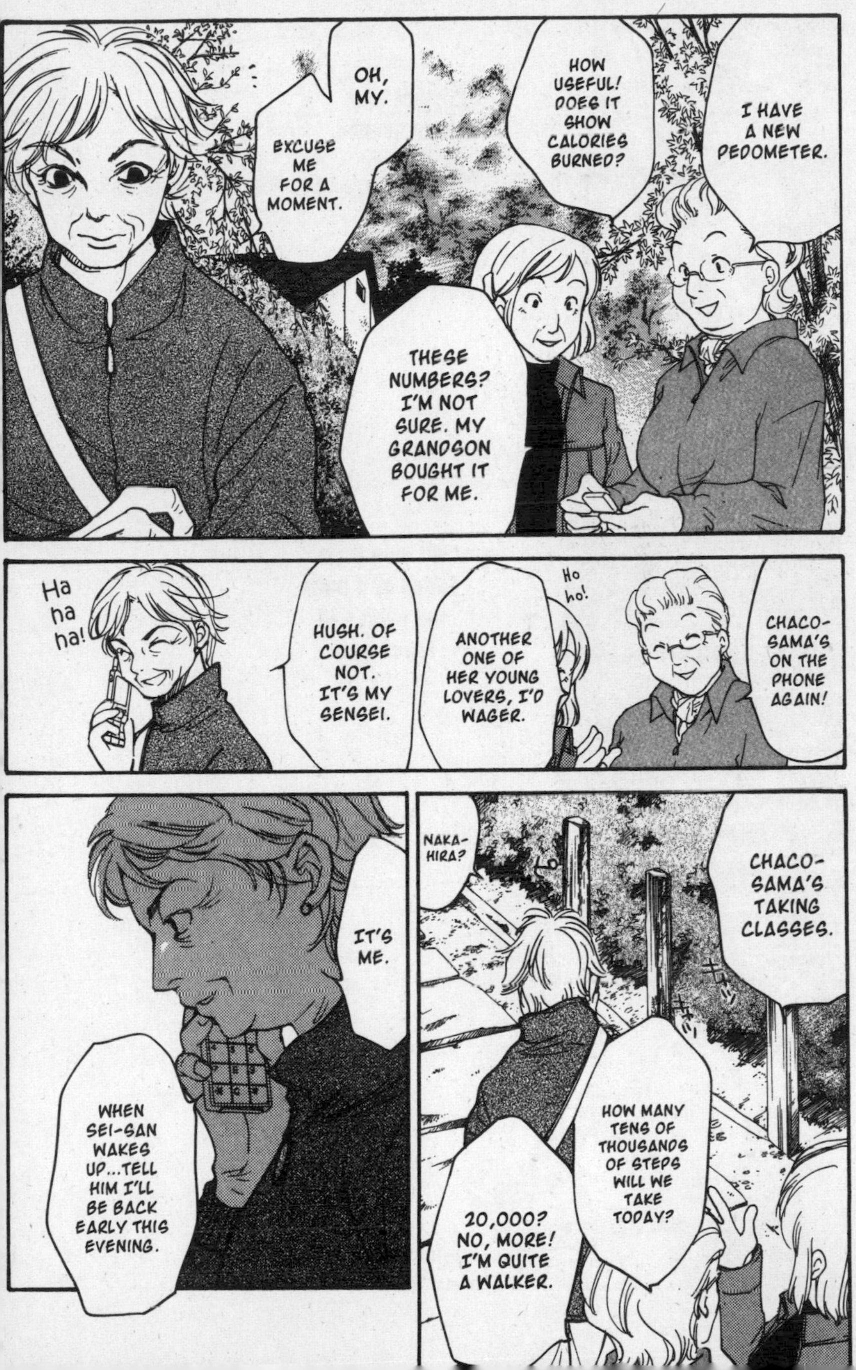
I HAVE A NEW PEDOMETER.
HOW USEFUL! DOES IT SHOW CALORIES BURNED?
THESE NUMBERS? I'M NOT SURE. MY GRANDSON BOUGHT IT FOR ME.
OH, MY.
EXCUSE ME FOR A MOMENT.
CHACO-SAMA'S ON THE PHONE AGAIN!
Ho ho!
ANOTHER ONE OF HER YOUNG LOVERS, I'D WAGER.
HUSH. OF COURSE NOT. IT'S MY SENSEI.
Ha ha ha!
CHACO-SAMA'S TAKING CLASSES.
NAKA-HIRA?
HOW MANY TENS OF THOUSANDS OF STEPS WILL WE TAKE TODAY?
20,000? NO, MORE! I'M QUITE A WALKER.
IT'S ME.
WHEN SEI-SAN WAKES UP...TELL HIM I'LL BE BACK EARLY THIS EVENING.

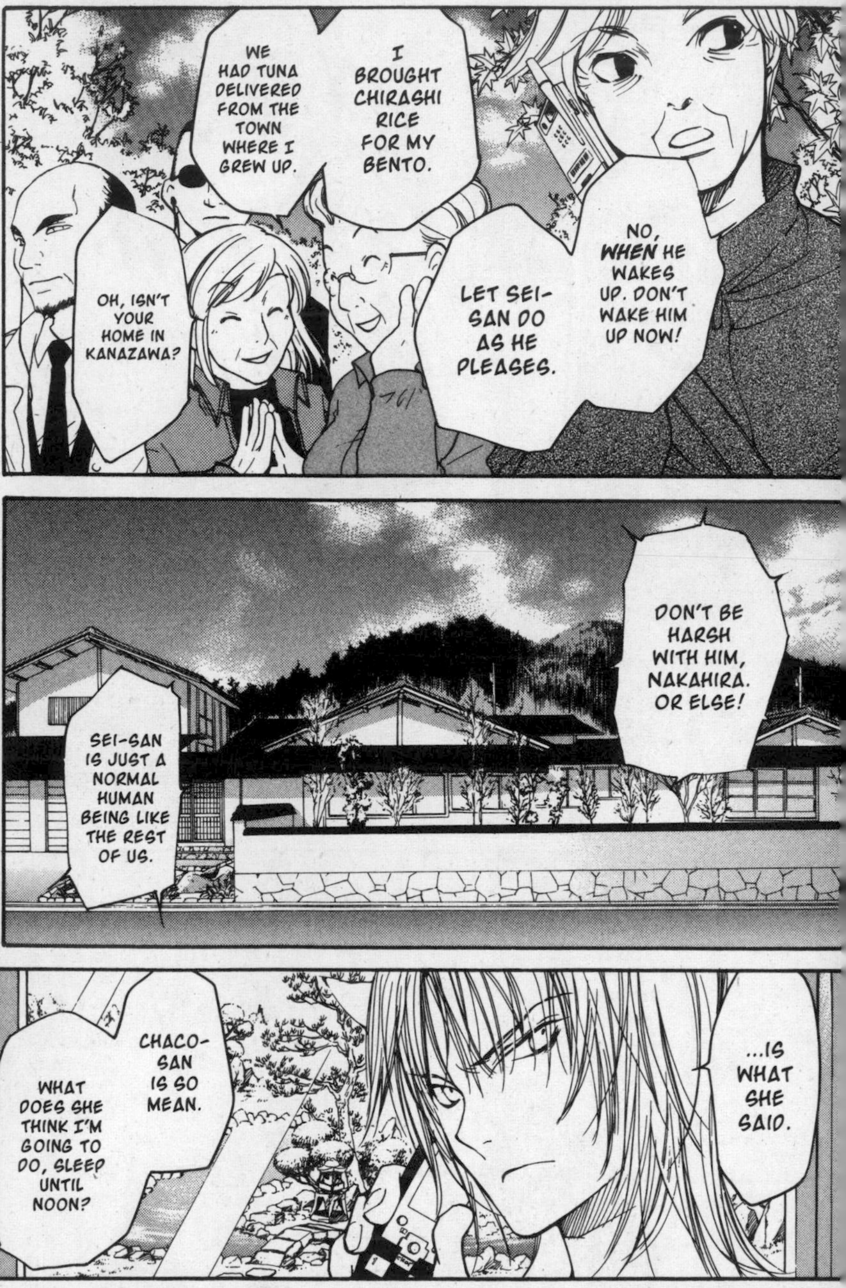
NO, *WHEN* HE WAKES UP. DON'T WAKE HIM UP NOW!
LET SEI-SAN DO AS HE PLEASES.
I BROUGHT CHIRASHI RICE FOR MY BENTO.
WE HAD TUNA DELIVERED FROM THE TOWN WHERE I GREW UP.
OH, ISN'T YOUR HOME IN KANAZAWA?
DON'T BE HARSH WITH HIM, NAKAHIRA. OR ELSE!
SEI-SAN IS JUST A NORMAL HUMAN BEING LIKE THE REST OF US.
...IS WHAT SHE SAID.
CHACO-SAN IS SO MEAN.
WHAT DOES SHE THINK I'M GOING TO DO, SLEEP UNTIL NOON?

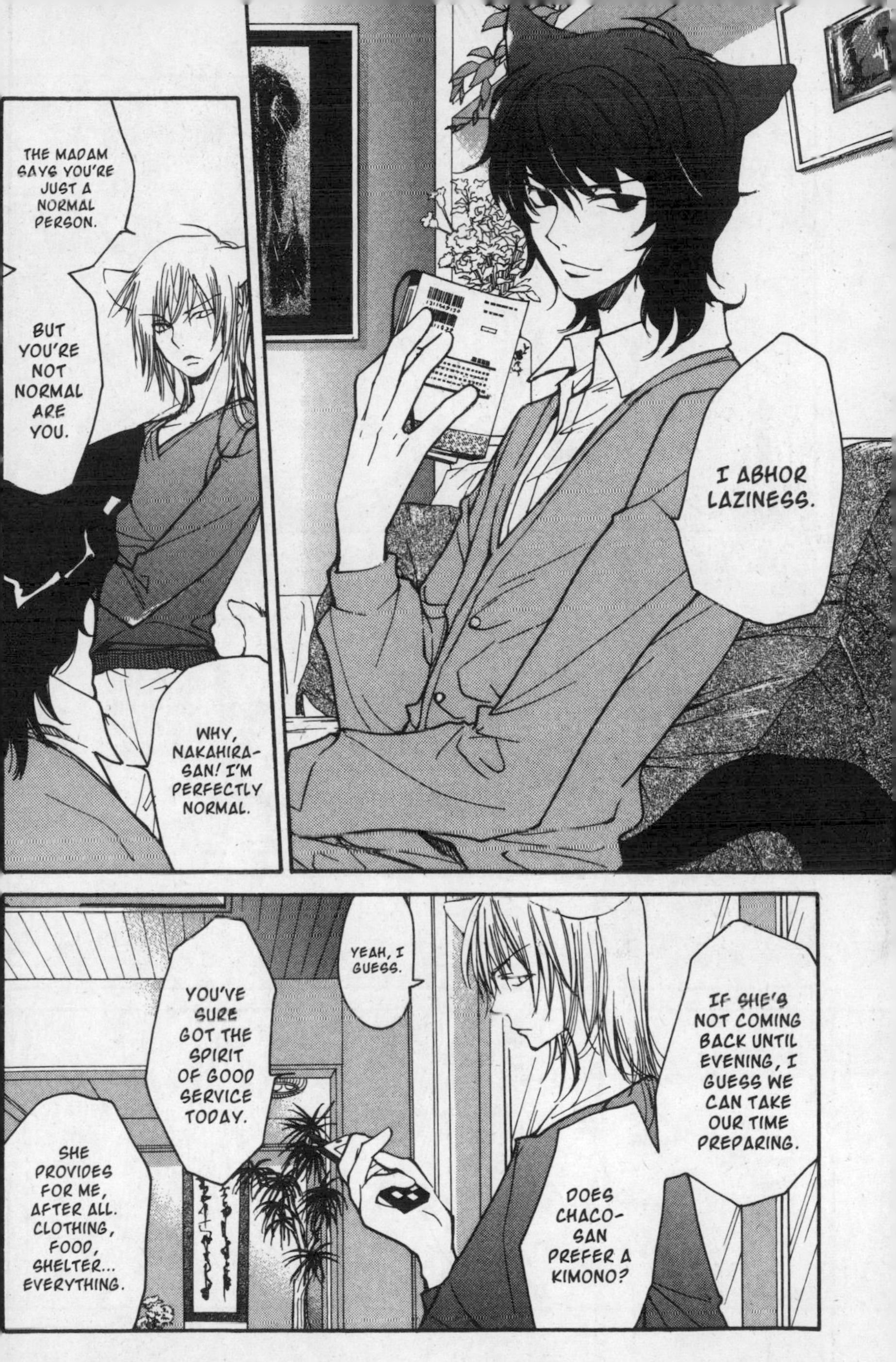
I ABHOR LAZINESS.
THE MADAM SAYS YOU'RE JUST A NORMAL PERSON.
BUT YOU'RE NOT NORMAL ARE YOU.
WHY, NAKAHIRA-SAN! I'M PERFECTLY NORMAL.
IF SHE'S NOT COMING BACK UNTIL EVENING, I GUESS WE CAN TAKE OUR TIME PREPARING.
YEAH, I GUESS.
YOU'VE SURE GOT THE SPIRIT OF GOOD SERVICE TODAY.
DOES CHACO-SAN PREFER A KIMONO?
SHE PROVIDES FOR ME, AFTER ALL. CLOTHING, FOOD, SHELTER... EVERYTHING.

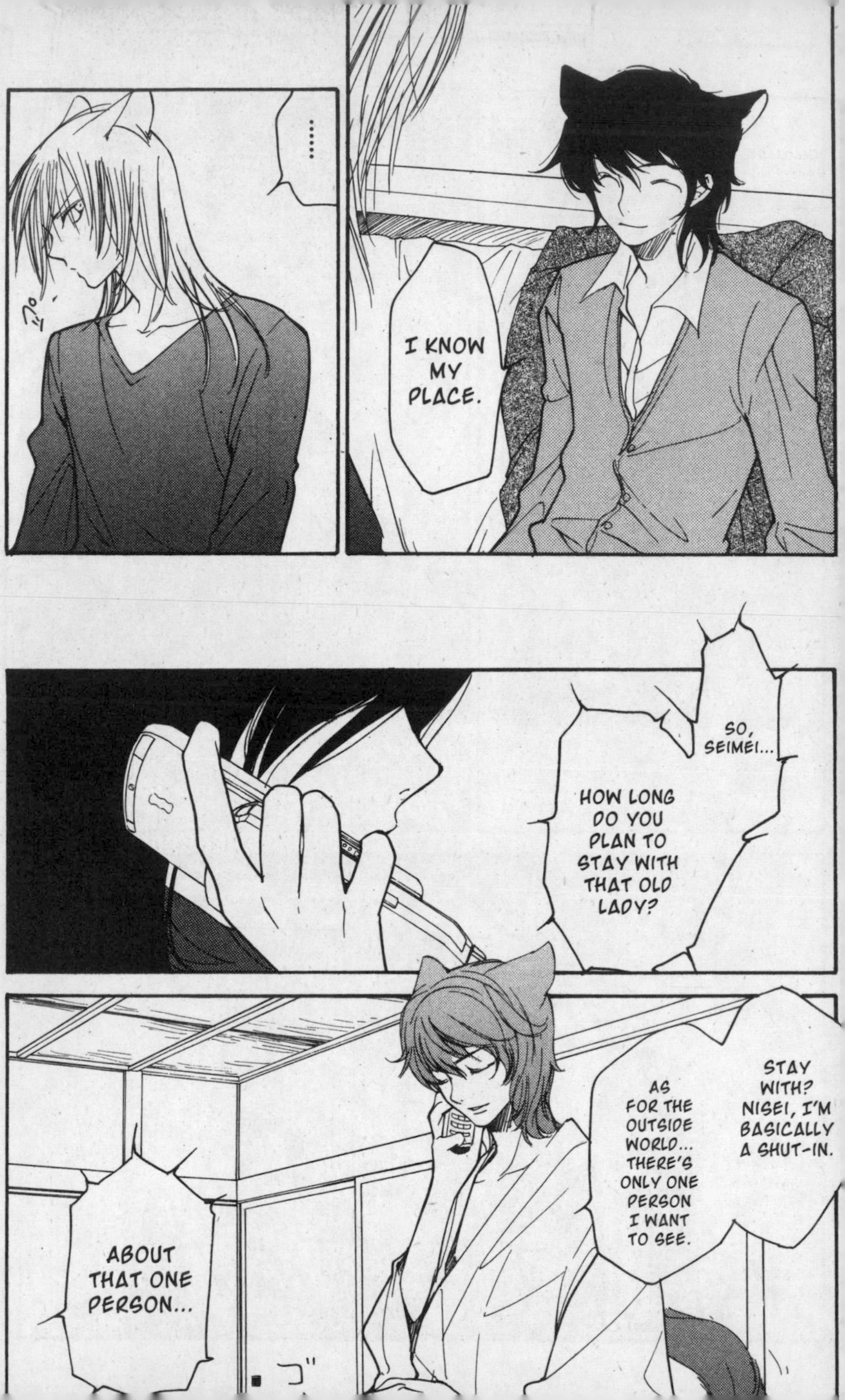
I KNOW MY PLACE.
......
SO, SEIMEI...
HOW LONG DO YOU PLAN TO STAY WITH THAT OLD LADY?
STAY WITH? NISEI, I'M BASICALLY A SHUT-IN.
AS FOR THE OUTSIDE WORLD... THERE'S ONLY ONE PERSON I WANT TO SEE.
ABOUT THAT ONE PERSON...

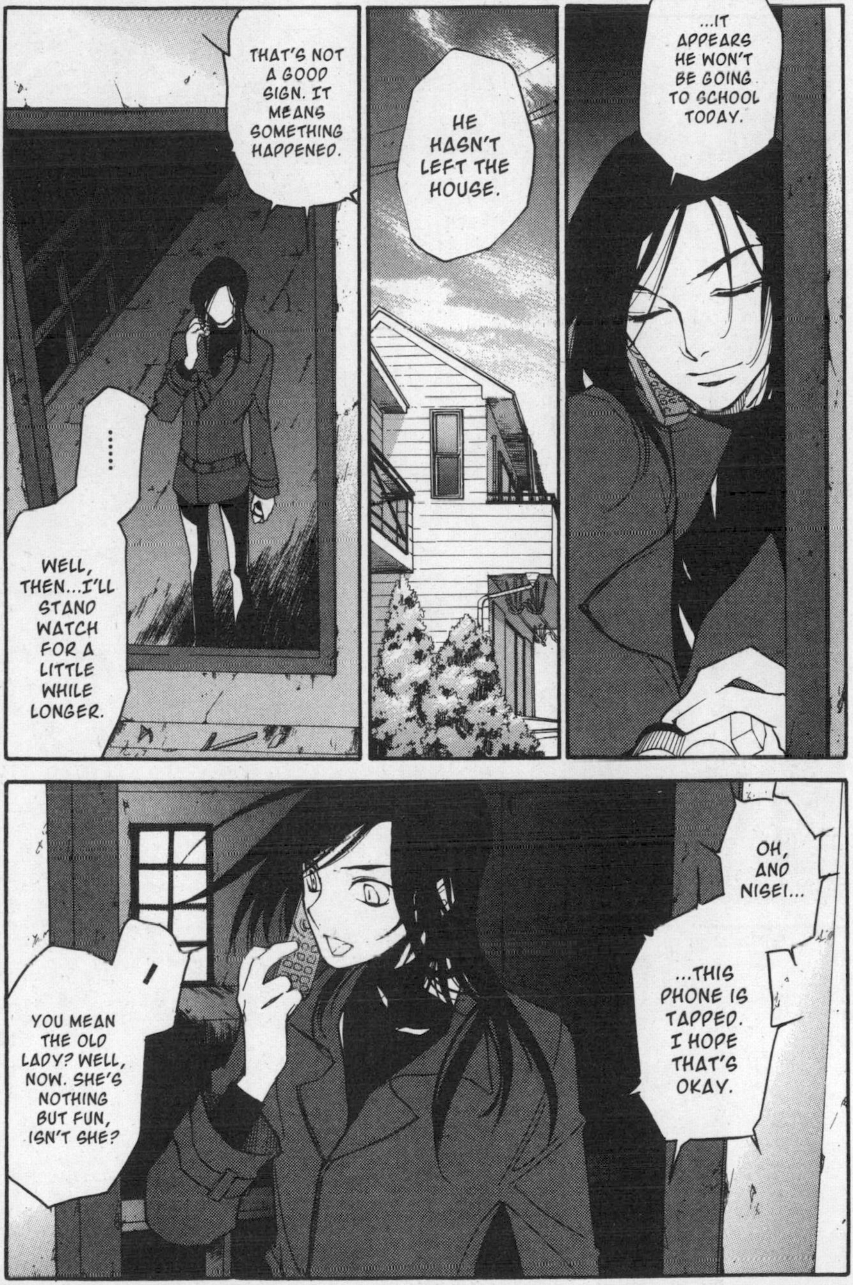
...IT APPEARS HE WON'T BE GOING TO SCHOOL TODAY.
HE HASN'T LEFT THE HOUSE.
THAT'S NOT A GOOD SIGN. IT MEANS SOMETHING HAPPENED.
......
WELL, THEN...I'LL STAND WATCH FOR A LITTLE WHILE LONGER.
OH, AND NISEI...
...THIS PHONE IS TAPPED. I HOPE THAT'S OKAY.
!
YOU MEAN THE OLD LADY? WELL, NOW. SHE'S NOTHING BUT FUN, ISN'T SHE?

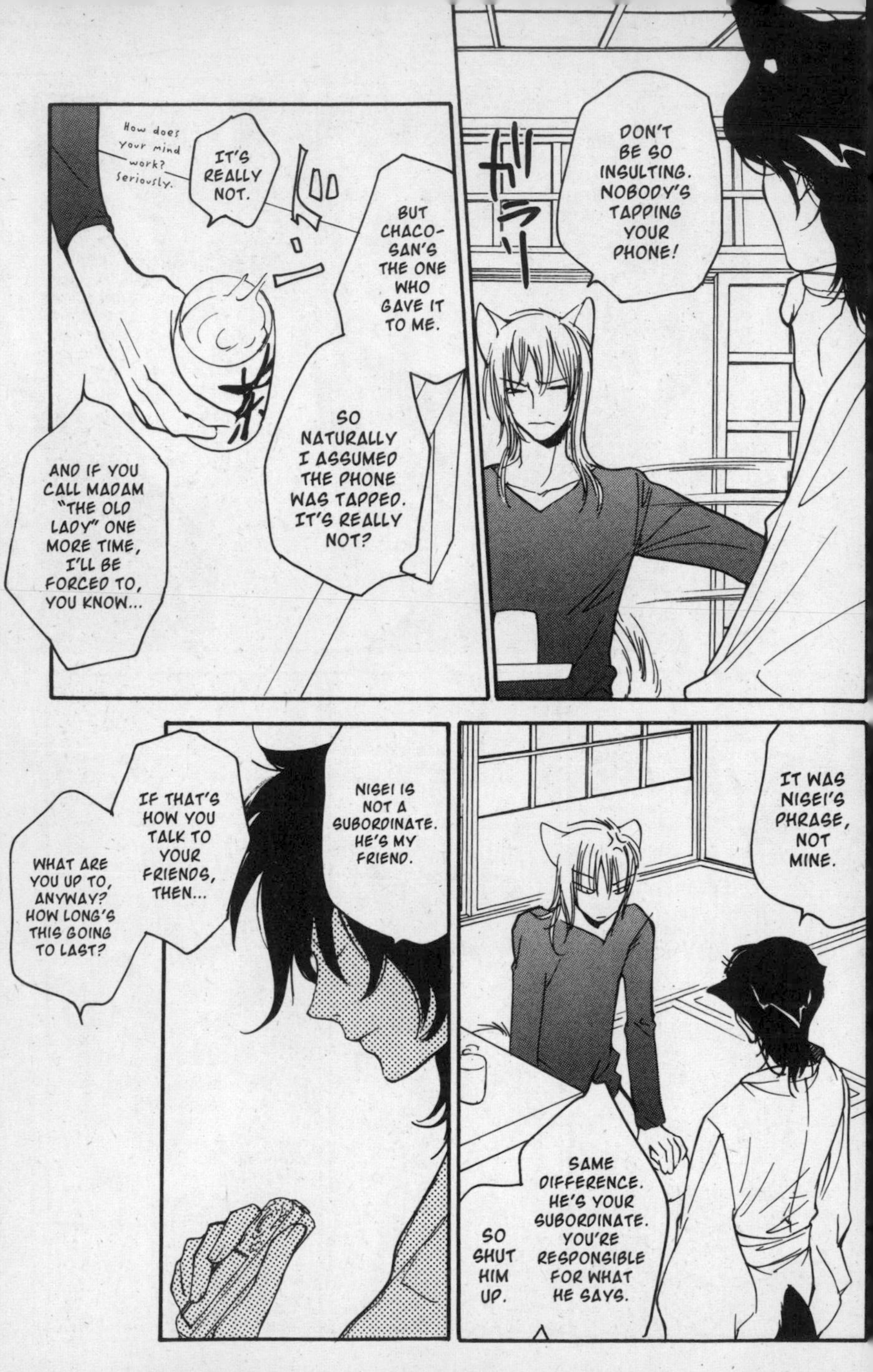
DON'T BE SO INSULTING. NOBODY'S TAPPING YOUR PHONE!
BUT CHACO-SAN'S THE ONE WHO GAVE IT TO ME.
SO NATURALLY I ASSUMED THE PHONE WAS TAPPED. IT'S REALLY NOT?
IT'S REALLY NOT.
How does your mind work? Seriously.
AND IF YOU CALL MADAM "THE OLD LADY" ONE MORE TIME, I'LL BE FORCED TO, YOU KNOW...
IT WAS NISEI'S PHRASE, NOT MINE.
SAME DIFFERENCE. HE'S YOUR SUBORDINATE. YOU'RE RESPONSIBLE FOR WHAT HE SAYS.
SO SHUT HIM UP.
NISEI IS NOT A SUBORDINATE. HE'S MY FRIEND.
IF THAT'S HOW YOU TALK TO YOUR FRIENDS, THEN...
WHAT ARE YOU UP TO, ANYWAY? HOW LONG'S THIS GOING TO LAST?

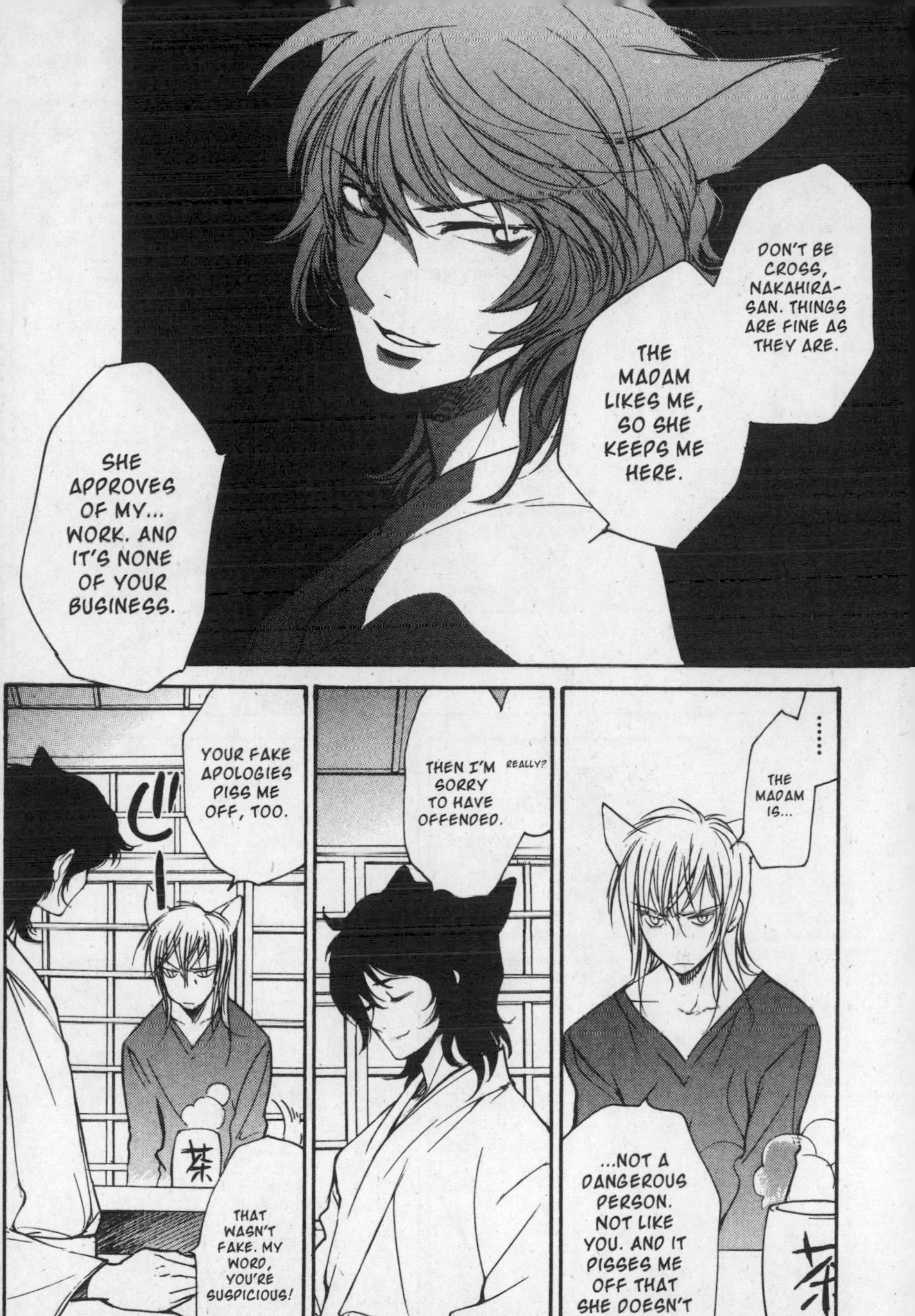
DON'T BE CROSS, NAKAHIRA-SAN. THINGS ARE FINE AS THEY ARE.
THE MADAM LIKES ME, SO SHE KEEPS ME HERE.
SHE APPROVES OF MY... WORK. AND IT'S NONE OF YOUR BUSINESS.
......
THE MADAM IS...
...NOT A DANGEROUS PERSON. NOT LIKE YOU. AND IT PISSES ME OFF THAT SHE DOESN'T SEE IT.
REALLY?
THEN I'M SORRY TO HAVE OFFENDED.
YOUR FAKE APOLOGIES PISS ME OFF, TOO.
THAT WASN'T FAKE. MY WORD, YOU'RE SUSPICIOUS!

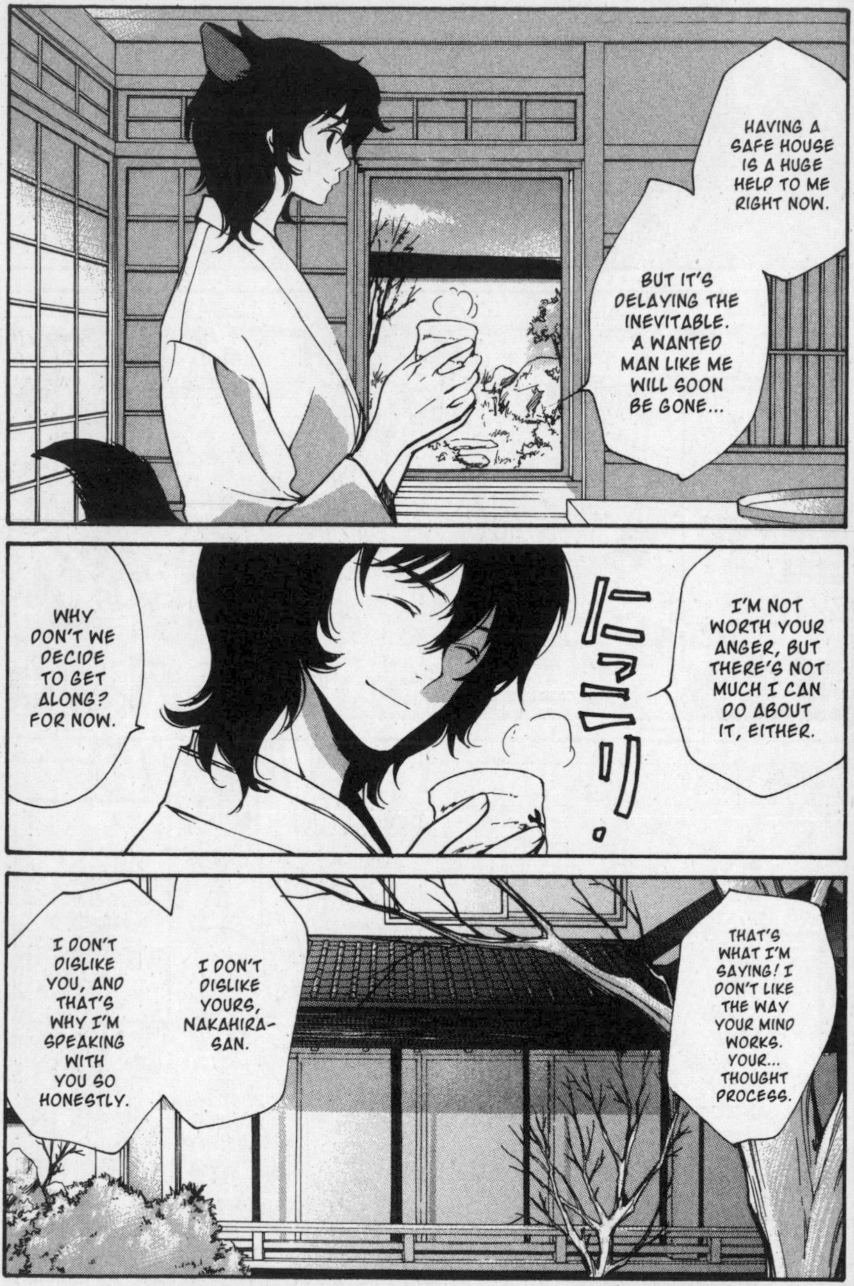
HAVING A SAFE HOUSE IS A HUGE HELP TO ME RIGHT NOW.
BUT IT'S DELAYING THE INEVITABLE. A WANTED MAN LIKE ME WILL SOON BE GONE...
I'M NOT WORTH YOUR ANGER, BUT THERE'S NOT MUCH I CAN DO ABOUT IT, EITHER.
WHY DON'T WE DECIDE TO GET ALONG? FOR NOW.
THAT'S WHAT I'M SAYING! I DON'T LIKE THE WAY YOUR MIND WORKS. YOUR... THOUGHT PROCESS.
I DON'T DISLIKE YOURS, NAKAHIRA-SAN.
I DON'T DISLIKE YOU, AND THAT'S WHY I'M SPEAKING WITH YOU SO HONESTLY.

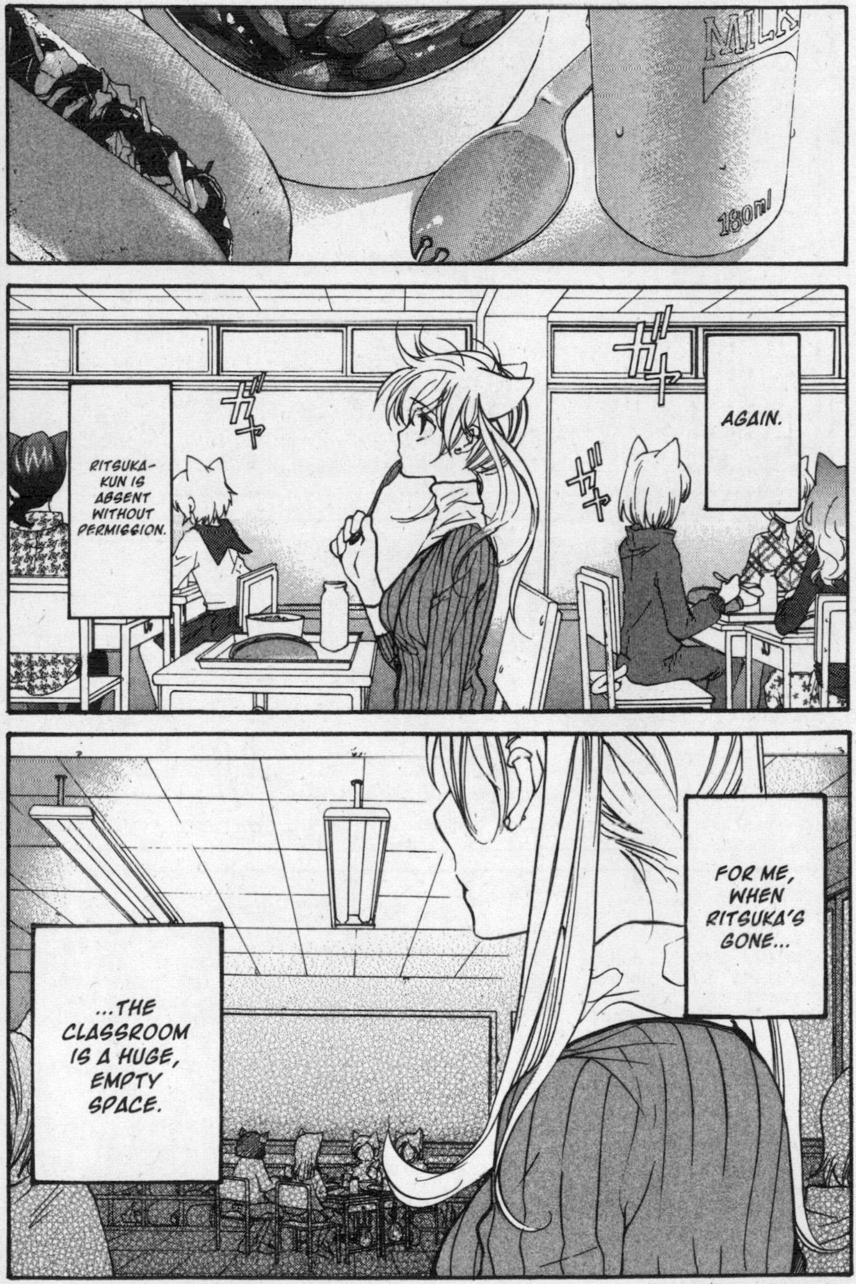
MILK
180ml
ガヤ
ガヤ
AGAIN.
ガヤ
RITSUKA-KUN IS ABSENT WITHOUT PERMISSION.
FOR ME, WHEN RITSUKA'S GONE...
...THE CLASSROOM IS A HUGE, EMPTY SPACE.

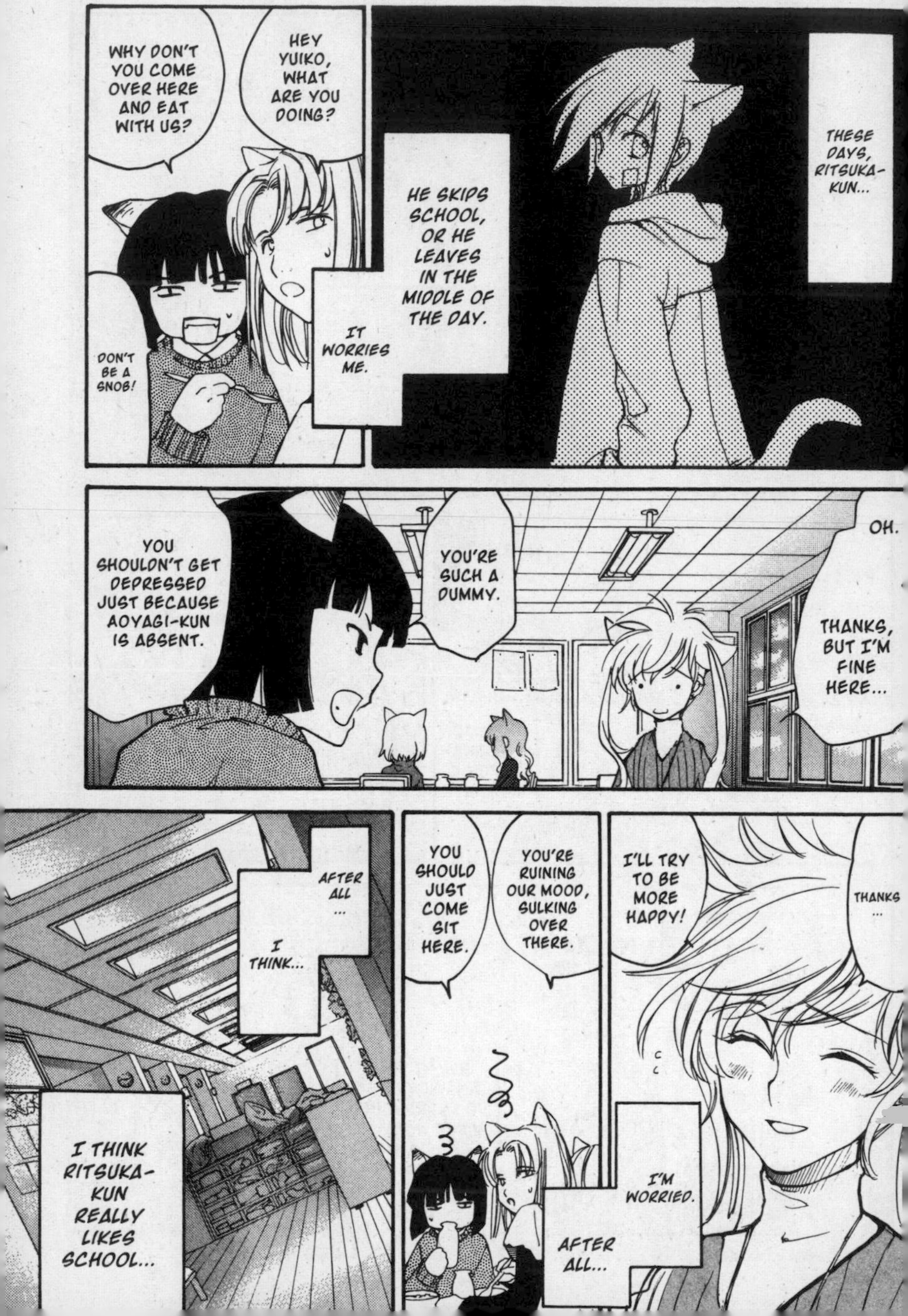
THESE DAYS, RITSUKA-KUN...
HE SKIPS SCHOOL, OR HE LEAVES IN THE MIDDLE OF THE DAY.
IT WORRIES ME.
HEY YUIKO, WHAT ARE YOU DOING?
WHY DON'T YOU COME OVER HERE AND EAT WITH US?
DON'T BE A SNOB!
OH.
THANKS, BUT I'M FINE HERE...
YOU'RE SUCH A DUMMY.
YOU SHOULDN'T GET DEPRESSED JUST BECAUSE AOYAGI-KUN IS ABSENT.
THANKS...
I'LL TRY TO BE MORE HAPPY!
I'M WORRIED.
AFTER ALL...
YOU'RE RUINING OUR MOOD, SULKING OVER THERE.
YOU SHOULD JUST COME SIT HERE.
AFTER ALL...
I THINK...
I THINK RITSUKA-KUN REALLY LIKES SCHOOL...

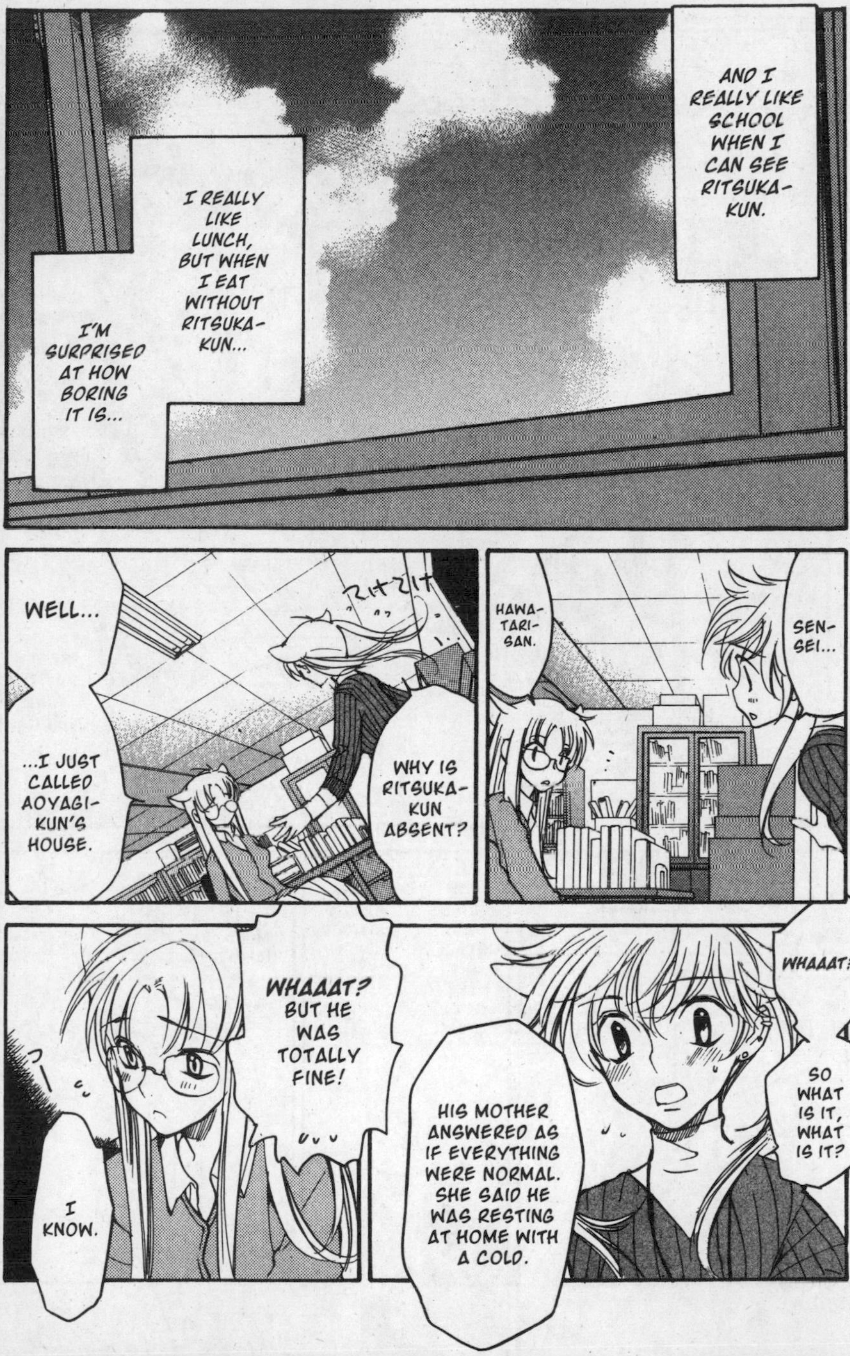
AND I REALLY LIKE SCHOOL WHEN I CAN SEE RITSUKA-KUN.
I REALLY LIKE LUNCH, BUT WHEN I EAT WITHOUT RITSUKA-KUN...
I'M SURPRISED AT HOW BORING IT IS...
SEN-SEI...
HAWA-TARI-SAN.
WHY IS RITSUKA-KUN ABSENT?
WELL...
...I JUST CALLED AOYAGI-KUN'S HOUSE.
WHAAAT?
SO WHAT IS IT, WHAT IS IT?
HIS MOTHER ANSWERED AS IF EVERYTHING WERE NORMAL. SHE SAID HE WAS RESTING AT HOME WITH A COLD.
WHAAAT? BUT HE WAS TOTALLY FINE!
I KNOW.

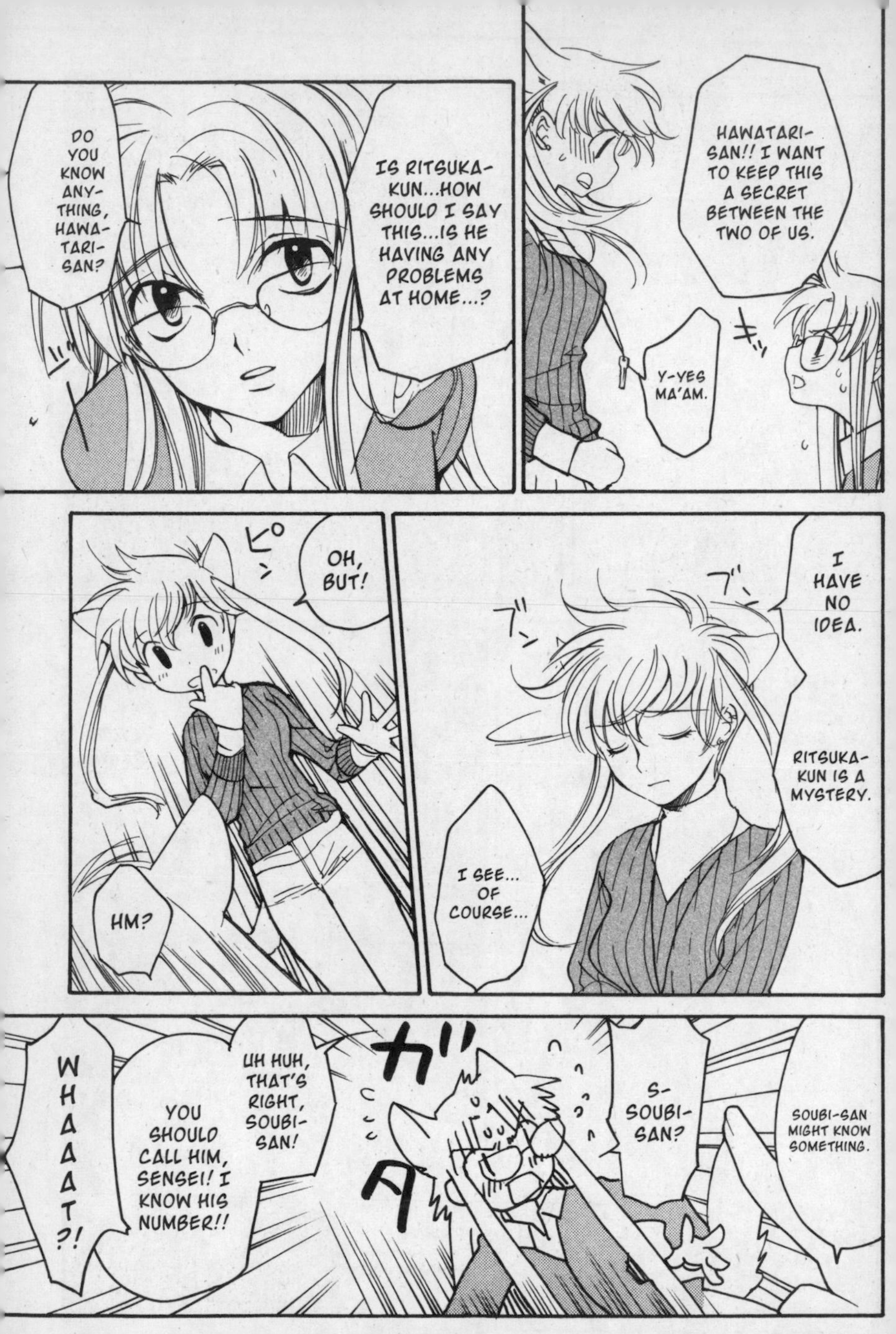
HAWATARI-SAN!! I WANT TO KEEP THIS A SECRET BETWEEN THE TWO OF US.
Y-YES MA'AM.
IS RITSUKA-KUN...HOW SHOULD I SAY THIS...IS HE HAVING ANY PROBLEMS AT HOME...?
DO YOU KNOW ANYTHING, HAWATARI-SAN?
I HAVE NO IDEA.
RITSUKA-KUN IS A MYSTERY.
I SEE... OF COURSE...
OH, BUT!
HM?
SOUBI-SAN MIGHT KNOW SOMETHING.
S-SOUBI-SAN?
UH HUH, THAT'S RIGHT, SOUBI-SAN!
YOU SHOULD CALL HIM, SENSEI! I KNOW HIS NUMBER!!
WHAAAAT?!

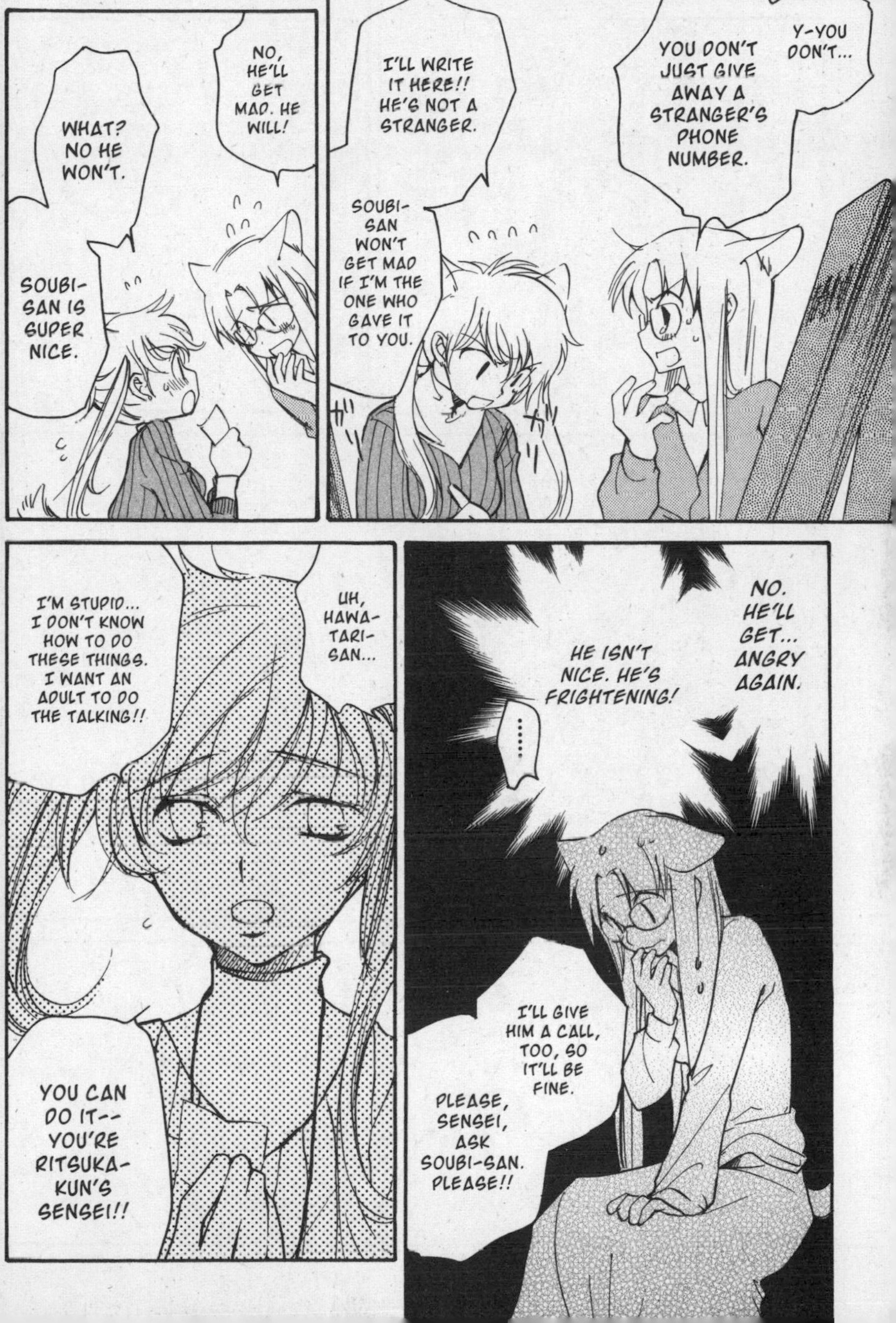
Y-YOU DON'T...
YOU DON'T JUST GIVE AWAY A STRANGER'S PHONE NUMBER.
I'LL WRITE IT HERE!! HE'S NOT A STRANGER.
SOUBI-SAN WON'T GET MAD IF I'M THE ONE WHO GAVE IT TO YOU.
NO, HE'LL GET MAD. HE WILL!
WHAT? NO HE WON'T.
SOUBI-SAN IS SUPER NICE.
NO. HE'LL GET... ANGRY AGAIN.
HE ISN'T NICE. HE'S FRIGHTENING!
......
I'LL GIVE HIM A CALL, TOO, SO IT'LL BE FINE.
PLEASE, SENSEI, ASK SOUBI-SAN. PLEASE!!
UH, HAWATARI-SAN...
I'M STUPID... I DON'T KNOW HOW TO DO THESE THINGS. I WANT AN ADULT TO DO THE TALKING!!
YOU CAN DO IT-- YOU'RE RITSUKA-KUN'S SENSEI!!

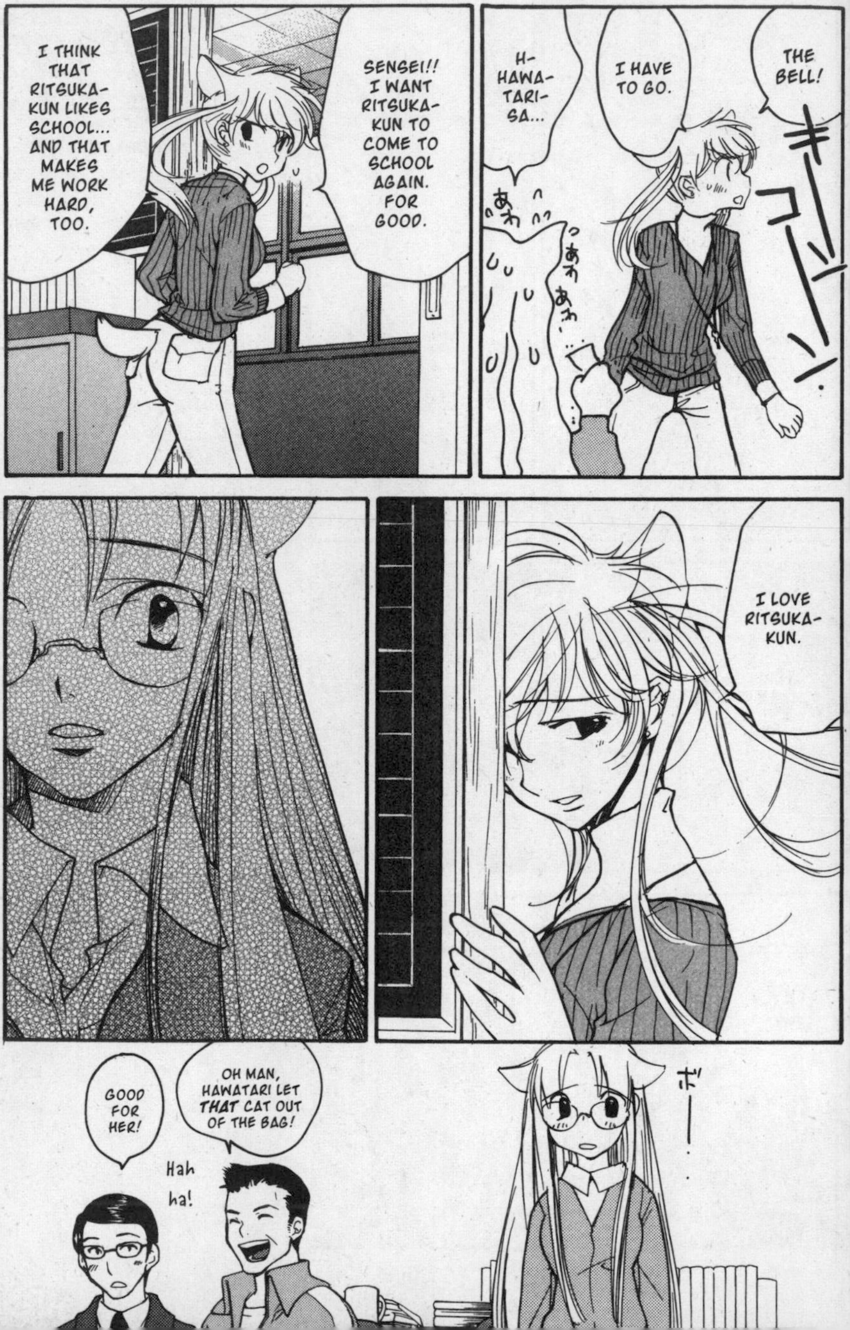
THE BELL!
キーンコーン
I HAVE TO GO.
H-HAWATARI-SA...
あわあわ
SENSEI!! I WANT RITSUKA-KUN TO COME TO SCHOOL AGAIN. FOR GOOD.
I THINK THAT RITSUKA-KUN LIKES SCHOOL... AND THAT MAKES ME WORK HARD, TOO.
I LOVE RITSUKA-KUN.
ボー・
OH MAN, HAWATARI LET *THAT* CAT OUT OF THE BAG!
GOOD FOR HER!
Hah ha!

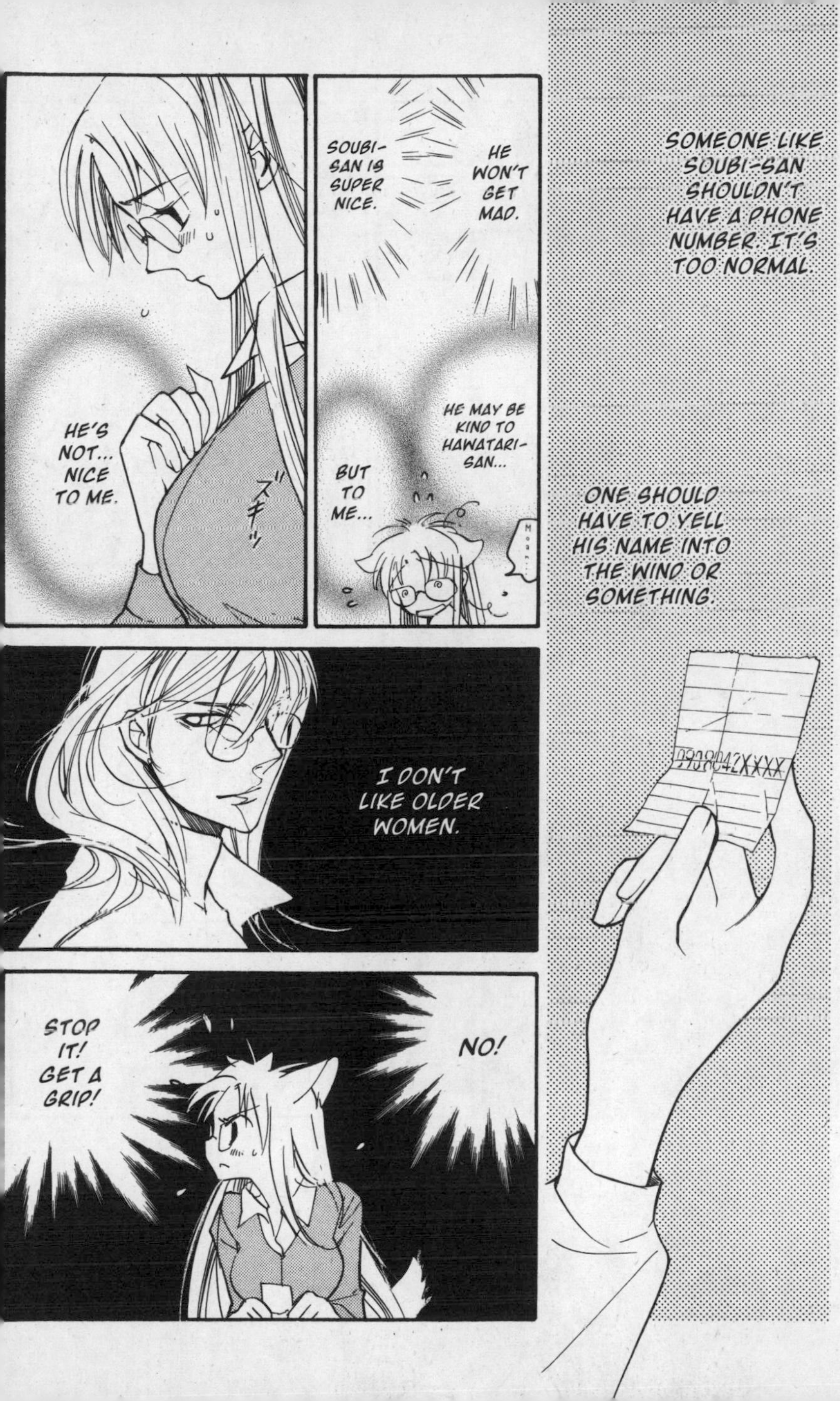
SOMEONE LIKE SOUBI-SAN SHOULDN'T HAVE A PHONE NUMBER. IT'S TOO NORMAL.
ONE SHOULD HAVE TO YELL HIS NAME INTO THE WIND OR SOMETHING.
HE WON'T GET MAD.
SOUBI-SAN IS SUPER NICE.
HE MAY BE KIND TO HAWATARI-SAN...
BUT TO ME...
HE'S NOT... NICE TO ME.
ズキッ
I DON'T LIKE OLDER WOMEN.
NO!
STOP IT! GET A GRIP!

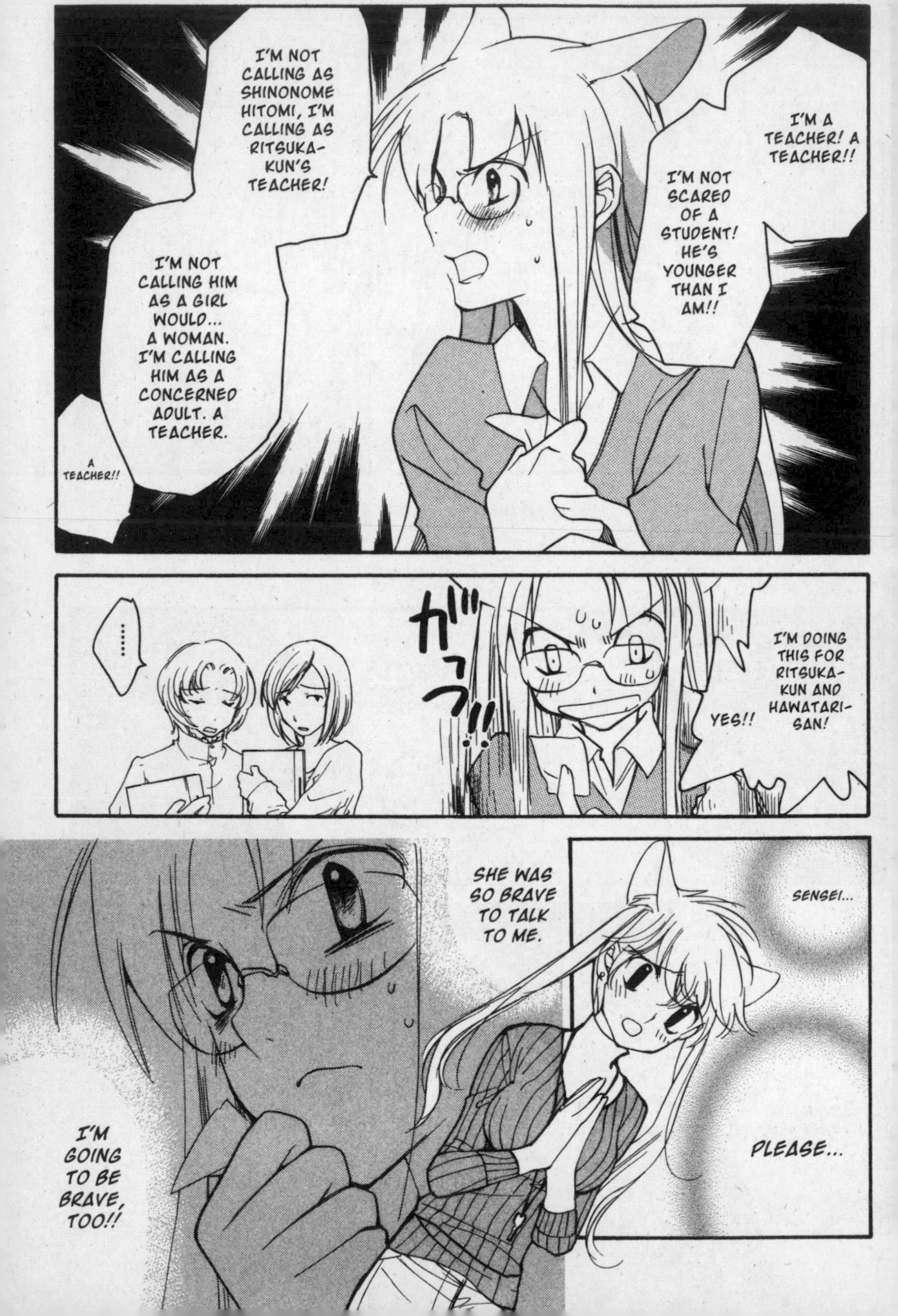
I'M A TEACHER! A TEACHER!!
I'M NOT SCARED OF A STUDENT! HE'S YOUNGER THAN I AM!!
I'M NOT CALLING AS SHINONOME HITOMI, I'M CALLING AS RITSUKA-KUN'S TEACHER!
I'M NOT CALLING HIM AS A GIRL WOULD... A WOMAN. I'M CALLING HIM AS A CONCERNED ADULT. A TEACHER.
A TEACHER!!
I'M DOING THIS FOR RITSUKA-KUN AND HAWATARI-SAN!
YES!!
ガッ!!
......
SENSEI...
SHE WAS SO BRAVE TO TALK TO ME.
PLEASE...
I'M GOING TO BE BRAVE, TOO!!

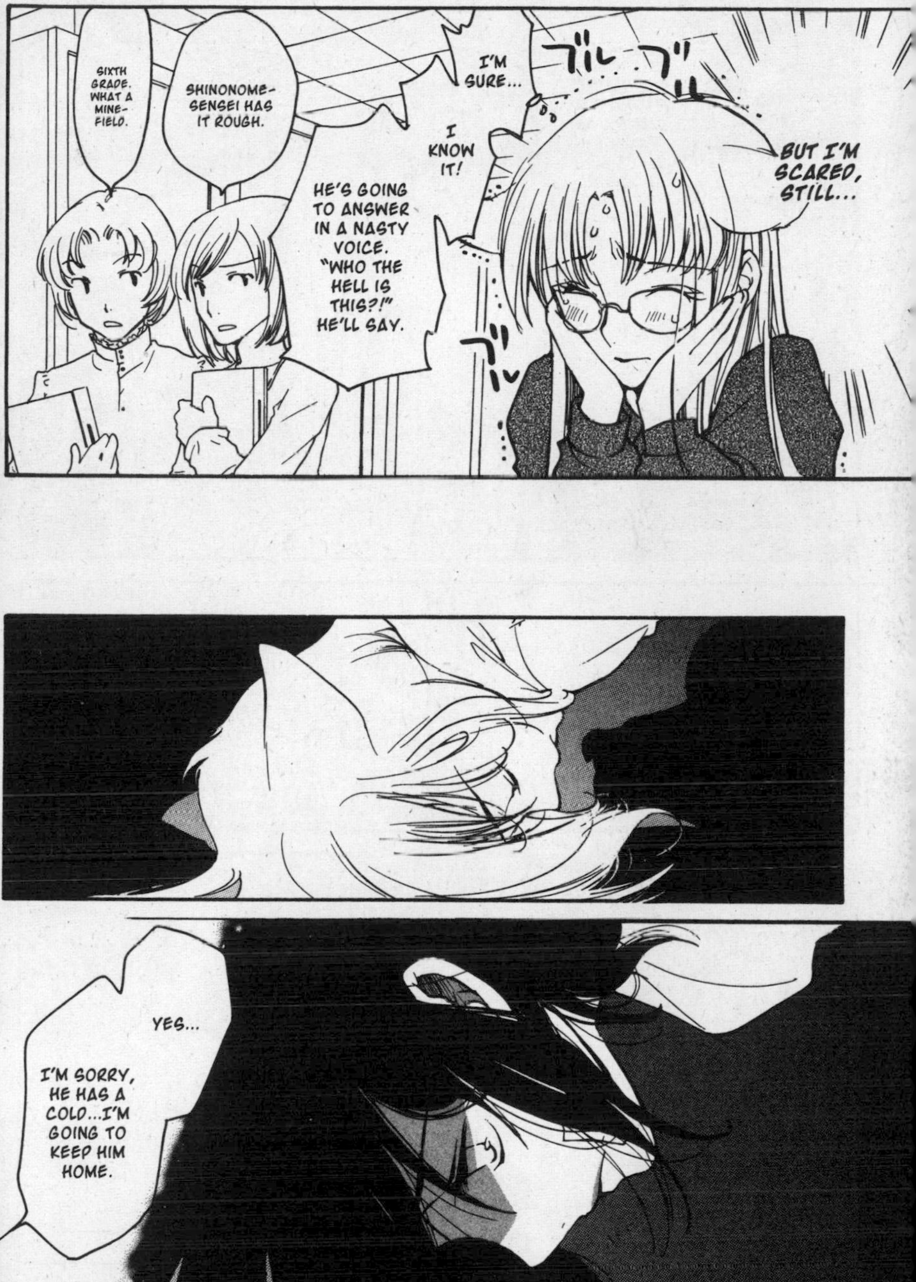
ブル ブル
I'M SURE...
I KNOW IT!
HE'S GOING TO ANSWER IN A NASTY VOICE. "WHO THE HELL IS THIS?!" HE'LL SAY.
BUT I'M SCARED, STILL...
ブル
SHINONOME-SENSEI HAS IT ROUGH.
SIXTH GRADE. WHAT A MINE-FIELD.
YES...
I'M SORRY, HE HAS A COLD...I'M GOING TO KEEP HIM HOME.

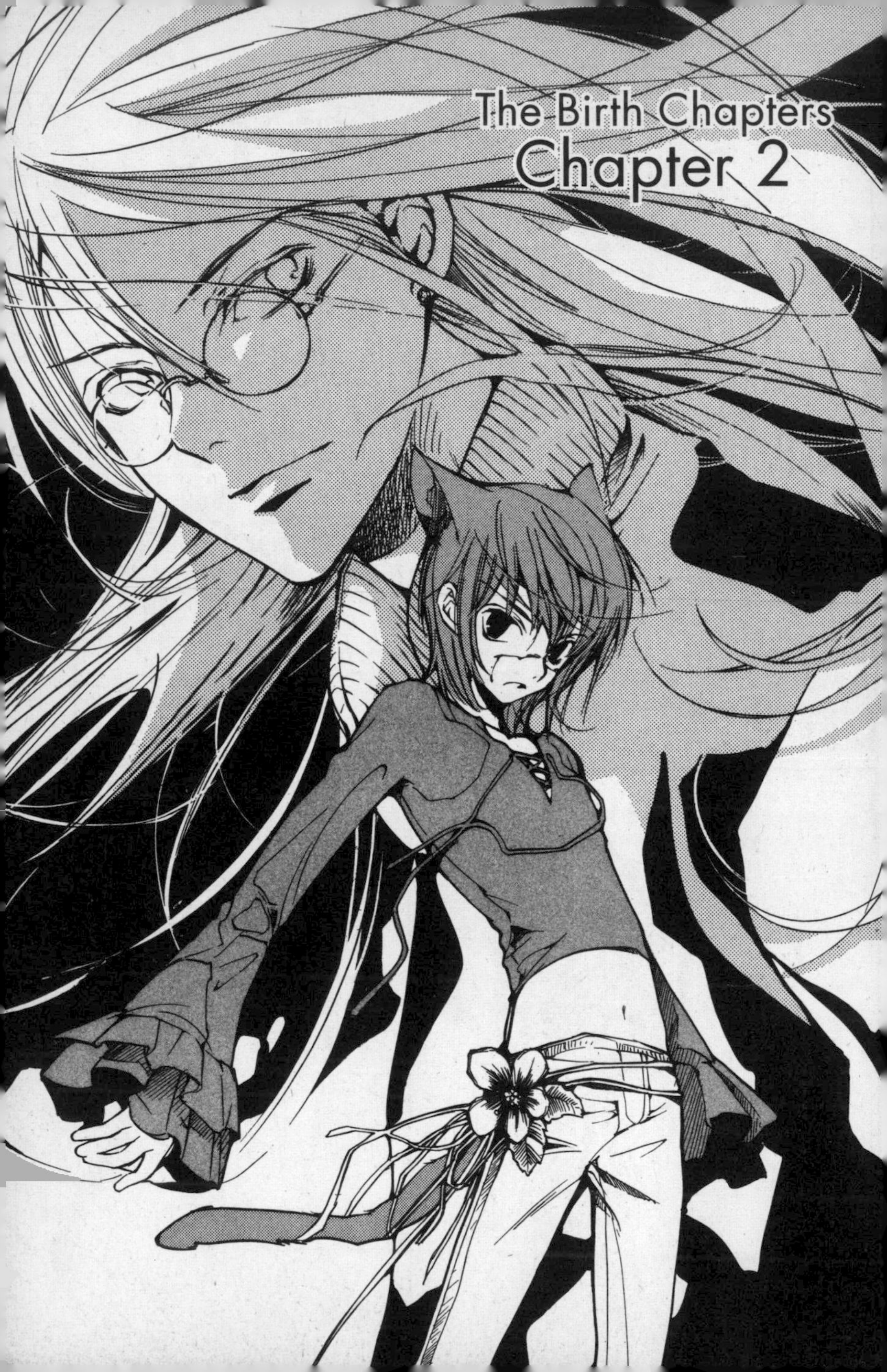
The Birth Chapters
Chapter 2

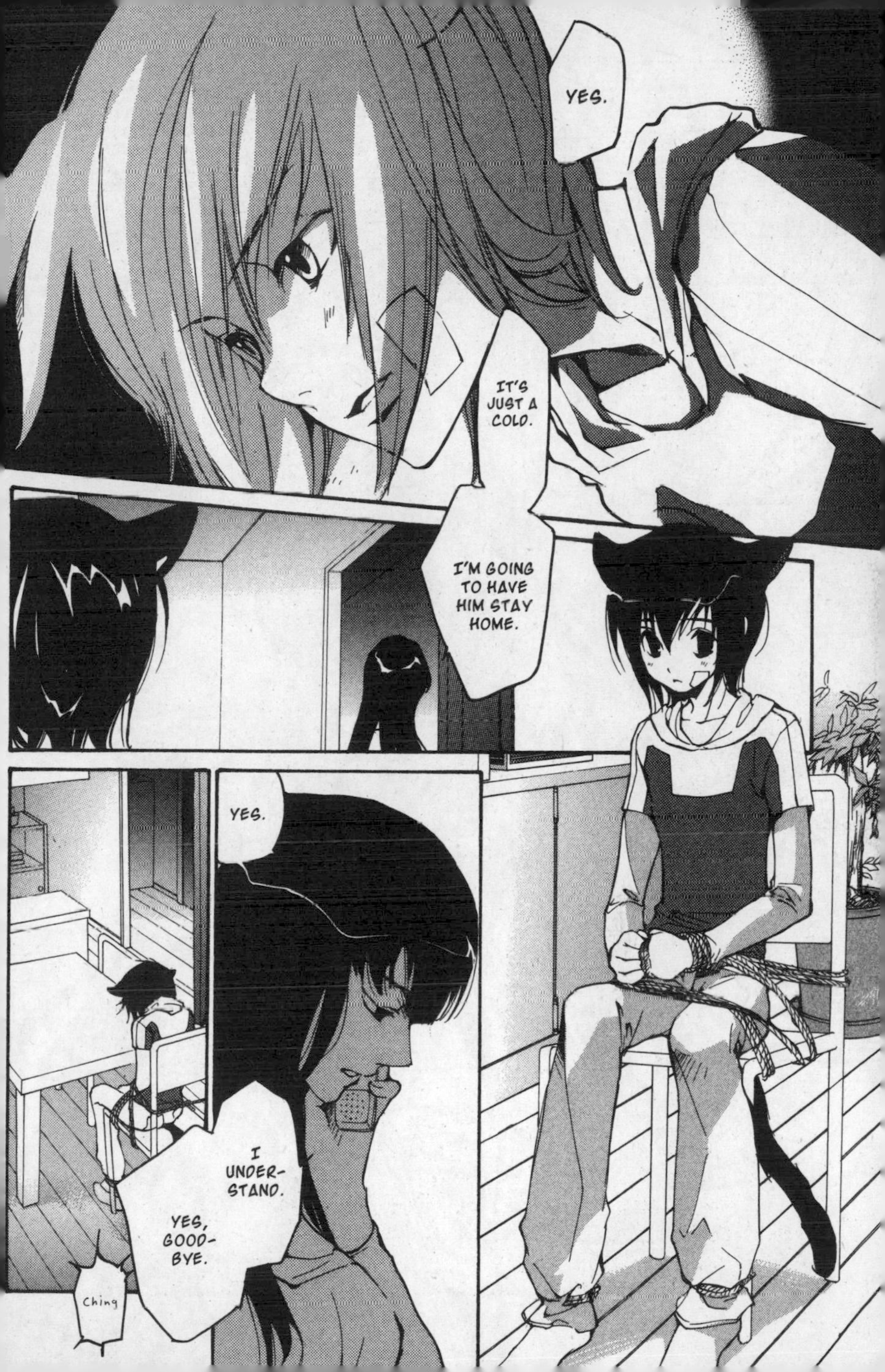
YES.
IT'S JUST A COLD.
I'M GOING TO HAVE HIM STAY HOME.
YES.
I UNDERSTAND.
YES, GOODBYE.
Ching

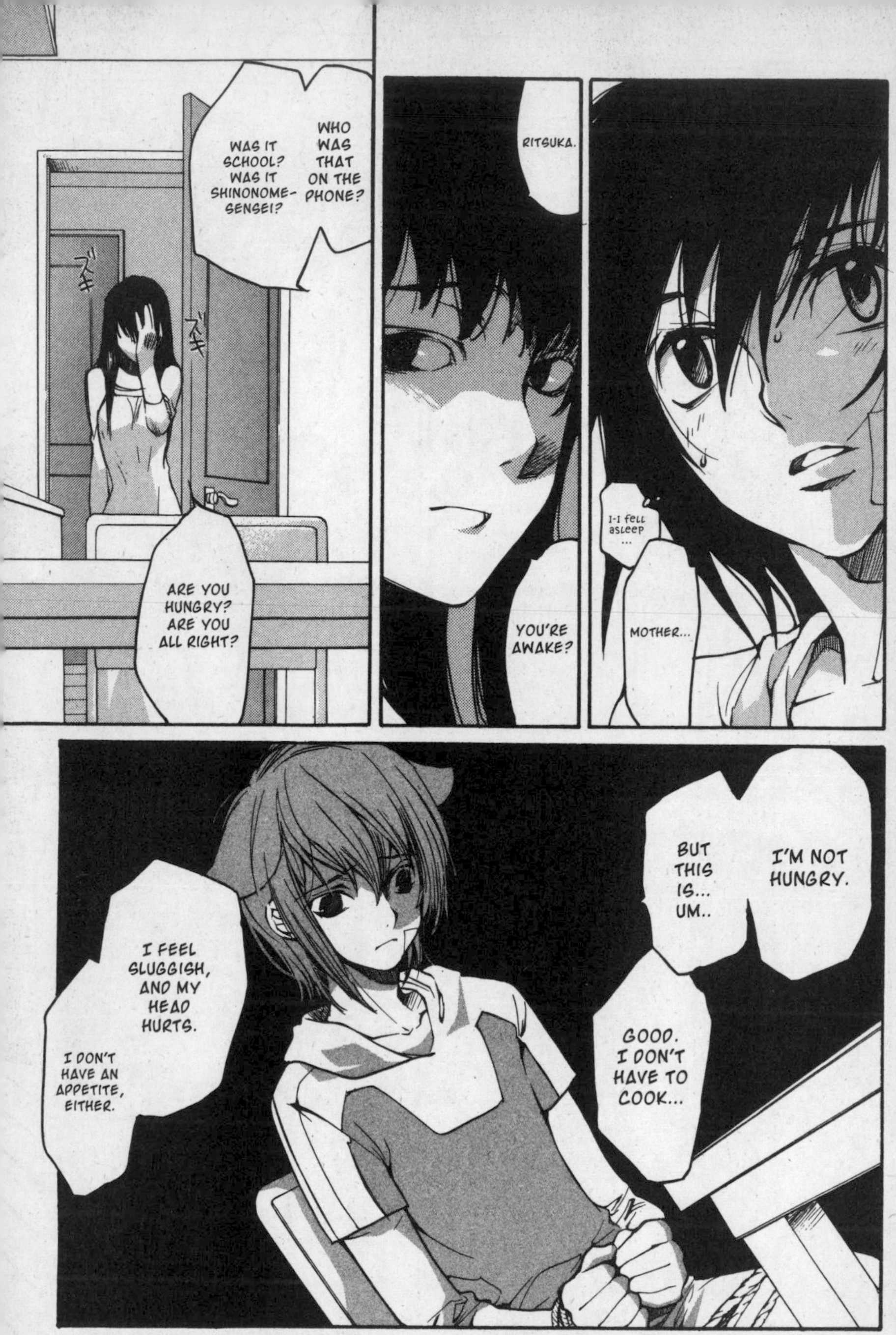
MOTHER...
I-I fell asleep...
RITSUKA.
YOU'RE AWAKE?
WHO WAS THAT ON THE PHONE?
WAS IT SCHOOL? WAS IT SHINONOME-SENSEI?
ズキ
ズキ
ARE YOU HUNGRY? ARE YOU ALL RIGHT?
I'M NOT HUNGRY.
BUT THIS IS... UM..
GOOD. I DON'T HAVE TO COOK...
I FEEL SLUGGISH, AND MY HEAD HURTS.
I DON'T HAVE AN APPETITE, EITHER.

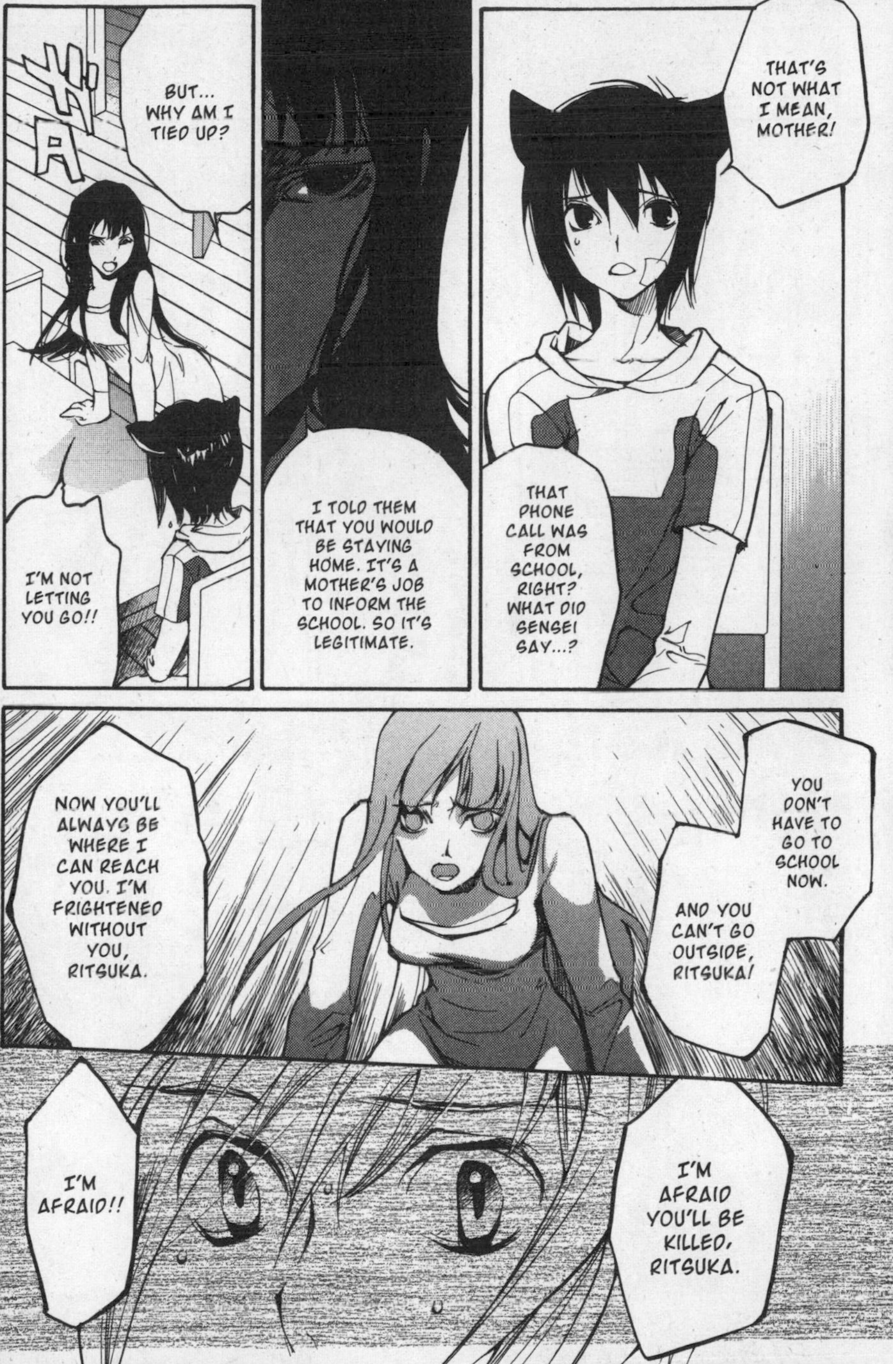
THAT'S NOT WHAT I MEAN, MOTHER!
THAT PHONE CALL WAS FROM SCHOOL, RIGHT? WHAT DID SENSEI SAY...?
I TOLD THEM THAT YOU WOULD BE STAYING HOME. IT'S A MOTHER'S JOB TO INFORM THE SCHOOL. SO IT'S LEGITIMATE.
BUT... WHY AM I TIED UP?
I'M NOT LETTING YOU GO!!
YOU DON'T HAVE TO GO TO SCHOOL NOW.
AND YOU CAN'T GO OUTSIDE, RITSUKA!
NOW YOU'LL ALWAYS BE WHERE I CAN REACH YOU. I'M FRIGHTENED WITHOUT YOU, RITSUKA.
I'M AFRAID YOU'LL BE KILLED, RITSUKA.
I'M AFRAID!!

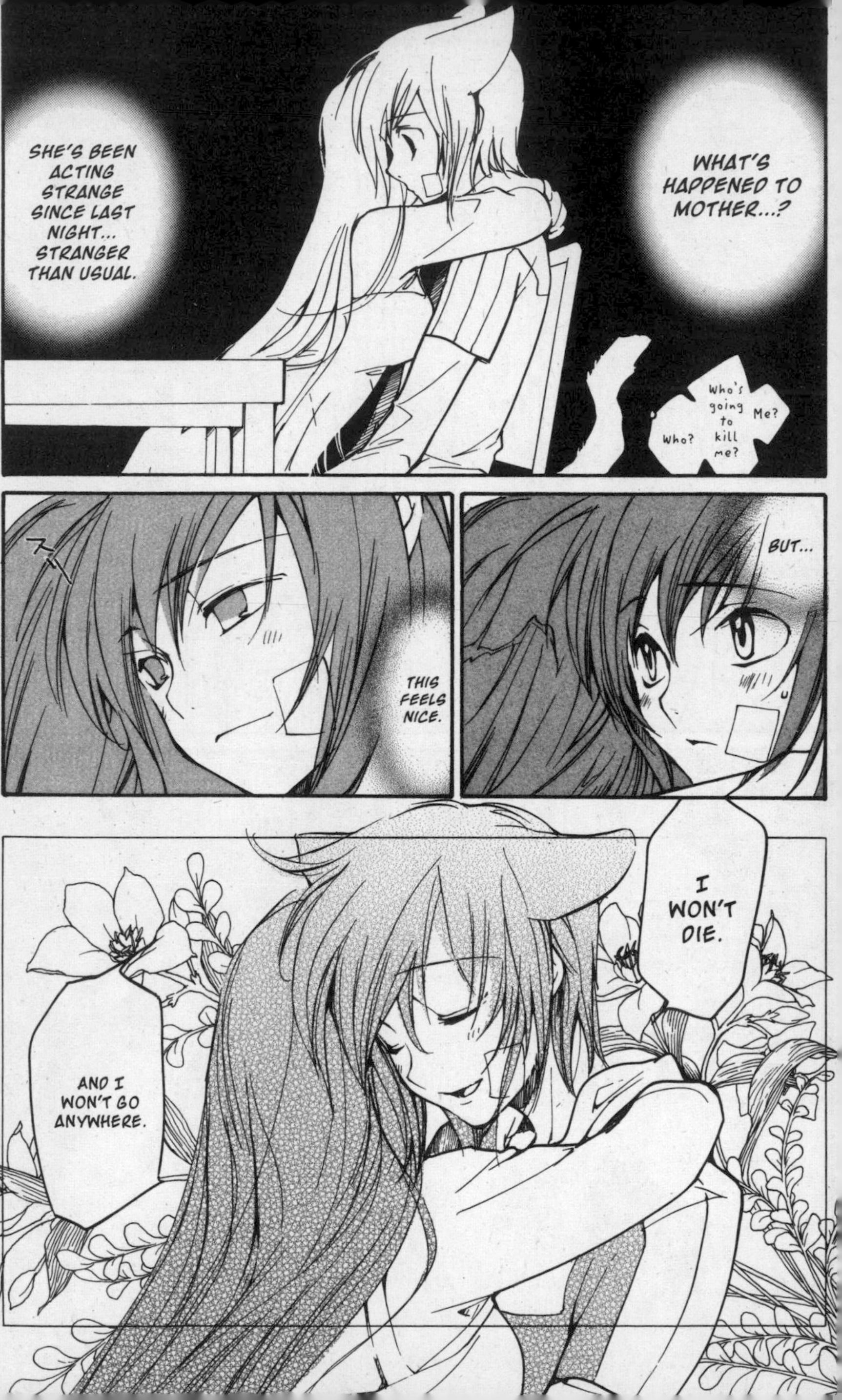
WHAT'S HAPPENED TO MOTHER...?
SHE'S BEEN ACTING STRANGE SINCE LAST NIGHT... STRANGER THAN USUAL.
Who's going to kill me? Me? Who?
BUT...
THIS FEELS NICE.
I WON'T DIE.
AND I WON'T GO ANYWHERE.

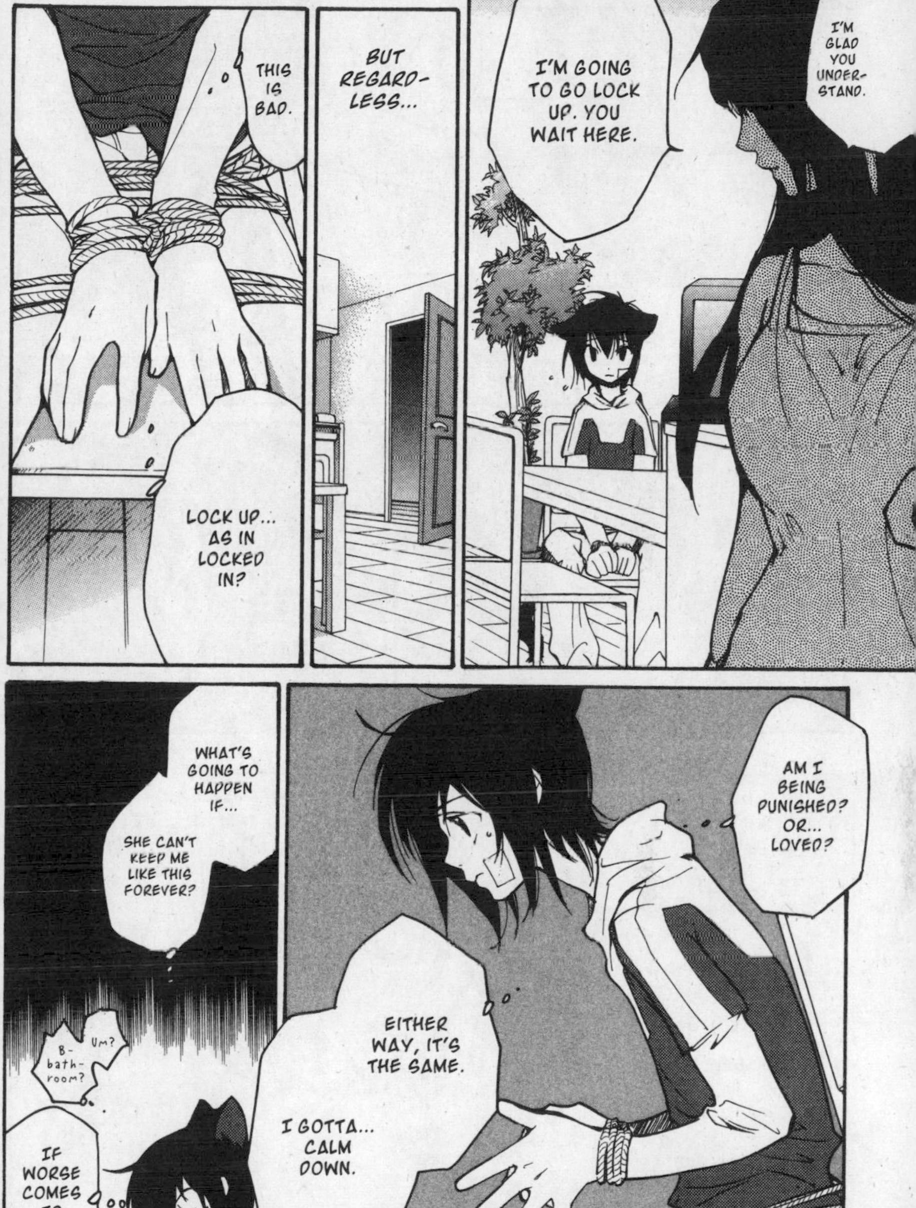
I'M GLAD YOU UNDER-STAND.
I'M GOING TO GO LOCK UP. YOU WAIT HERE.
BUT REGARD-LESS...
THIS IS BAD.
LOCK UP... AS IN LOCKED IN?
AM I BEING PUNISHED? OR... LOVED?
EITHER WAY, IT'S THE SAME.
I GOTTA... CALM DOWN.
WHAT'S GOING TO HAPPEN IF...
SHE CAN'T KEEP ME LIKE THIS FOREVER?
Um?
B-bath-room?
IF WORSE COMES TO WORST...

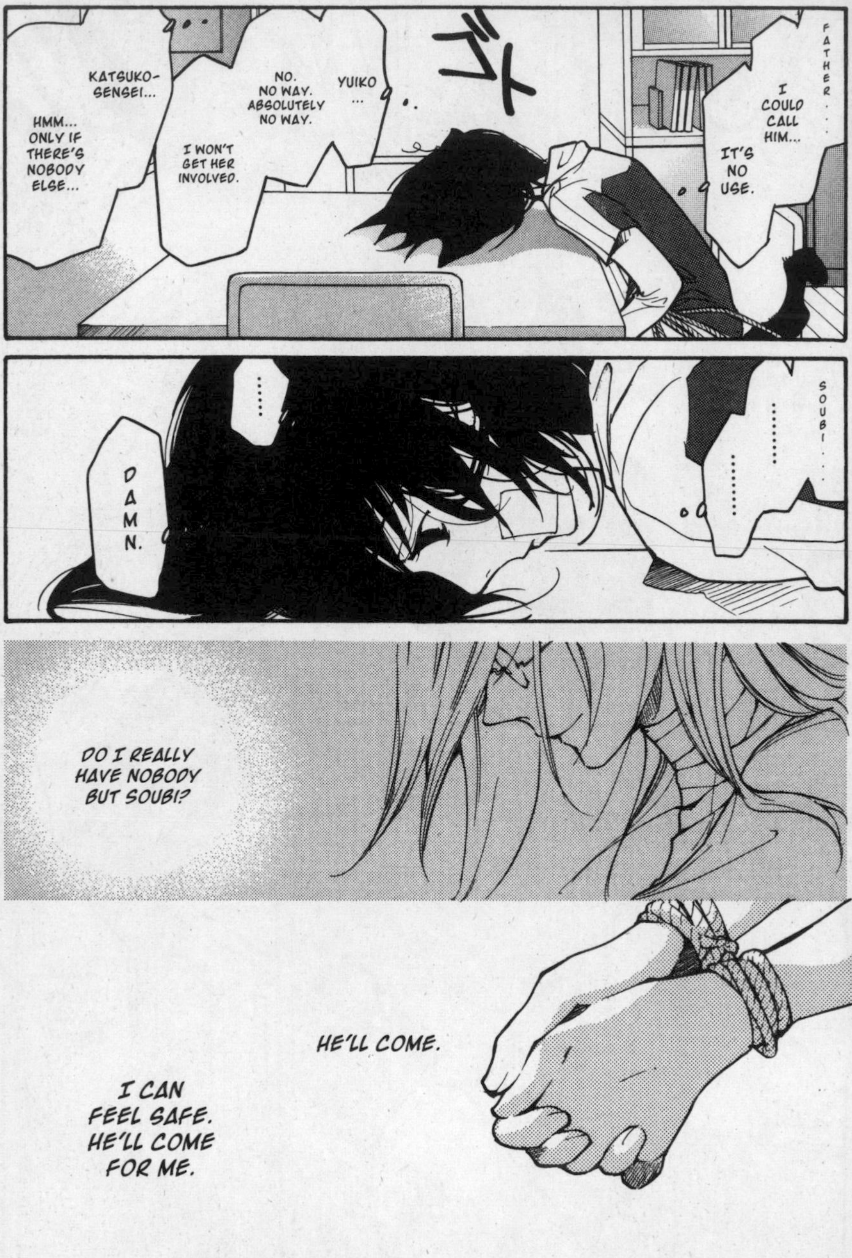
FATHER...
I COULD CALL HIM...
IT'S NO USE.
YUIKO...
NO. NO WAY. ABSOLUTELY NO WAY.
I WON'T GET HER INVOLVED.
KATSUKO-SENSEI...
HMM... ONLY IF THERE'S NOBODY ELSE...
SOUBI...
....
....
......
DAMN.
DO I REALLY HAVE NOBODY BUT SOUBI?
HE'LL COME.
I CAN FEEL SAFE. HE'LL COME FOR ME.

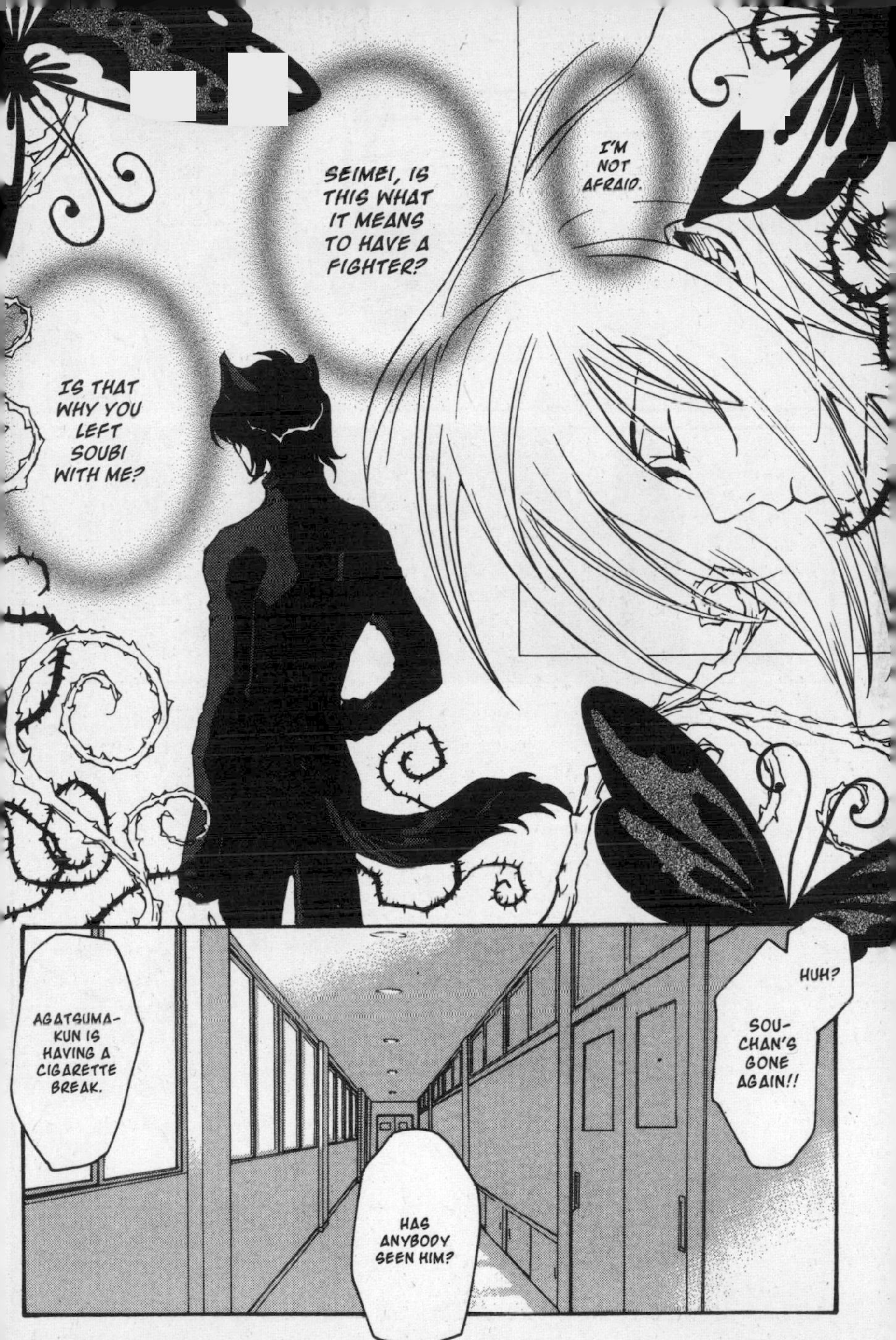
I'M NOT AFRAID.
SEIMEI, IS THIS WHAT IT MEANS TO HAVE A FIGHTER?
IS THAT WHY YOU LEFT SOUBI WITH ME?
HUH?
SOU-CHAN'S GONE AGAIN!!
HAS ANYBODY SEEN HIM?
AGATSUMA-KUN IS HAVING A CIGARETTE BREAK.

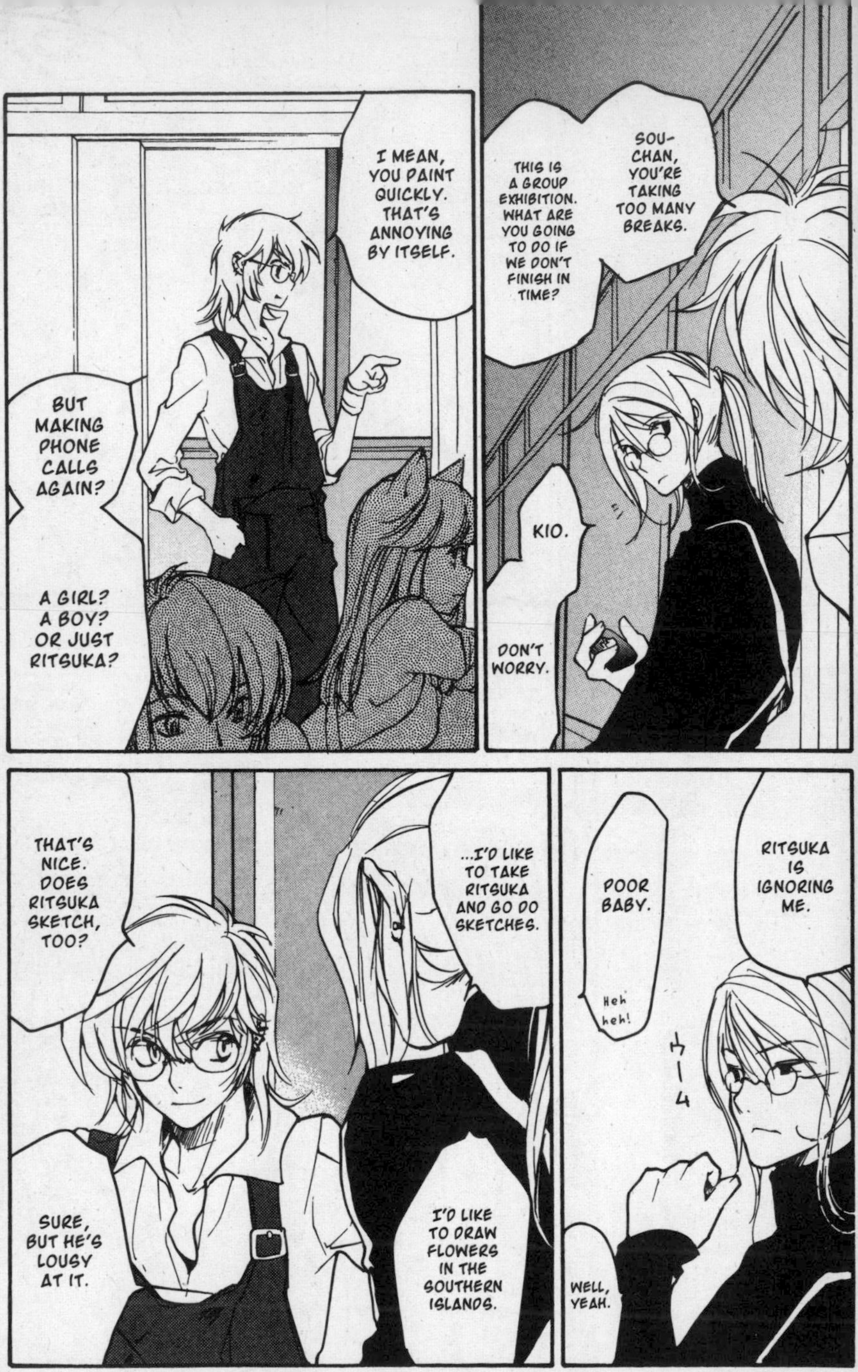
SOU-CHAN, YOU'RE TAKING TOO MANY BREAKS.
THIS IS A GROUP EXHIBITION. WHAT ARE YOU GOING TO DO IF WE DON'T FINISH IN TIME?
KIO.
DON'T WORRY.
I MEAN, YOU PAINT QUICKLY. THAT'S ANNOYING BY ITSELF.
BUT MAKING PHONE CALLS AGAIN?
A GIRL? A BOY? OR JUST RITSUKA?
RITSUKA IS IGNORING ME.
POOR BABY.
Heh heh!
ウーム
WELL, YEAH.
...I'D LIKE TO TAKE RITSUKA AND GO DO SKETCHES.
THAT'S NICE. DOES RITSUKA SKETCH, TOO?
I'D LIKE TO DRAW FLOWERS IN THE SOUTHERN ISLANDS.
SURE, BUT HE'S LOUSY AT IT.

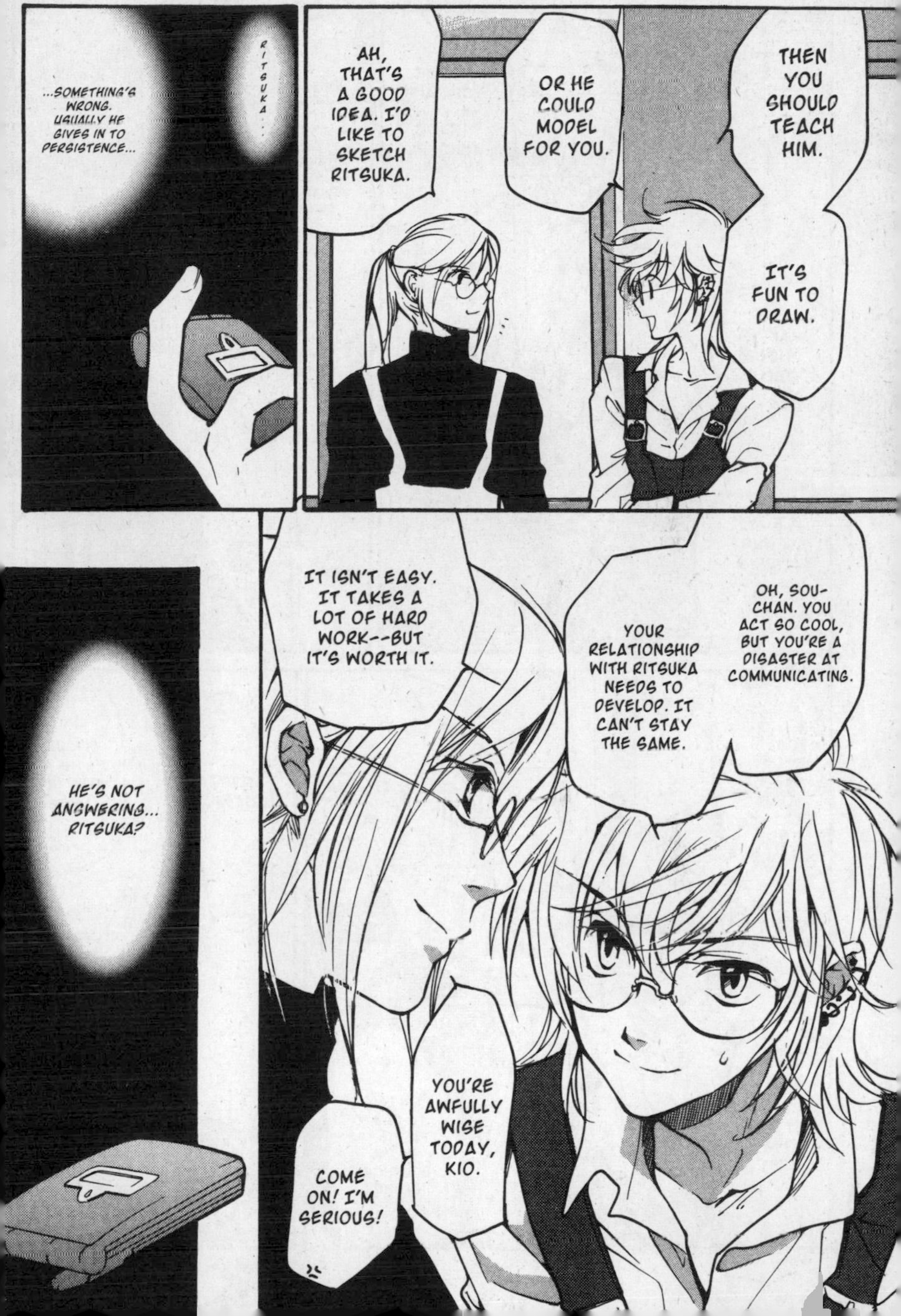
THEN YOU SHOULD TEACH HIM.
IT'S FUN TO DRAW.
OR HE COULD MODEL FOR YOU.
AH, THAT'S A GOOD IDEA. I'D LIKE TO SKETCH RITSUKA.
RITSUKA...
...SOMETHING'S WRONG. USUALLY HE GIVES IN TO PERSISTENCE...
OH, SOU-CHAN. YOU ACT SO COOL, BUT YOU'RE A DISASTER AT COMMUNICATING.
YOUR RELATIONSHIP WITH RITSUKA NEEDS TO DEVELOP. IT CAN'T STAY THE SAME.
IT ISN'T EASY. IT TAKES A LOT OF HARD WORK--BUT IT'S WORTH IT.
YOU'RE AWFULLY WISE TODAY, KIO.
COME ON! I'M SERIOUS!
HE'S NOT ANSWERING... RITSUKA?

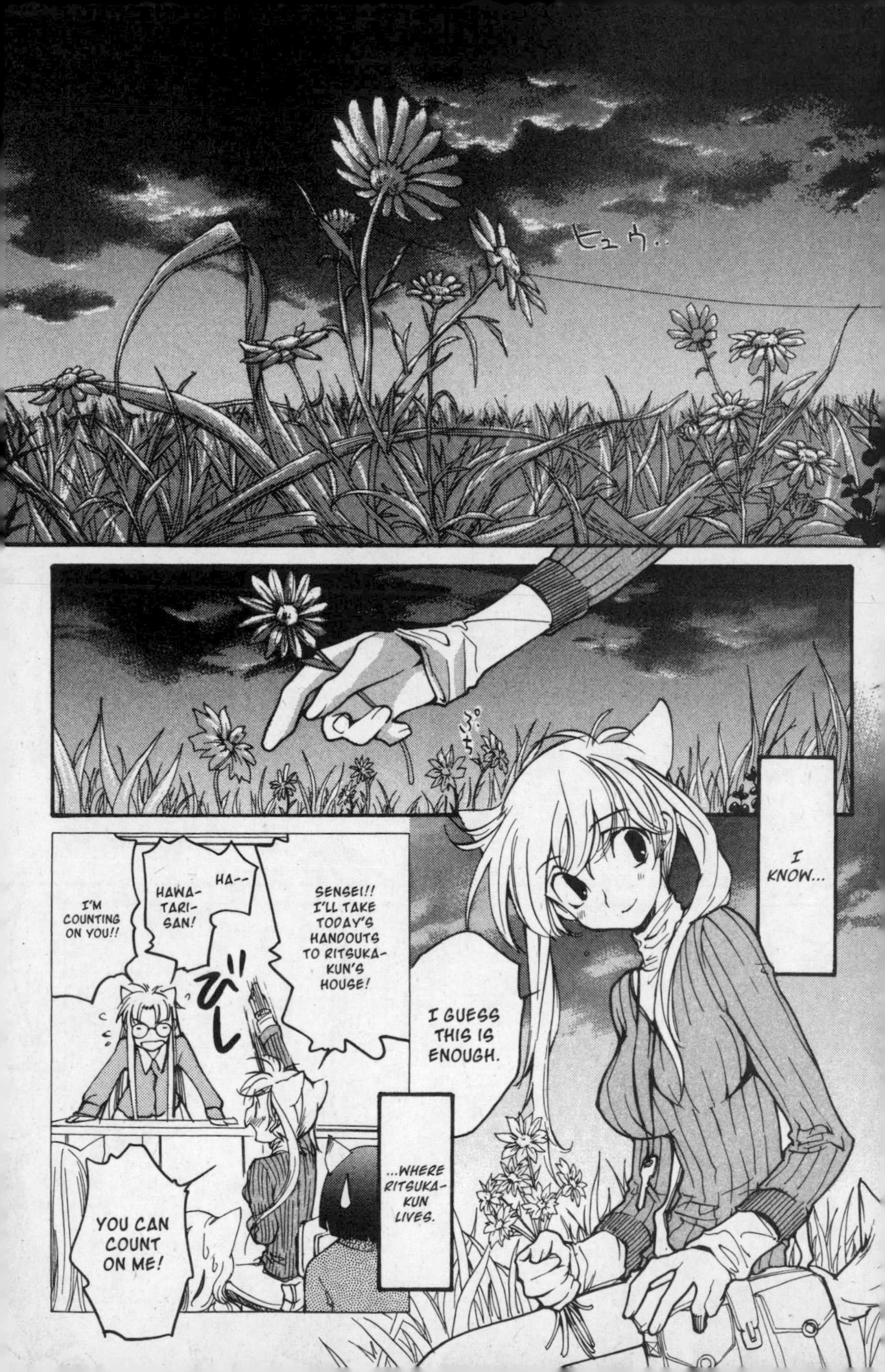
ヒュゥ..
ぷち
I KNOW...
I GUESS THIS IS ENOUGH.
...WHERE RITSUKA-KUN LIVES.
SENSEI!! I'LL TAKE TODAY'S HANDOUTS TO RITSUKA-KUN'S HOUSE!
HA--
HAWATARI-SAN!
I'M COUNTING ON YOU!!
びし
YOU CAN COUNT ON ME!

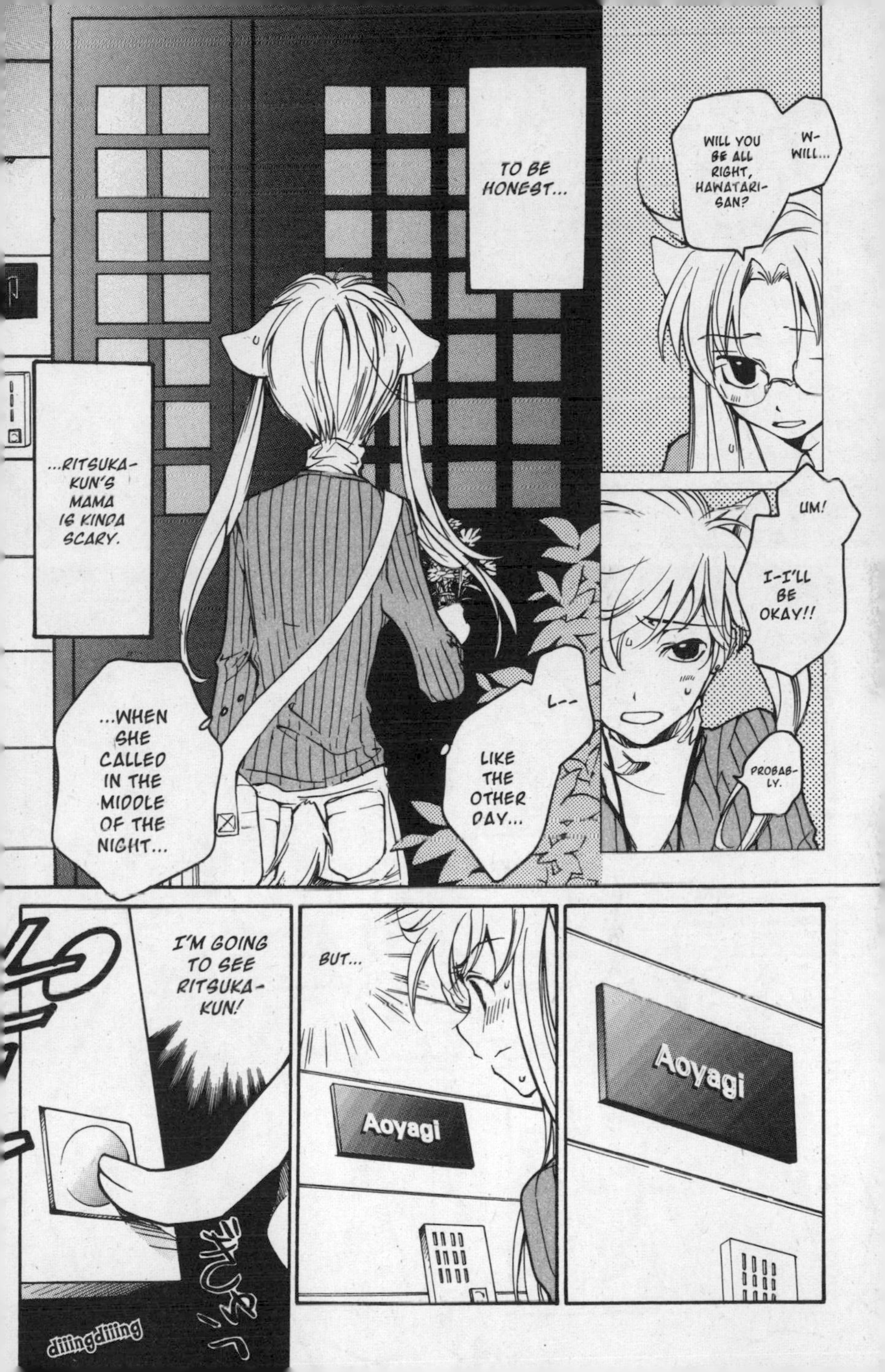
W-WILL...
WILL YOU BE ALL RIGHT, HAWATARI-SAN?
UM!
I-I'LL BE OKAY!!
PROBABLY.
TO BE HONEST...
...RITSUKA-KUN'S MAMA IS KINDA SCARY.
L--
LIKE THE OTHER DAY...
...WHEN SHE CALLED IN THE MIDDLE OF THE NIGHT...
Aoyagi
BUT...
Aoyagi
I'M GOING TO SEE RITSUKA-KUN!
diiingdiiing

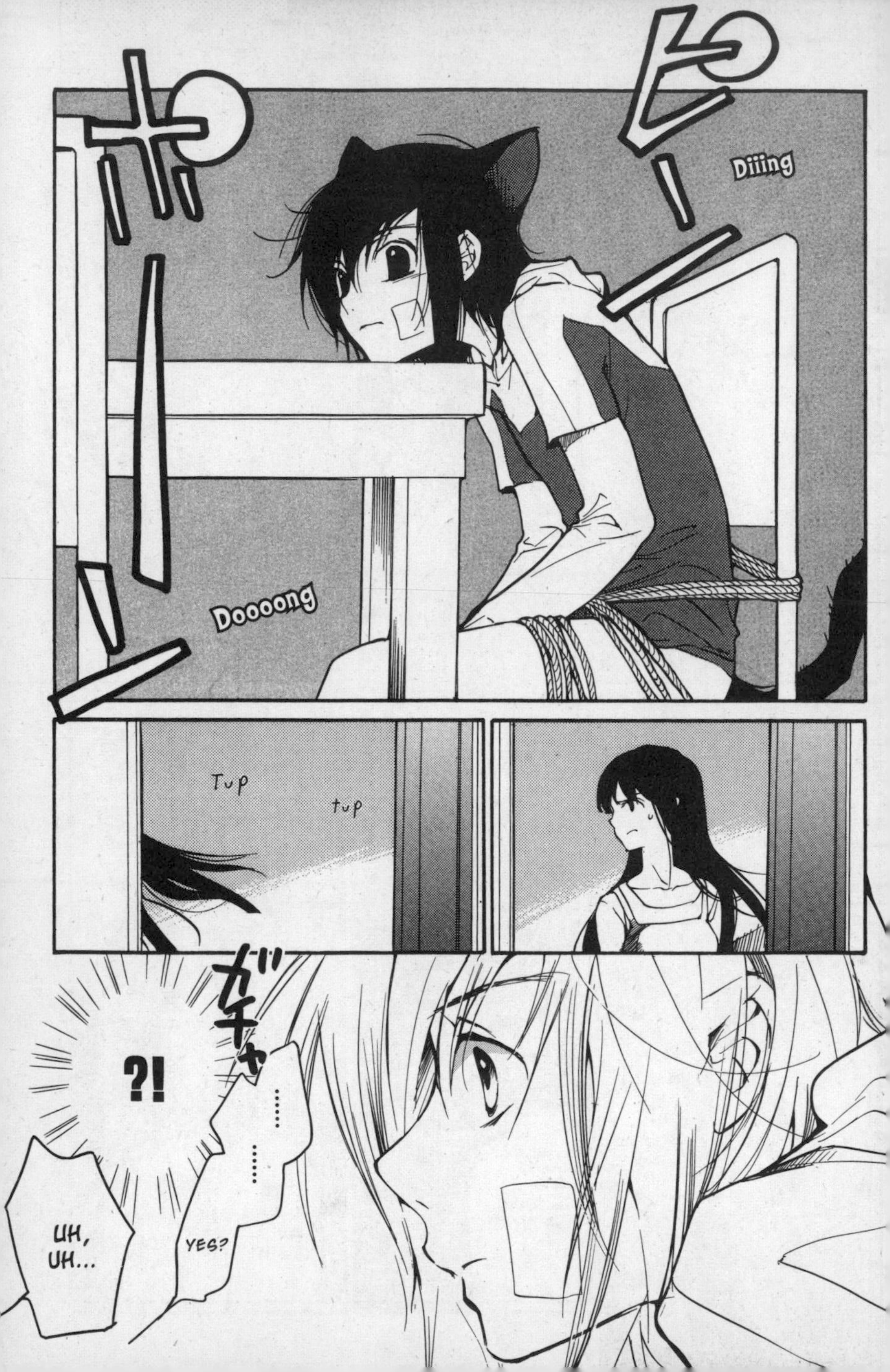
Diiing
Doooong
Tup
tup
ガチャ
......
......
YES?
?!
UH,
UH...

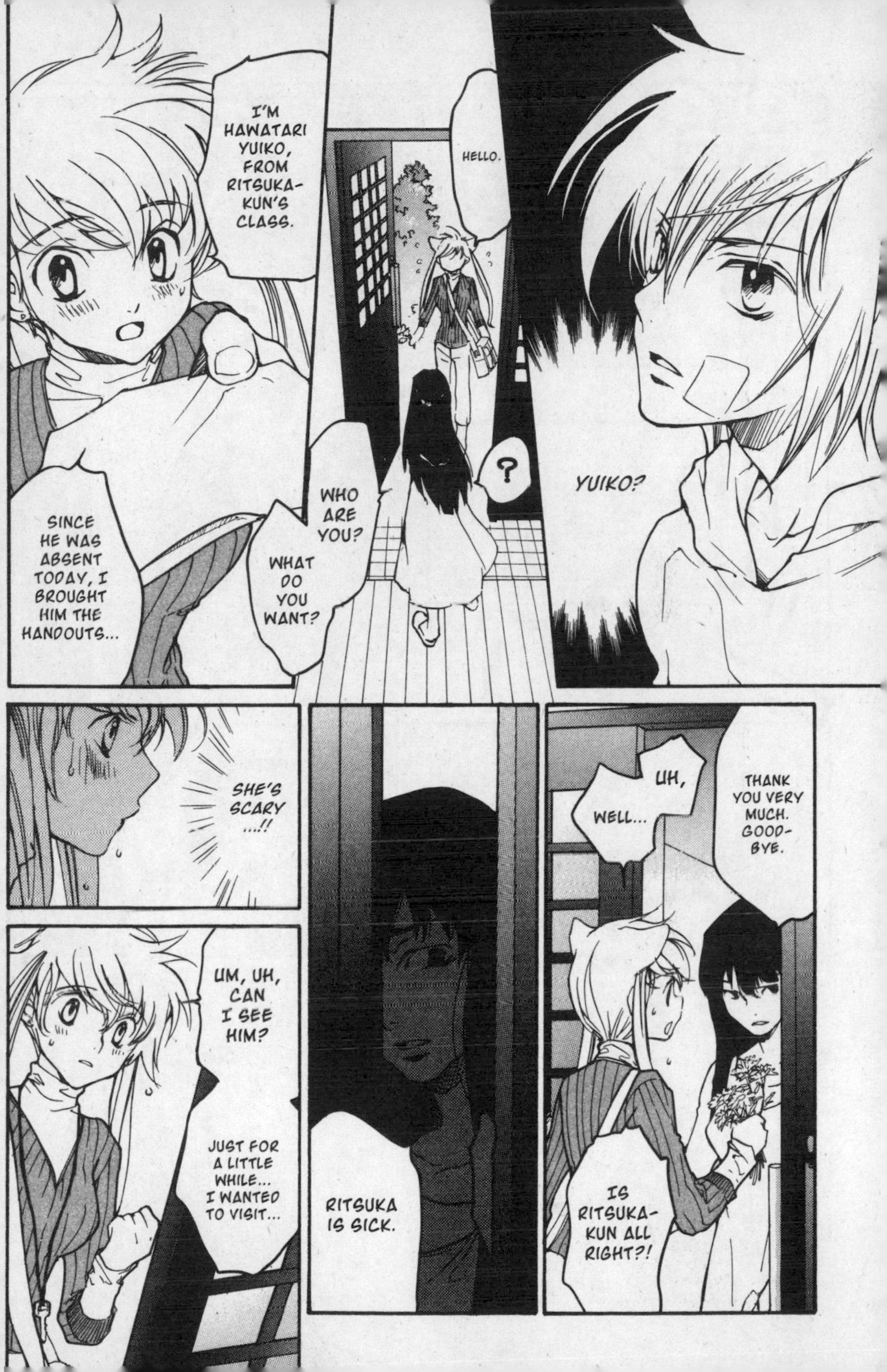
YUIKO?
HELLO.
?
WHO ARE YOU?
WHAT DO YOU WANT?
I'M HAWATARI YUIKO, FROM RITSUKA-KUN'S CLASS.
SINCE HE WAS ABSENT TODAY, I BROUGHT HIM THE HANDOUTS...
THANK YOU VERY MUCH. GOOD-BYE.
UH, WELL...
IS RITSUKA-KUN ALL RIGHT?!
RITSUKA IS SICK.
SHE'S SCARY ...!!
UM, UH, CAN I SEE HIM?
JUST FOR A LITTLE WHILE... I WANTED TO VISIT...

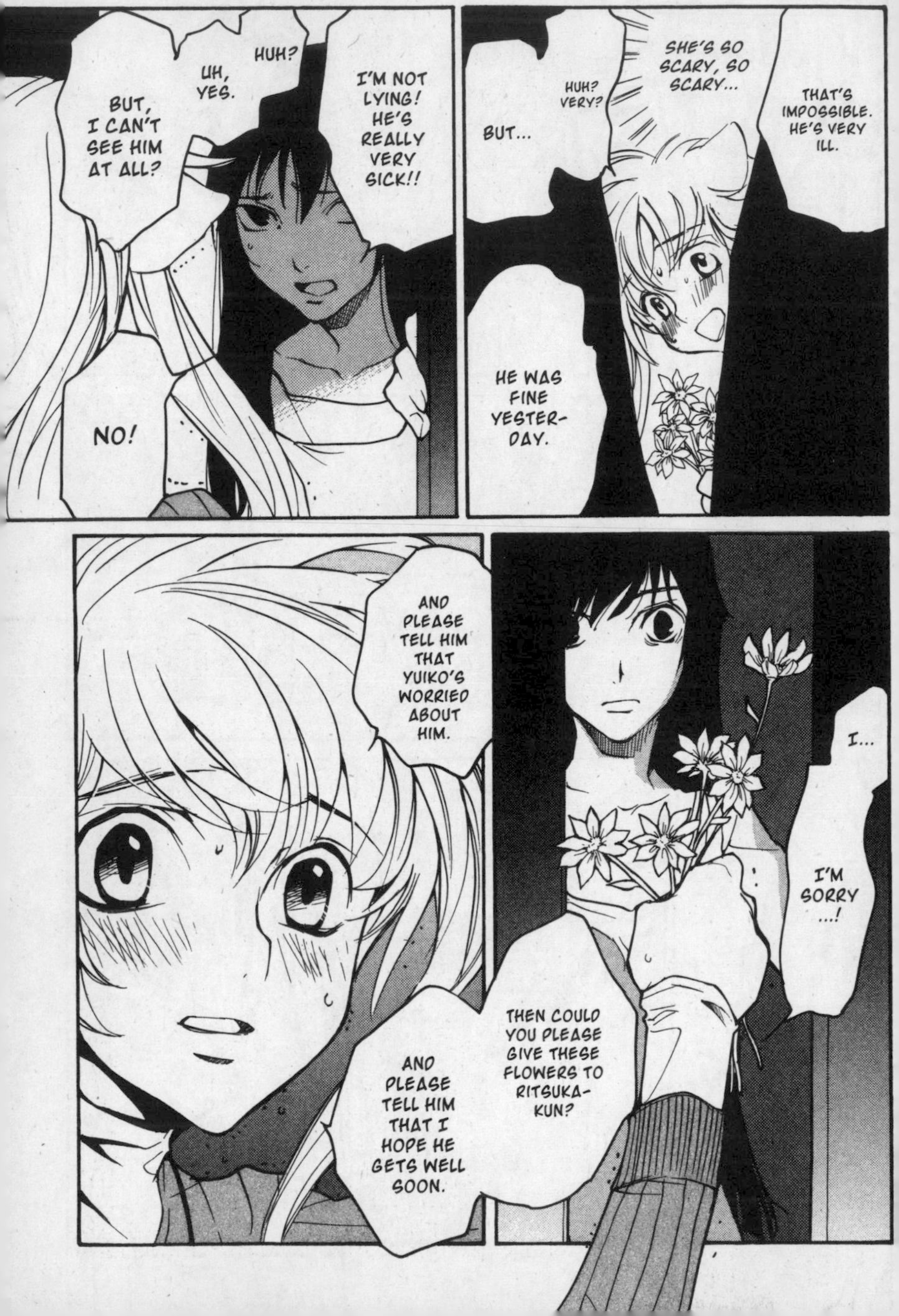
THAT'S IMPOSSIBLE. HE'S VERY ILL.
SHE'S SO SCARY, SO SCARY...
HUH? VERY?
BUT...
HE WAS FINE YESTER-DAY.
I'M NOT LYING! HE'S REALLY VERY SICK!!
HUH?
UH, YES.
BUT, I CAN'T SEE HIM AT ALL?
NO!
I...
I'M SORRY ...!
THEN COULD YOU PLEASE GIVE THESE FLOWERS TO RITSUKA-KUN?
AND PLEASE TELL HIM THAT YUIKO'S WORRIED ABOUT HIM.
AND PLEASE TELL HIM THAT I HOPE HE GETS WELL SOON.

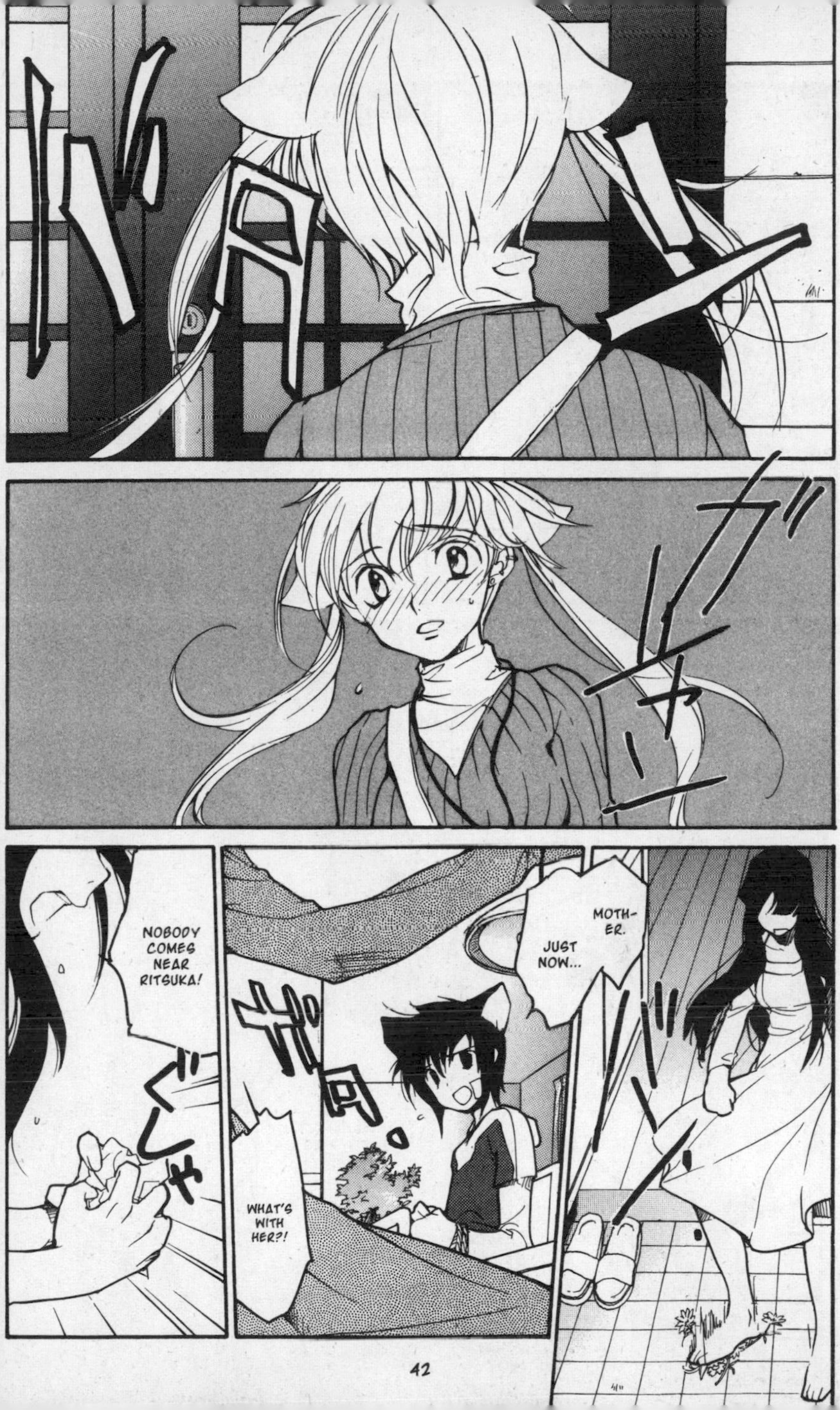
MOTH- ER.
JUST NOW...
WHAT'S WITH HER?!
NOBODY COMES NEAR RITSUKA!

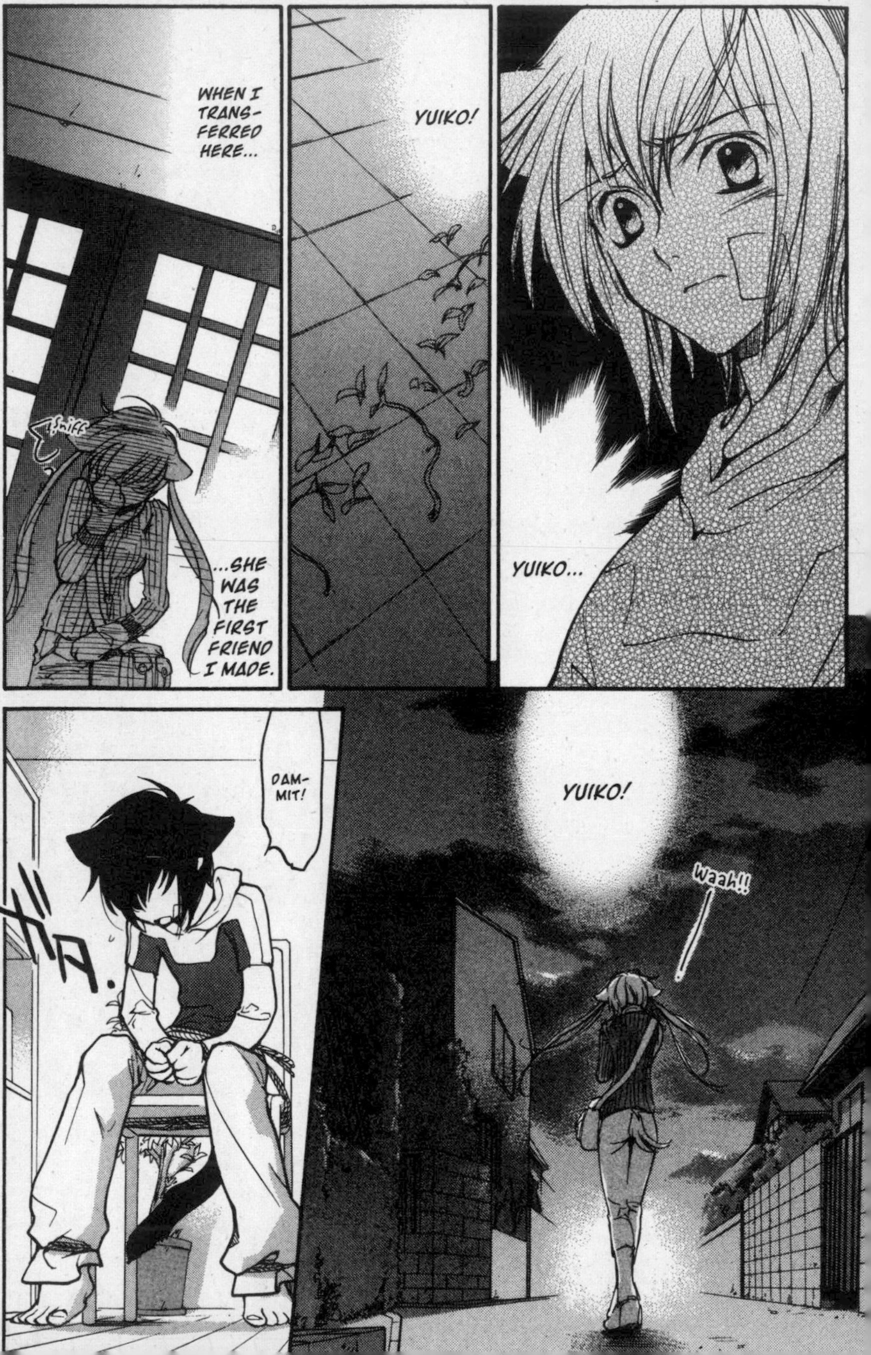
YUIKO...
YUIKO!
WHEN I TRANSFERRED HERE...
Sniff
...SHE WAS THE FIRST FRIEND I MADE.
YUIKO!
Waah!!
DAMMIT!

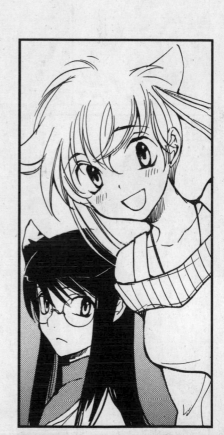

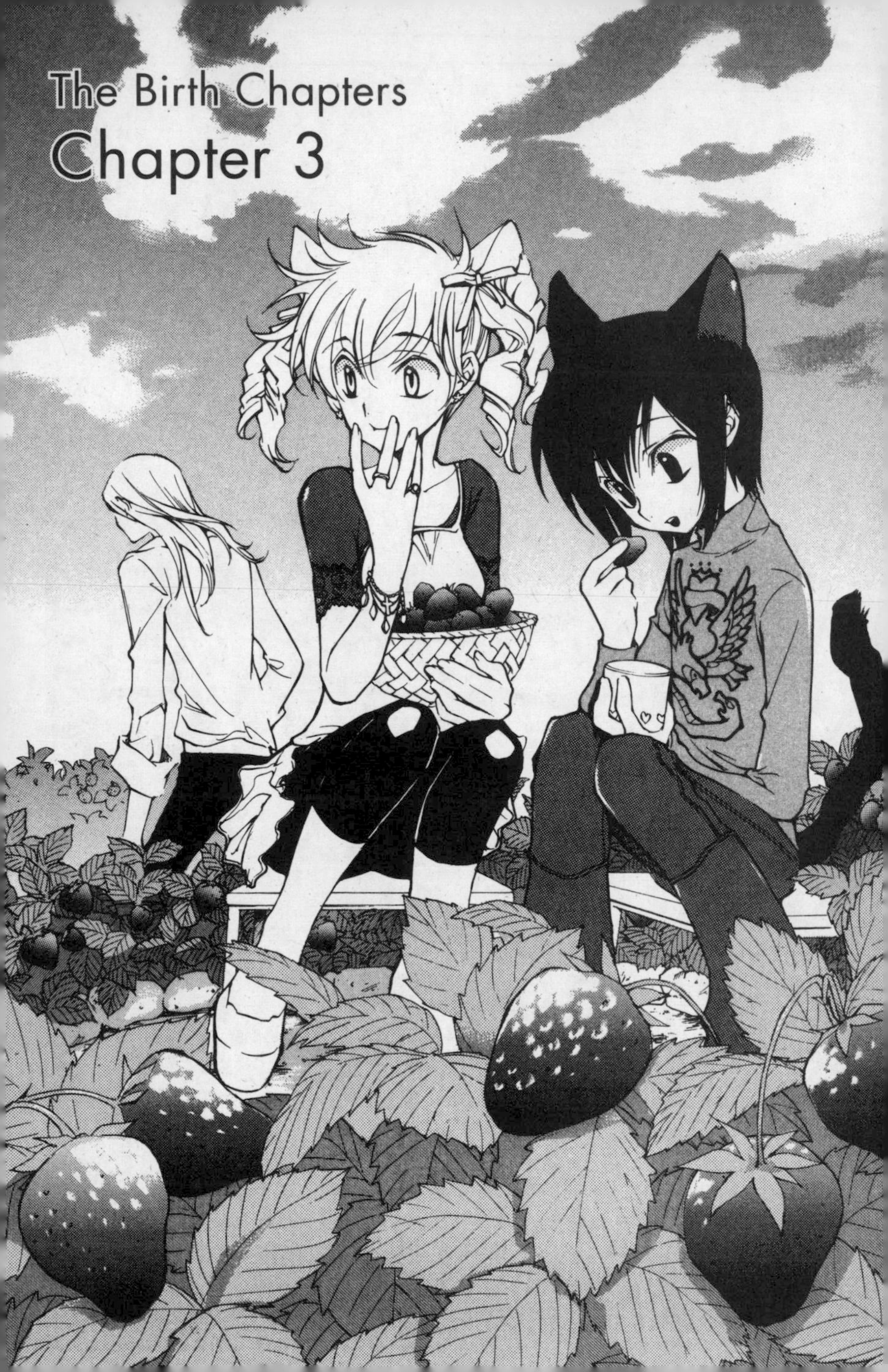
The Birth Chapters
Chapter 3

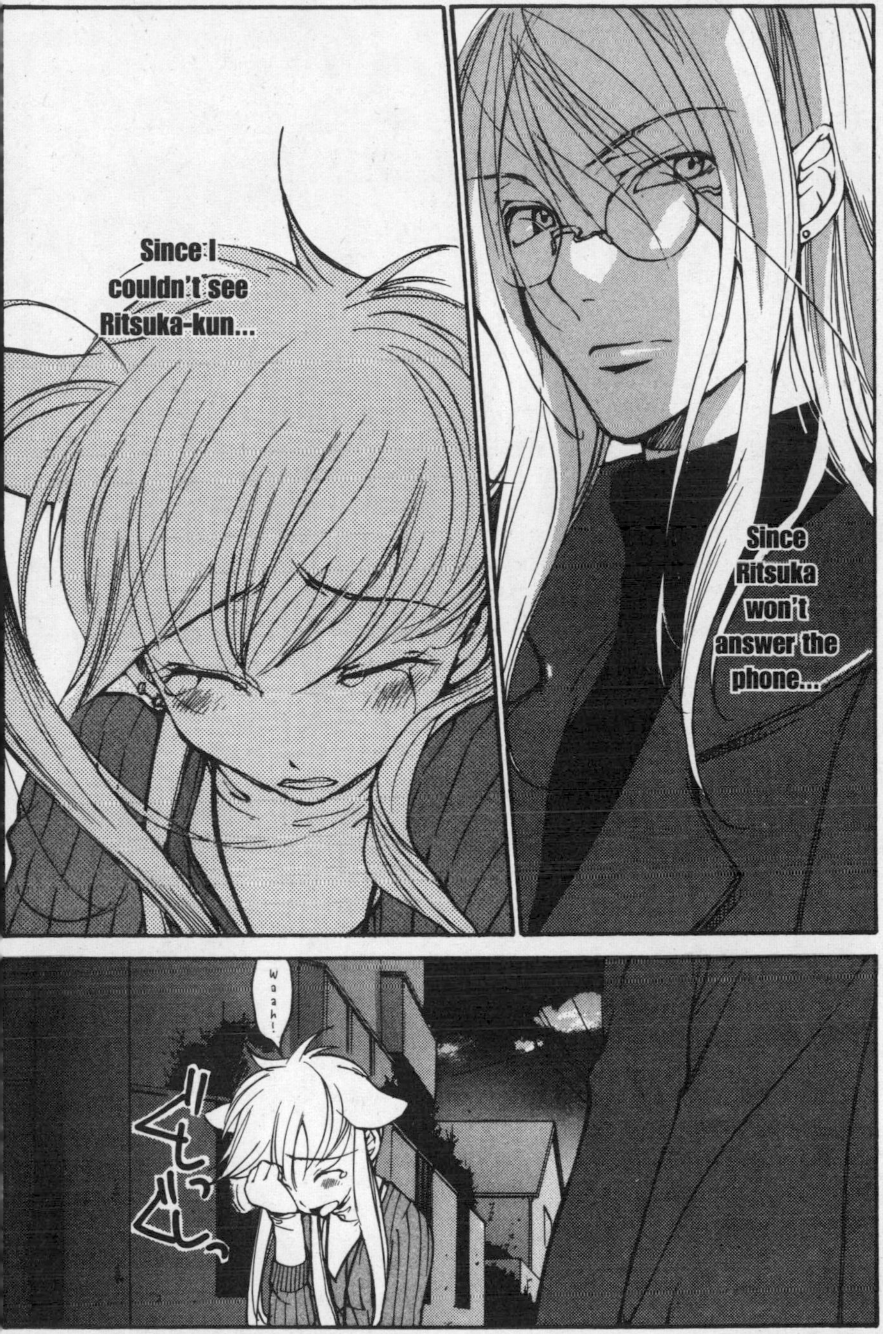
Since Ritsuka won't answer the phone...
Since I couldn't see Ritsuka-kun...
Woah!

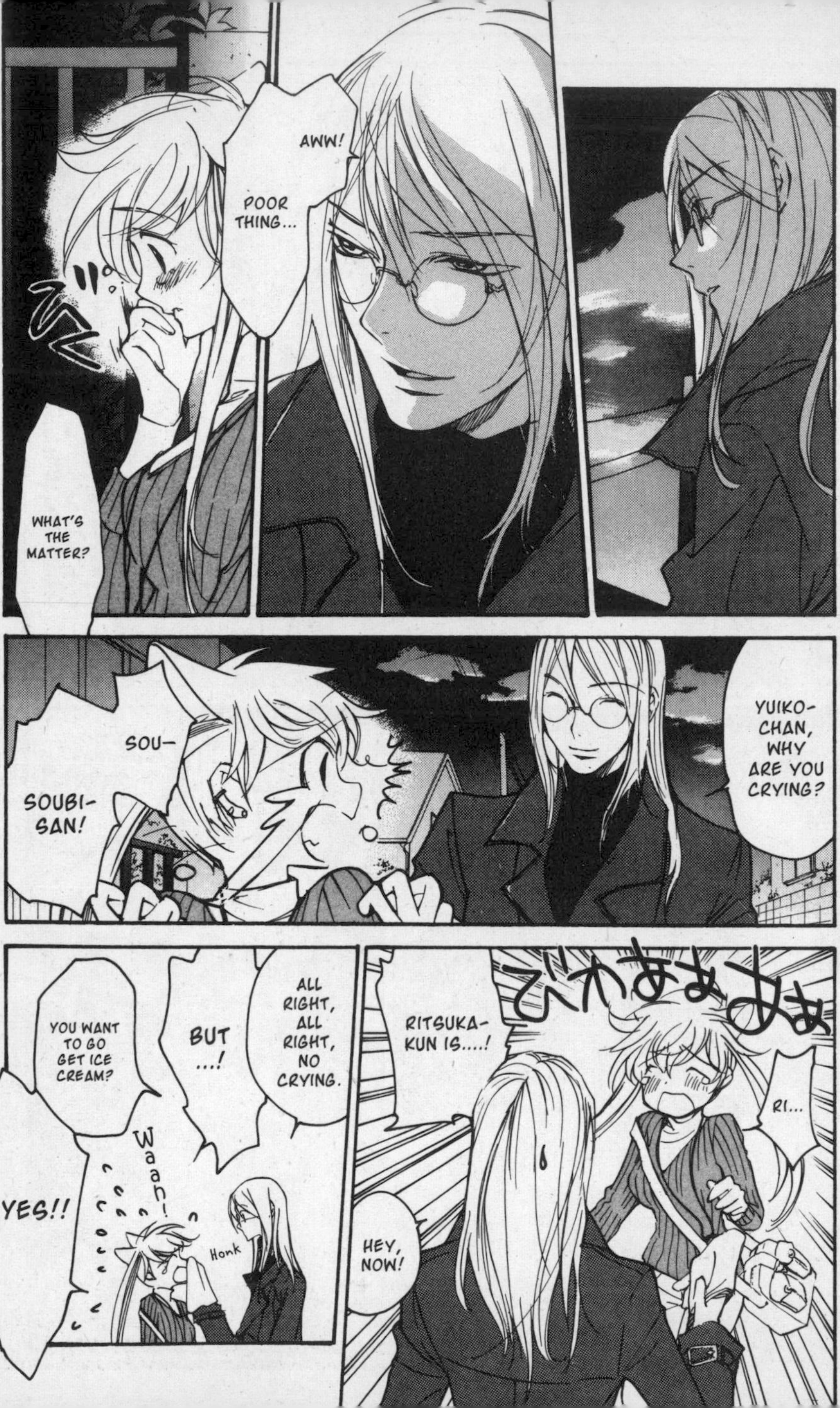

AWW!
POOR THING...
WHAT'S THE MATTER?
YUIKO-CHAN, WHY ARE YOU CRYING?
SOU-
SOUBI-SAN!
RI...
RITSUKA-KUN IS.....!
HEY, NOW!
ALL RIGHT, ALL RIGHT, NO CRYING.
BUT ...!
YOU WANT TO GO GET ICE CREAM?
Waah!
Honk
YES!!

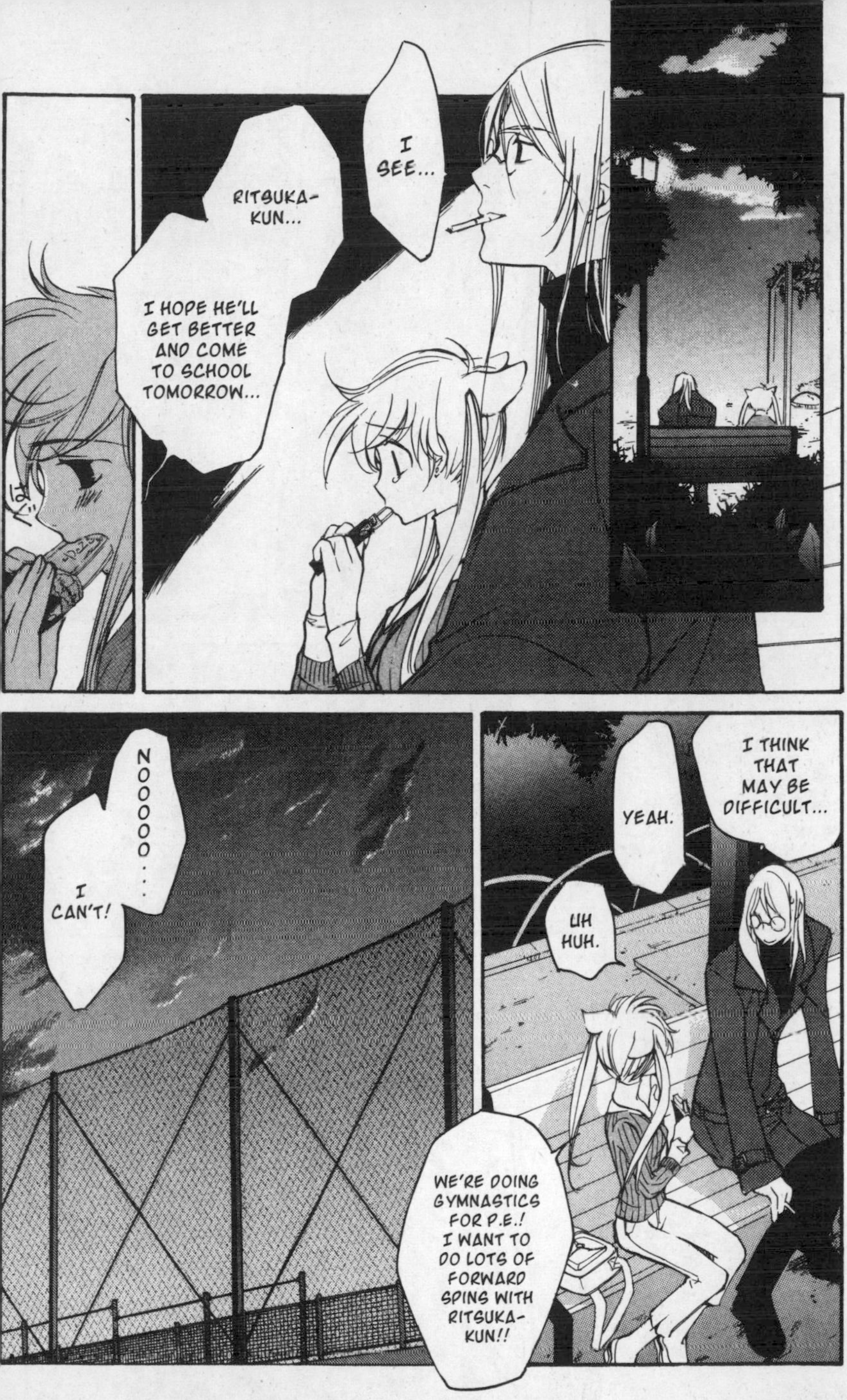
I SEE...
RITSUKA-KUN...
I HOPE HE'LL GET BETTER AND COME TO SCHOOL TOMORROW...
I THINK THAT MAY BE DIFFICULT...
YEAH.
UH HUH.
WE'RE DOING GYMNASTICS FOR P.E.! I WANT TO DO LOTS OF FORWARD SPINS WITH RITSUKA-KUN!!
NOOOOOO...
I CAN'T!

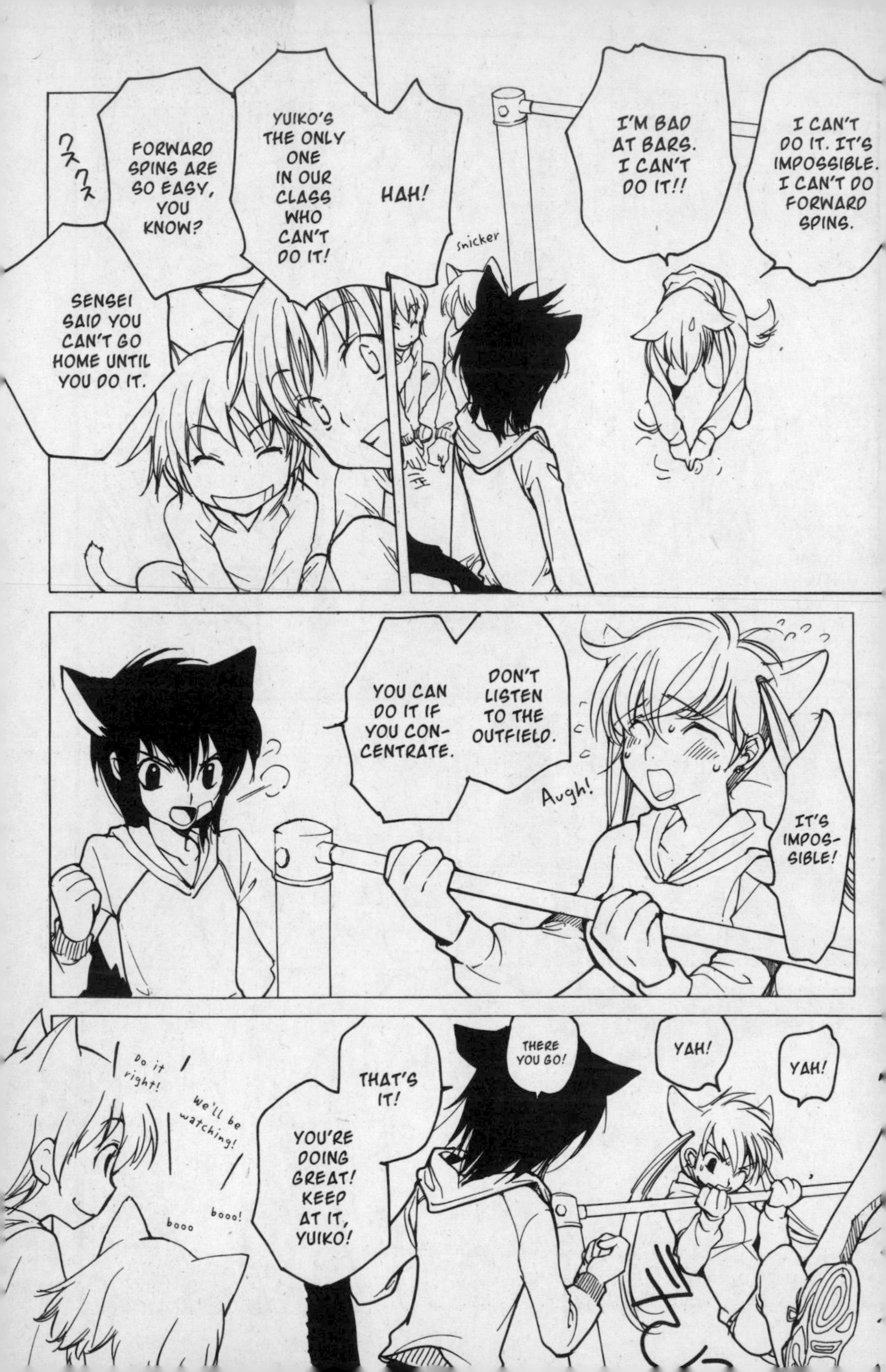
I CAN'T DO IT. IT'S IMPOSSIBLE. I CAN'T DO FORWARD SPINS.
I'M BAD AT BARS. I CAN'T DO IT!!
snicker
HAH!
YUIKO'S THE ONLY ONE IN OUR CLASS WHO CAN'T DO IT!
FORWARD SPINS ARE SO EASY, YOU KNOW?
クスクス
SENSEI SAID YOU CAN'T GO HOME UNTIL YOU DO IT.
IT'S IMPOS-SIBLE!
Augh!
DON'T LISTEN TO THE OUTFIELD.
YOU CAN DO IT IF YOU CON-CENTRATE.
YAH!
YAH!
THERE YOU GO!
THAT'S IT!
YOU'RE DOING GREAT! KEEP AT IT, YUIKO!
We'll be watching!
Do it right!
booo!
booo

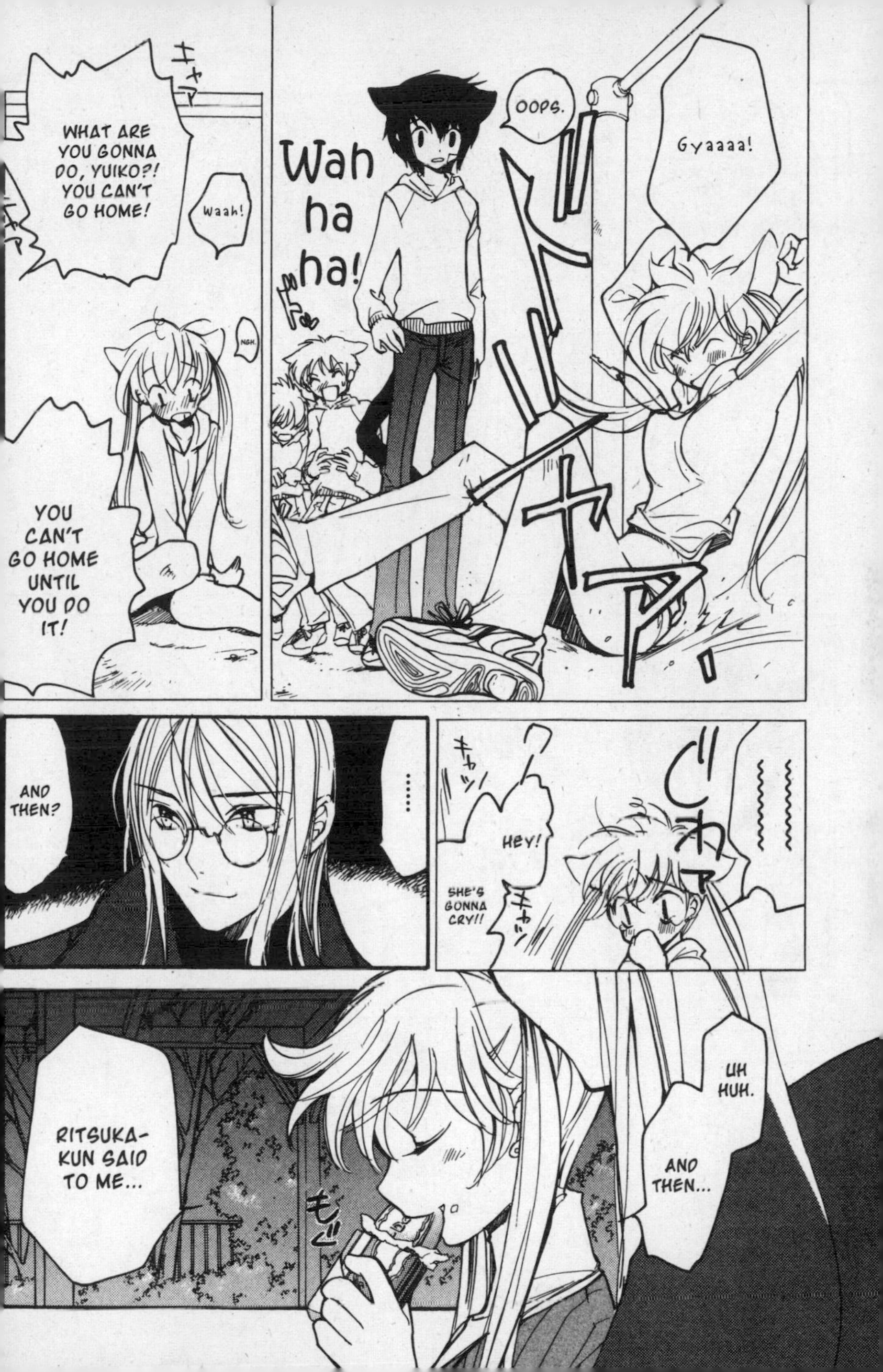
Gyaaaa!
OOPS.
Wah ha ha!
Waah!
WHAT ARE YOU GONNA DO, YUIKO?! YOU CAN'T GO HOME!
NGH.
YOU CAN'T GO HOME UNTIL YOU DO IT!
じわァ
HEY!
SHE'S GONNA CRY!!
......
AND THEN?
UH HUH.
AND THEN...
RITSUKA-KUN SAID TO ME...
もぐ

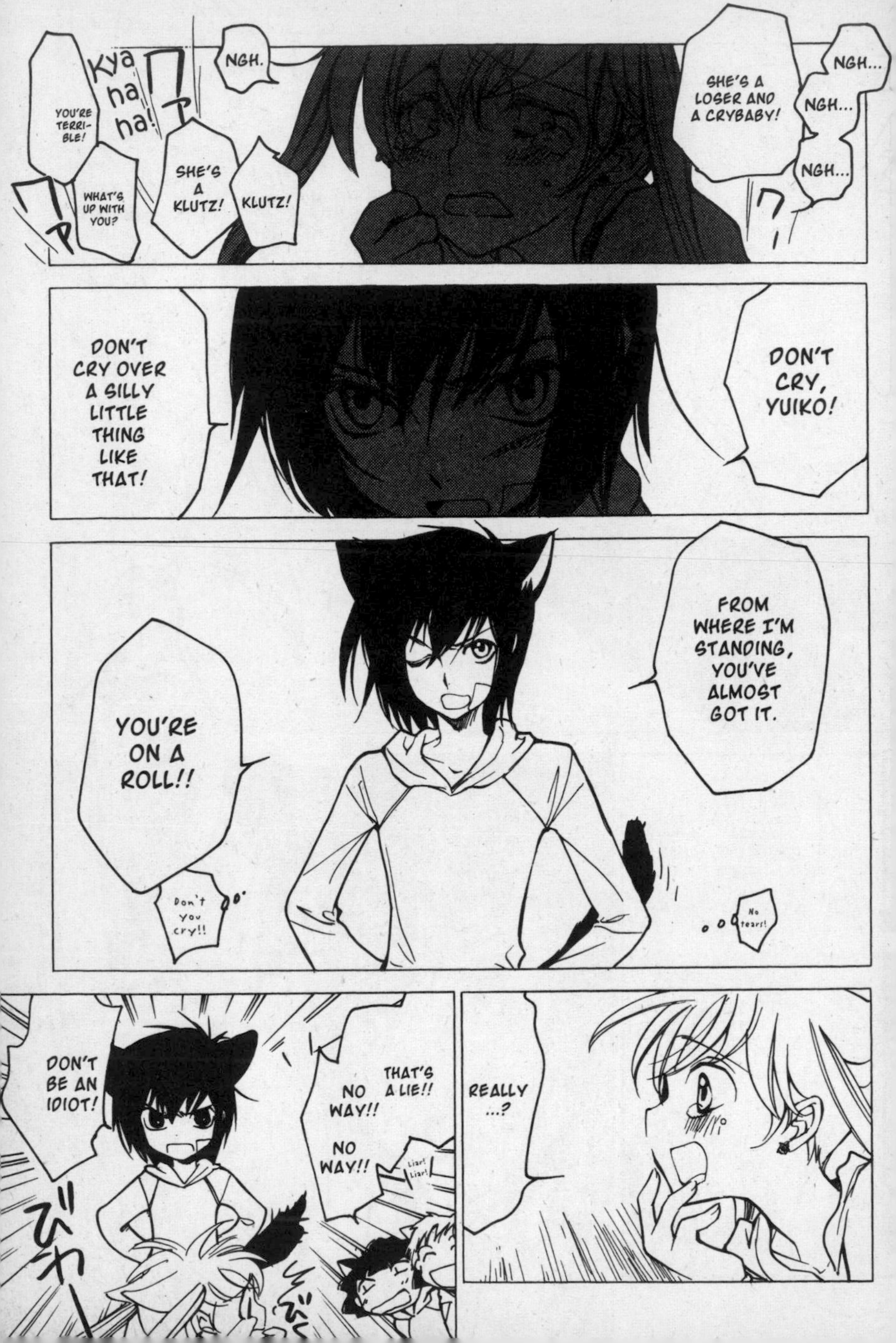
SHE'S A LOSER AND A CRYBABY!
NGH...
NGH...
NGH...
NGH.
KLUTZ!
SHE'S A KLUTZ!
Kya ha ha!
YOU'RE TERRI-BLE!
WHAT'S UP WITH YOU?
DON'T CRY, YUIKO!
DON'T CRY OVER A SILLY LITTLE THING LIKE THAT!
FROM WHERE I'M STANDING, YOU'VE ALMOST GOT IT.
YOU'RE ON A ROLL!!
No tears!
Don't you cry!!
REALLY ...?
THAT'S A LIE!!
NO WAY!!
NO WAY!!
Liar! Liar!
DON'T BE AN IDIOT!

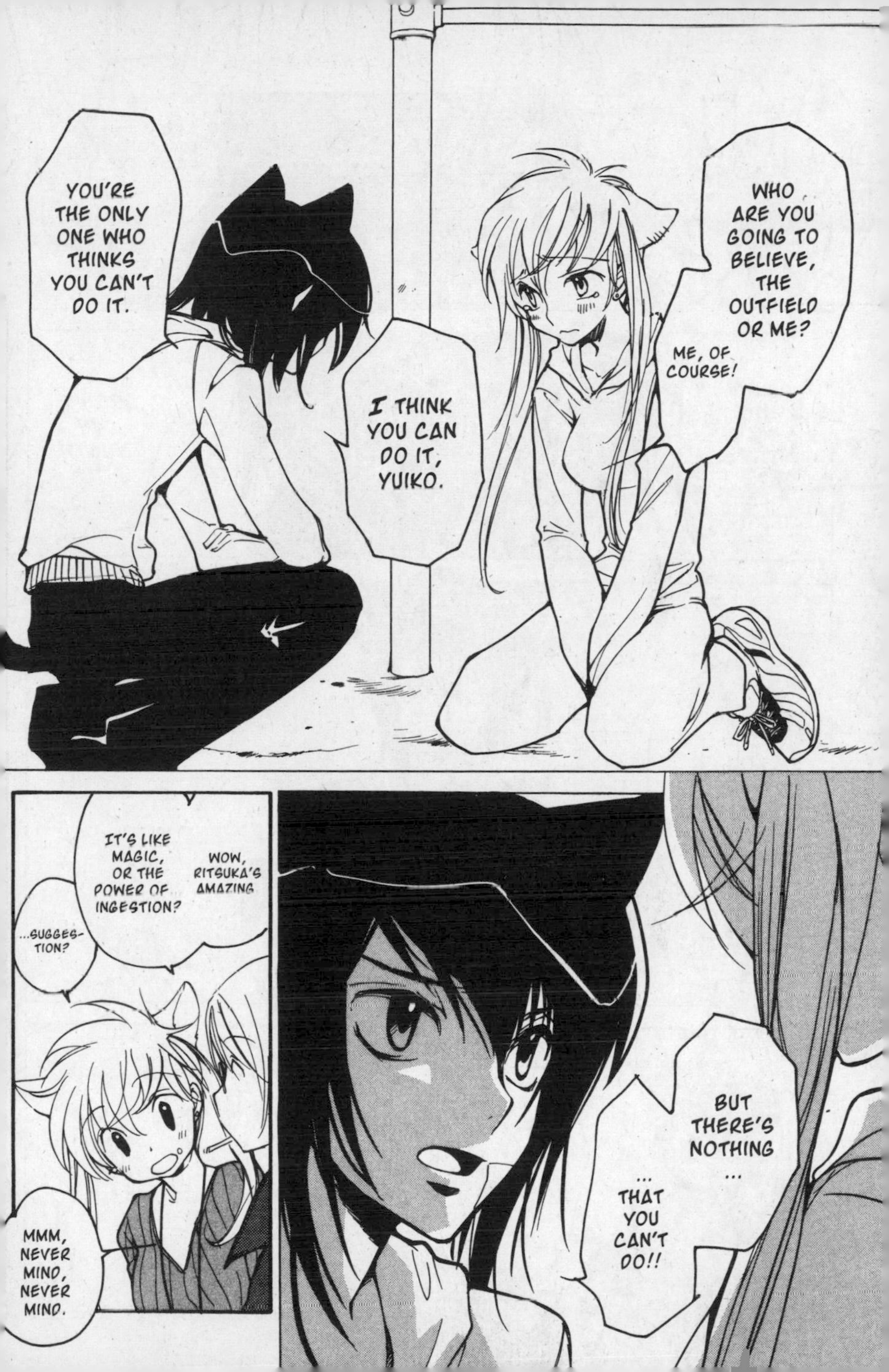
WHO ARE YOU GOING TO BELIEVE, THE OUTFIELD OR ME?
ME, OF COURSE!
YOU'RE THE ONLY ONE WHO THINKS YOU CAN'T DO IT.
I THINK YOU CAN DO IT, YUIKO.
BUT THERE'S NOTHING ... ... THAT YOU CAN'T DO!!
WOW, RITSUKA'S AMAZING
IT'S LIKE MAGIC, OR THE POWER OF INGESTION?
...SUGGESTION?
MMM, NEVER MIND, NEVER MIND.

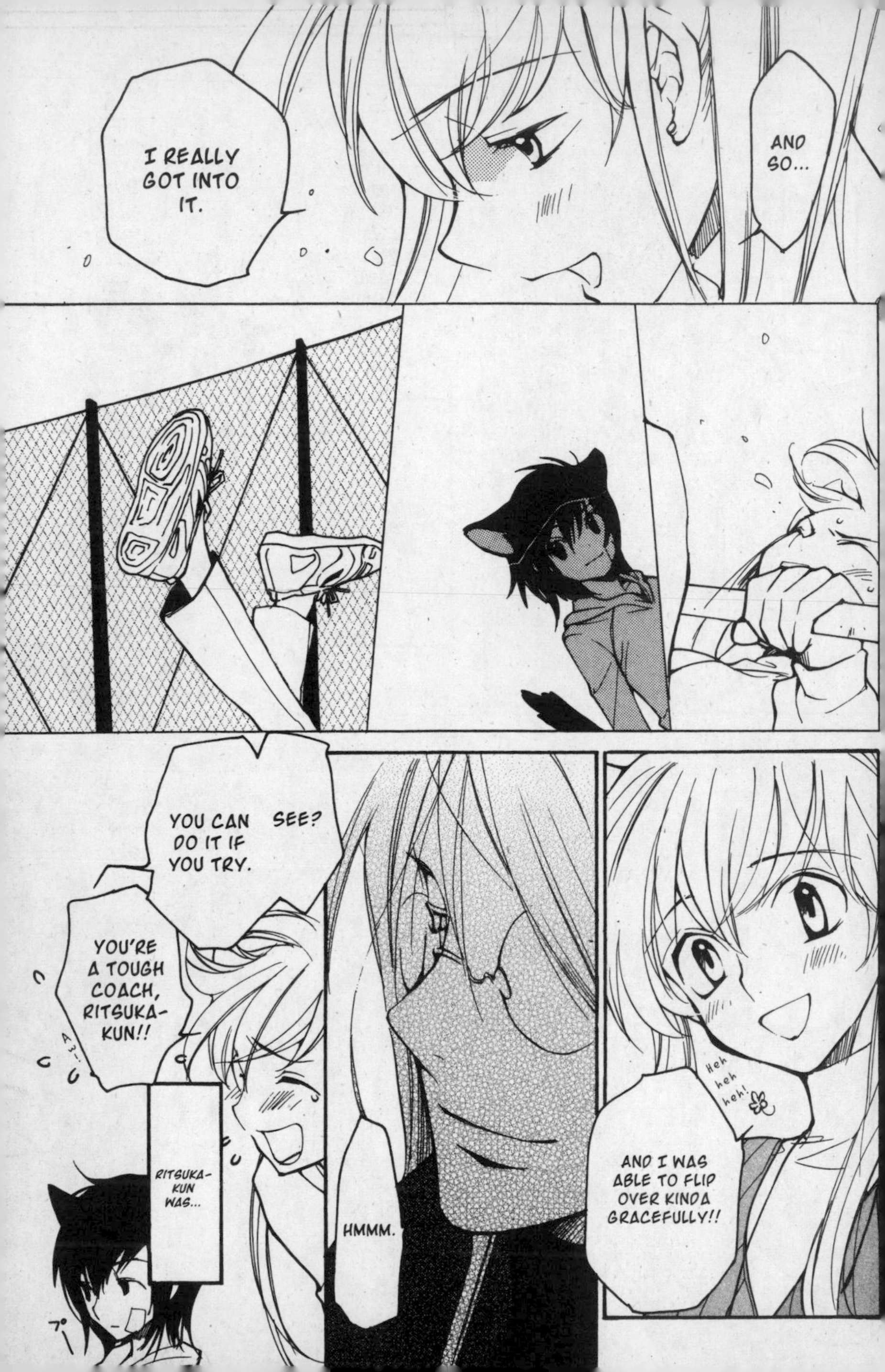
AND SO...
I REALLY GOT INTO IT.
Heh heh heh!
AND I WAS ABLE TO FLIP OVER KINDA GRACEFULLY!!
HMMM.
SEE?
YOU CAN DO IT IF YOU TRY.
YOU'RE A TOUGH COACH, RITSUKA-KUN!!
RITSUKA-KUN WAS...

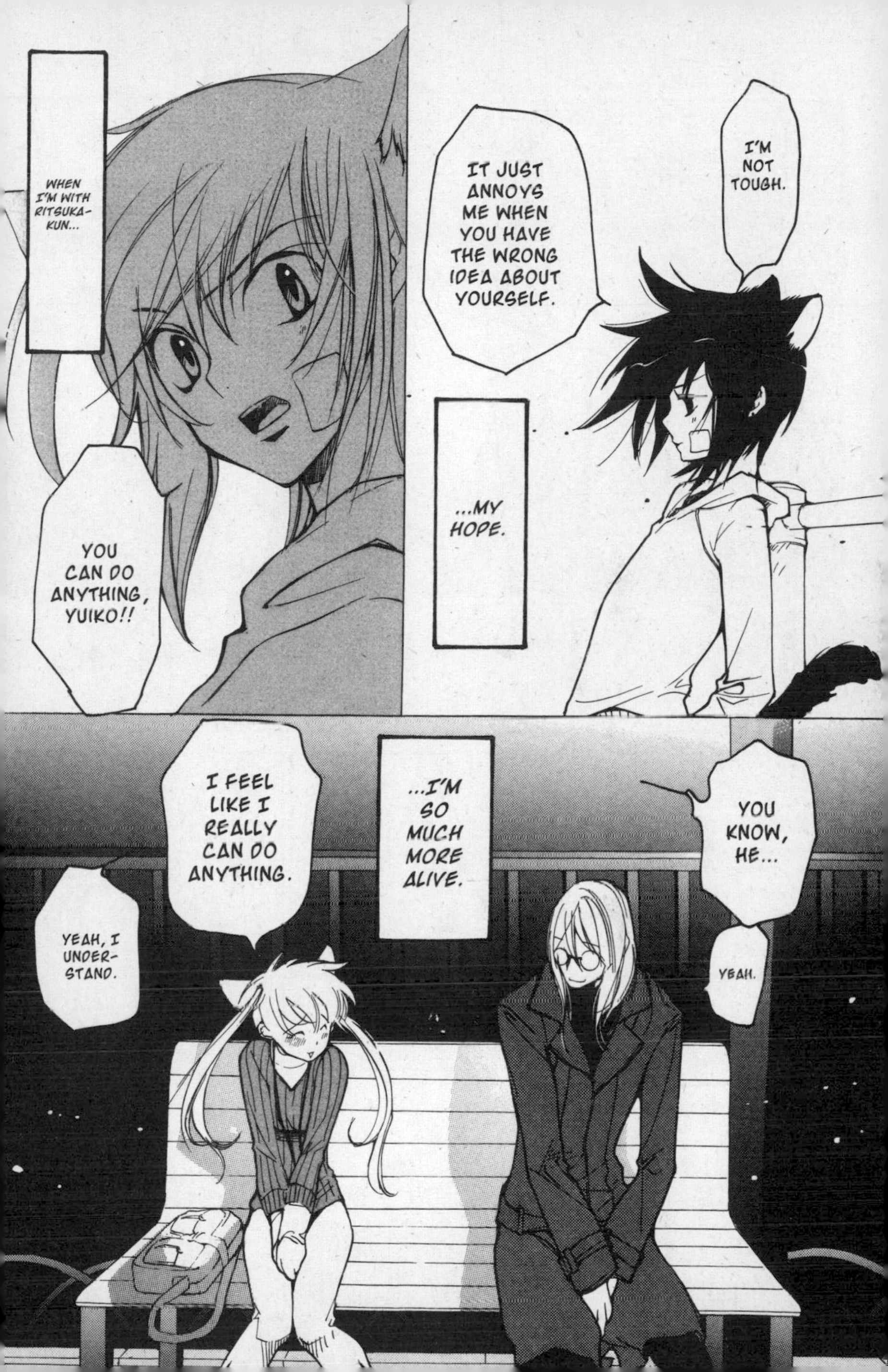
I'M NOT TOUGH.
IT JUST ANNOYS ME WHEN YOU HAVE THE WRONG IDEA ABOUT YOURSELF.
...MY HOPE.
WHEN I'M WITH RITSUKA-KUN...
YOU CAN DO ANYTHING, YUIKO!!
YOU KNOW, HE...
YEAH.
...I'M SO MUCH MORE ALIVE.
I FEEL LIKE I REALLY CAN DO ANYTHING.
YEAH, I UNDERSTAND.

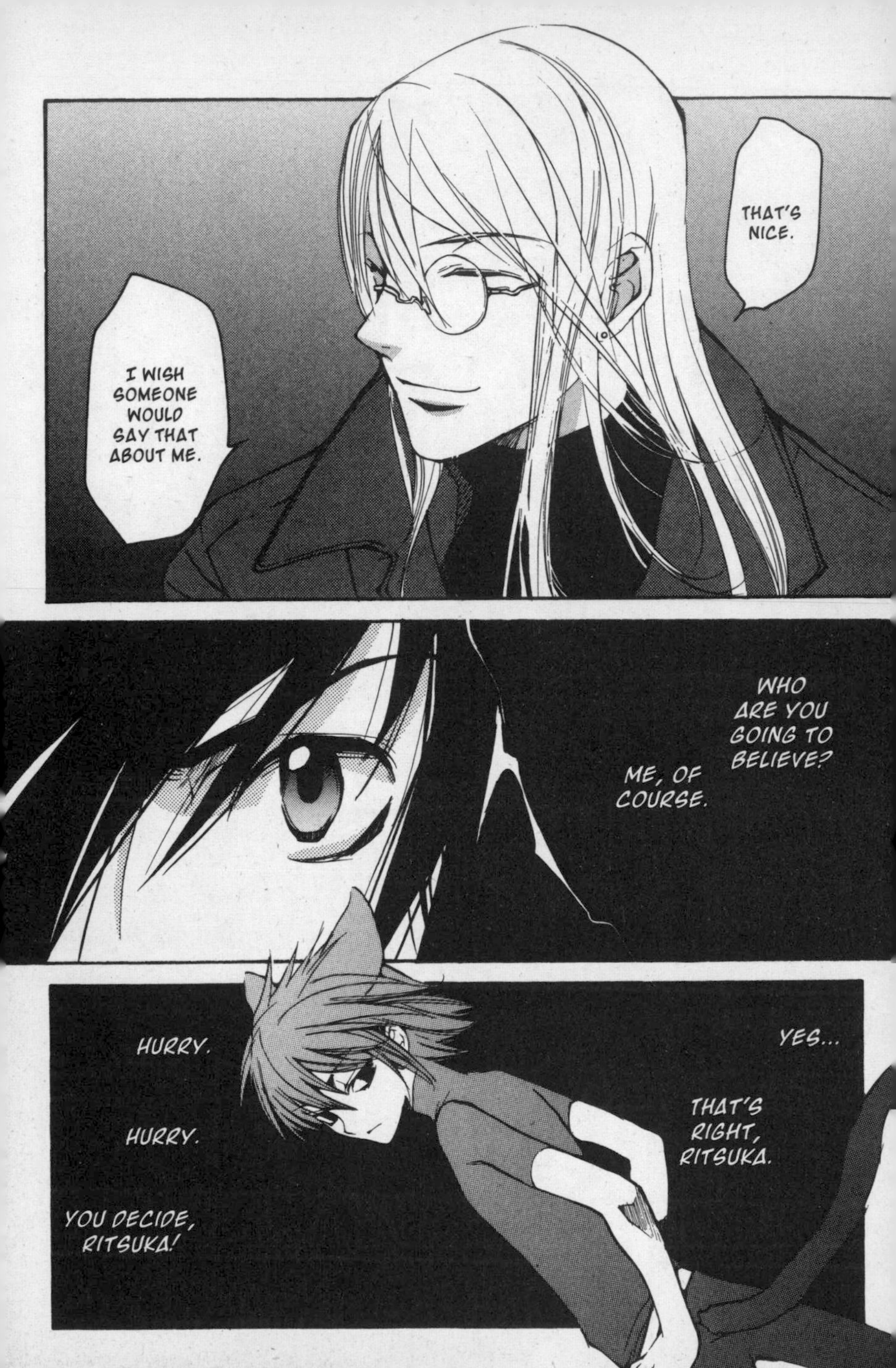
THAT'S NICE.
I WISH SOMEONE WOULD SAY THAT ABOUT ME.
WHO ARE YOU GOING TO BELIEVE?
ME, OF COURSE.
YES...
THAT'S RIGHT, RITSUKA.
HURRY.
HURRY.
YOU DECIDE, RITSUKA!

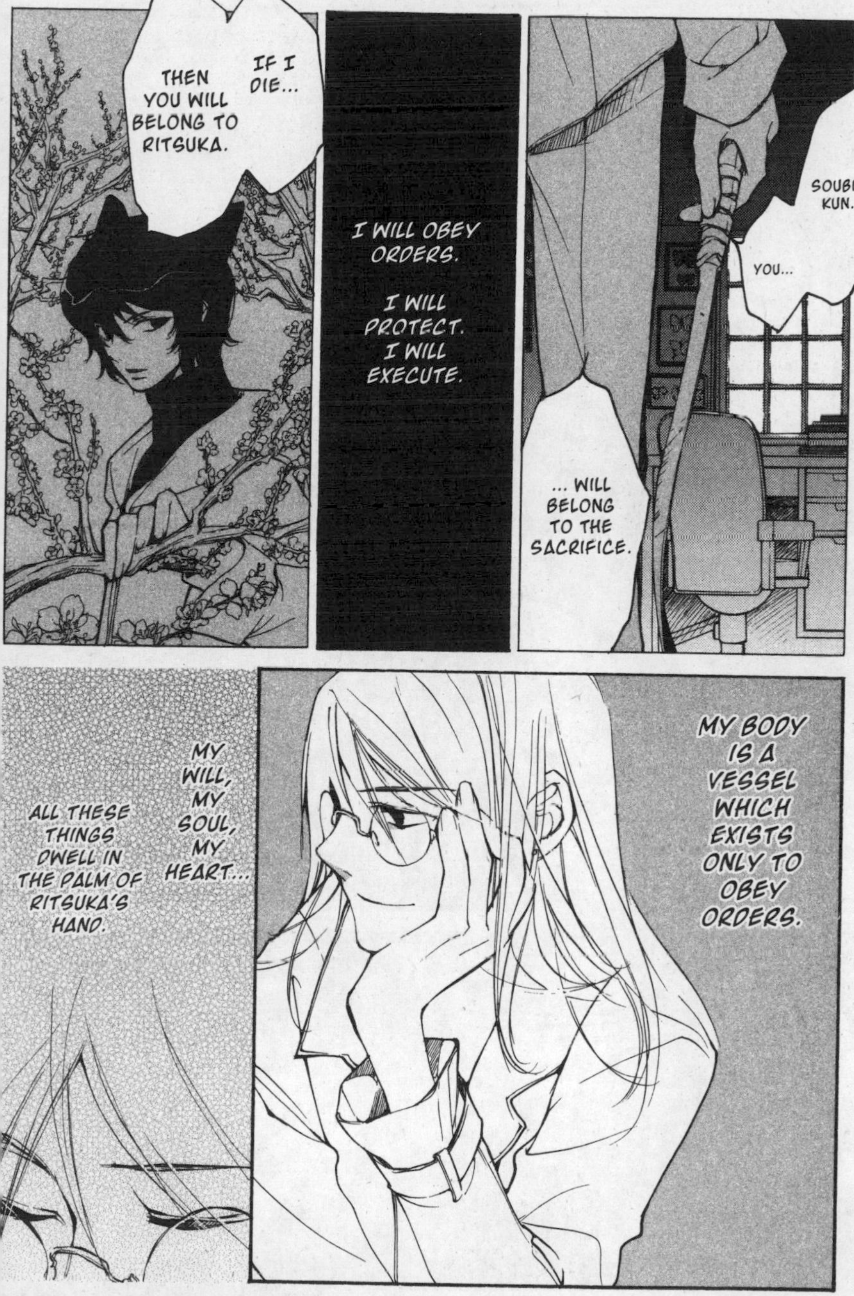
SOUBI-KUN.
YOU...
... WILL BELONG TO THE SACRIFICE.
I WILL OBEY ORDERS.
I WILL PROTECT. I WILL EXECUTE.
IF I DIE...
THEN YOU WILL BELONG TO RITSUKA.
MY BODY IS A VESSEL WHICH EXISTS ONLY TO OBEY ORDERS.
MY WILL, MY SOUL, MY HEART...
ALL THESE THINGS DWELL IN THE PALM OF RITSUKA'S HAND.

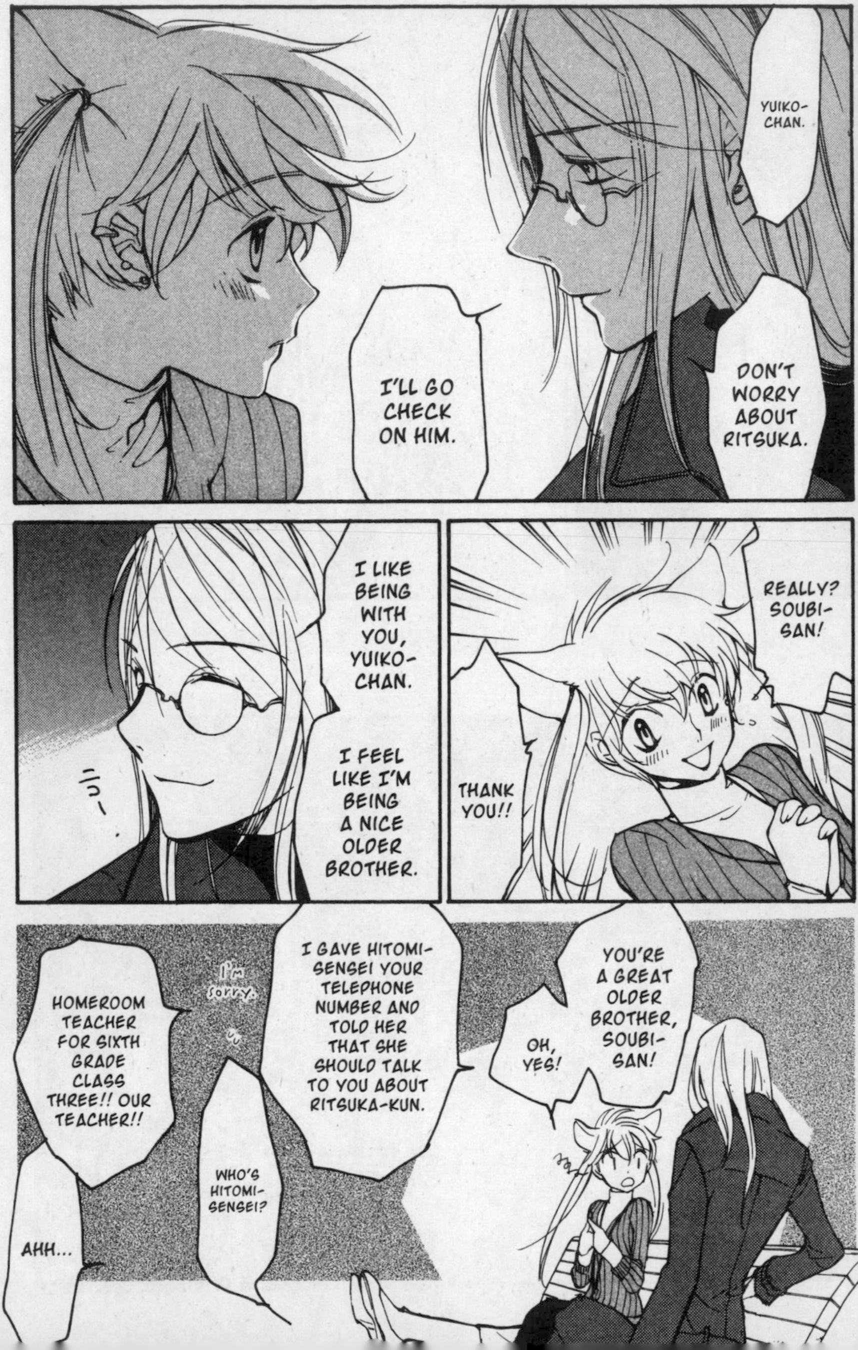
YUIKO-CHAN.
DON'T WORRY ABOUT RITSUKA.
I'LL GO CHECK ON HIM.
REALLY? SOUBI-SAN!
THANK YOU!!
I LIKE BEING WITH YOU, YUIKO-CHAN.
I FEEL LIKE I'M BEING A NICE OLDER BROTHER.
YOU'RE A GREAT OLDER BROTHER, SOUBI-SAN!
OH, YES!
I GAVE HITOMI-SENSEI YOUR TELEPHONE NUMBER AND TOLD HER THAT SHE SHOULD TALK TO YOU ABOUT RITSUKA-KUN.
I'm sorry.
WHO'S HITOMI-SENSEI?
HOMEROOM TEACHER FOR SIXTH GRADE CLASS THREE!! OUR TEACHER!!
AHH...

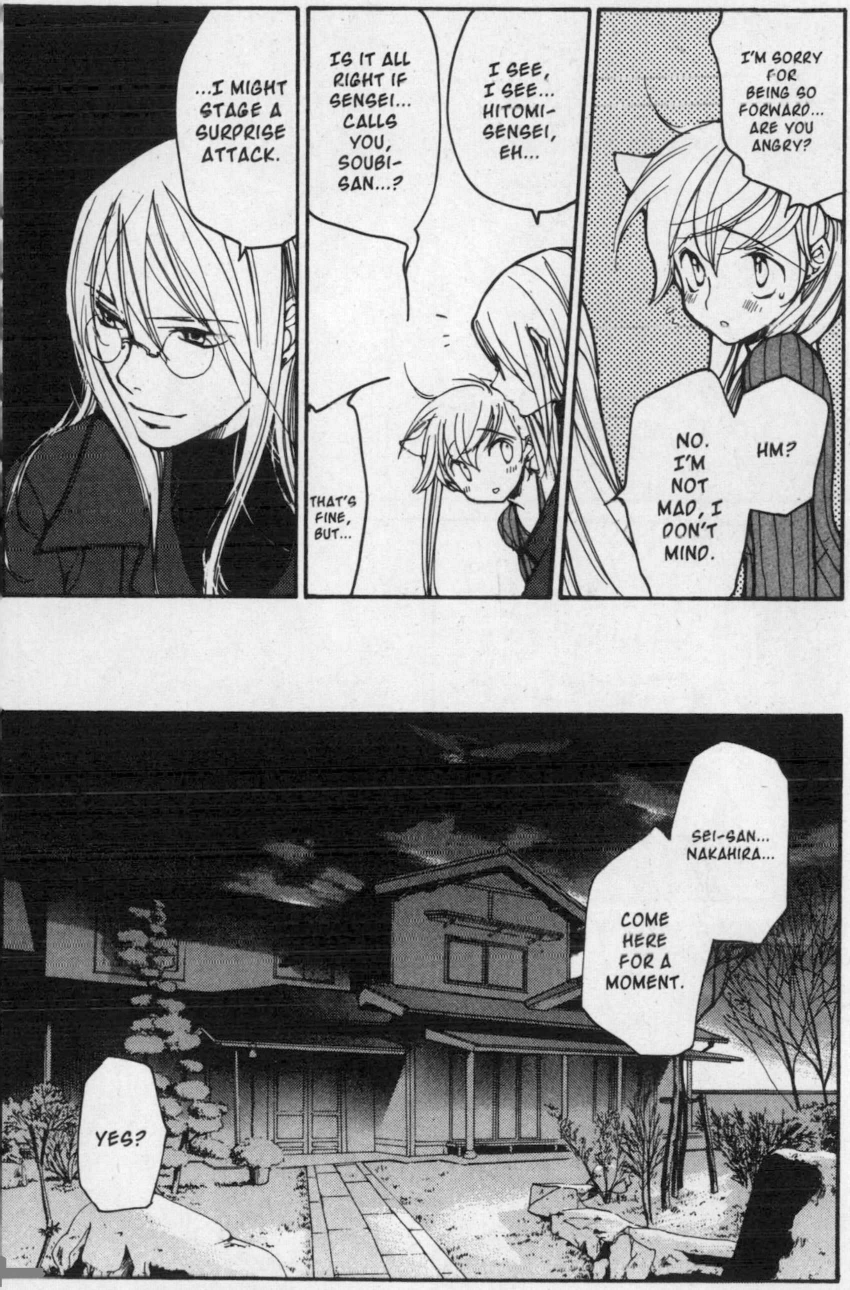
I'M SORRY FOR BEING SO FORWARD... ARE YOU ANGRY?
HM?
NO. I'M NOT MAD, I DON'T MIND.
I SEE, I SEE... HITOMI-SENSEI, EH...
IS IT ALL RIGHT IF SENSEI... CALLS YOU, SOUBI-SAN...?
THAT'S FINE, BUT...
...I MIGHT STAGE A SURPRISE ATTACK.
SEI-SAN... NAKAHIRA...
COME HERE FOR A MOMENT.
YES?

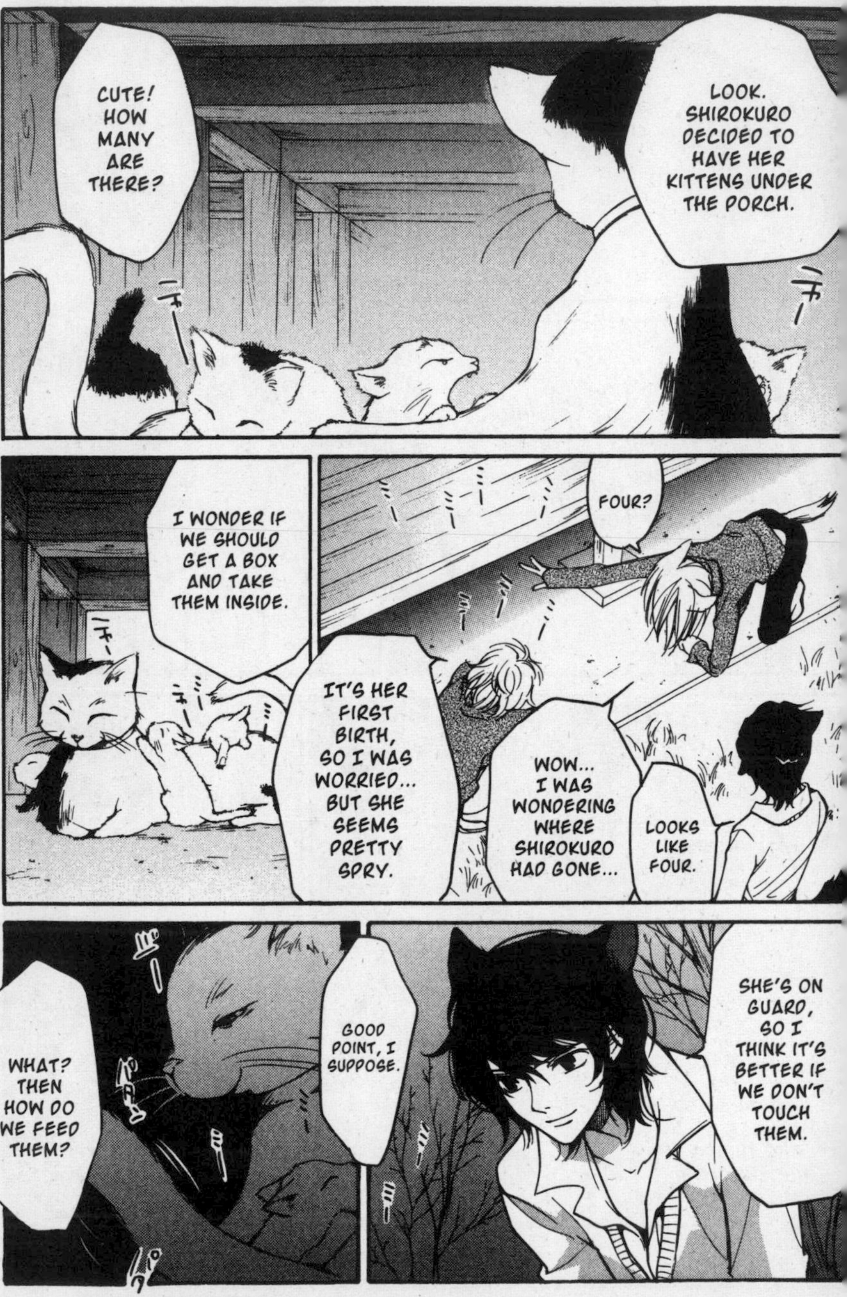
LOOK. SHIROKURO DECIDED TO HAVE HER KITTENS UNDER THE PORCH.
CUTE! HOW MANY ARE THERE?
FOUR?
LOOKS LIKE FOUR.
WOW... I WAS WONDERING WHERE SHIROKURO HAD GONE...
IT'S HER FIRST BIRTH, SO I WAS WORRIED... BUT SHE SEEMS PRETTY SPRY.
I WONDER IF WE SHOULD GET A BOX AND TAKE THEM INSIDE.
SHE'S ON GUARD, SO I THINK IT'S BETTER IF WE DON'T TOUCH THEM.
GOOD POINT, I SUPPOSE.
WHAT? THEN HOW DO WE FEED THEM?

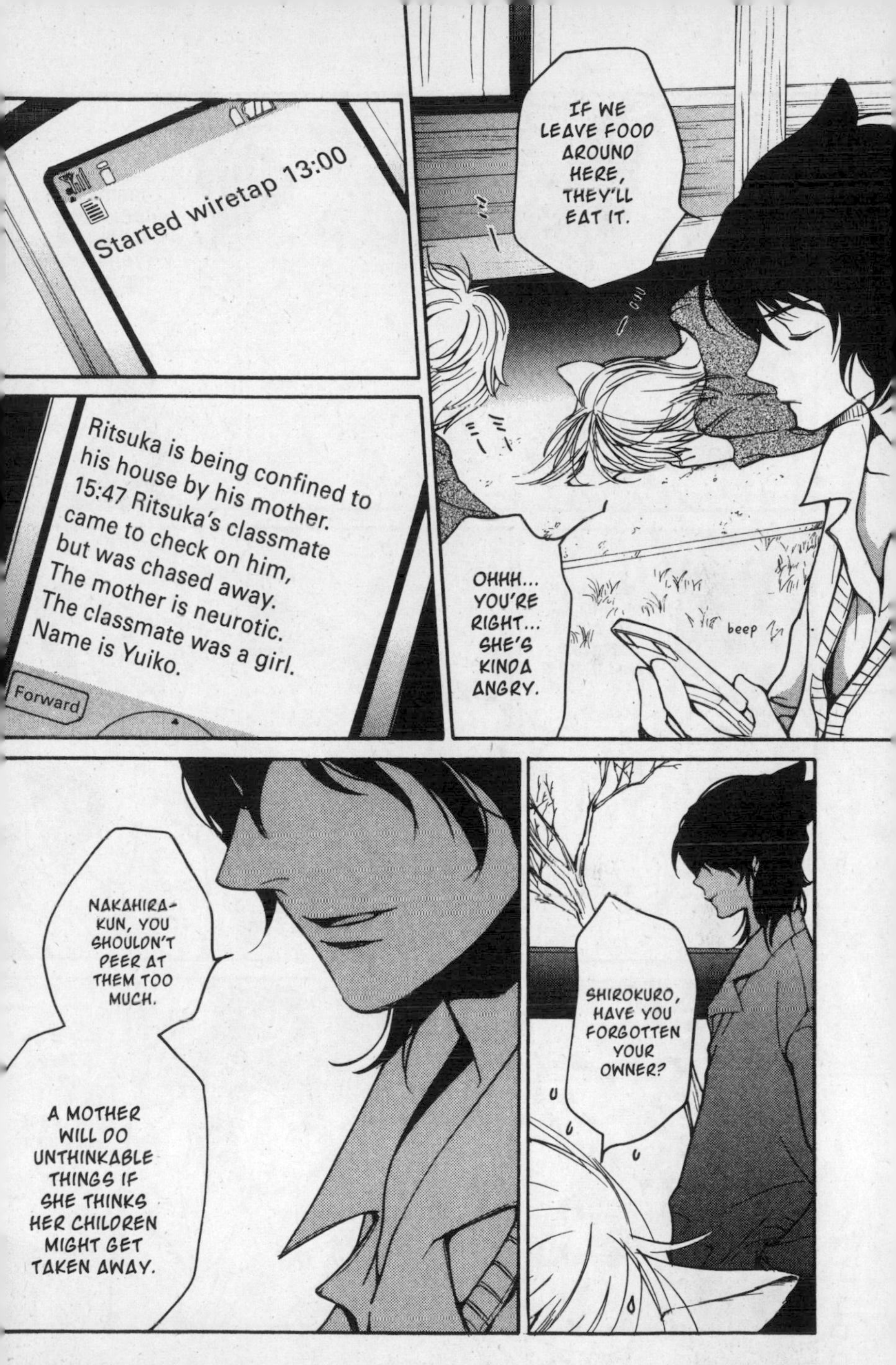

IF WE LEAVE FOOD AROUND HERE, THEY'LL EAT IT.
OHHH... YOU'RE RIGHT... SHE'S KINDA ANGRY.
beep
Started wiretap 13:00
Ritsuka is being confined to his house by his mother. 15:47 Ritsuka's classmate came to check on him, but was chased away. The mother is neurotic. The classmate was a girl. Name is Yuiko.
Forward
SHIROKURO, HAVE YOU FORGOTTEN YOUR OWNER?
NAKAHIRA-KUN, YOU SHOULDN'T PEER AT THEM TOO MUCH.
A MOTHER WILL DO UNTHINKABLE THINGS IF SHE THINKS HER CHILDREN MIGHT GET TAKEN AWAY.

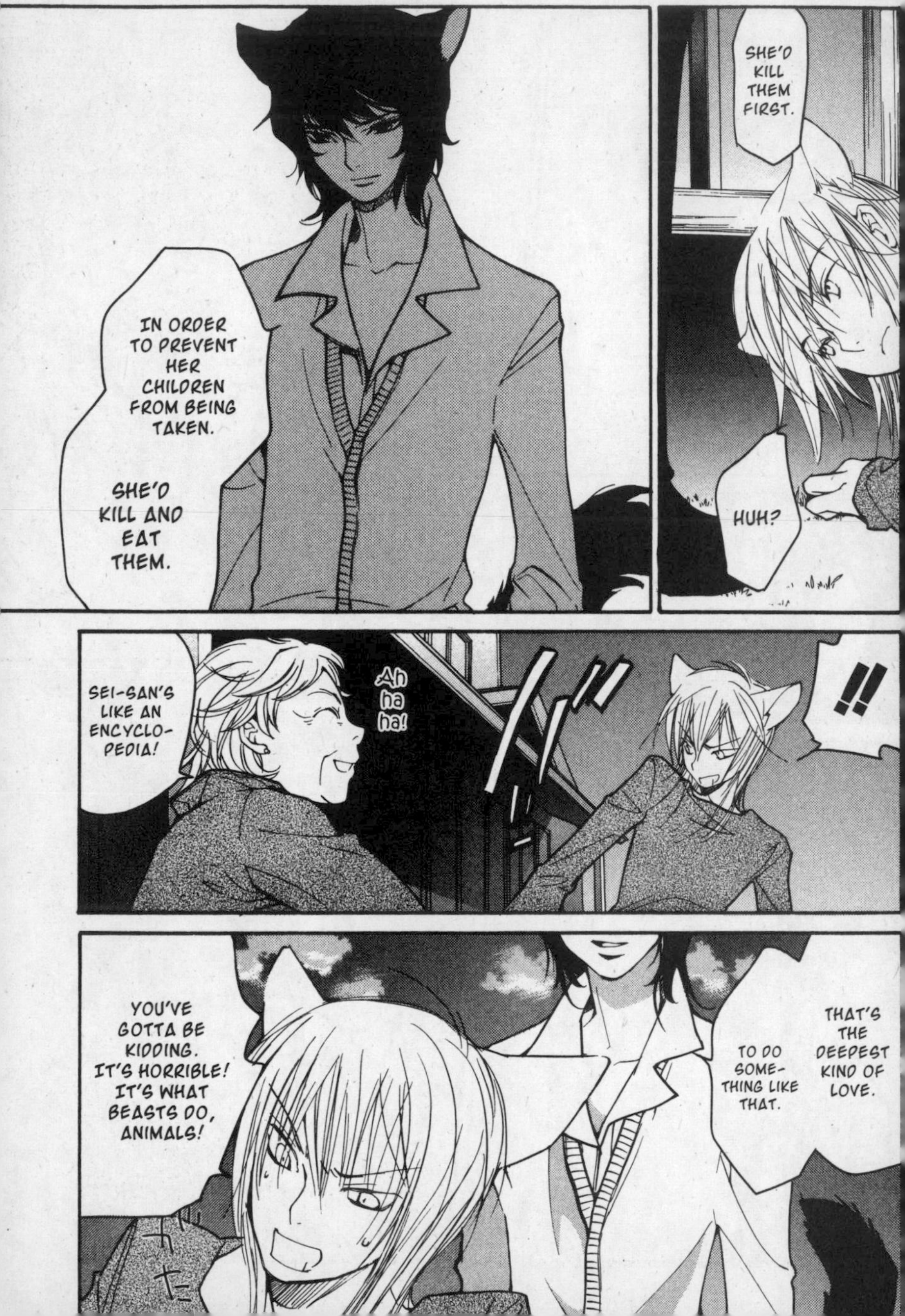
SHE'D KILL THEM FIRST.
HUH?
IN ORDER TO PREVENT HER CHILDREN FROM BEING TAKEN.
SHE'D KILL AND EAT THEM.
!!
Ah ha ha!
SEI-SAN'S LIKE AN ENCYCLO-PEDIA!
THAT'S THE DEEPEST KIND OF LOVE.
TO DO SOME-THING LIKE THAT.
YOU'VE GOTTA BE KIDDING. IT'S HORRIBLE! IT'S WHAT BEASTS DO, ANIMALS!

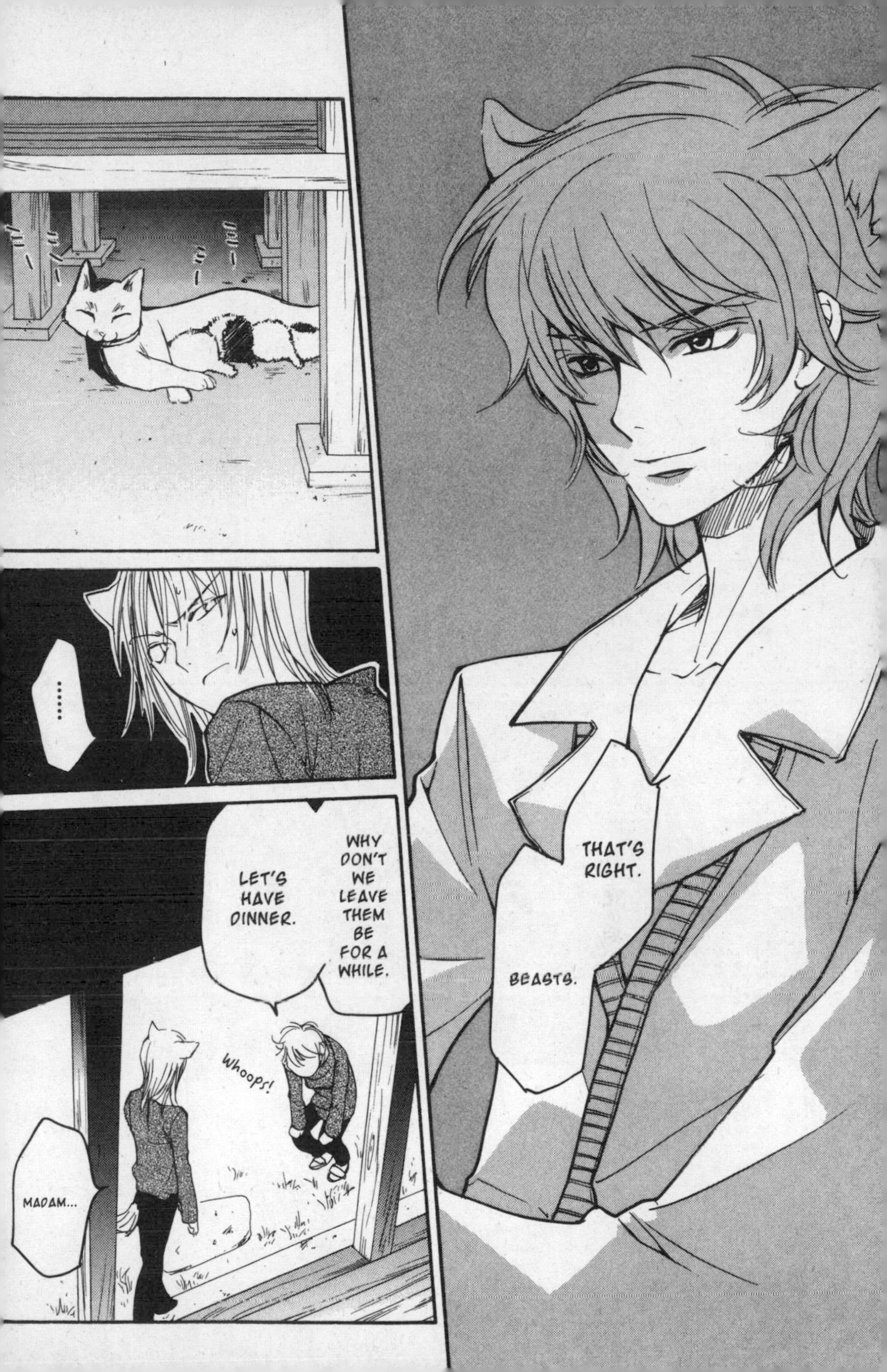
THAT'S RIGHT.
BEASTS.
......
WHY DON'T WE LEAVE THEM BE FOR A WHILE.
LET'S HAVE DINNER.
Whoops!
MADAM...

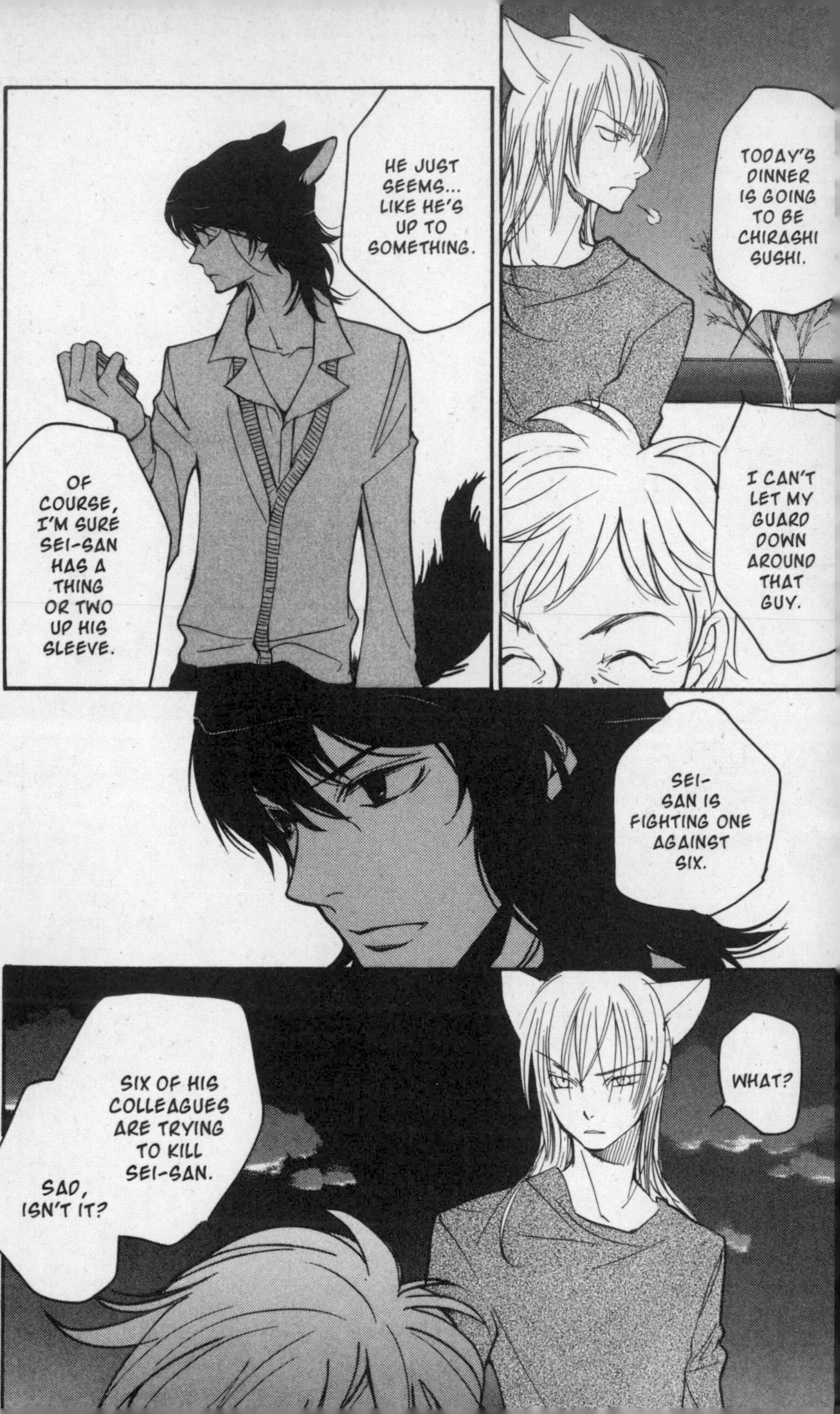
TODAY'S DINNER IS GOING TO BE CHIRASHI SUSHI.
I CAN'T LET MY GUARD DOWN AROUND THAT GUY.
HE JUST SEEMS... LIKE HE'S UP TO SOMETHING.
OF COURSE, I'M SURE SEI-SAN HAS A THING OR TWO UP HIS SLEEVE.
SEI-SAN IS FIGHTING ONE AGAINST SIX.
WHAT?
SIX OF HIS COLLEAGUES ARE TRYING TO KILL SEI-SAN.
SAD, ISN'T IT?

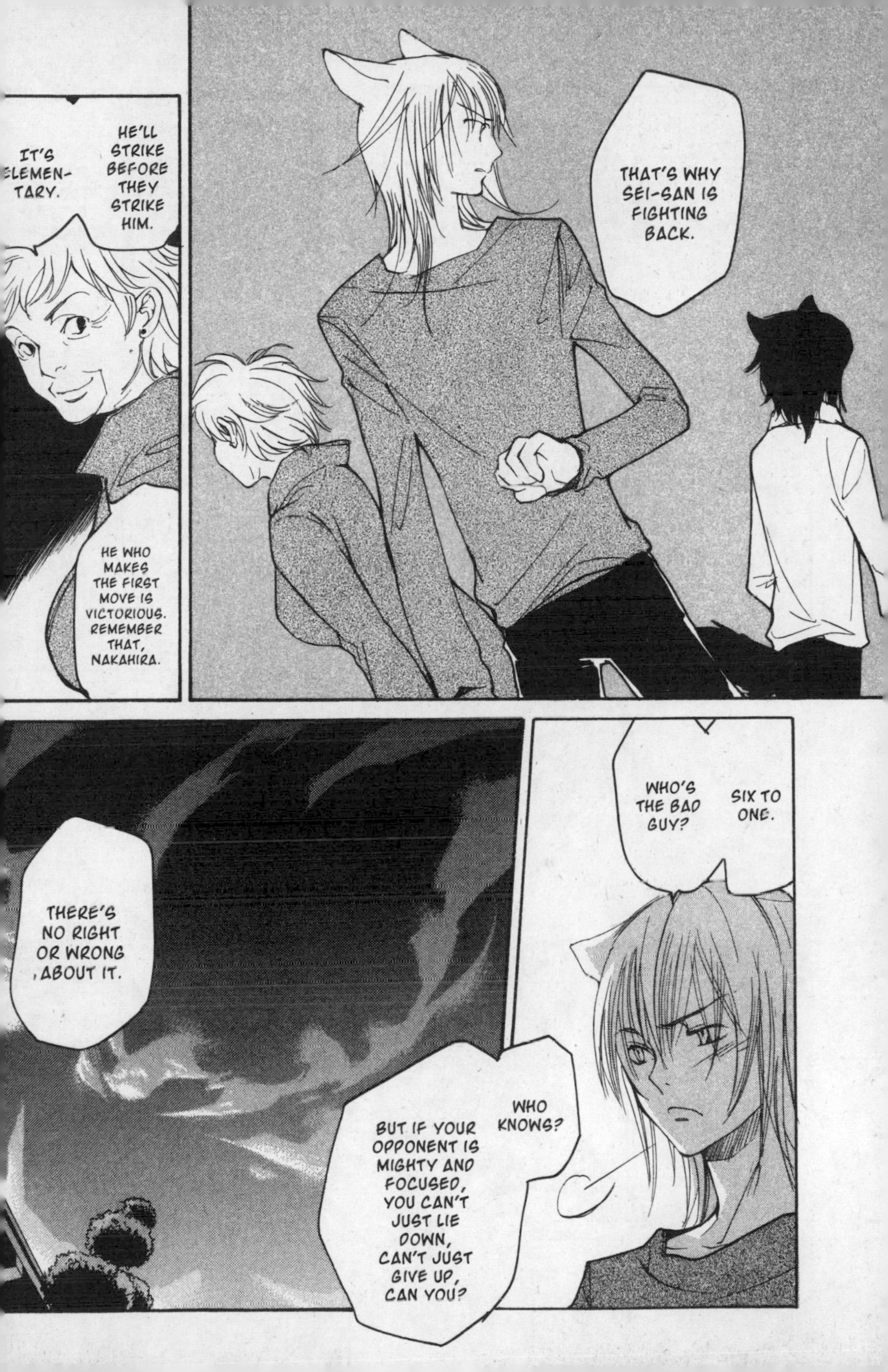
THAT'S WHY SEI-SAN IS FIGHTING BACK.
HE'LL STRIKE BEFORE THEY STRIKE HIM.
IT'S ELEMENTARY.
HE WHO MAKES THE FIRST MOVE IS VICTORIOUS. REMEMBER THAT, NAKAHIRA.
SIX TO ONE.
WHO'S THE BAD GUY?
WHO KNOWS?
BUT IF YOUR OPPONENT IS MIGHTY AND FOCUSED, YOU CAN'T JUST LIE DOWN, CAN'T JUST GIVE UP, CAN YOU?
THERE'S NO RIGHT OR WRONG ABOUT IT.

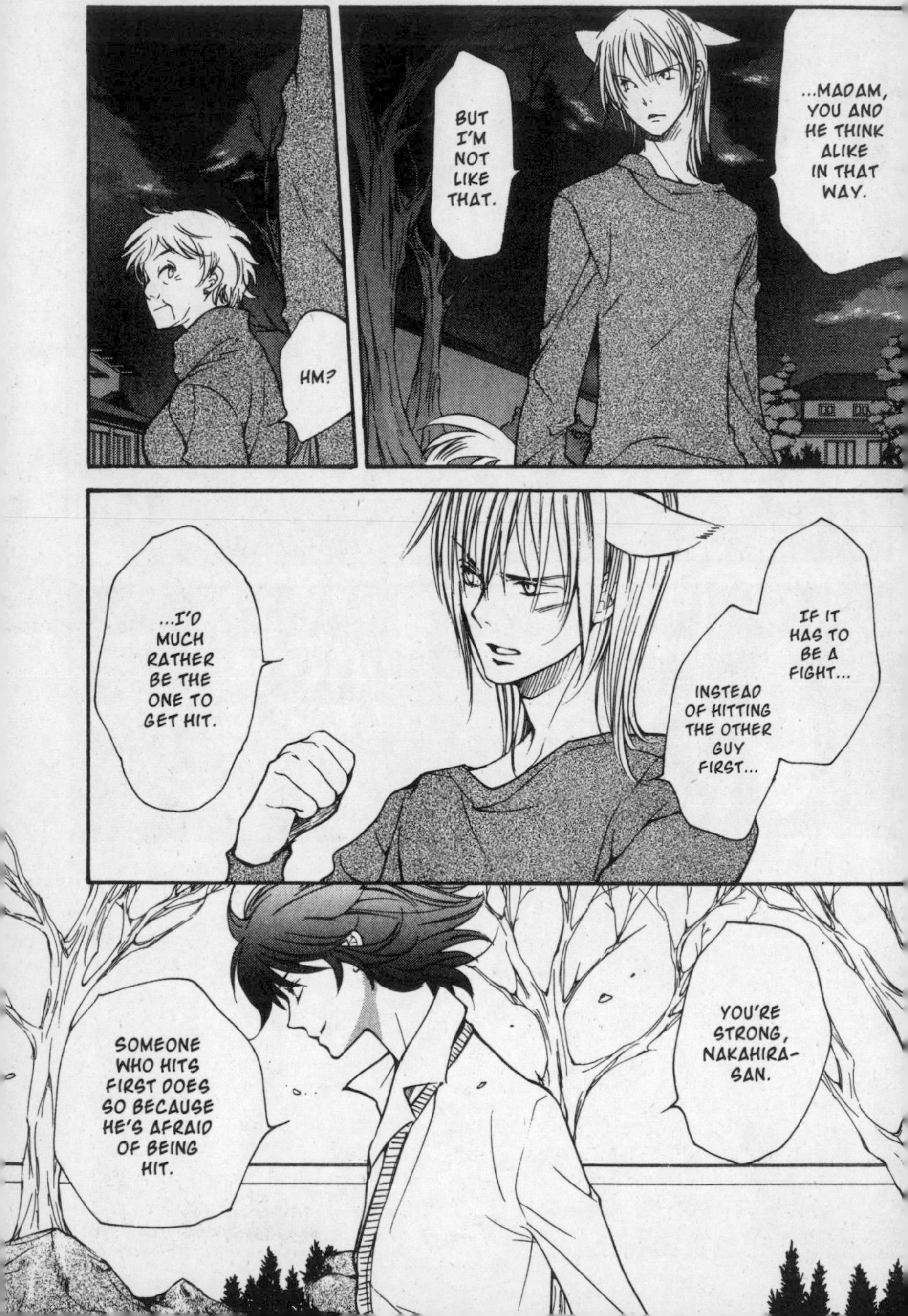
...MADAM, YOU AND HE THINK ALIKE IN THAT WAY.
BUT I'M NOT LIKE THAT.
HM?
IF IT HAS TO BE A FIGHT...
INSTEAD OF HITTING THE OTHER GUY FIRST...
...I'D MUCH RATHER BE THE ONE TO GET HIT.
YOU'RE STRONG, NAKAHIRA-SAN.
SOMEONE WHO HITS FIRST DOES SO BECAUSE HE'S AFRAID OF BEING HIT.

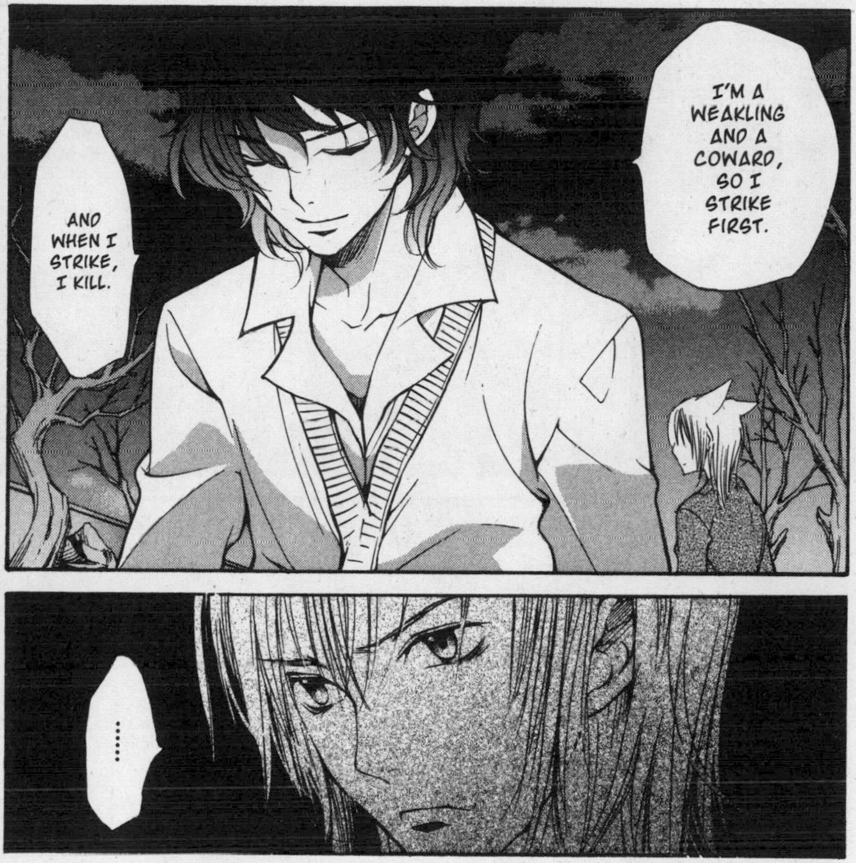
I'M A WEAKLING AND A COWARD, SO I STRIKE FIRST.
AND WHEN I STRIKE, I KILL.
……

The Birth Chapters
Chapter 4

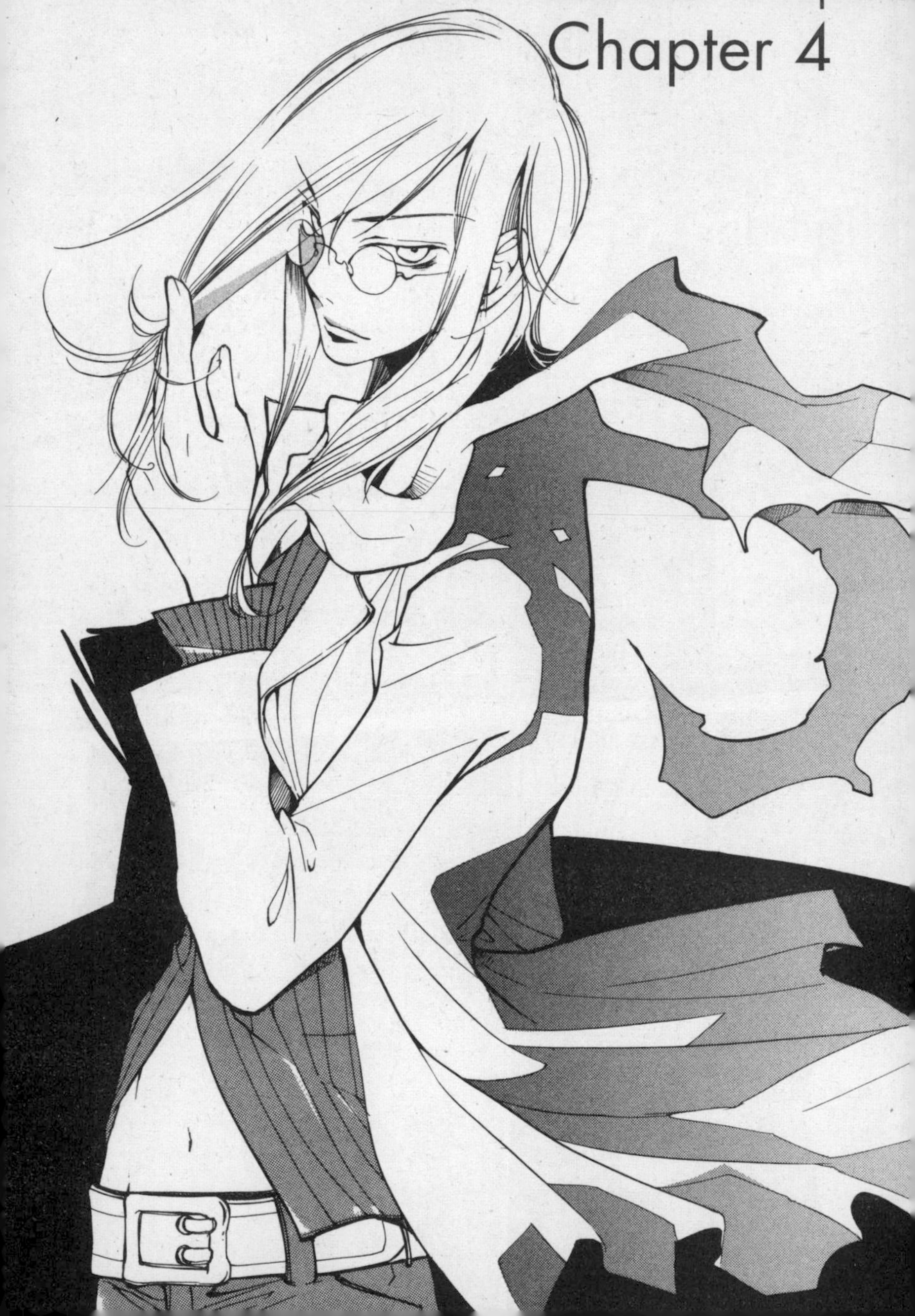

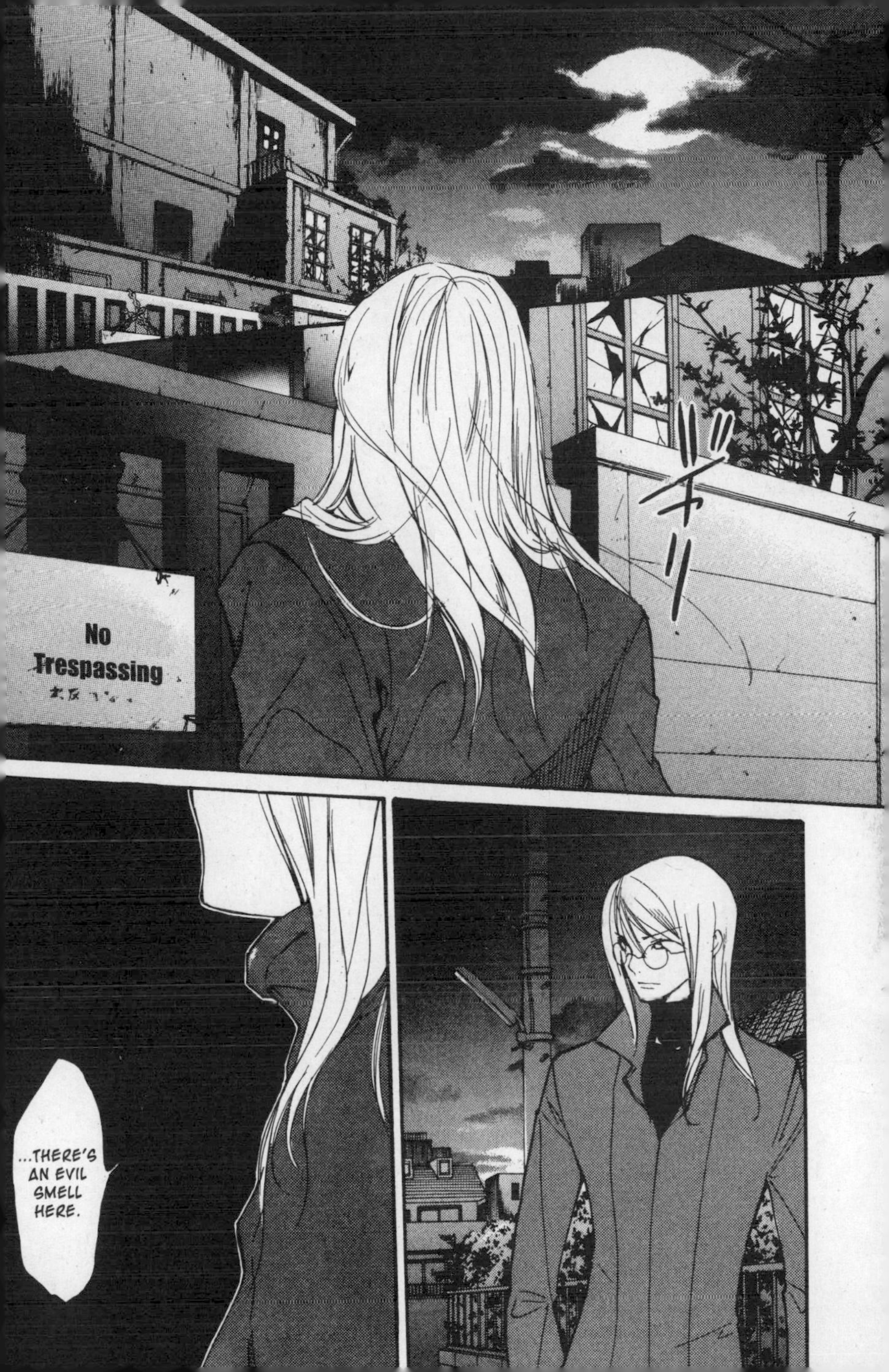
ジャリ
No Trespassing
...THERE'S AN EVIL SMELL HERE.

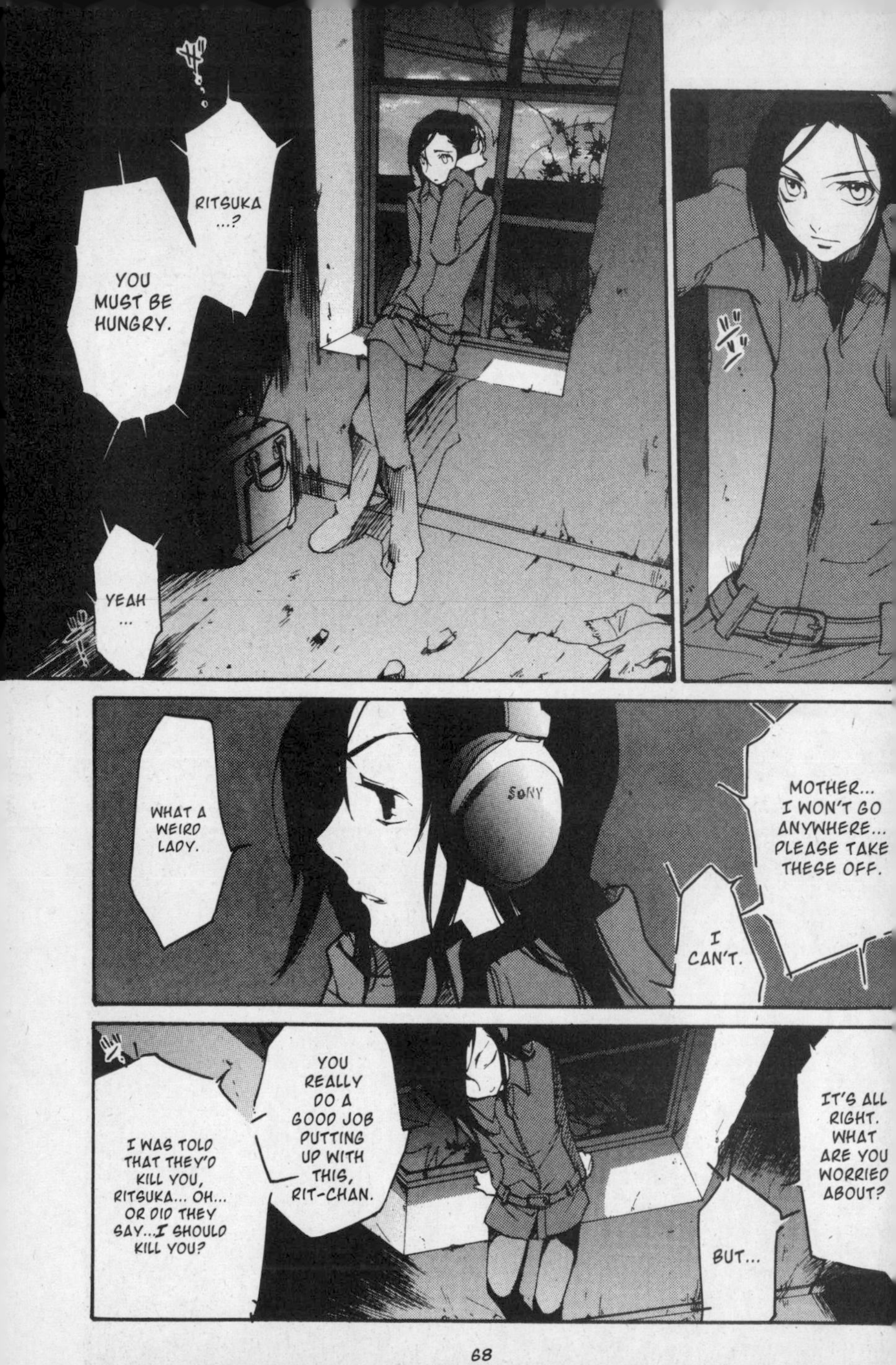
RITSUKA ...?
YOU MUST BE HUNGRY.
YEAH ...
MOTHER... I WON'T GO ANYWHERE... PLEASE TAKE THESE OFF.
I CAN'T.
WHAT A WEIRD LADY.
IT'S ALL RIGHT. WHAT ARE YOU WORRIED ABOUT?
BUT...
YOU REALLY DO A GOOD JOB PUTTING UP WITH THIS, RIT-CHAN.
I WAS TOLD THAT THEY'D KILL YOU, RITSUKA... OH... OR DID THEY SAY...I SHOULD KILL YOU?

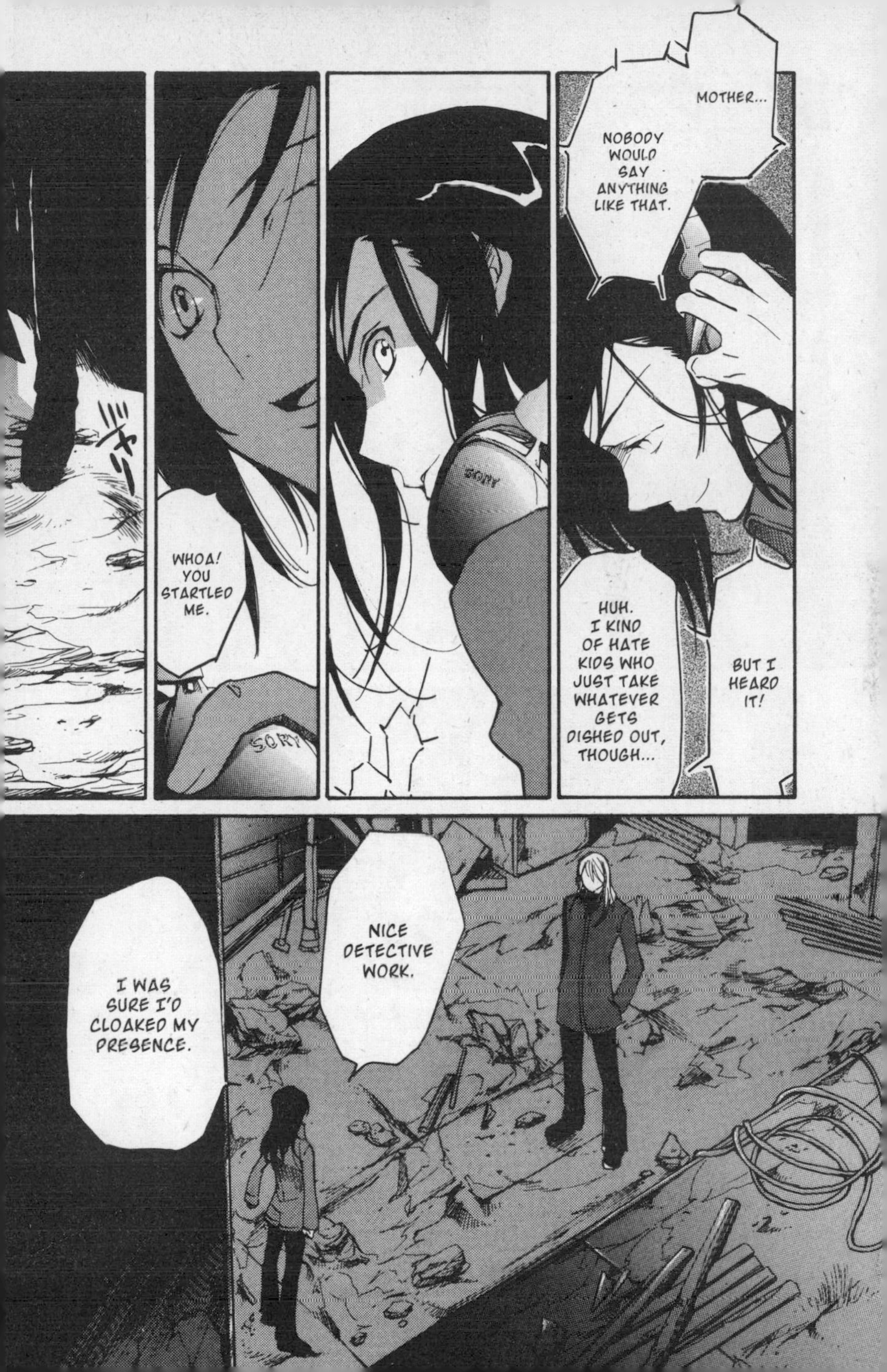
MOTHER...
NOBODY WOULD SAY ANYTHING LIKE THAT.
BUT I HEARD IT!
HUH. I KIND OF HATE KIDS WHO JUST TAKE WHATEVER GETS DISHED OUT, THOUGH...
SORY
WHOA! YOU STARTLED ME.
SORY
ジャリ
NICE DETECTIVE WORK.
I WAS SURE I'D CLOAKED MY PRESENCE.

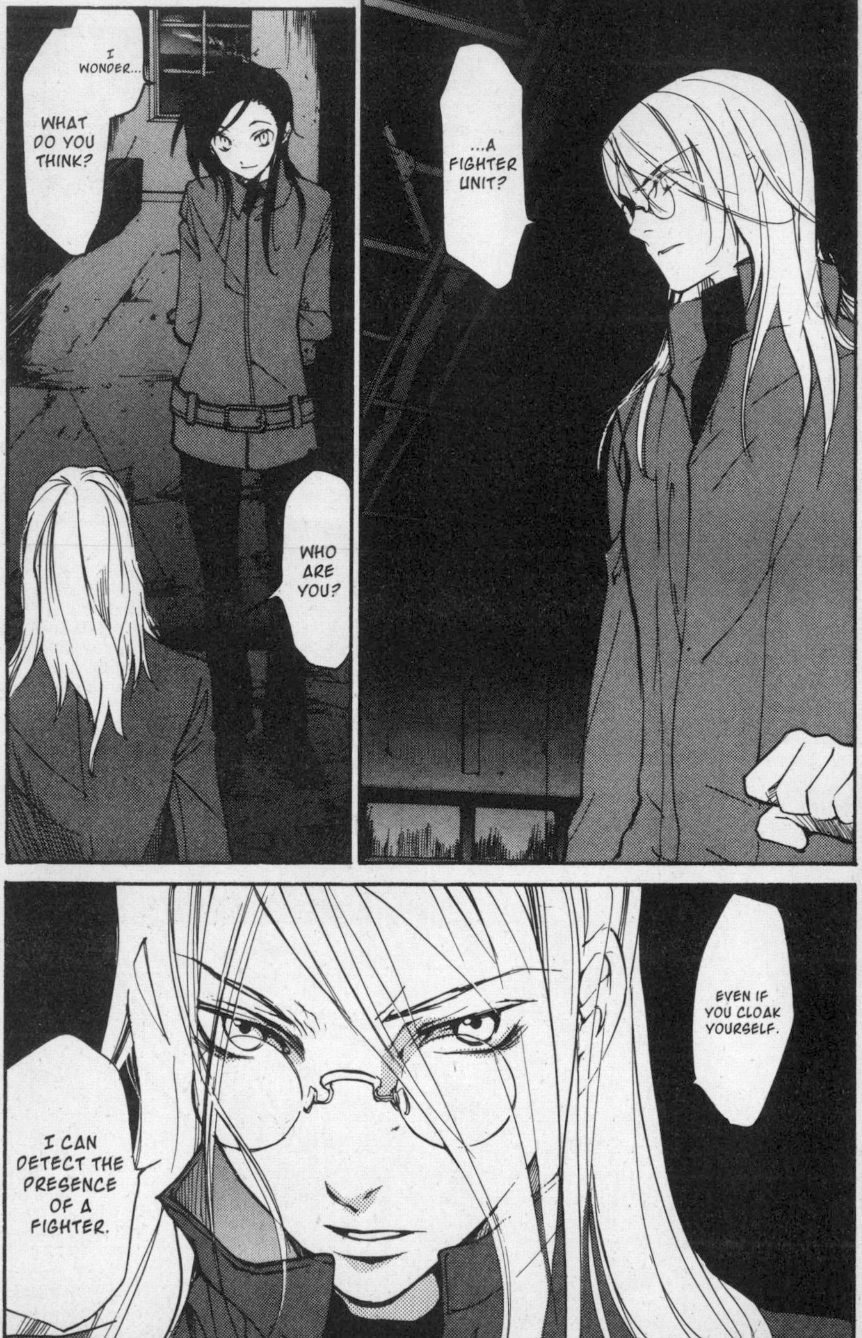
...A FIGHTER UNIT?
I WONDER...
WHAT DO YOU THINK?
WHO ARE YOU?
EVEN IF YOU CLOAK YOURSELF.
I CAN DETECT THE PRESENCE OF A FIGHTER.

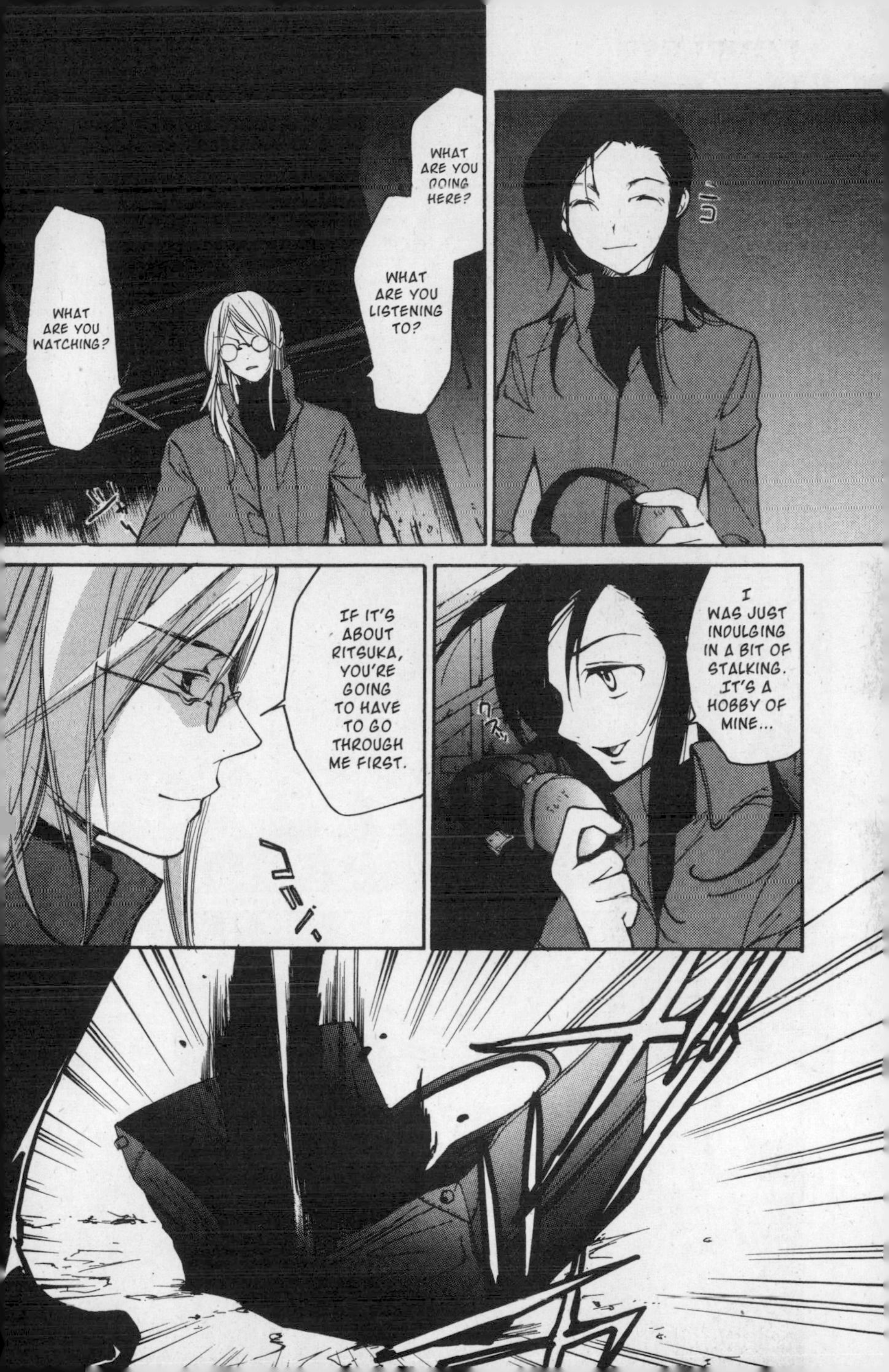
WHAT ARE YOU DOING HERE?
WHAT ARE YOU LISTENING TO?
WHAT ARE YOU WATCHING?
I WAS JUST INDULGING IN A BIT OF STALKING. IT'S A HOBBY OF MINE...
IF IT'S ABOUT RITSUKA, YOU'RE GOING TO HAVE TO GO THROUGH ME FIRST.

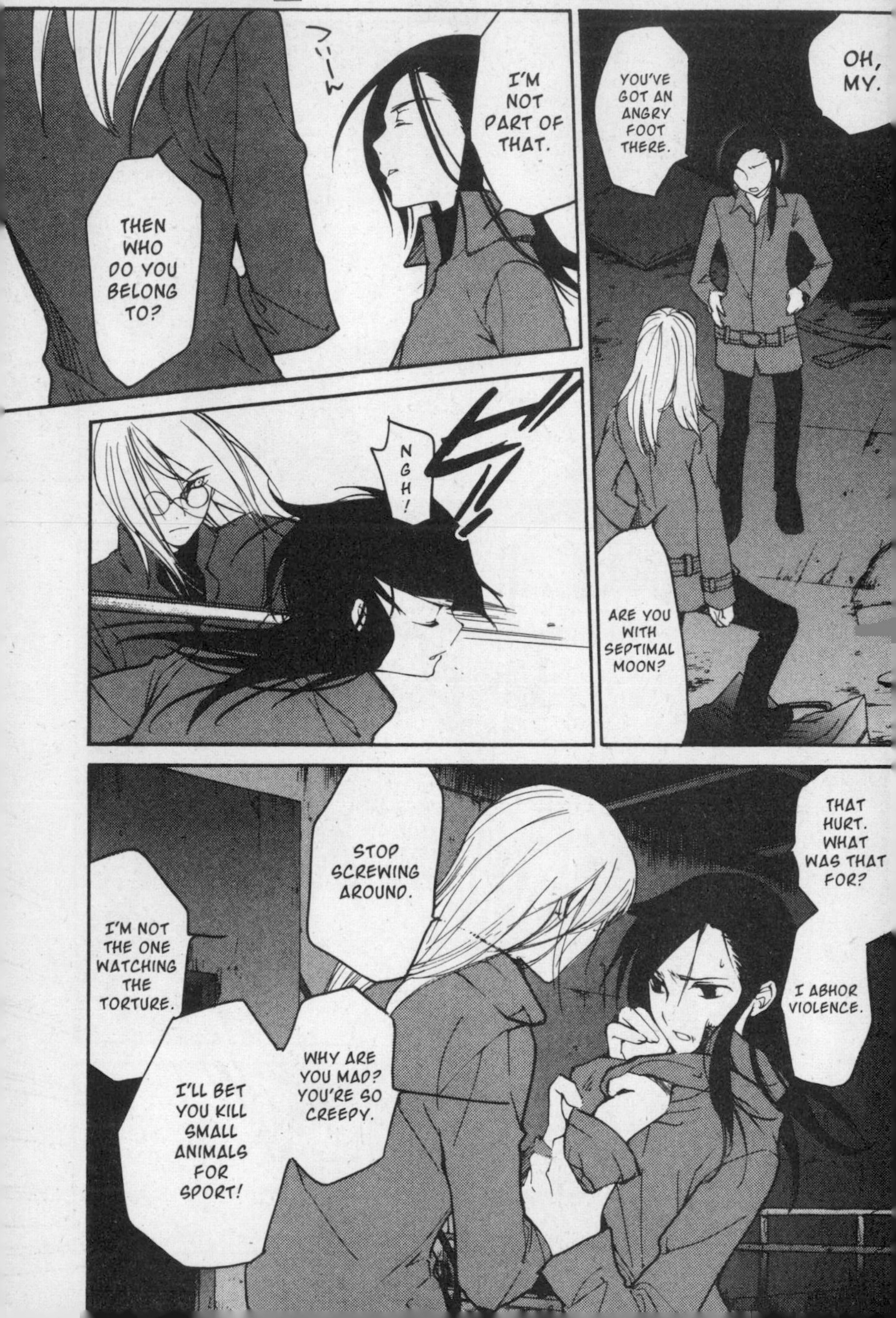
OH, MY.
YOU'VE GOT AN ANGRY FOOT THERE.
ARE YOU WITH SEPTIMAL MOON?
I'M NOT PART OF THAT.
THEN WHO DO YOU BELONG TO?
NGH!
THAT HURT. WHAT WAS THAT FOR?
I ABHOR VIOLENCE.
STOP SCREWING AROUND.
I'M NOT THE ONE WATCHING THE TORTURE.
WHY ARE YOU MAD? YOU'RE SO CREEPY.
I'LL BET YOU KILL SMALL ANIMALS FOR SPORT!

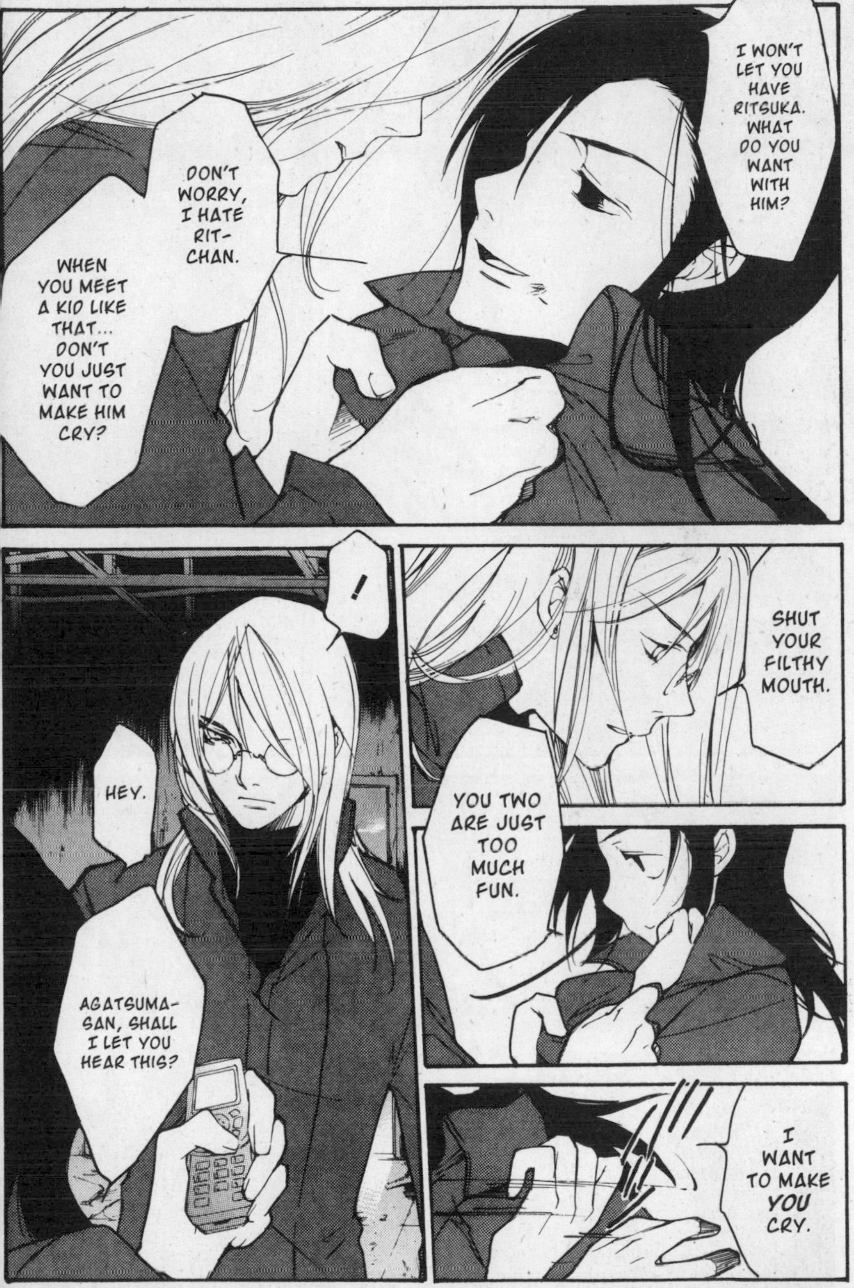
I WON'T LET YOU HAVE RITSUKA. WHAT DO YOU WANT WITH HIM?
DON'T WORRY, I HATE RIT-CHAN.
WHEN YOU MEET A KID LIKE THAT... DON'T YOU JUST WANT TO MAKE HIM CRY?
SHUT YOUR FILTHY MOUTH.
YOU TWO ARE JUST TOO MUCH FUN.
I WANT TO MAKE *YOU* CRY.
!
HEY.
AGATSUMA-SAN, SHALL I LET YOU HEAR THIS?

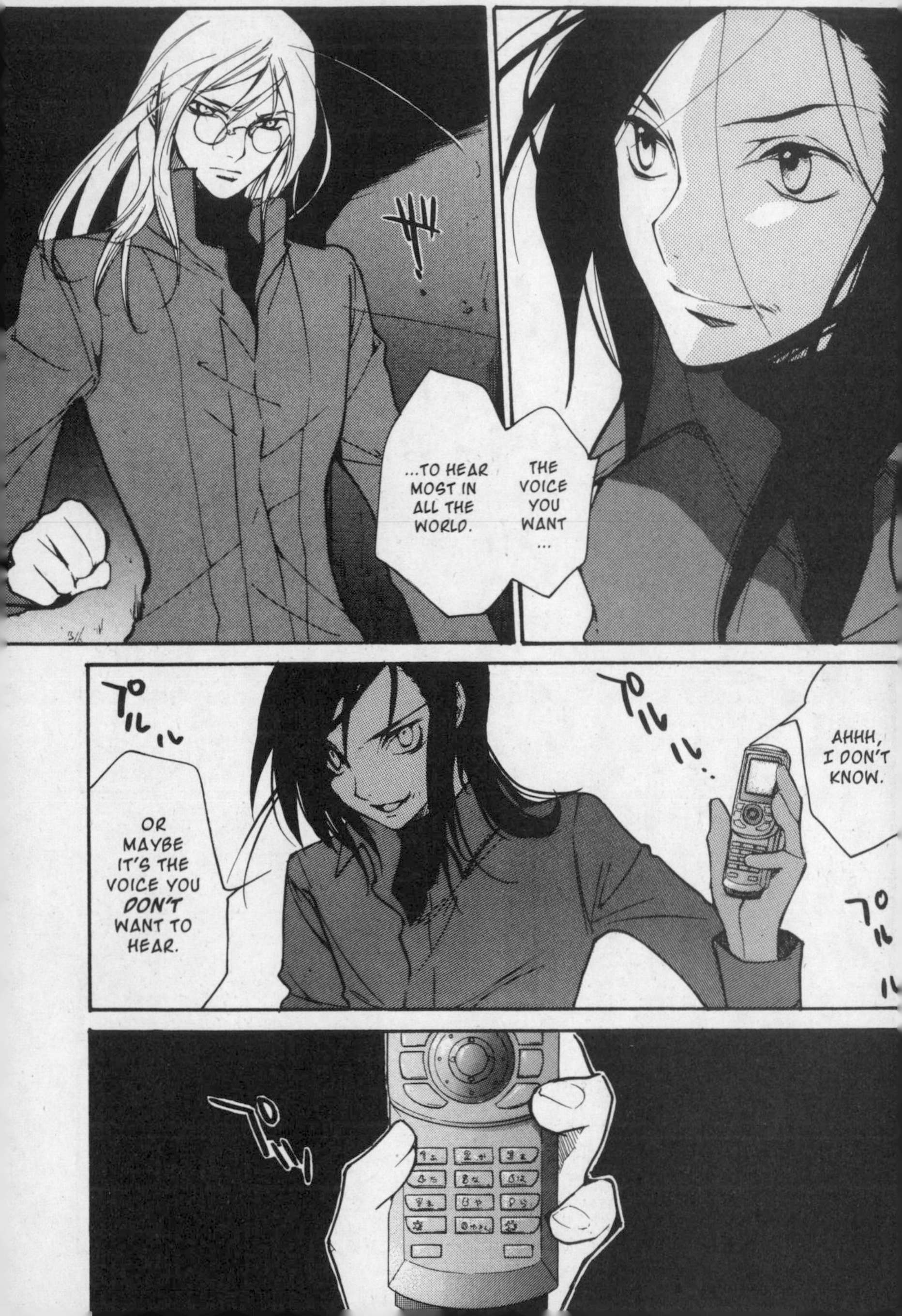

THE VOICE YOU WANT ...
...TO HEAR MOST IN ALL THE WORLD.
プルル…
AHHH, I DON'T KNOW.
プルル
プルル
OR MAYBE IT'S THE VOICE YOU *DON'T* WANT TO HEAR.

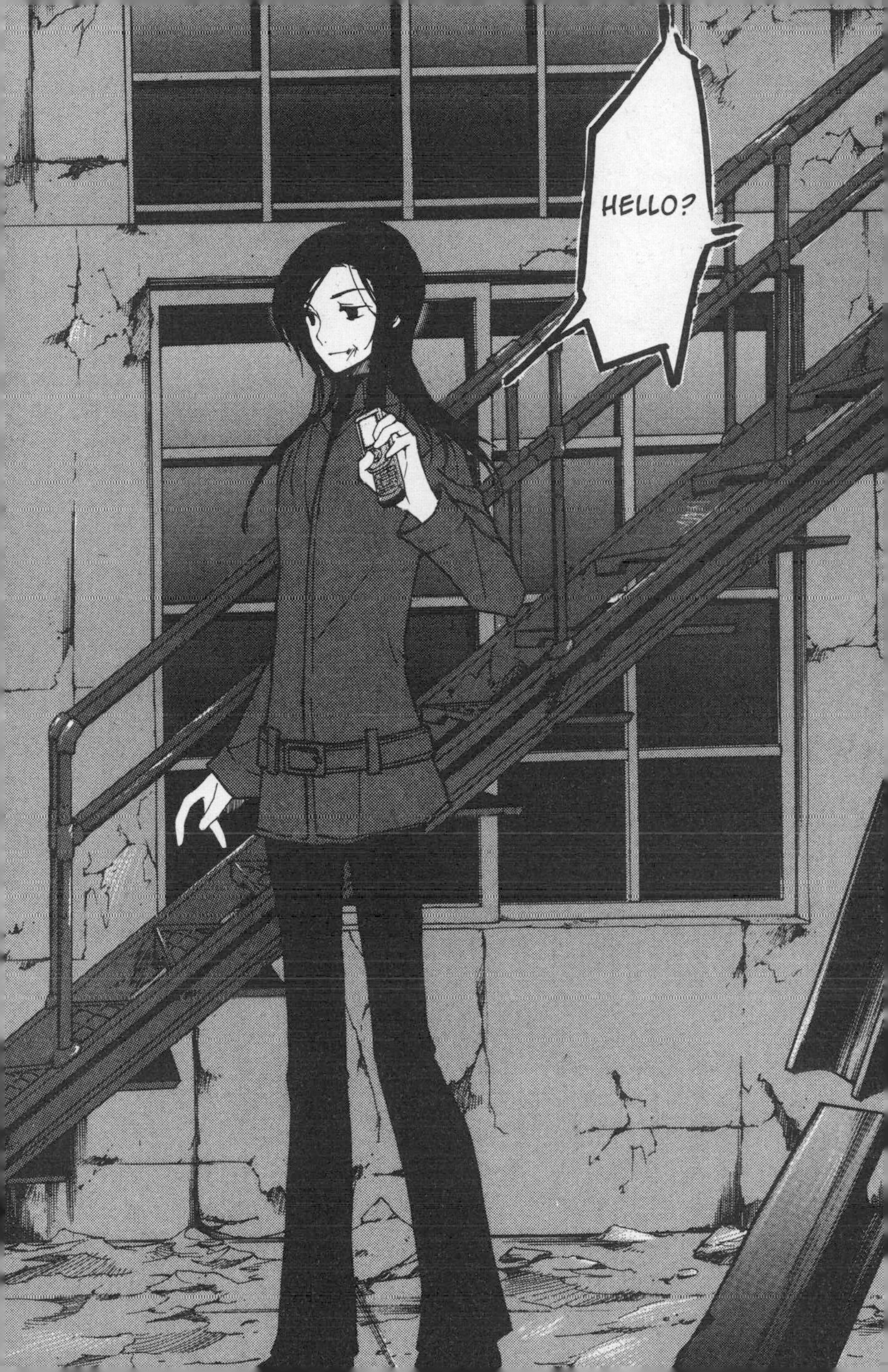
HELLO?

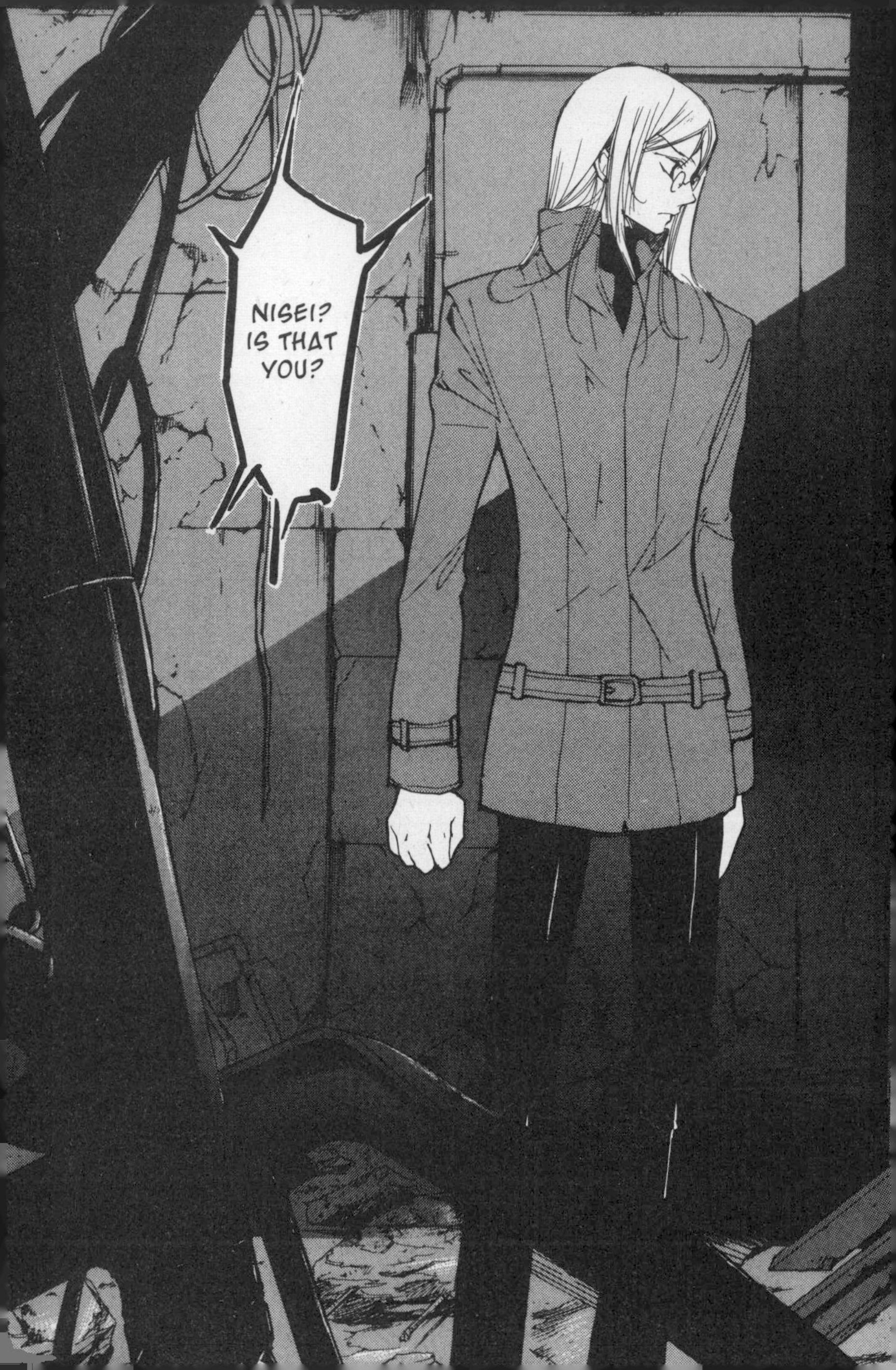
NISEI!? IS THAT YOU?

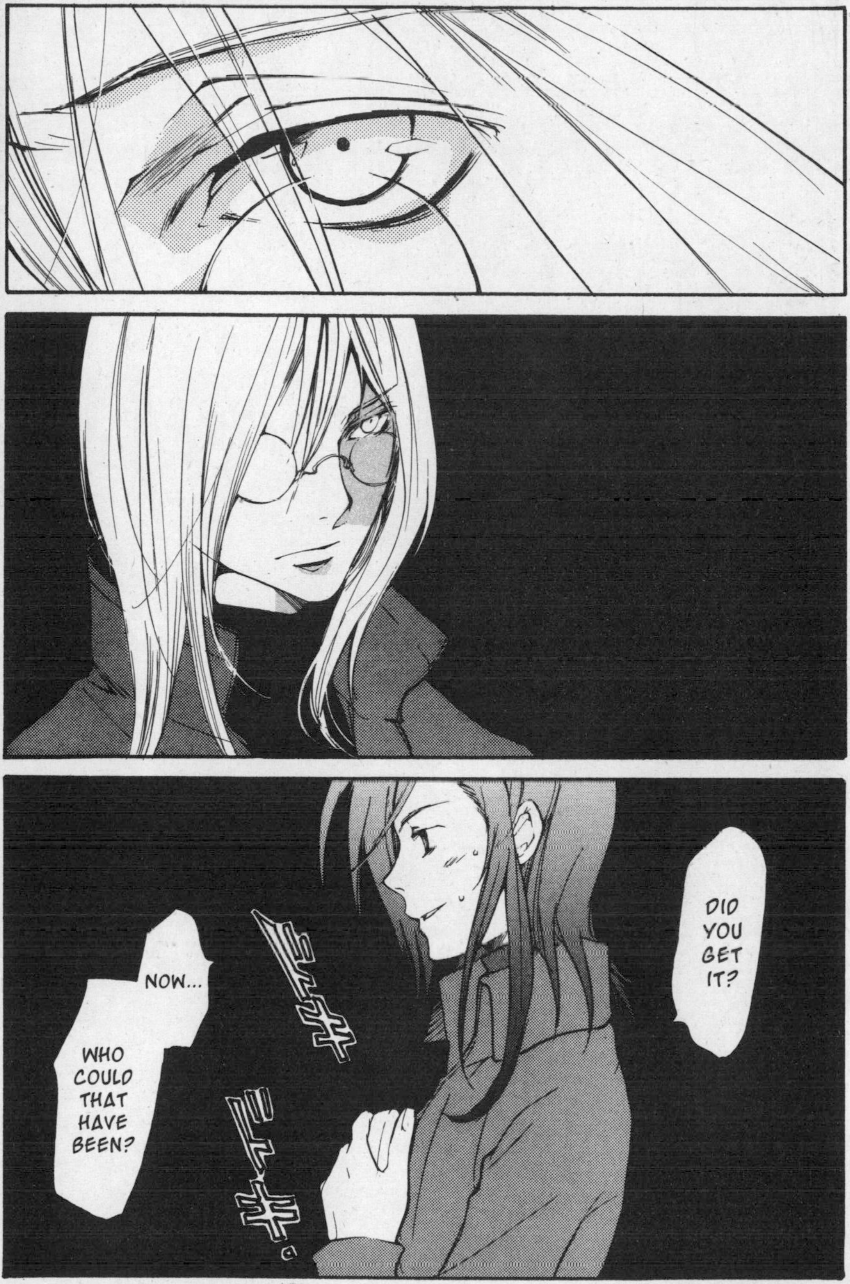
DID YOU GET IT?
NOW...
WHO COULD THAT HAVE BEEN?

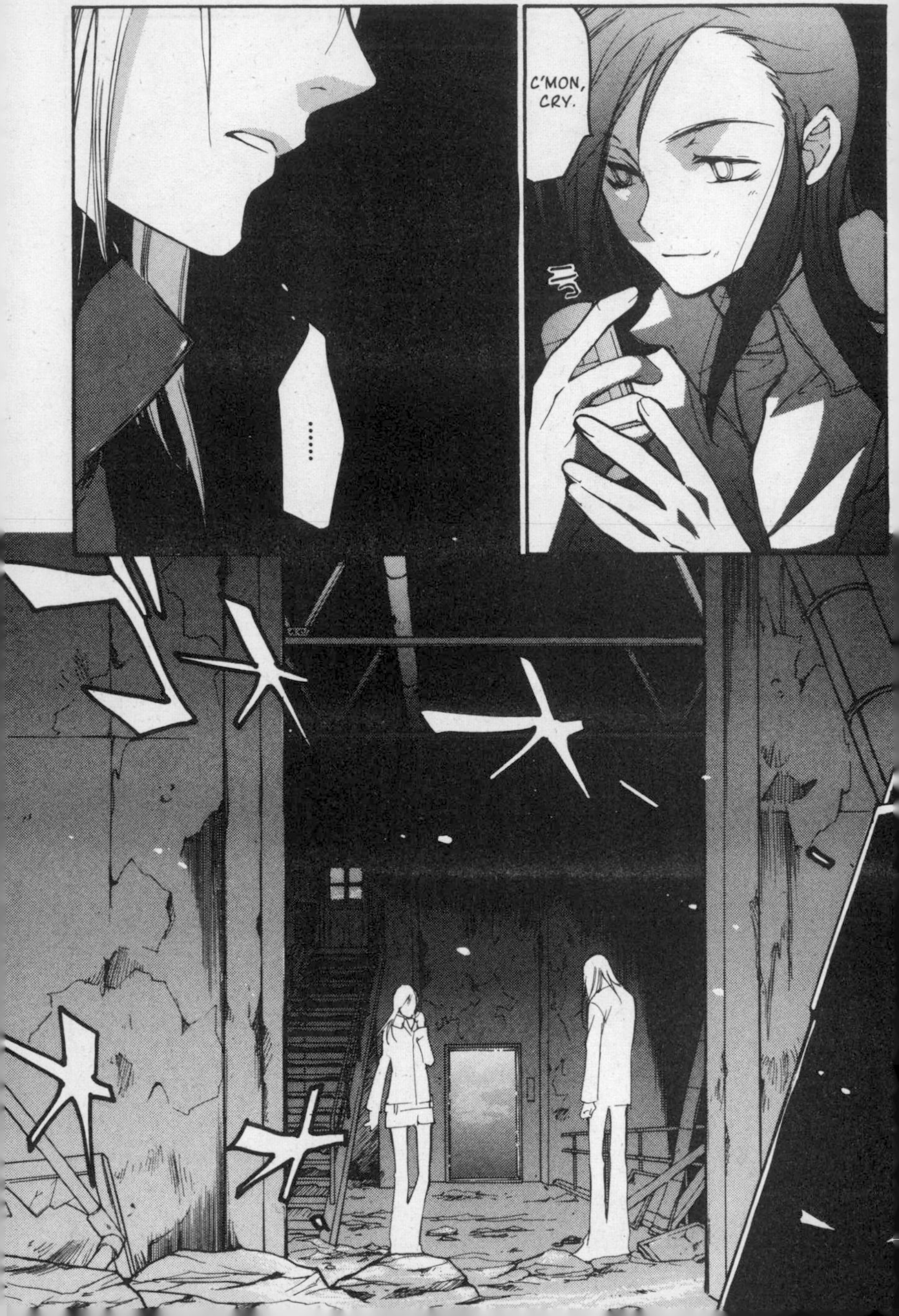
C'MON, CRY.
......

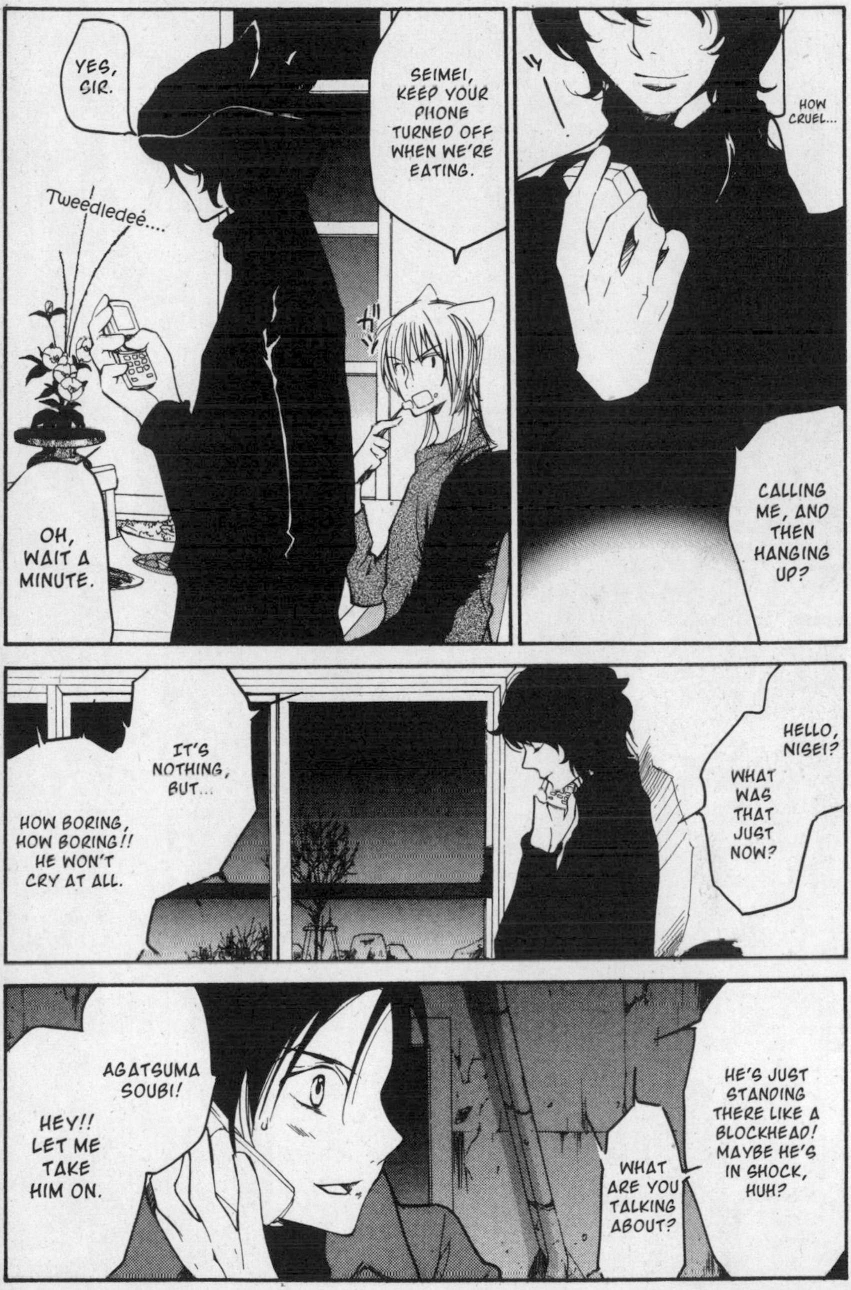
HOW CRUEL...
CALLING ME, AND THEN HANGING UP?
SEIMEI, KEEP YOUR PHONE TURNED OFF WHEN WE'RE EATING.
YES, SIR.
Tweedledeé....
OH, WAIT A MINUTE.
HELLO, NISEI?
WHAT WAS THAT JUST NOW?
IT'S NOTHING, BUT...
HOW BORING, HOW BORING!! HE WON'T CRY AT ALL.
HE'S JUST STANDING THERE LIKE A BLOCKHEAD! MAYBE HE'S IN SHOCK, HUH?
WHAT ARE YOU TALKING ABOUT?
AGATSUMA SOUBI!
HEY!! LET ME TAKE HIM ON.

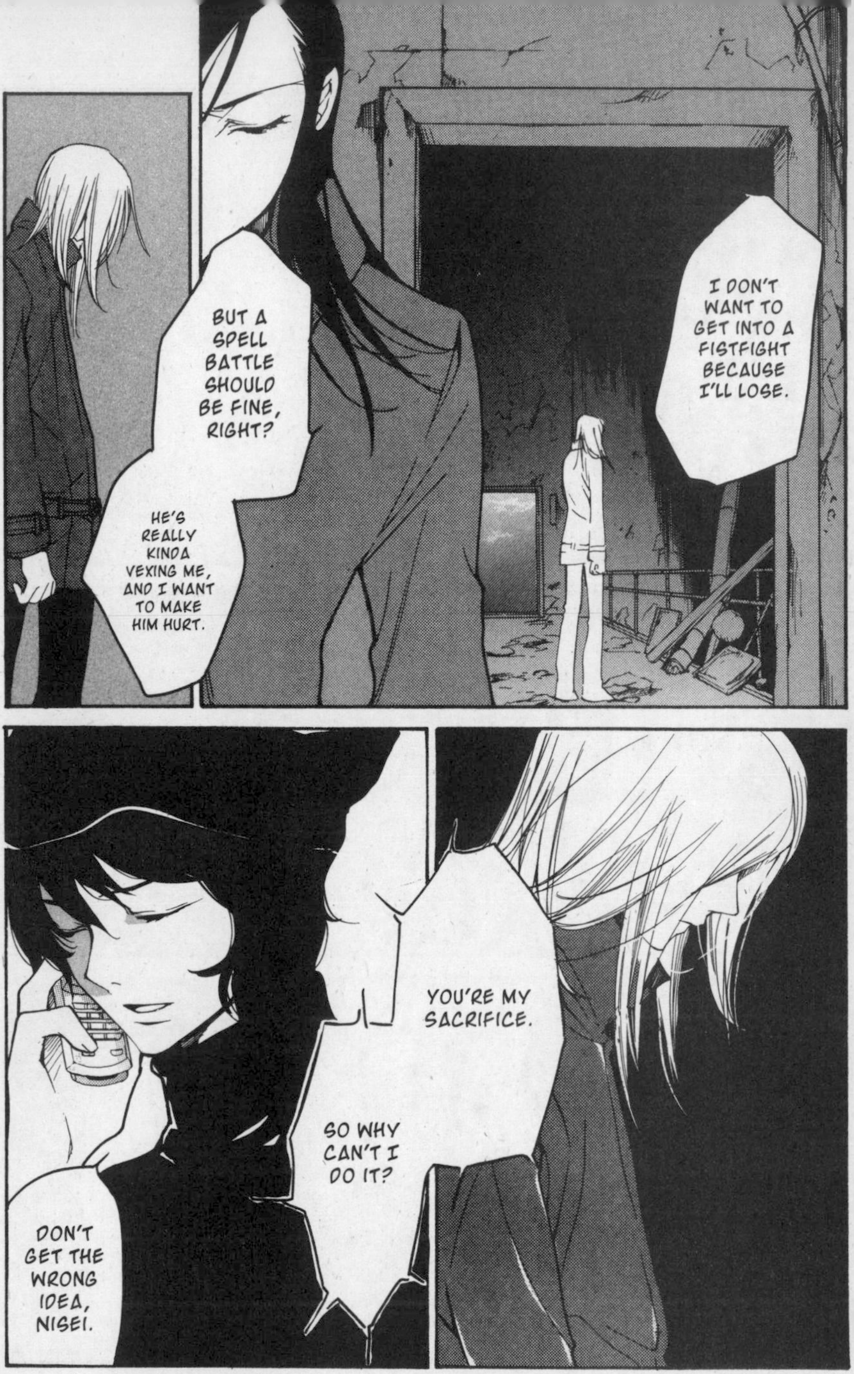
I DON'T WANT TO GET INTO A FISTFIGHT BECAUSE I'LL LOSE.
BUT A SPELL BATTLE SHOULD BE FINE, RIGHT?
HE'S REALLY KINDA VEXING ME, AND I WANT TO MAKE HIM HURT.
YOU'RE MY SACRIFICE.
SO WHY CAN'T I DO IT?
DON'T GET THE WRONG IDEA, NISEI.

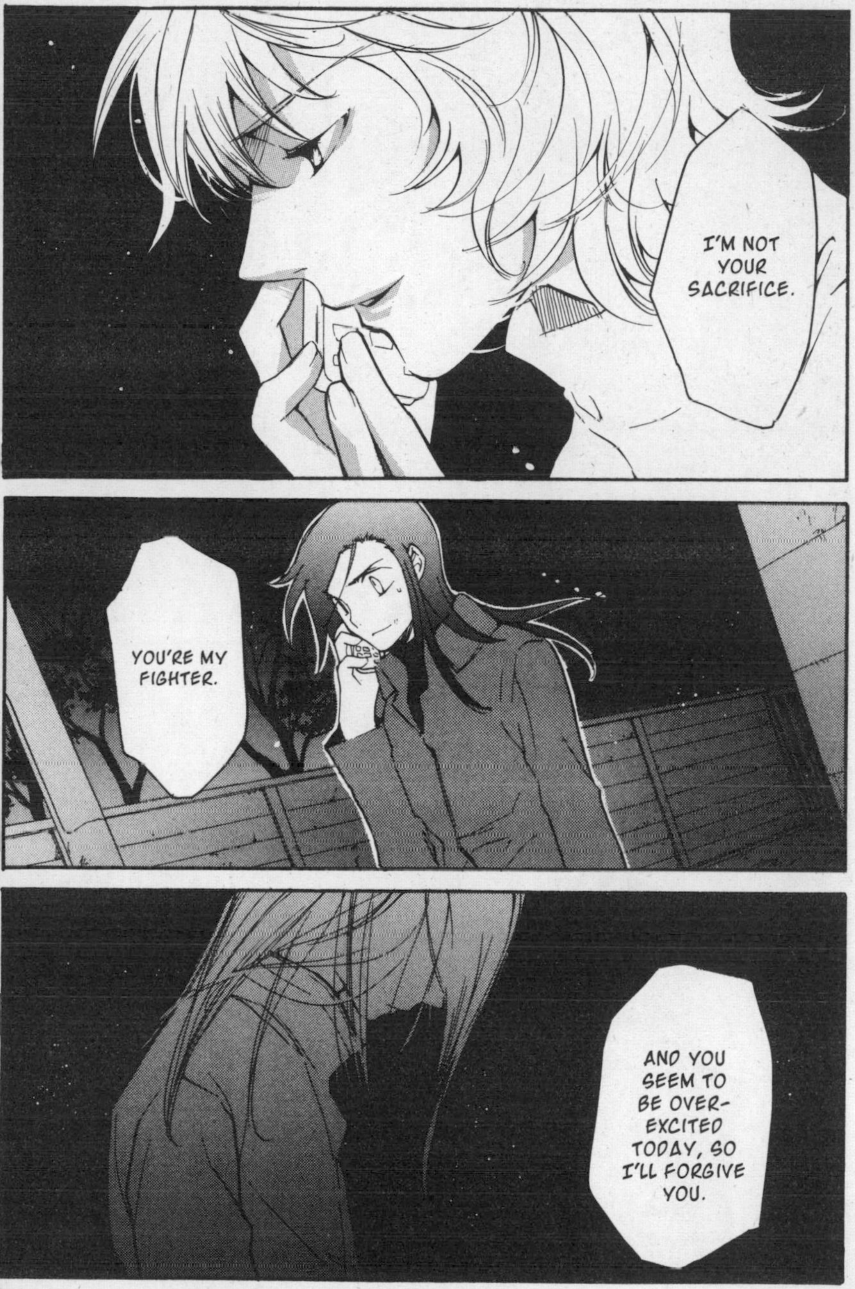
I'M NOT YOUR SACRIFICE.
YOU'RE MY FIGHTER.
AND YOU SEEM TO BE OVER-EXCITED TODAY, SO I'LL FORGIVE YOU.

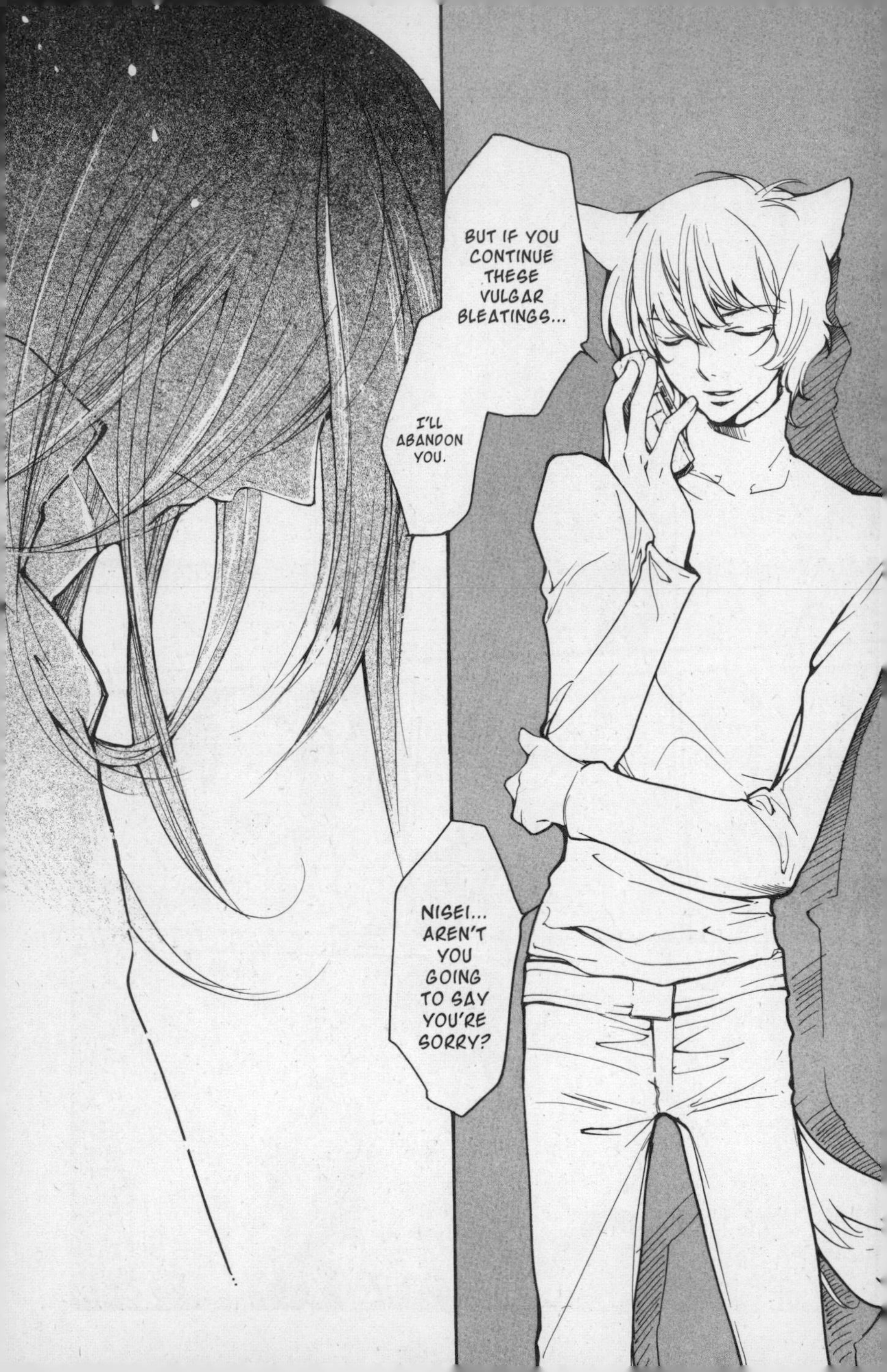
BUT IF YOU CONTINUE THESE VULGAR BLEATINGS...
I'LL ABANDON YOU.
NISEI... AREN'T YOU GOING TO SAY YOU'RE SORRY?

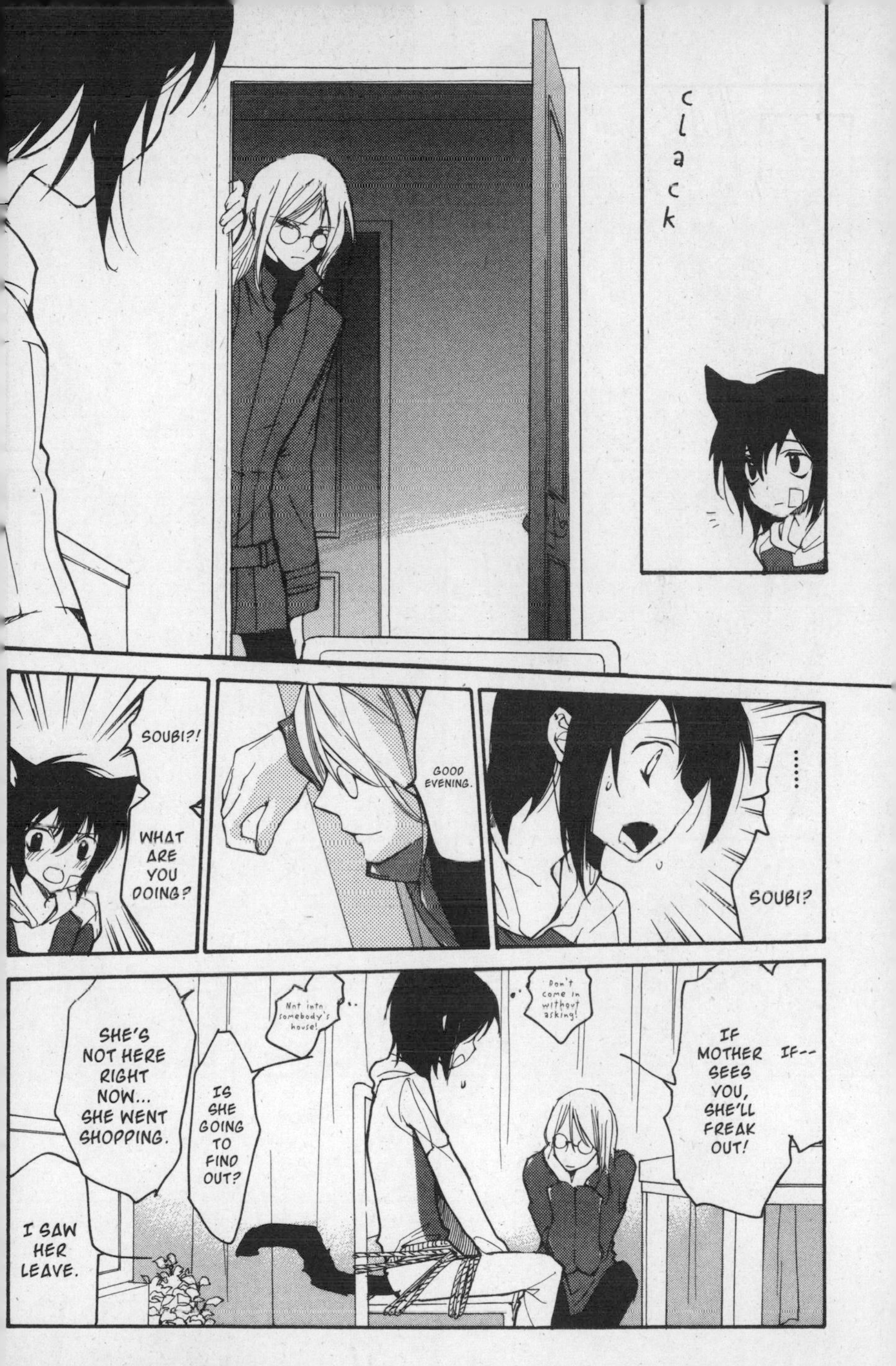
clack
......
SOUBI?
GOOD EVENING.
SOUBI?!
WHAT ARE YOU DOING?
IF MOTHER SEES YOU, SHE'LL FREAK OUT!
IF--
Don't come in without asking!
Not into somebody's house!
IS SHE GOING TO FIND OUT?
SHE'S NOT HERE RIGHT NOW... SHE WENT SHOPPING.
I SAW HER LEAVE.

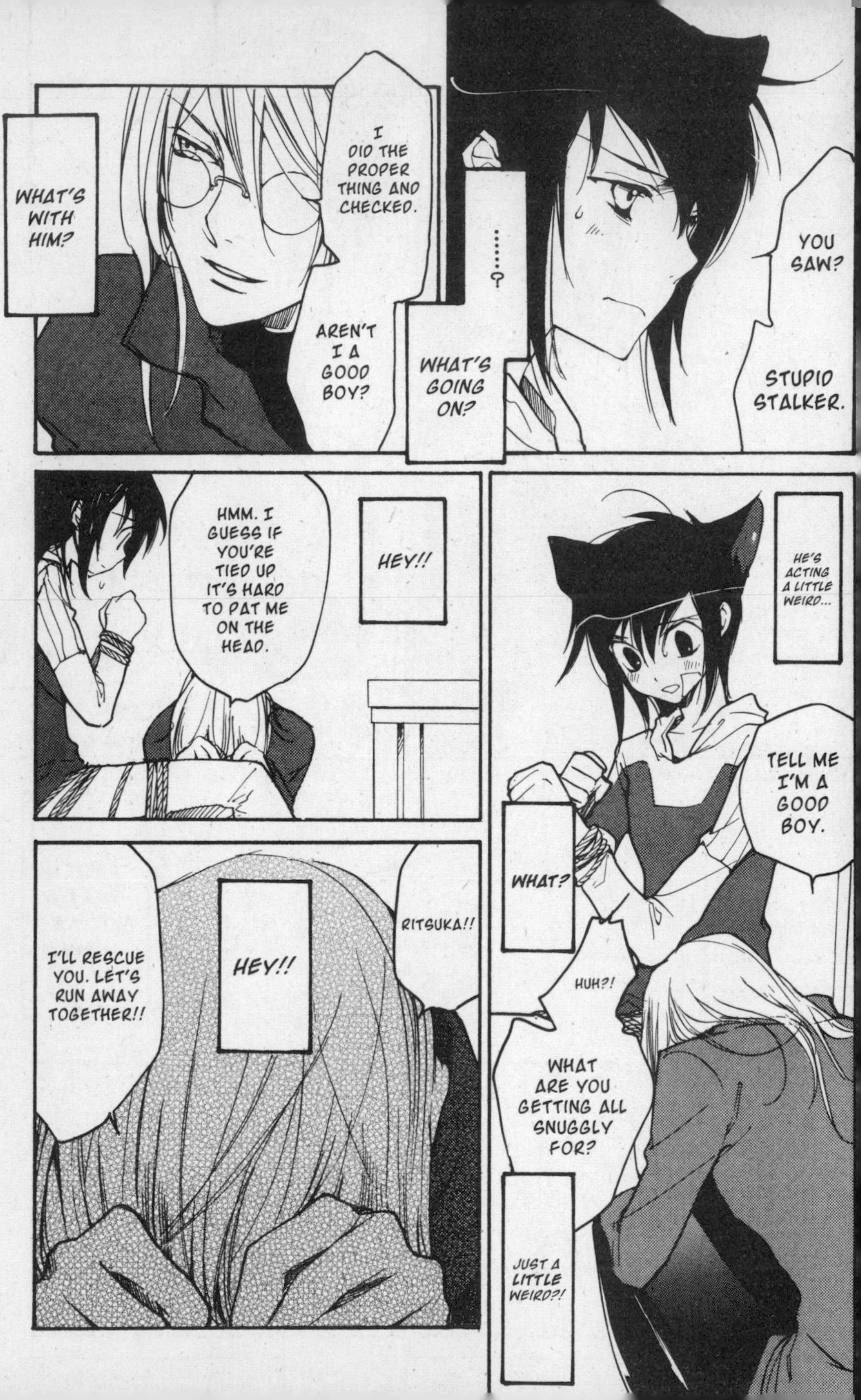
YOU SAW?
STUPID STALKER.
......?
WHAT'S GOING ON?
I DID THE PROPER THING AND CHECKED.
AREN'T I A GOOD BOY?
WHAT'S WITH HIM?
HE'S ACTING A LITTLE WEIRD...
TELL ME I'M A GOOD BOY.
WHAT?
HUH?!
WHAT ARE YOU GETTING ALL SNUGGLY FOR?
JUST A LITTLE WEIRD?!
HEY!!
HMM. I GUESS IF YOU'RE TIED UP IT'S HARD TO PAT ME ON THE HEAD.
RITSUKA!!
HEY!!
I'LL RESCUE YOU. LET'S RUN AWAY TOGETHER!!

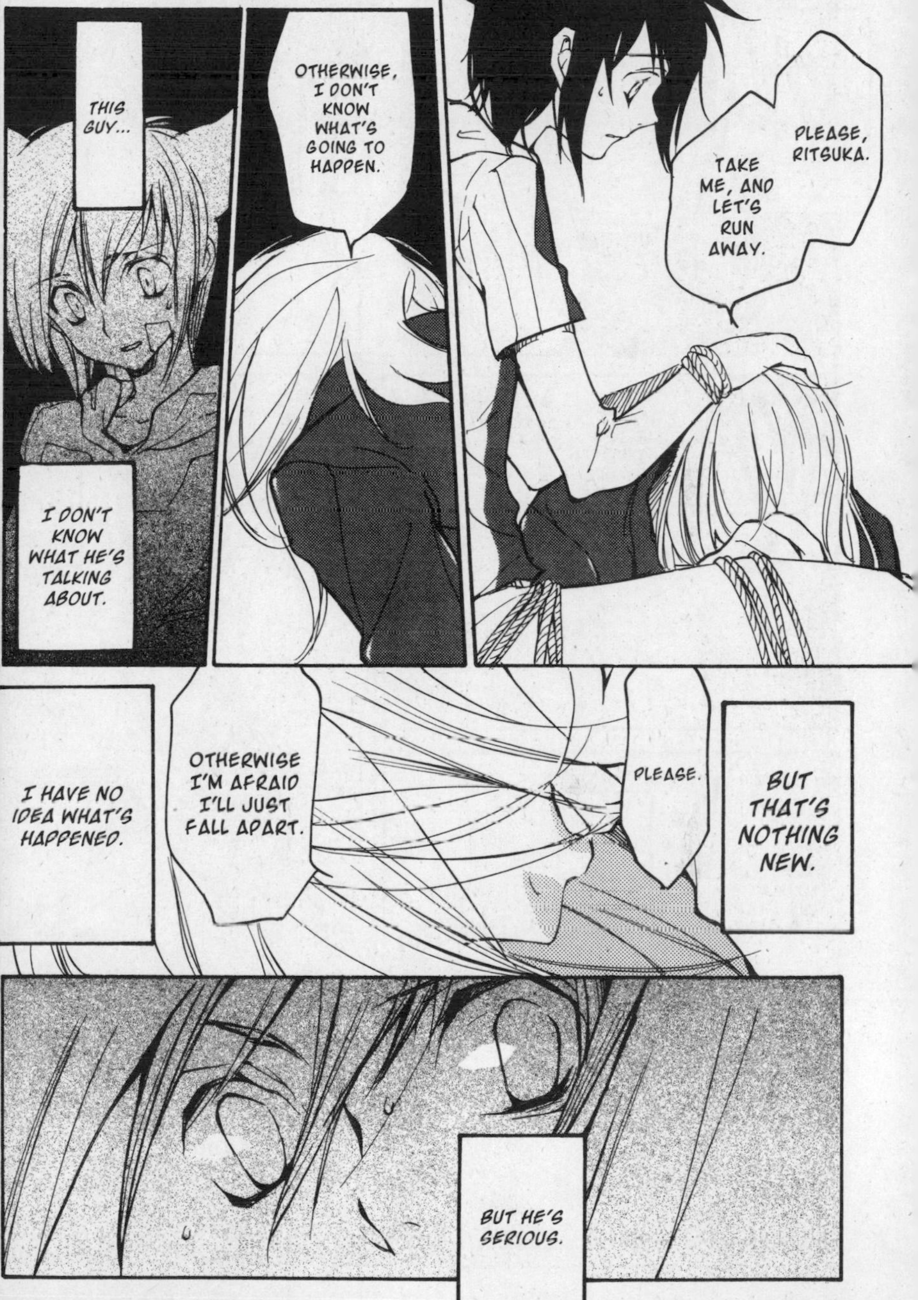
PLEASE, RITSUKA.
TAKE ME, AND LET'S RUN AWAY.
OTHERWISE, I DON'T KNOW WHAT'S GOING TO HAPPEN.
THIS GUY...
I DON'T KNOW WHAT HE'S TALKING ABOUT.
BUT THAT'S NOTHING NEW.
PLEASE.
OTHERWISE I'M AFRAID I'LL JUST FALL APART.
I HAVE NO IDEA WHAT'S HAPPENED.
BUT HE'S SERIOUS.

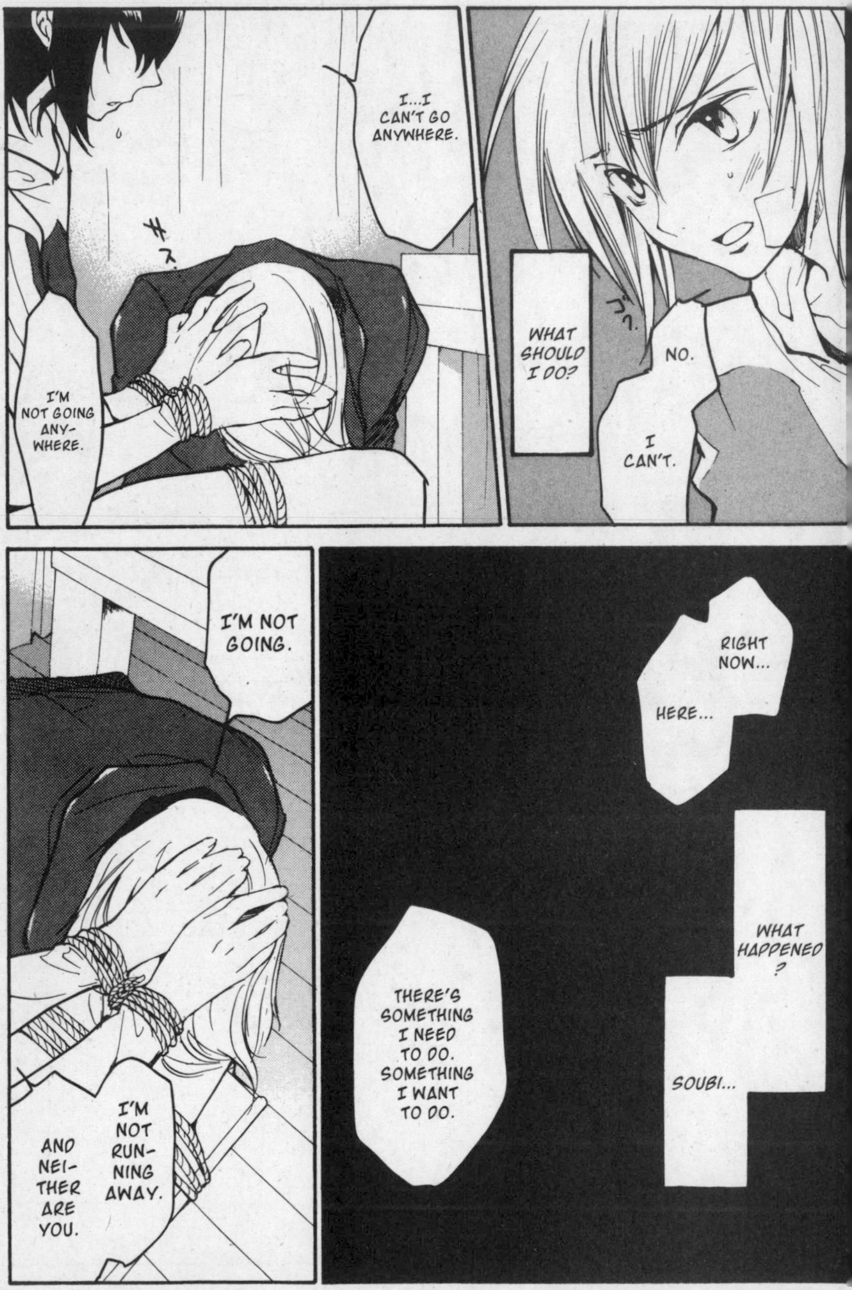
NO.
I CAN'T.
WHAT SHOULD I DO?
I...I CAN'T GO ANYWHERE.
I'M NOT GOING ANYWHERE.
RIGHT NOW...
HERE...
WHAT HAPPENED?
SOUBI...
THERE'S SOMETHING I NEED TO DO. SOMETHING I WANT TO DO.
I'M NOT GOING.
I'M NOT RUNNING AWAY.
AND NEITHER ARE YOU.

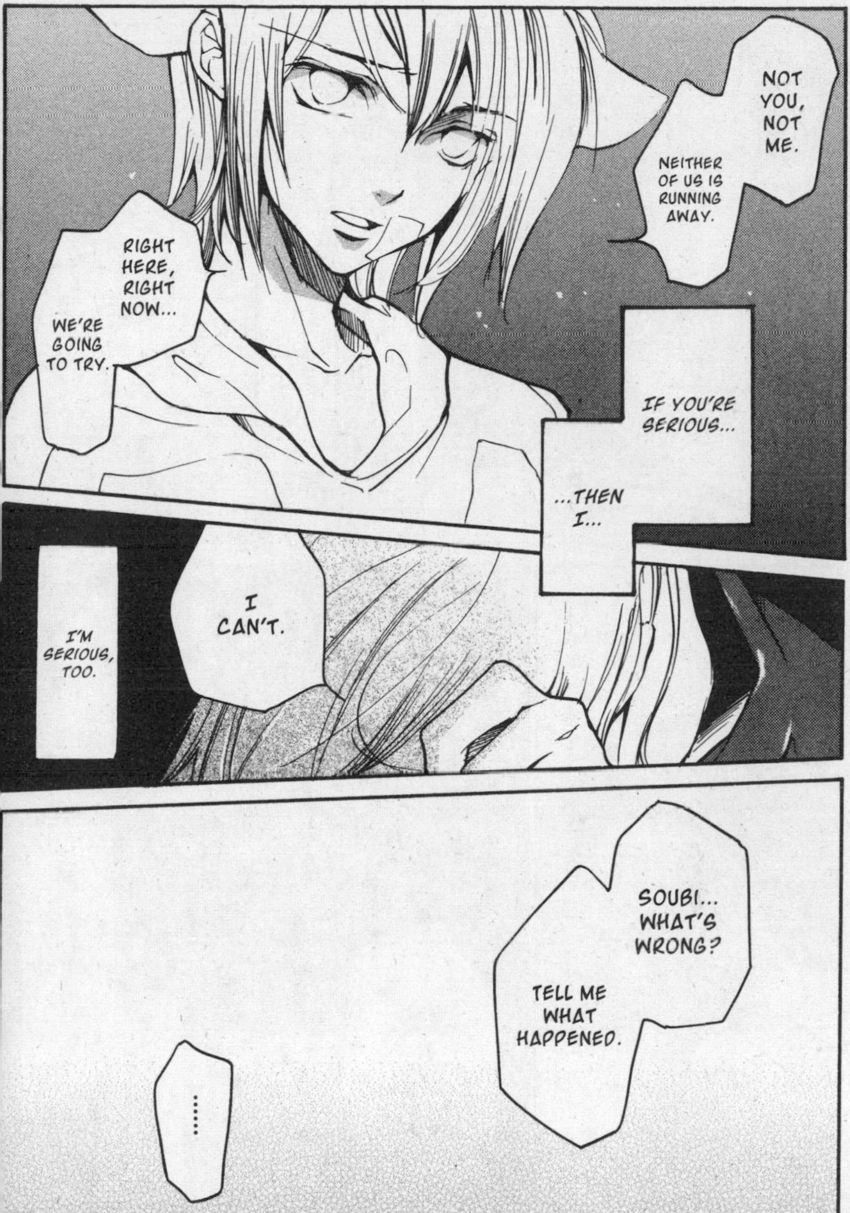
NOT YOU, NOT ME.
NEITHER OF US IS RUNNING AWAY.
RIGHT HERE, RIGHT NOW...
WE'RE GOING TO TRY.
IF YOU'RE SERIOUS...
...THEN I...
I CAN'T.
I'M SERIOUS, TOO.
SOUBI... WHAT'S WRONG?
TELL ME WHAT HAPPENED.
......

Even though I only want to believe in Ritsuka...

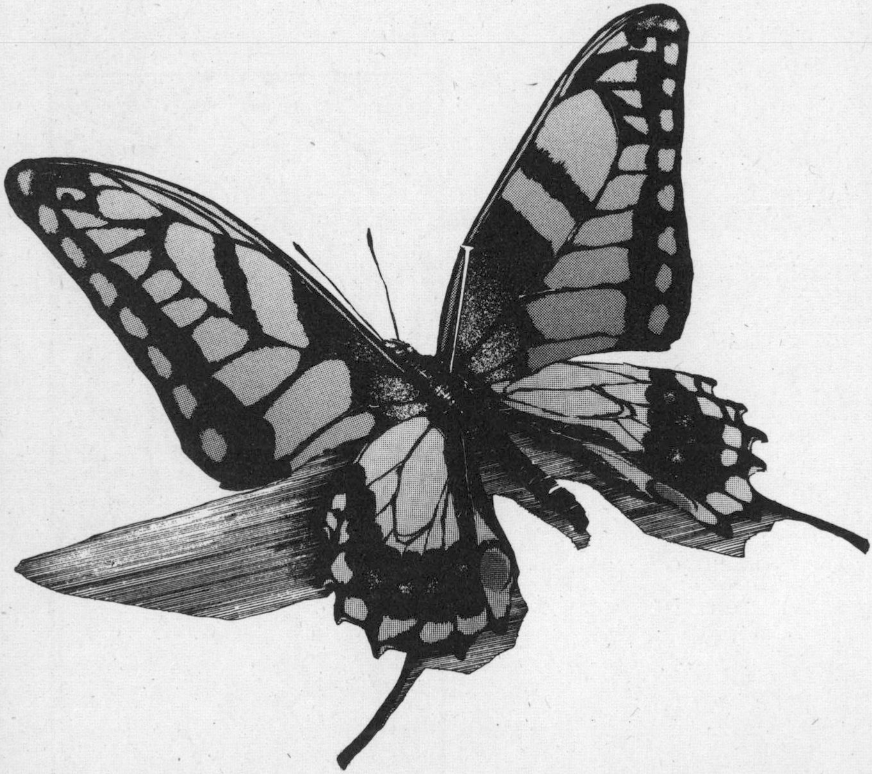

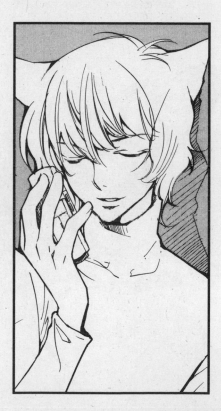

The Birth Chapters

Chapter 5

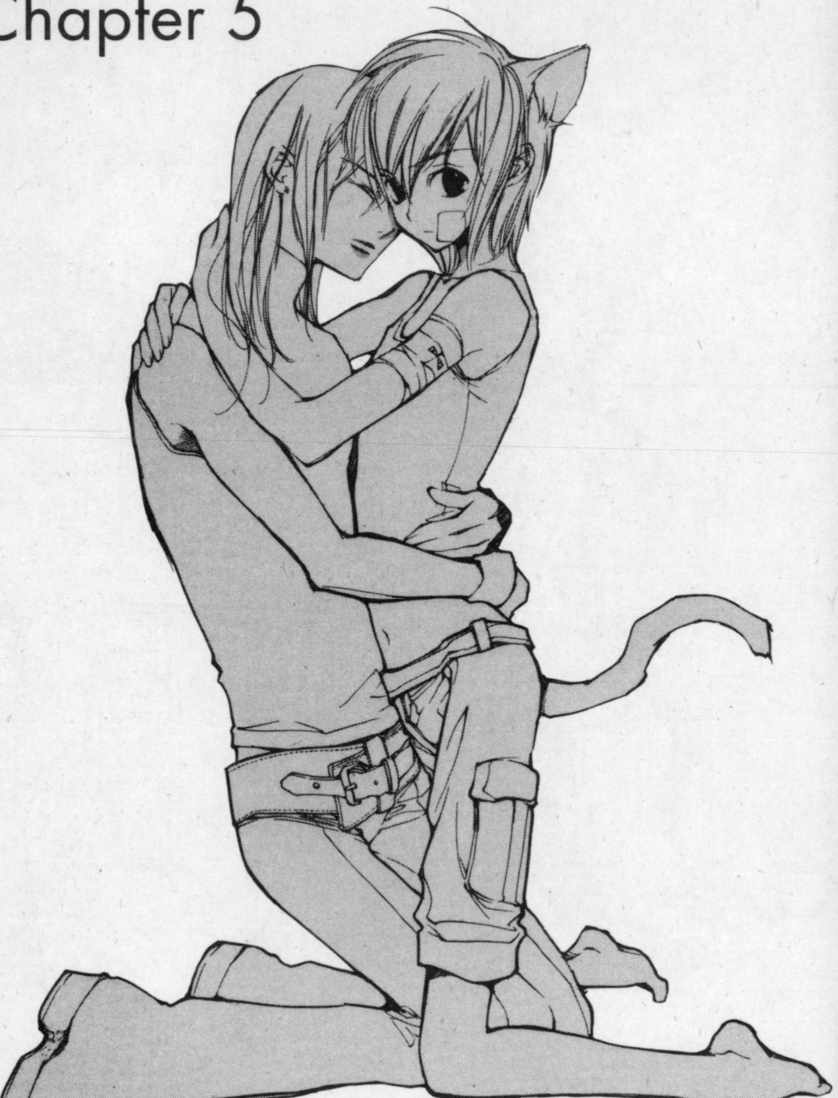

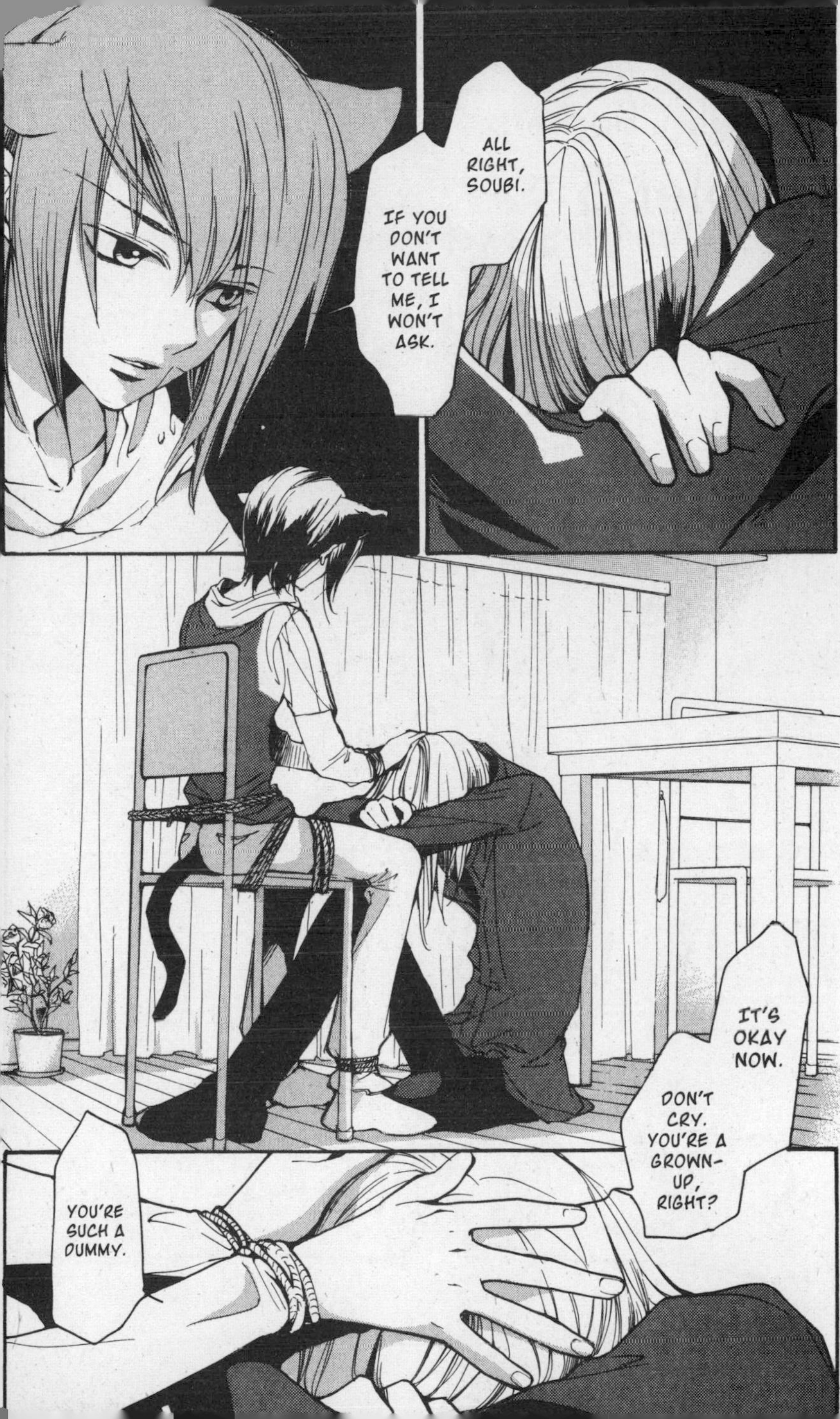
ALL RIGHT, SOUBI.
IF YOU DON'T WANT TO TELL ME, I WON'T ASK.
IT'S OKAY NOW.
DON'T CRY. YOU'RE A GROWN-UP, RIGHT?
YOU'RE SUCH A DUMMY.

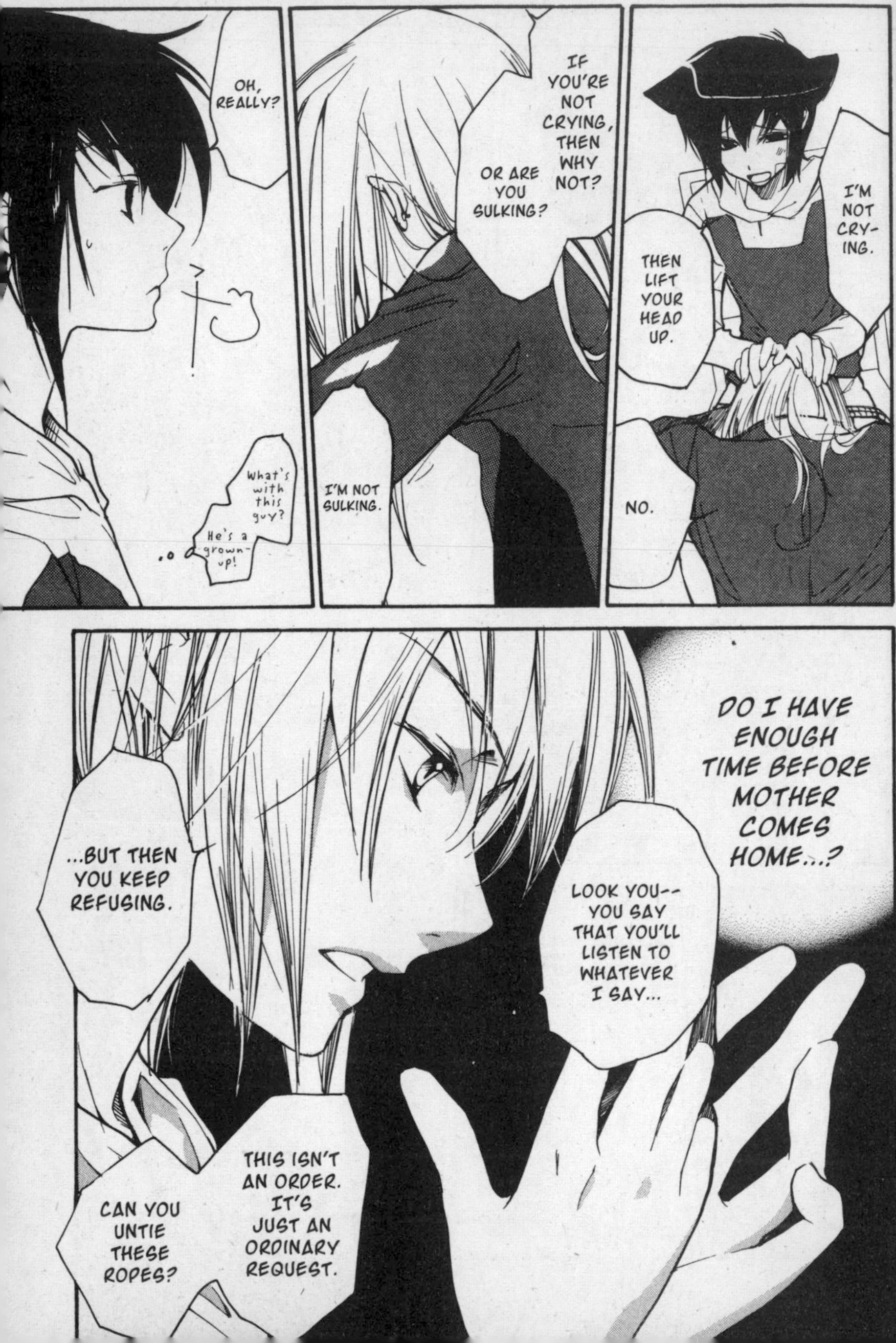

I'M NOT CRYING.
THEN LIFT YOUR HEAD UP.
NO.
IF YOU'RE NOT CRYING, THEN WHY NOT?
OR ARE YOU SULKING?
I'M NOT SULKING.
OH, REALLY?
What's with this guy?
He's a grown-up!
DO I HAVE ENOUGH TIME BEFORE MOTHER COMES HOME...?
LOOK YOU-- YOU SAY THAT YOU'LL LISTEN TO WHATEVER I SAY...
...BUT THEN YOU KEEP REFUSING.
THIS ISN'T AN ORDER. IT'S JUST AN ORDINARY REQUEST.
CAN YOU UNTIE THESE ROPES?

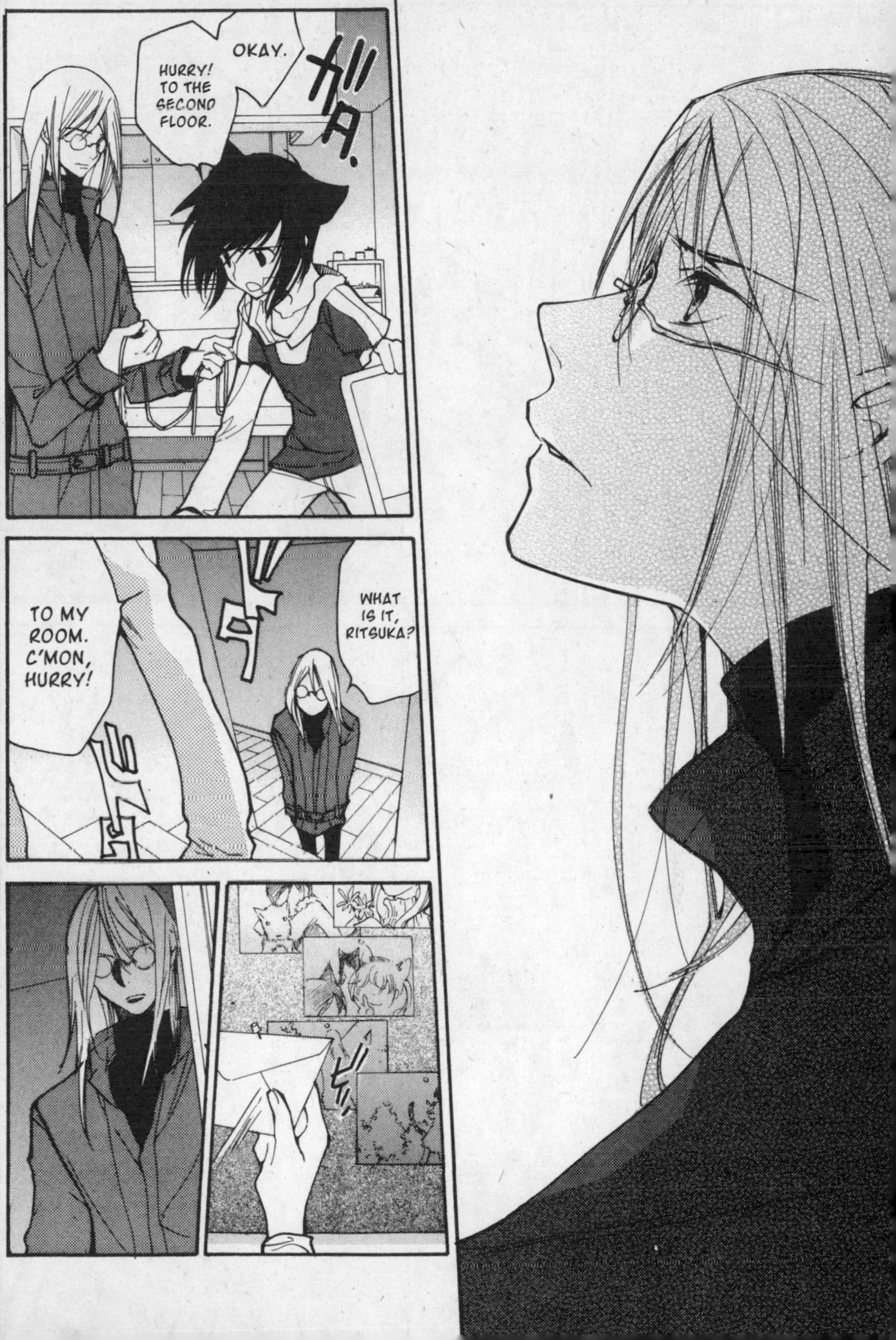
HURRY! TO THE SECOND FLOOR.
OKAY.
WHAT IS IT, RITSUKA?
TO MY ROOM. C'MON, HURRY!

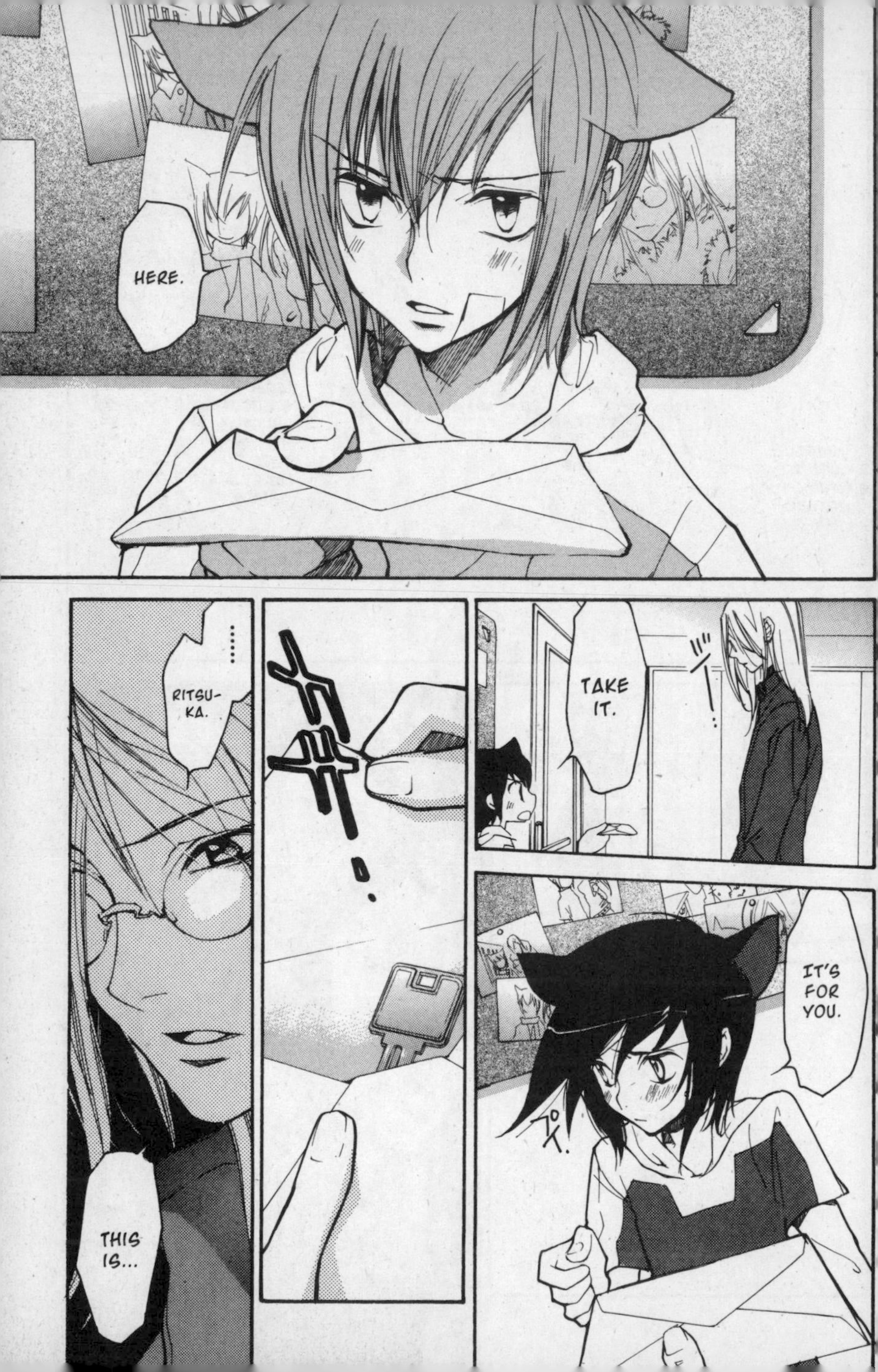
HERE.
TAKE IT.
IT'S FOR YOU.
......
RITSUKA.
THIS IS...

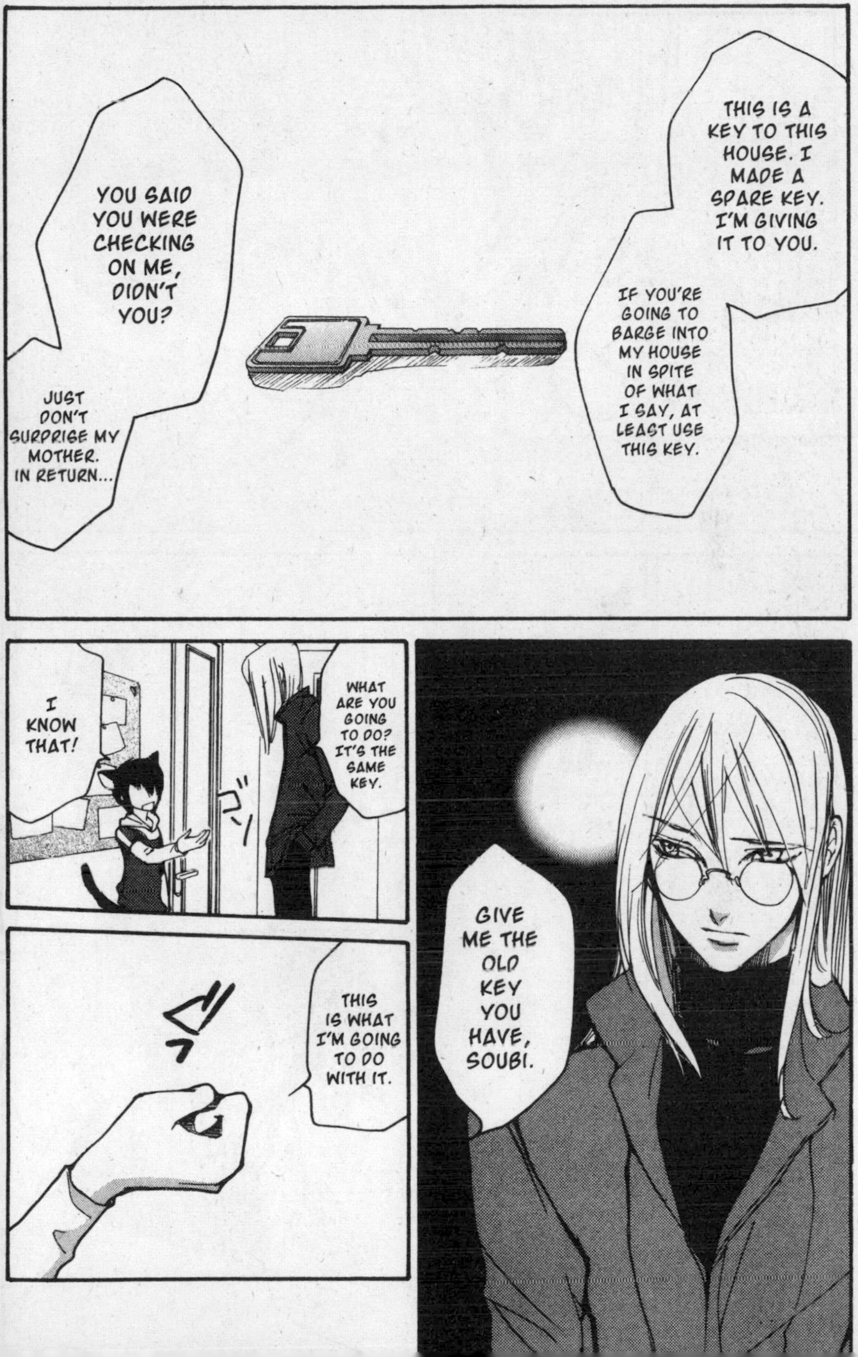
THIS IS A KEY TO THIS HOUSE. I MADE A SPARE KEY. I'M GIVING IT TO YOU.
IF YOU'RE GOING TO BARGE INTO MY HOUSE IN SPITE OF WHAT I SAY, AT LEAST USE THIS KEY.
YOU SAID YOU WERE CHECKING ON ME, DIDN'T YOU?
JUST DON'T SURPRISE MY MOTHER. IN RETURN...
GIVE ME THE OLD KEY YOU HAVE, SOUBI.
WHAT ARE YOU GOING TO DO? IT'S THE SAME KEY.
I KNOW THAT!
THIS IS WHAT I'M GOING TO DO WITH IT.

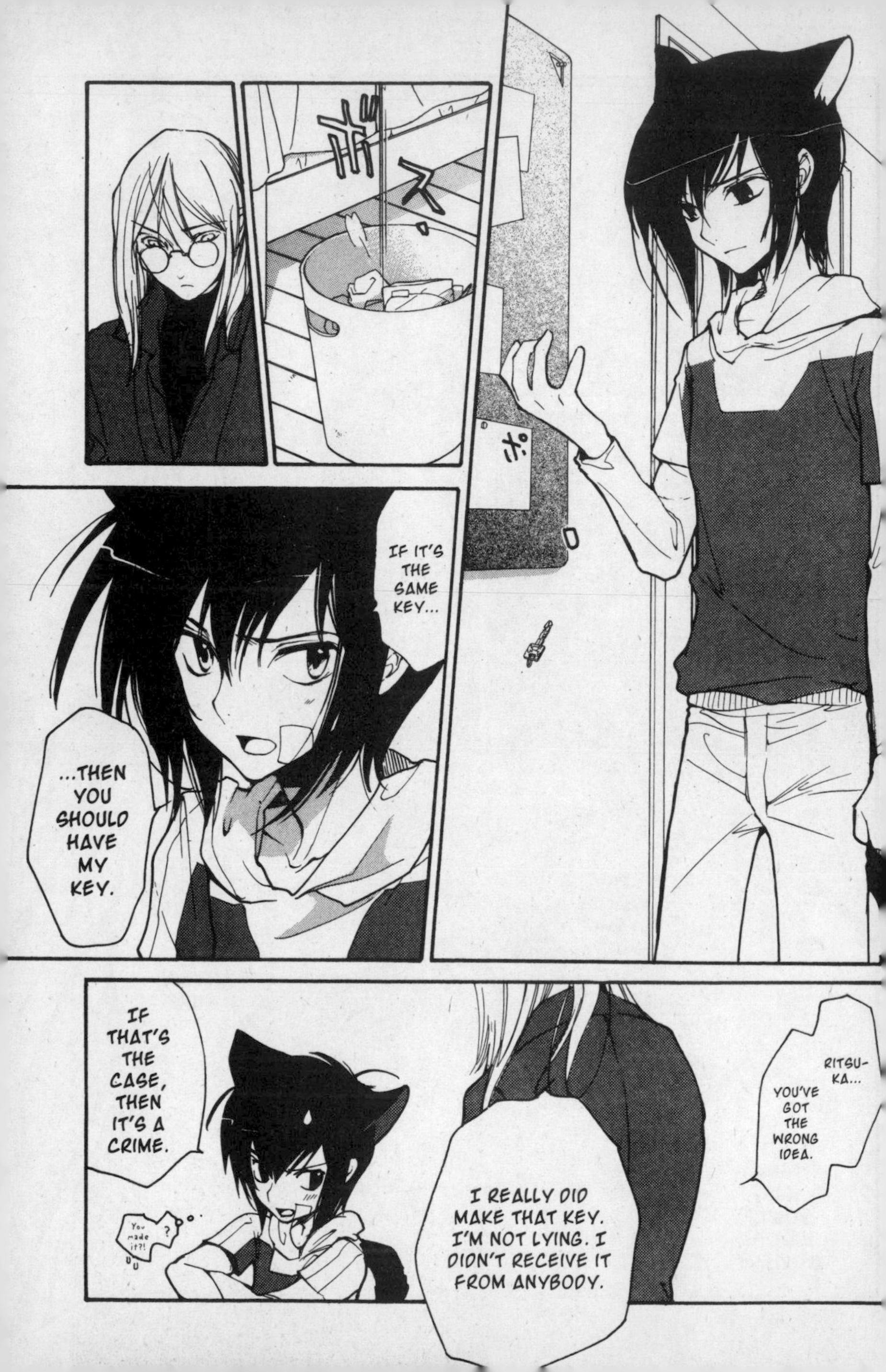
IF IT'S THE SAME KEY...
...THEN YOU SHOULD HAVE MY KEY.
RITSUKA... YOU'VE GOT THE WRONG IDEA.
I REALLY DID MAKE THAT KEY. I'M NOT LYING. I DIDN'T RECEIVE IT FROM ANYBODY.
IF THAT'S THE CASE, THEN IT'S A CRIME.
You made it?!
?

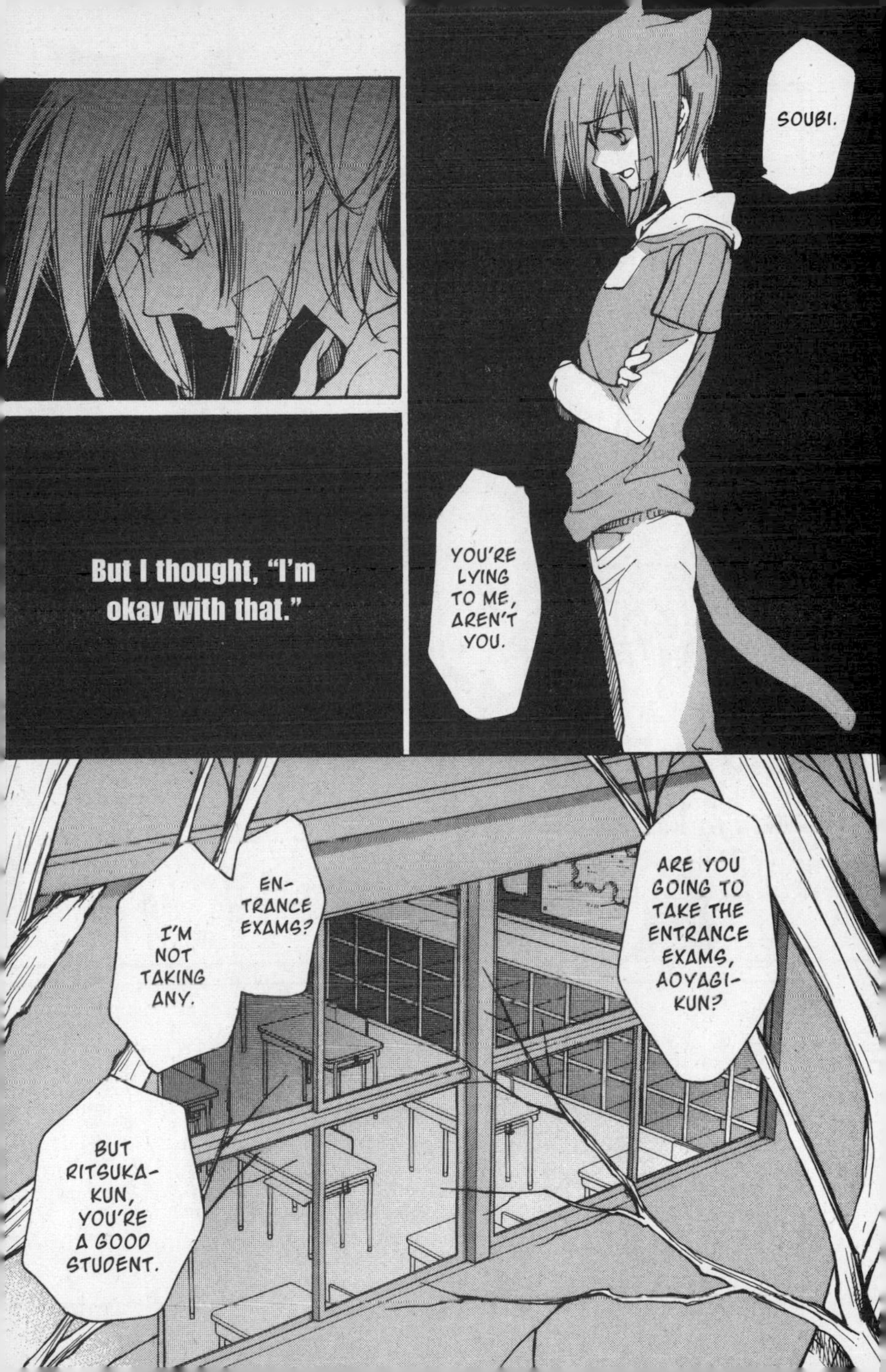
SOUBI.
YOU'RE LYING TO ME, AREN'T YOU.
But I thought, "I'm okay with that."
ARE YOU GOING TO TAKE THE ENTRANCE EXAMS, AOYAGI-KUN?
ENTRANCE EXAMS?
I'M NOT TAKING ANY.
BUT RITSUKA-KUN, YOU'RE A GOOD STUDENT.

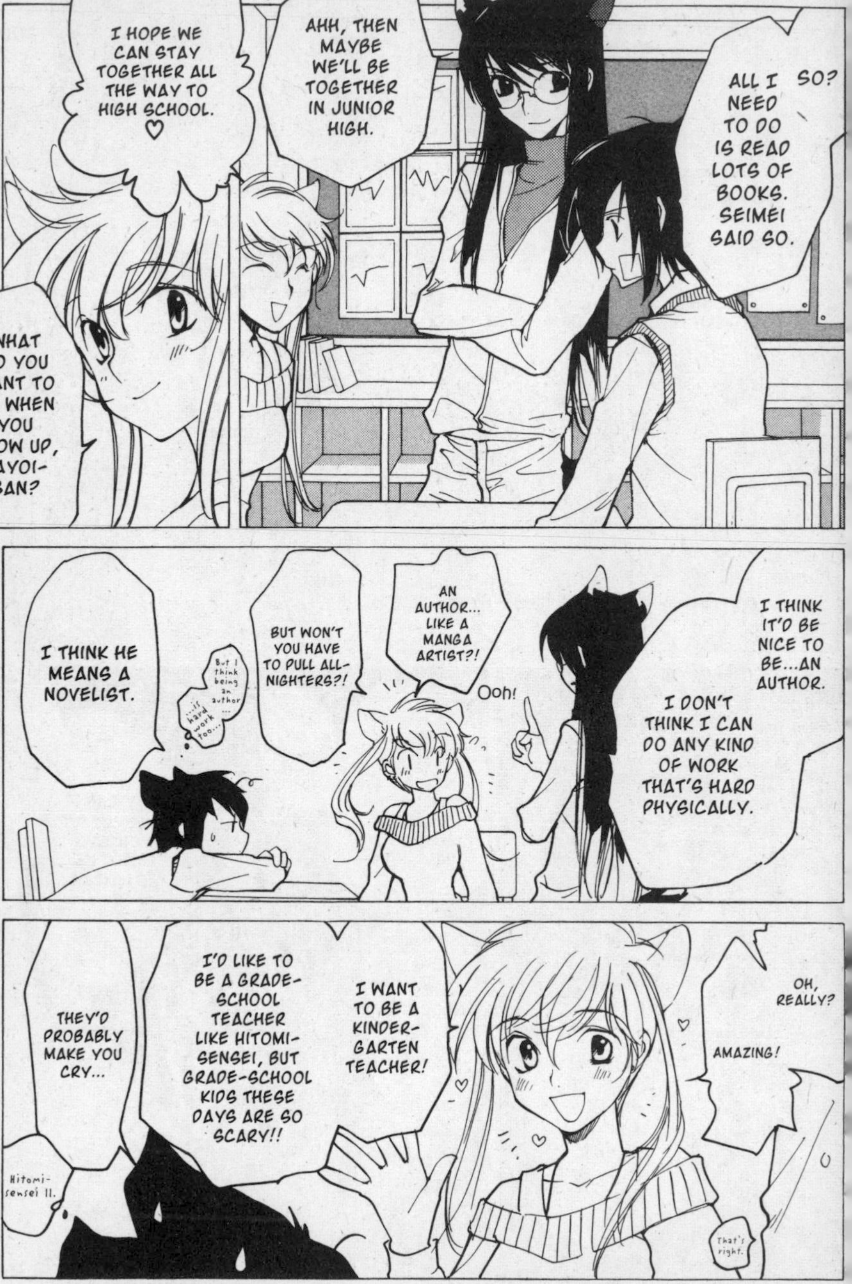
SO?
ALL I NEED TO DO IS READ LOTS OF BOOKS. SEIMEI SAID SO.
AHH, THEN MAYBE WE'LL BE TOGETHER IN JUNIOR HIGH.
I HOPE WE CAN STAY TOGETHER ALL THE WAY TO HIGH SCHOOL. ♡
WHAT DO YOU WANT TO BE WHEN YOU GROW UP, YAYOI-SAN?
I THINK IT'D BE NICE TO BE...AN AUTHOR.
I DON'T THINK I CAN DO ANY KIND OF WORK THAT'S HARD PHYSICALLY.
Ooh!
AN AUTHOR... LIKE A MANGA ARTIST?!
BUT WON'T YOU HAVE TO PULL ALL-NIGHTERS?!
But I think being an author...
...is hard work too...
I THINK HE MEANS A NOVELIST.
OH, REALLY?
AMAZING!
That's right.
I WANT TO BE A KINDER-GARTEN TEACHER!
I'D LIKE TO BE A GRADE-SCHOOL TEACHER LIKE HITOMI-SENSEI, BUT GRADE-SCHOOL KIDS THESE DAYS ARE SO SCARY!!
THEY'D PROBABLY MAKE YOU CRY...
Hitomi-sensei!!.

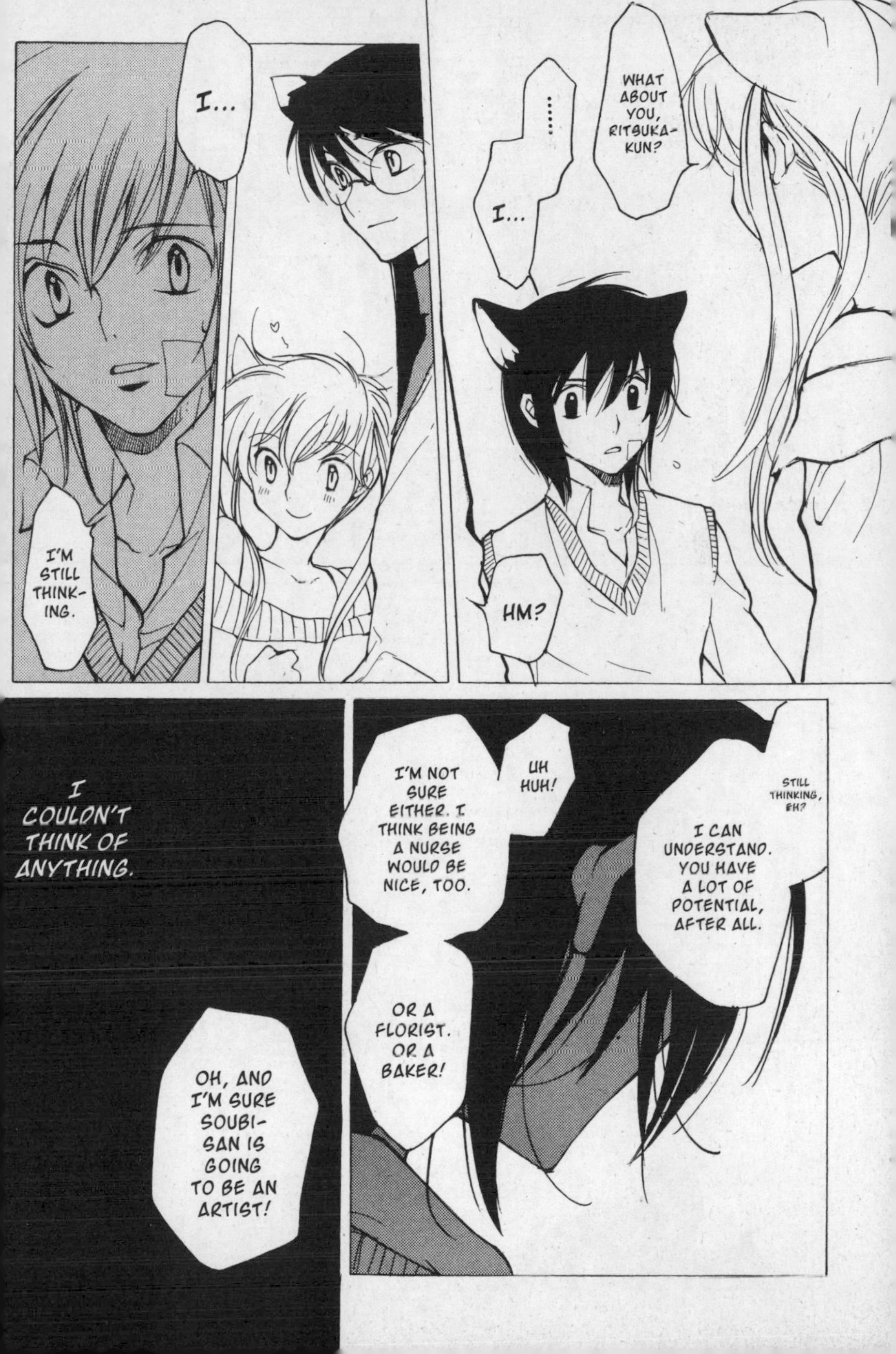
WHAT ABOUT YOU, RITSUKA-KUN?
......
I...
HM?
I...
I'M STILL THINKING.
STILL THINKING, EH?
I CAN UNDERSTAND. YOU HAVE A LOT OF POTENTIAL, AFTER ALL.
UH HUH!
I'M NOT SURE EITHER. I THINK BEING A NURSE WOULD BE NICE, TOO.
OR A FLORIST. OR A BAKER!
OH, AND I'M SURE SOUBI-SAN IS GOING TO BE AN ARTIST!
I COULDN'T THINK OF ANYTHING.

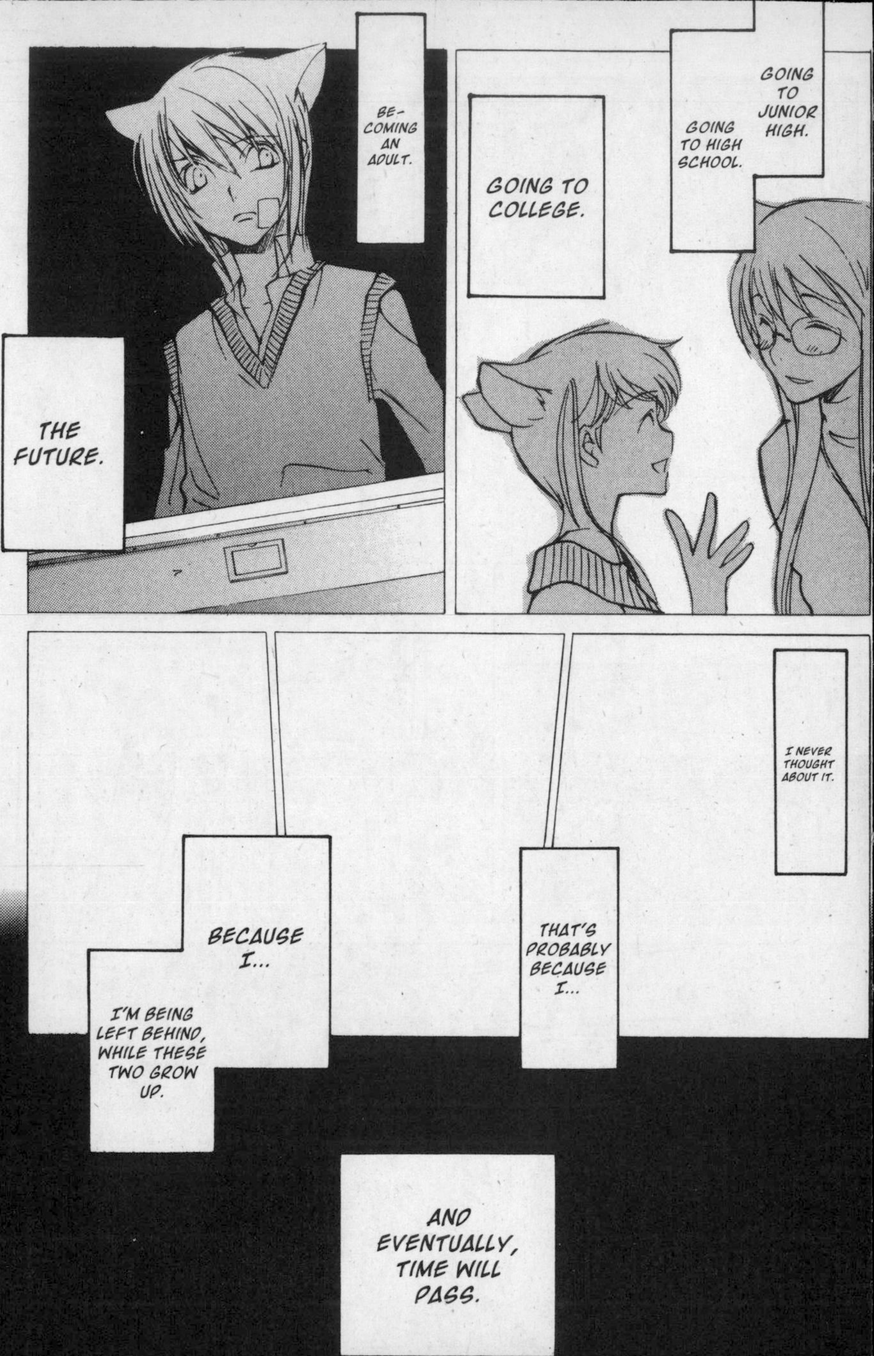
GOING TO JUNIOR HIGH.
GOING TO HIGH SCHOOL.
GOING TO COLLEGE.
BE-COMING AN ADULT.
THE FUTURE.
I NEVER THOUGHT ABOUT IT.
THAT'S PROBABLY BECAUSE I...
BECAUSE I...
I'M BEING LEFT BEHIND, WHILE THESE TWO GROW UP.
AND EVENTUALLY, TIME WILL PASS.

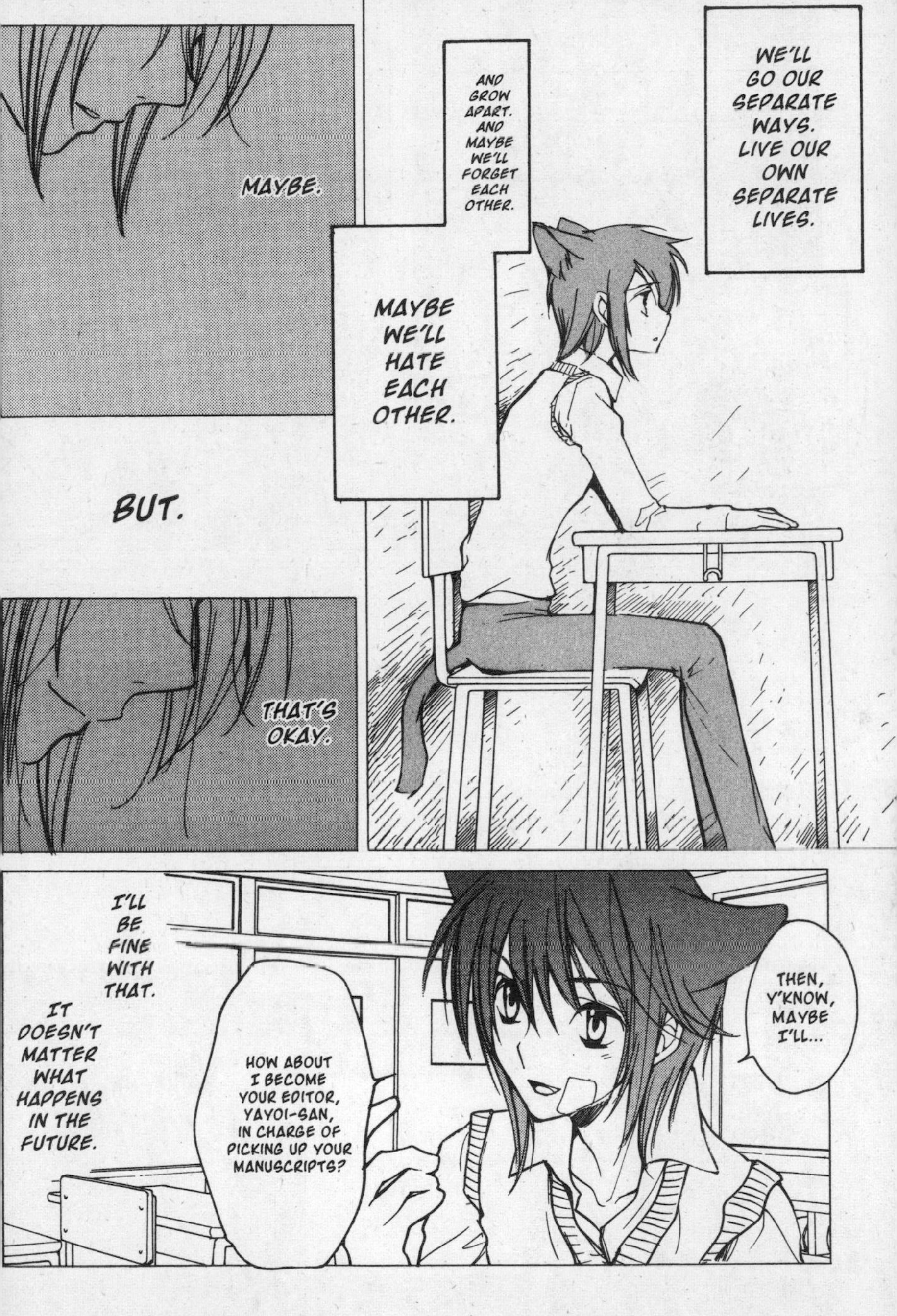
WE'LL GO OUR SEPARATE WAYS. LIVE OUR OWN SEPARATE LIVES.
AND GROW APART. AND MAYBE WE'LL FORGET EACH OTHER.
MAYBE WE'LL HATE EACH OTHER.
MAYBE.
BUT.
THAT'S OKAY.
THEN, Y'KNOW, MAYBE I'LL...
HOW ABOUT I BECOME YOUR EDITOR, YAYOI-SAN, IN CHARGE OF PICKING UP YOUR MANUSCRIPTS?
I'LL BE FINE WITH THAT.
IT DOESN'T MATTER WHAT HAPPENS IN THE FUTURE.

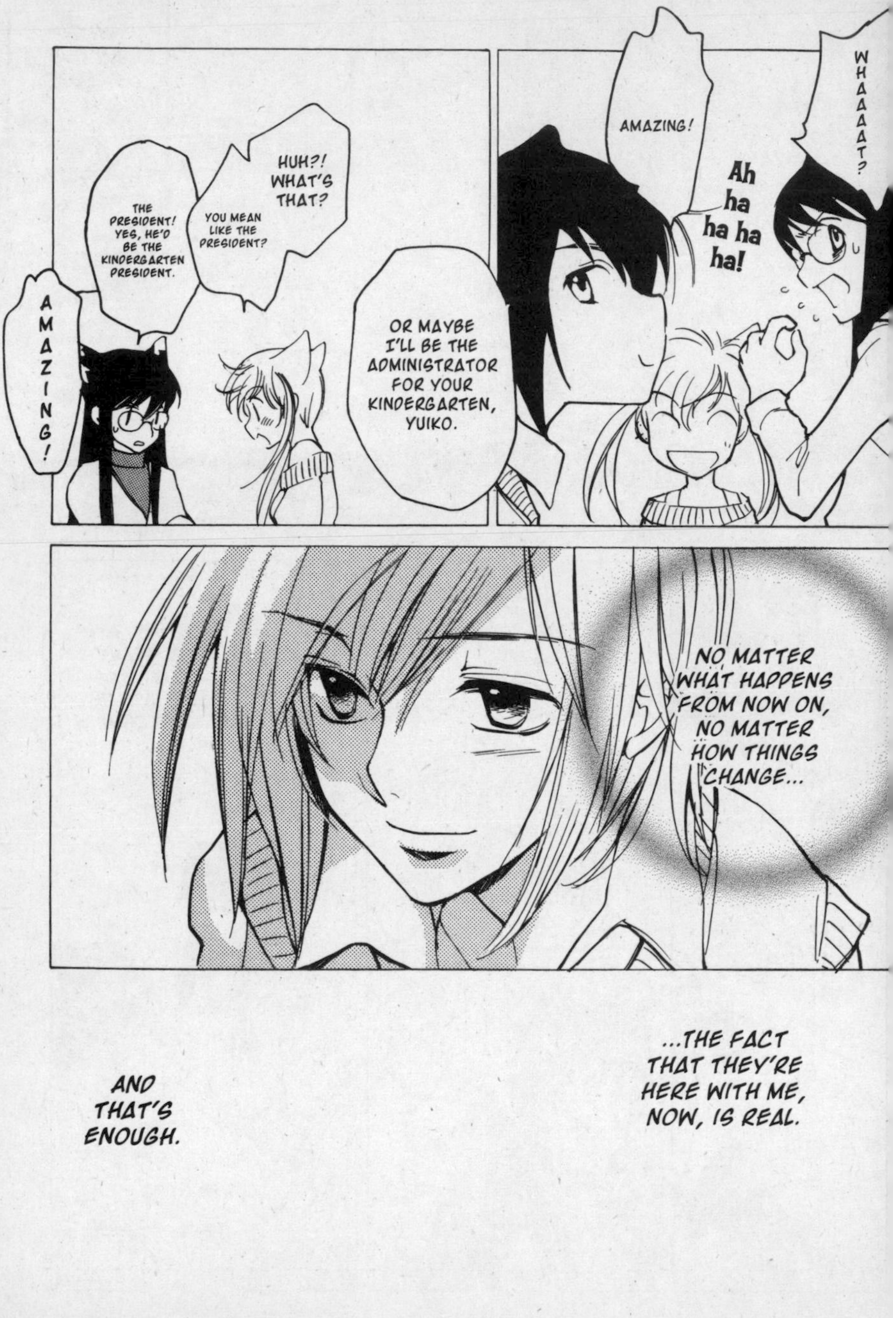
OR MAYBE I'LL BE THE ADMINISTRATOR FOR YOUR KINDERGARTEN, YUIKO.
HUH?! WHAT'S THAT?
YOU MEAN LIKE THE PRESIDENT?
THE PRESIDENT! YES, HE'D BE THE KINDERGARTEN PRESIDENT.
AMAZING!
AMAZING!
Ah ha ha ha ha!
WHAAAAAT?
NO MATTER WHAT HAPPENS FROM NOW ON, NO MATTER HOW THINGS CHANGE...
...THE FACT THAT THEY'RE HERE WITH ME, NOW, IS REAL.
AND THAT'S ENOUGH.

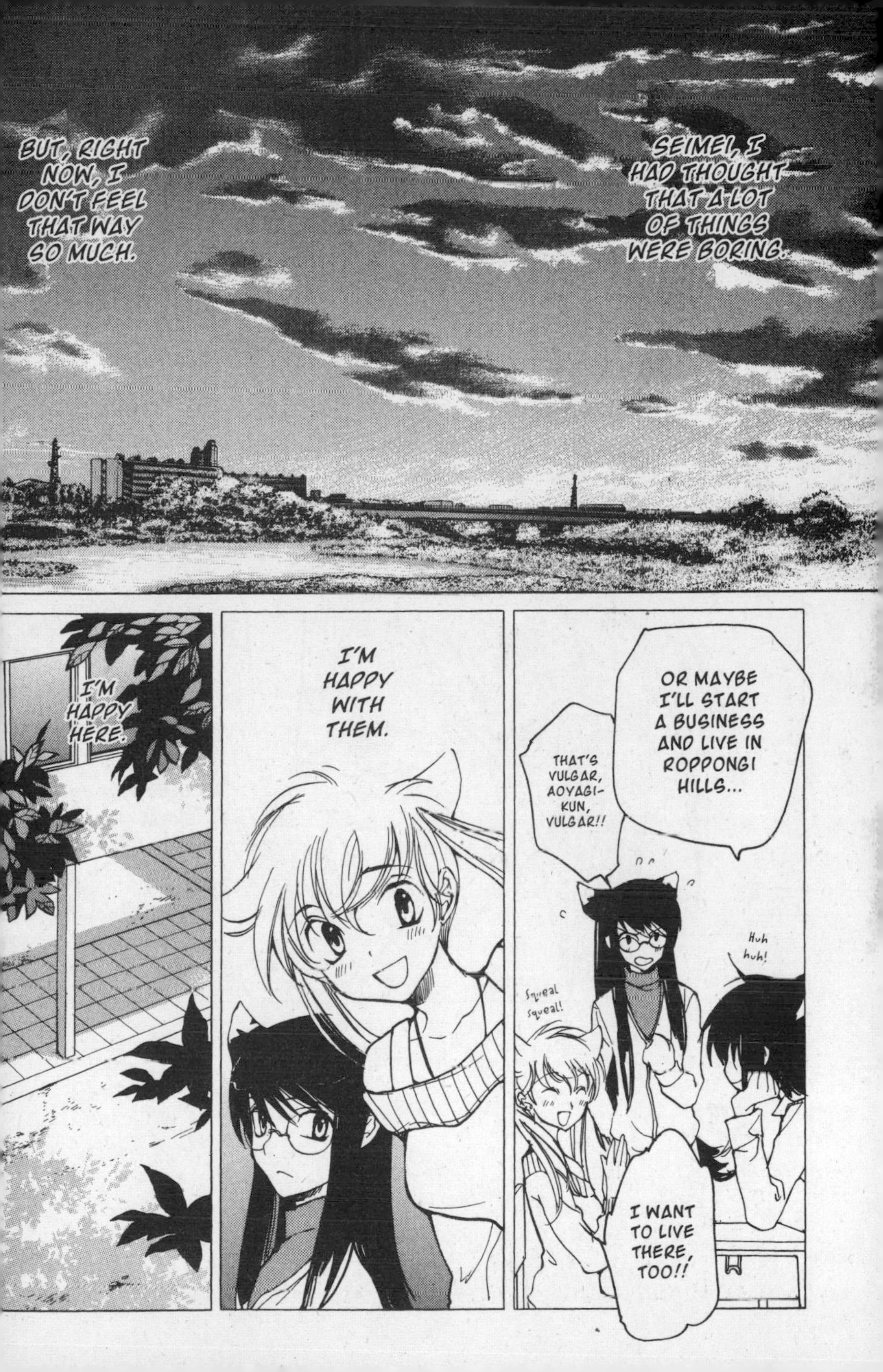
SEIMEI, I HAD THOUGHT THAT A LOT OF THINGS WERE BORING.
BUT, RIGHT NOW, I DON'T FEEL THAT WAY SO MUCH.
OR MAYBE I'LL START A BUSINESS AND LIVE IN ROPPONGI HILLS...
THAT'S VULGAR, AOYAGI-KUN, VULGAR!!
Huh huh!
Squeal squeal!
I WANT TO LIVE THERE, TOO!!
I'M HAPPY WITH THEM.
I'M HAPPY HERE.

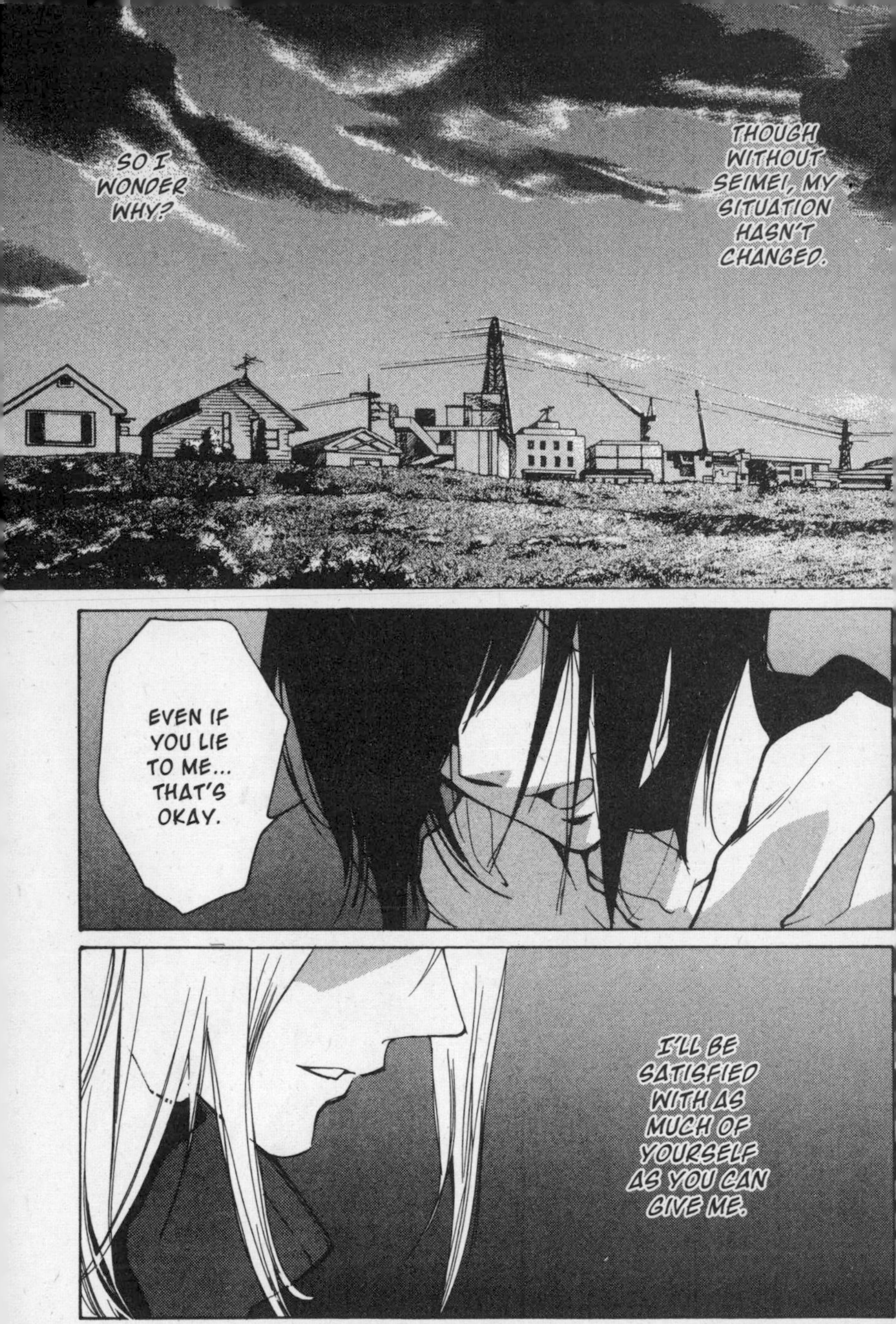
THOUGH WITHOUT SEIMEI, MY SITUATION HASN'T CHANGED.
SO I WONDER WHY?
EVEN IF YOU LIE TO ME... THAT'S OKAY.
I'LL BE SATISFIED WITH AS MUCH OF YOURSELF AS YOU CAN GIVE ME.

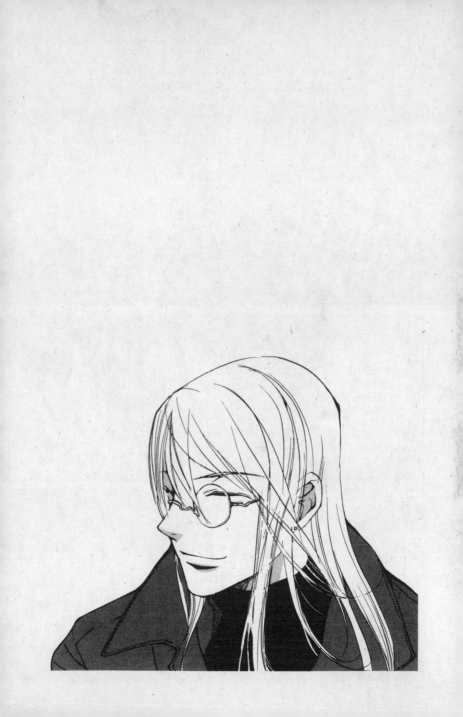

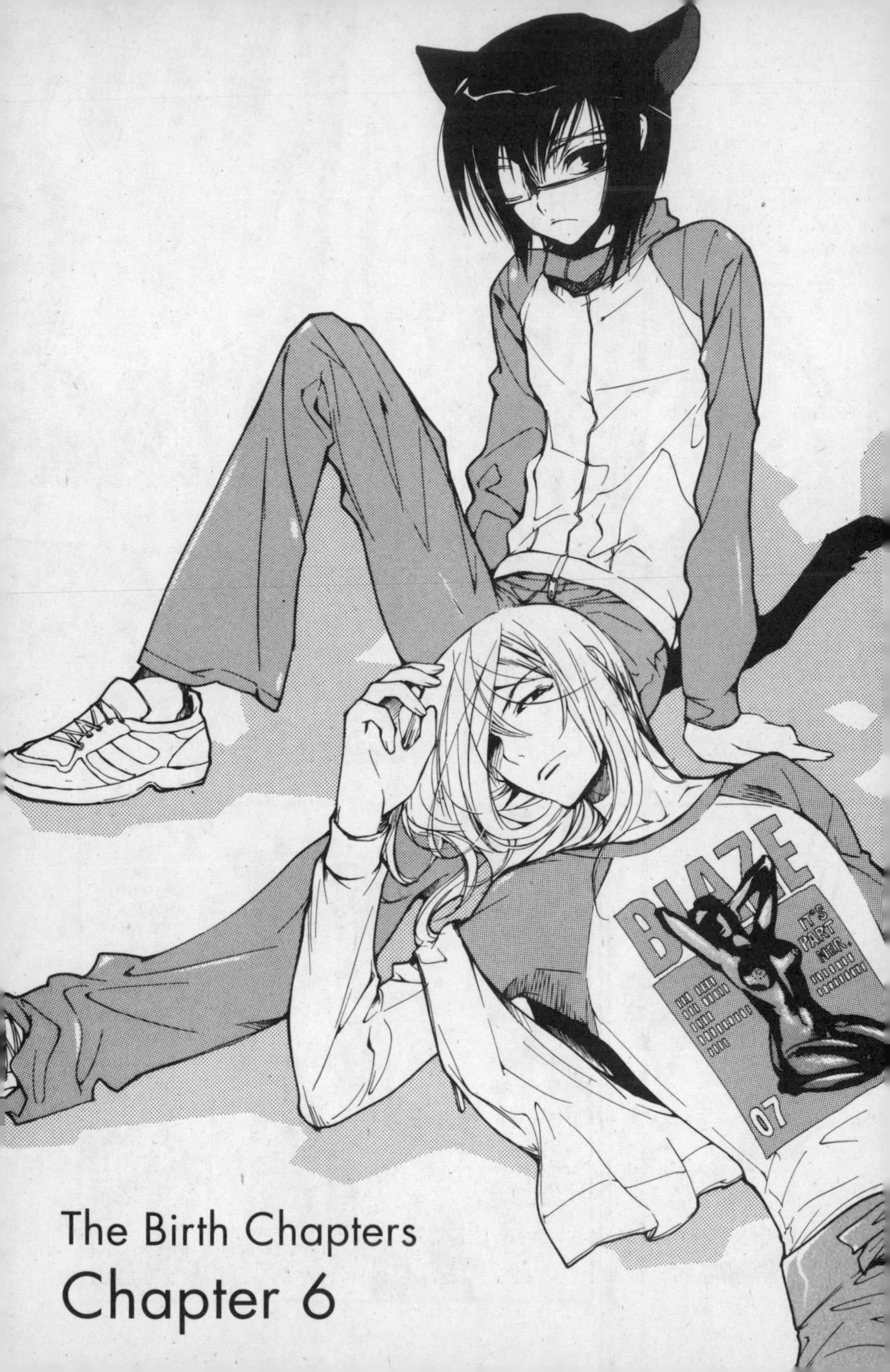
BLAZE
IT'S PART
NER.
07

The Birth Chapters

Chapter 6

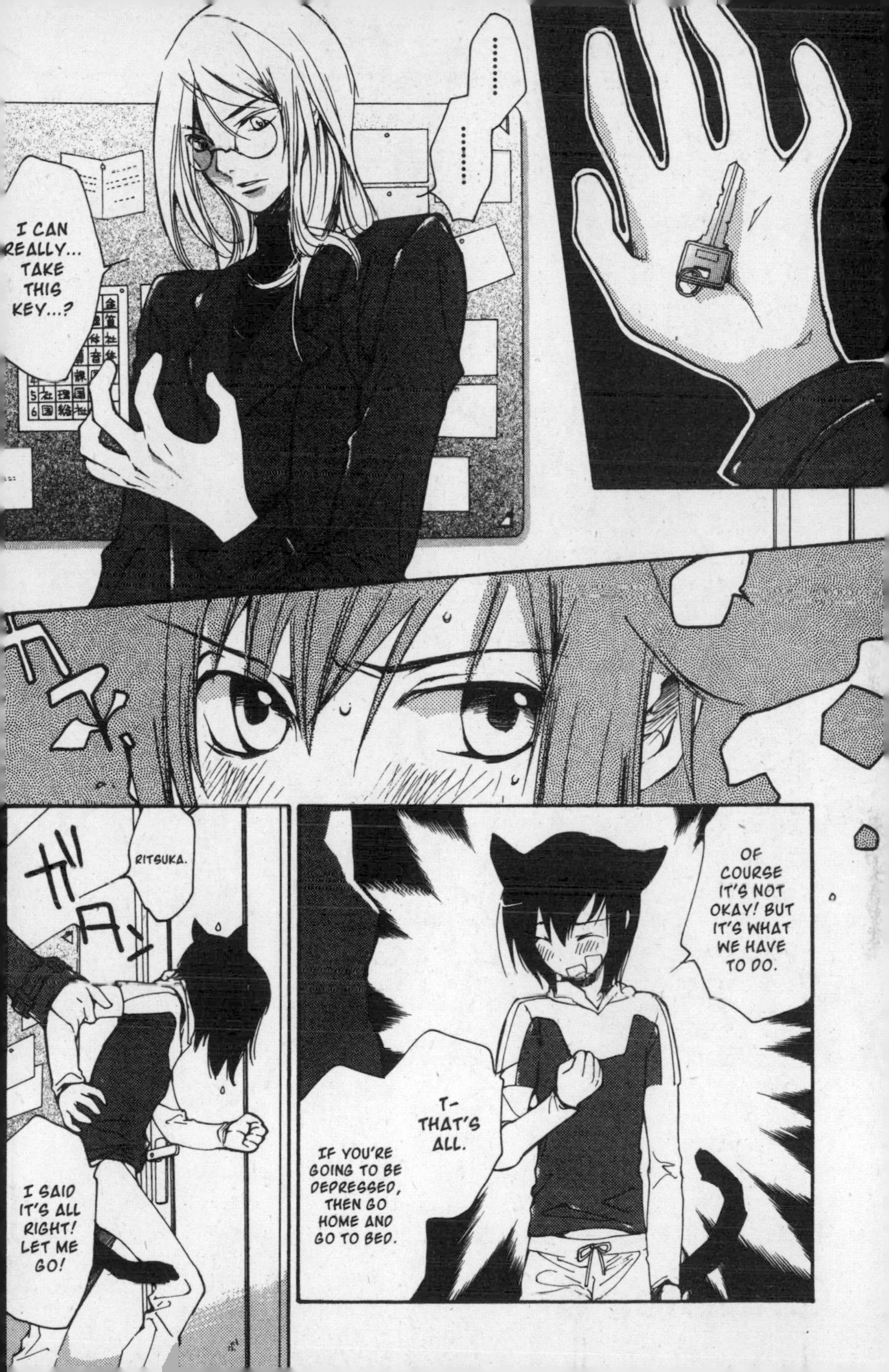
......
......
I CAN REALLY... TAKE THIS KEY...?
OF COURSE IT'S NOT OKAY! BUT IT'S WHAT WE HAVE TO DO.
T-THAT'S ALL.
IF YOU'RE GOING TO BE DEPRESSED, THEN GO HOME AND GO TO BED.
RITSUKA.
I SAID IT'S ALL RIGHT! LET ME GO!

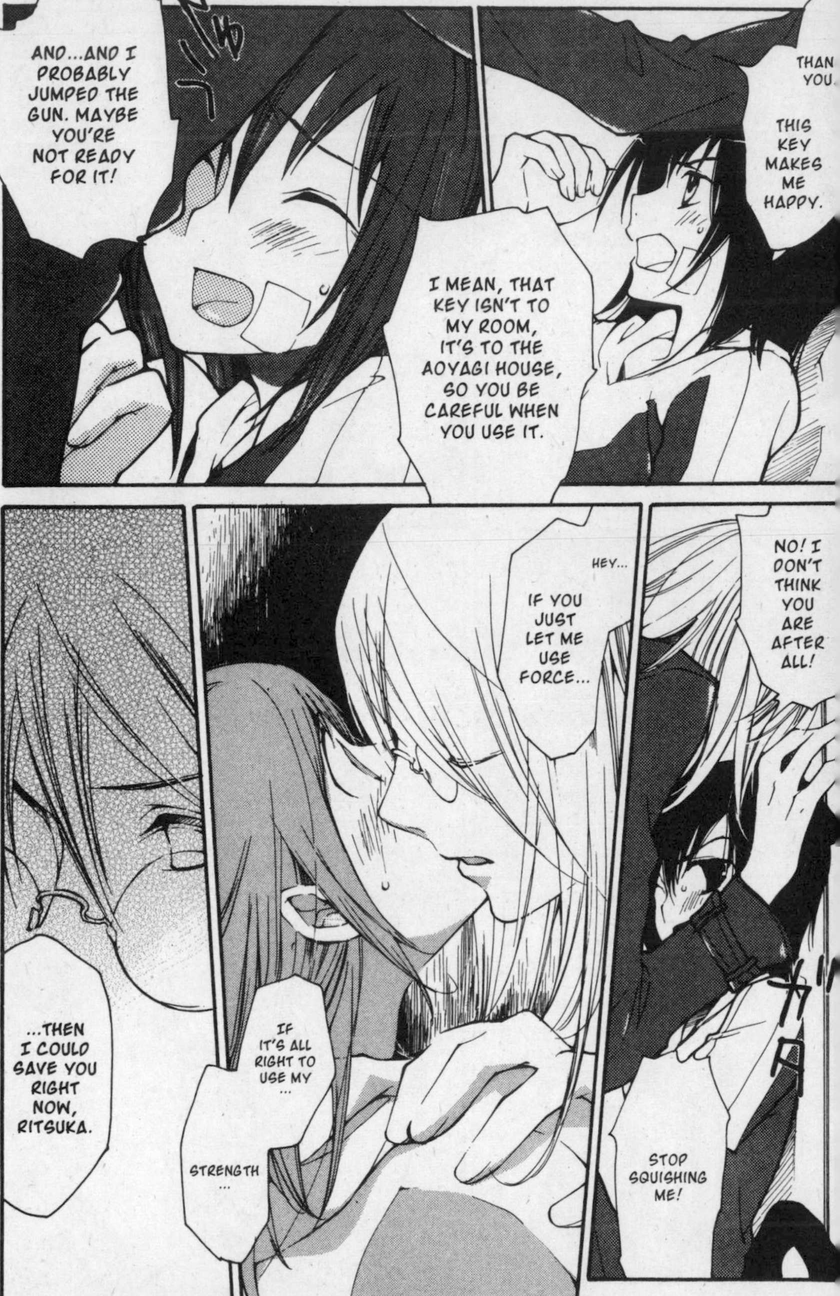
THAN YOU.
THIS KEY MAKES ME HAPPY.
I MEAN, THAT KEY ISN'T TO MY ROOM, IT'S TO THE AOYAGI HOUSE, SO YOU BE CAREFUL WHEN YOU USE IT.
AND...AND I PROBABLY JUMPED THE GUN. MAYBE YOU'RE NOT READY FOR IT!
NO! I DON'T THINK YOU ARE AFTER ALL!
STOP SQUISHING ME!
HEY...
IF YOU JUST LET ME USE FORCE...
IF IT'S ALL RIGHT TO USE MY ...
STRENGTH ...
...THEN I COULD SAVE YOU RIGHT NOW, RITSUKA.

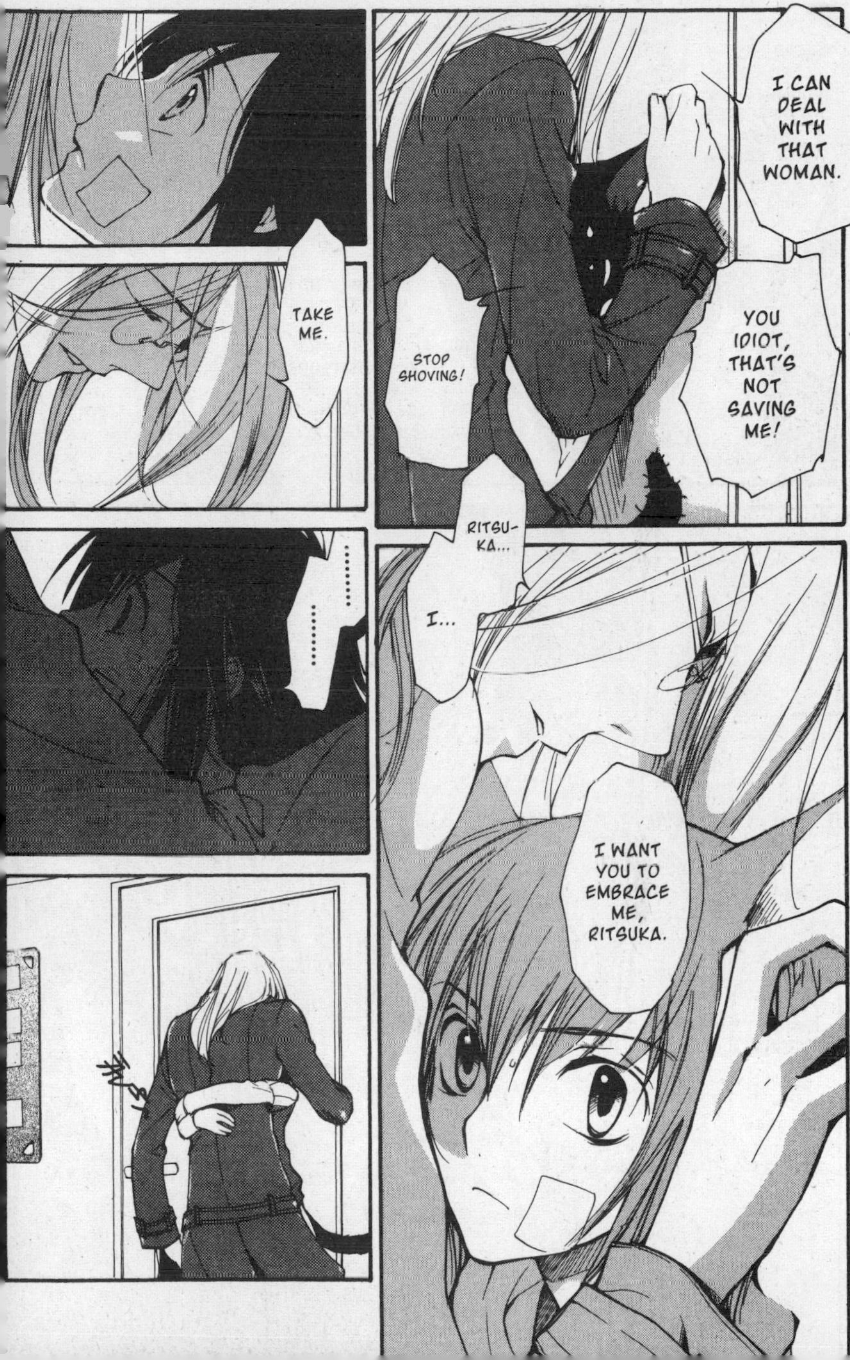
I CAN DEAL WITH THAT WOMAN.
YOU IDIOT, THAT'S NOT SAVING ME!
STOP SHOVING!
TAKE ME.
RITSU-KA...
I...
I WANT YOU TO EMBRACE ME, RITSUKA.
......
......

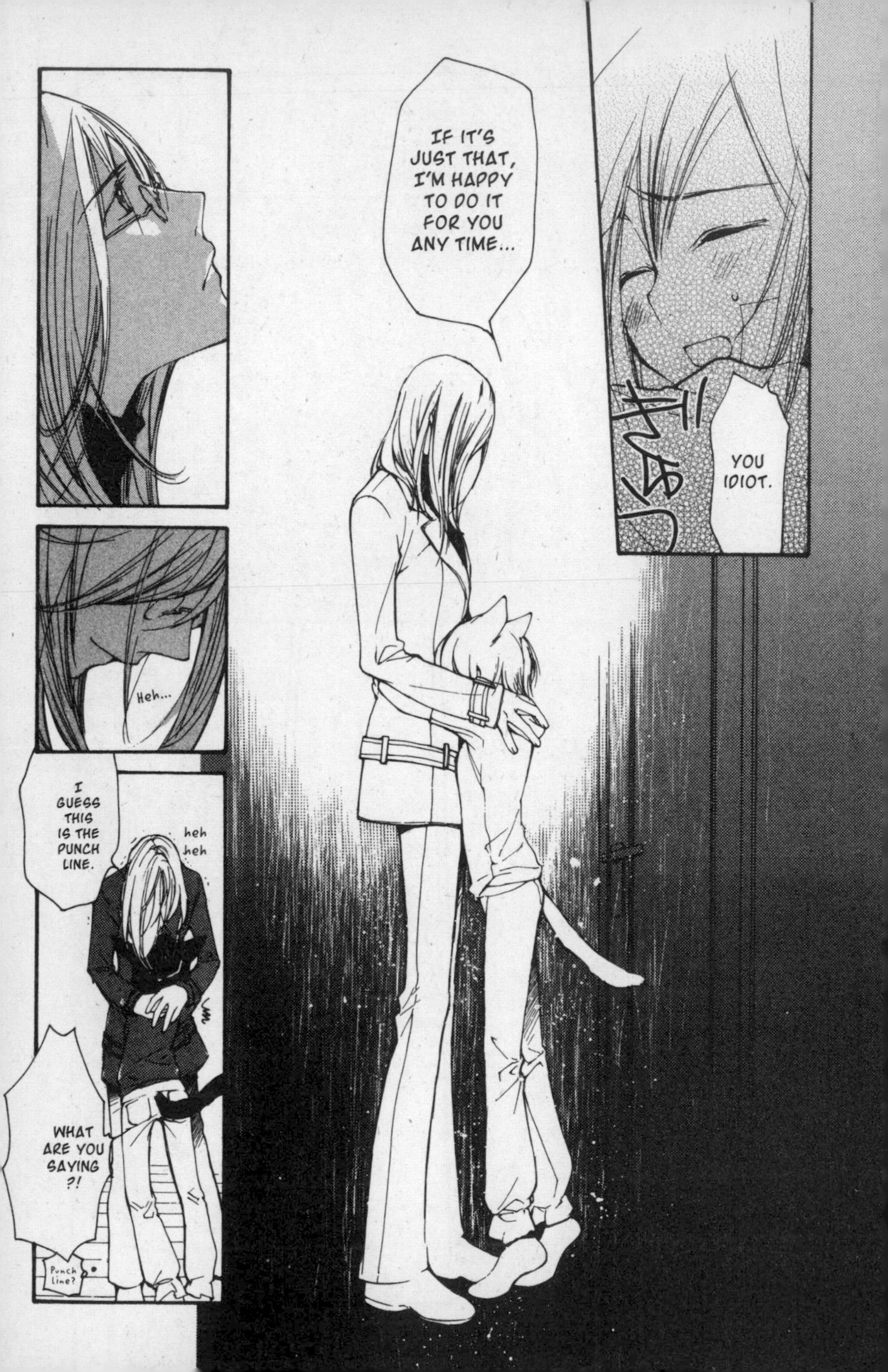
YOU IDIOT.
IF IT'S JUST THAT, I'M HAPPY TO DO IT FOR YOU ANY TIME...
Heh...
I GUESS THIS IS THE PUNCH LINE.
heh heh
WHAT ARE YOU SAYING ?!
Punch line?

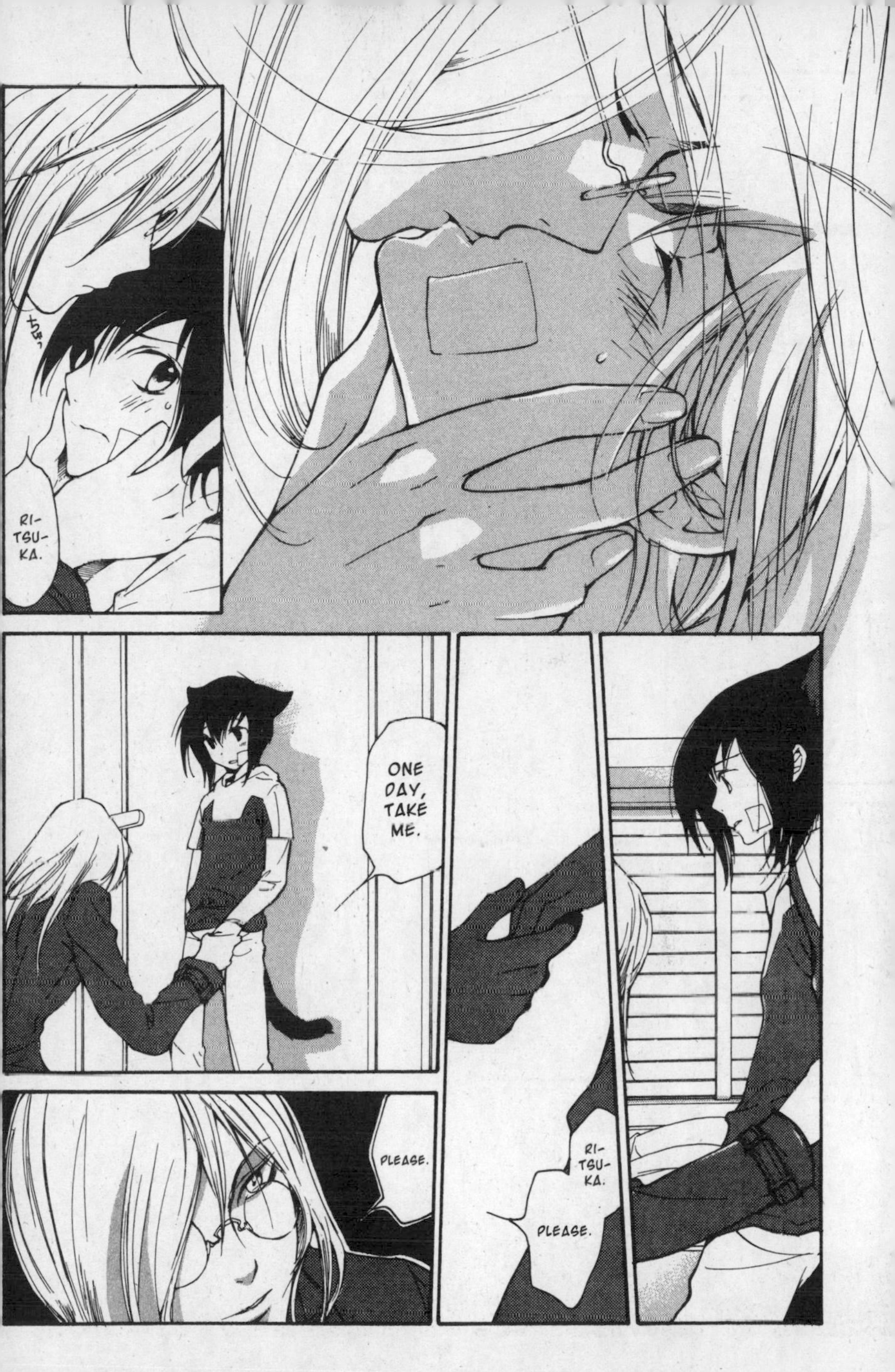
RI-TSU-KA.
RI-TSU-KA.
PLEASE.
ONE DAY, TAKE ME.
PLEASE.

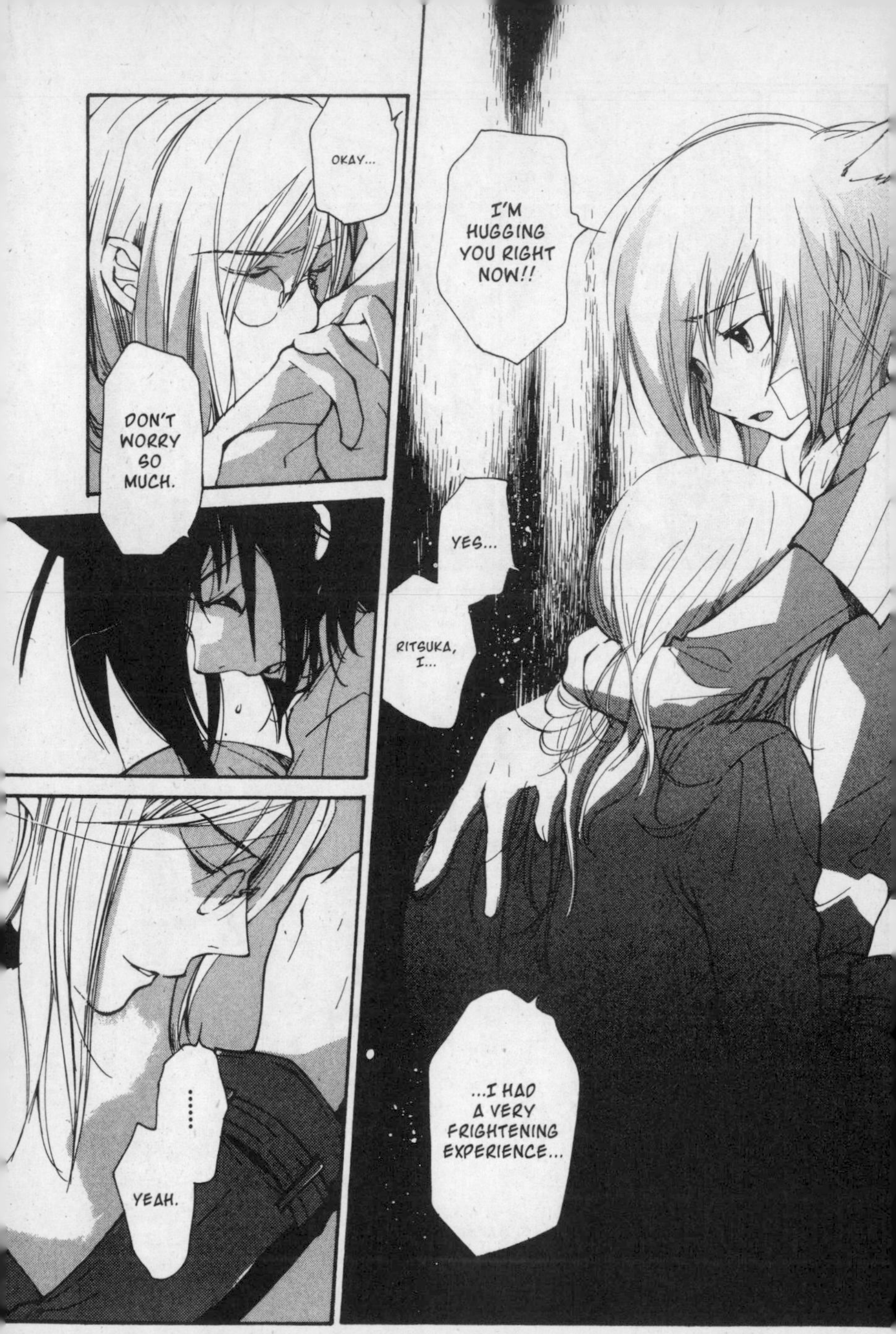
I'M HUGGING YOU RIGHT NOW!!
YES...
RITSUKA, I...
...I HAD A VERY FRIGHTENING EXPERIENCE...
OKAY...
DON'T WORRY SO MUCH.
......
YEAH.

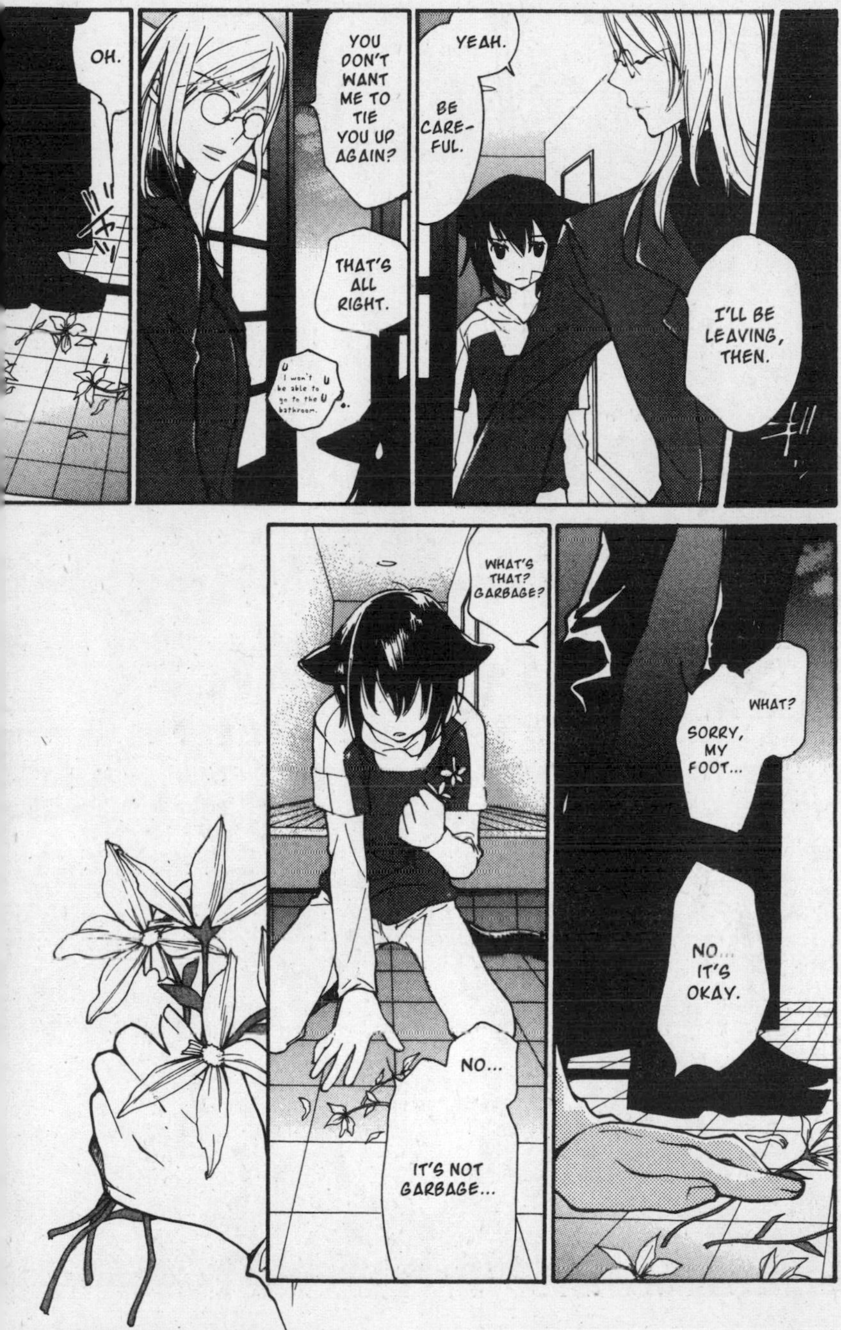
I'LL BE LEAVING, THEN.
YEAH.
BE CAREFUL.
YOU DON'T WANT ME TO TIE YOU UP AGAIN?
THAT'S ALL RIGHT.
I won't be able to go to the bathroom.
OH.
WHAT?
SORRY, MY FOOT...
NO... IT'S OKAY.
WHAT'S THAT? GARBAGE?
NO...
IT'S NOT GARBAGE...

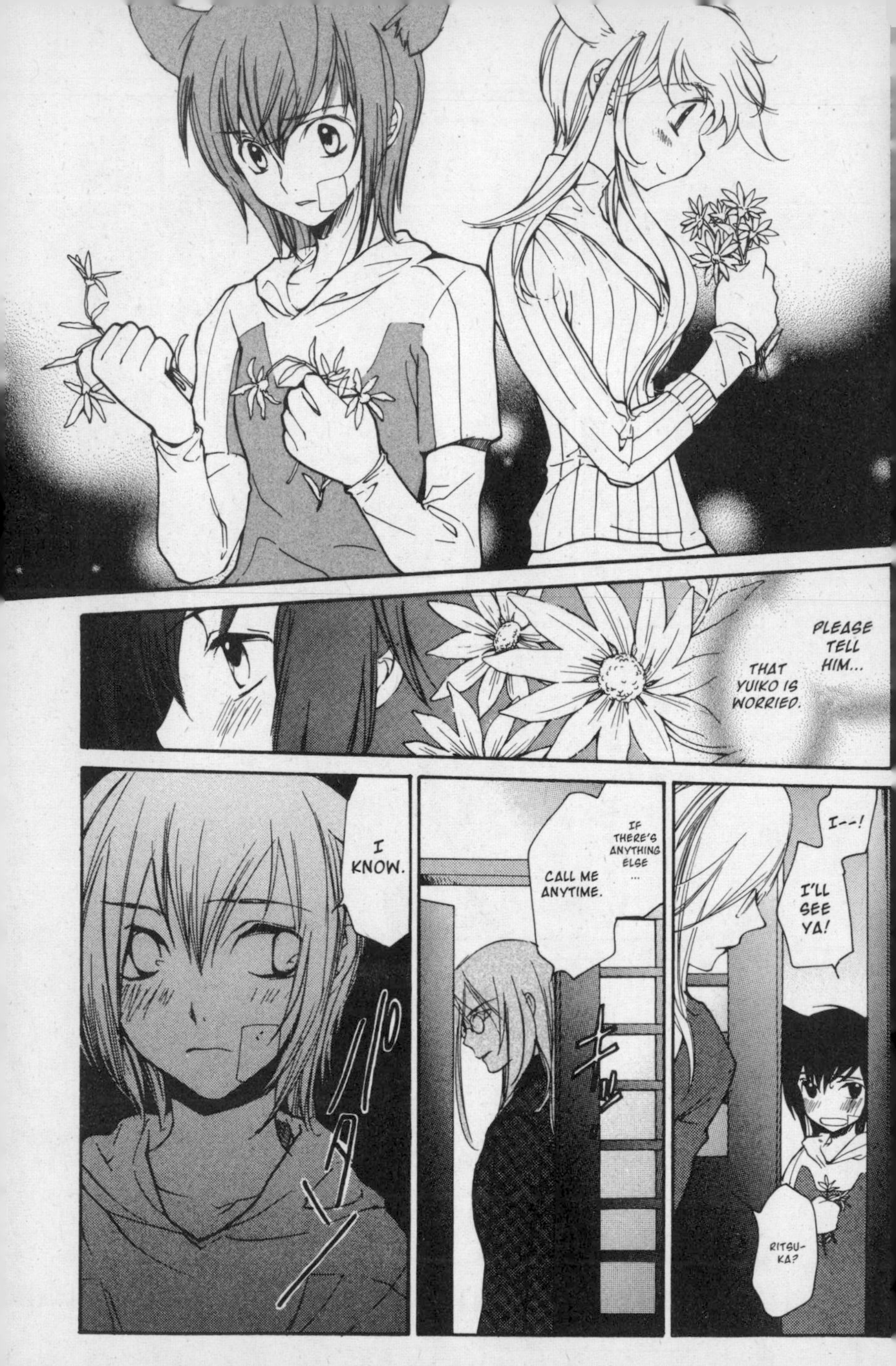
PLEASE TELL HIM...
THAT YUIKO IS WORRIED.
I--!
I'LL SEE YA!
RITSU-KA?
IF THERE'S ANYTHING ELSE ...
CALL ME ANYTIME.
I KNOW.

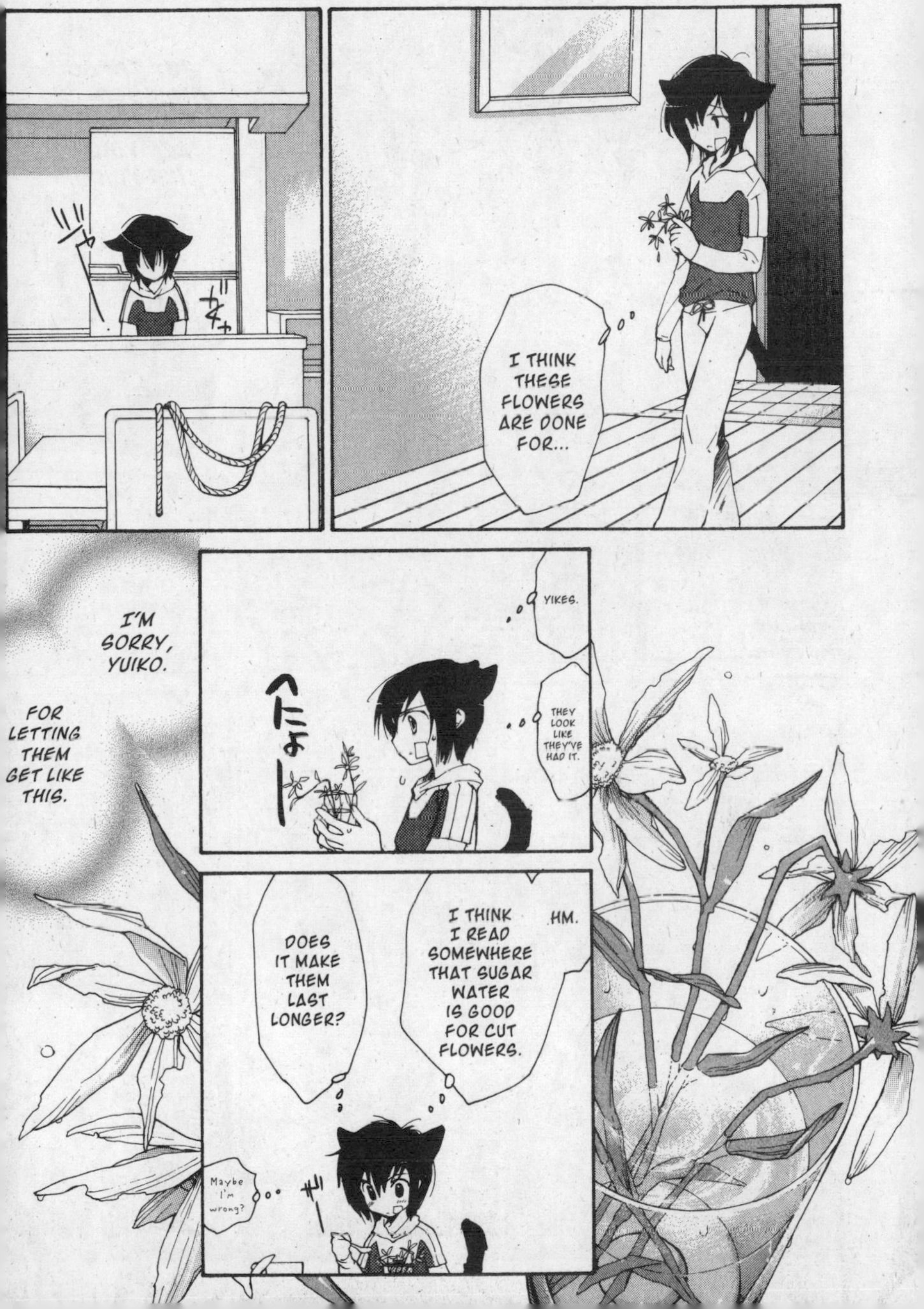

I THINK THESE FLOWERS ARE DONE FOR...
YIKES.
THEY LOOK LIKE THEY'VE HAD IT.
I'M SORRY, YUIKO.
FOR LETTING THEM GET LIKE THIS.
HM.
I THINK I READ SOMEWHERE THAT SUGAR WATER IS GOOD FOR CUT FLOWERS.
DOES IT MAKE THEM LAST LONGER?
Maybe I'm wrong?

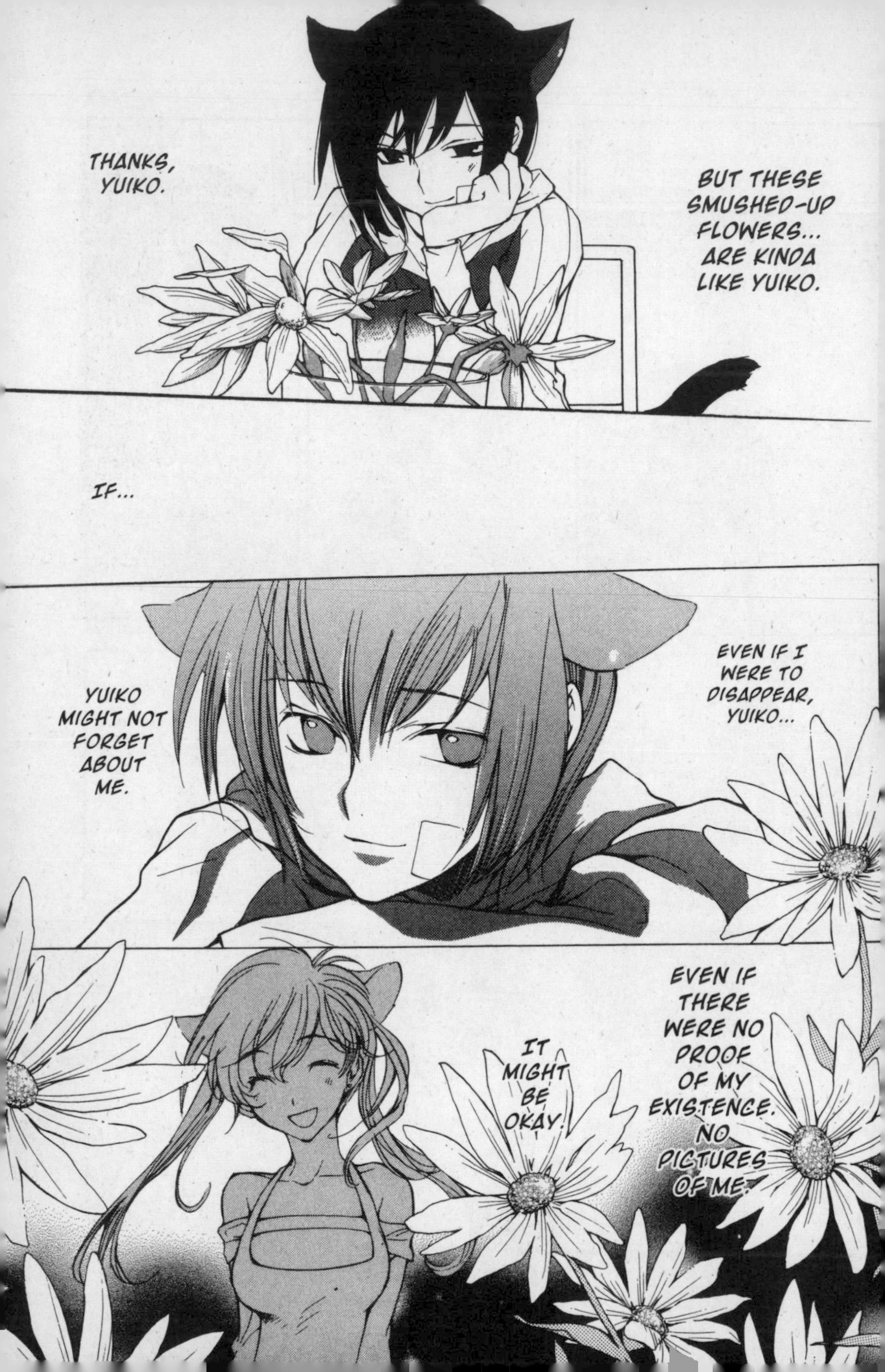
THANKS, YUIKO.
BUT THESE SMUSHED-UP FLOWERS... ARE KINDA LIKE YUIKO.
IF...
EVEN IF I WERE TO DISAPPEAR, YUIKO...
YUIKO MIGHT NOT FORGET ABOUT ME.
EVEN IF THERE WERE NO PROOF OF MY EXISTENCE. NO PICTURES OF ME.
IT MIGHT BE OKAY!

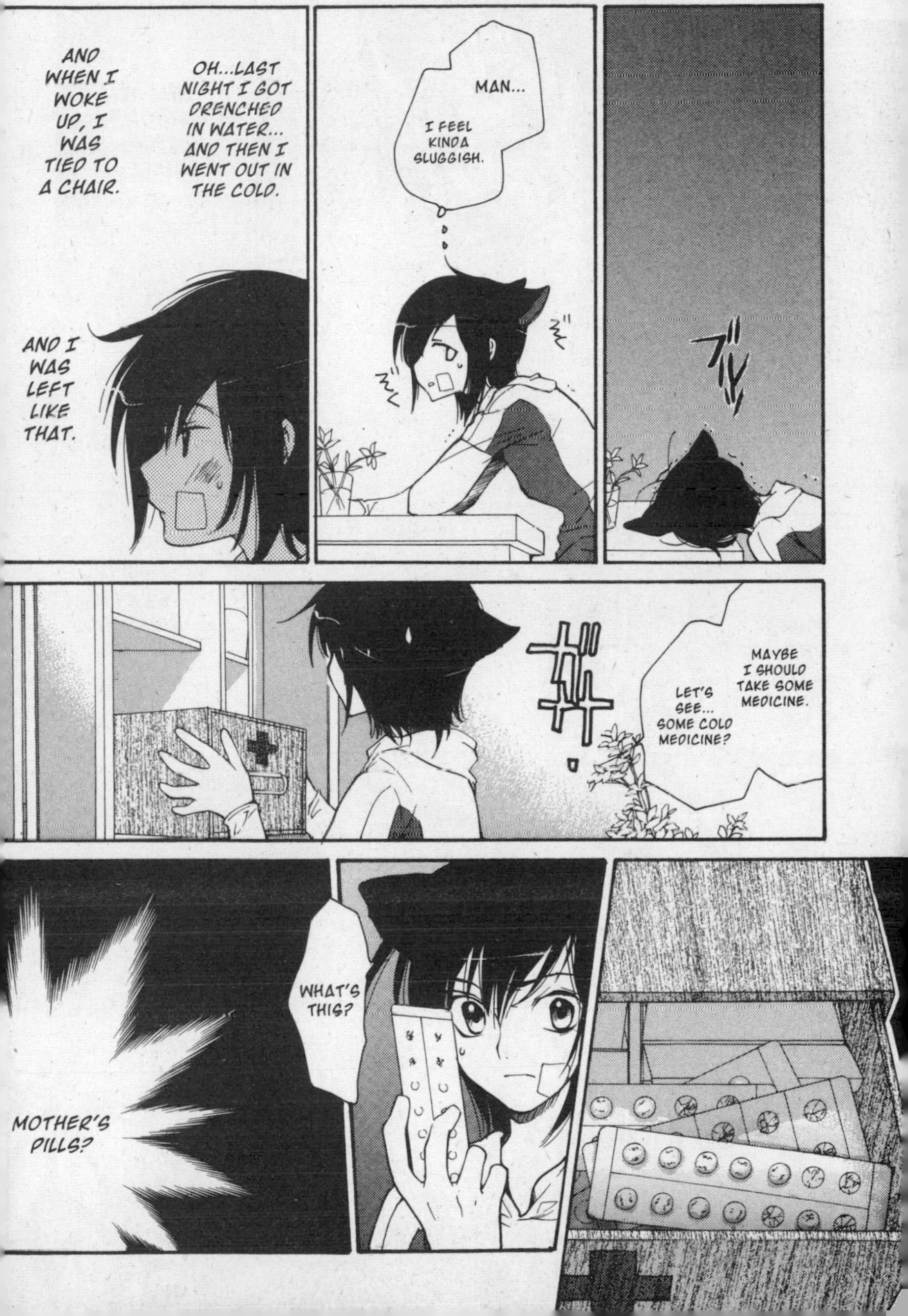
MAN...
I FEEL KINDA SLUGGISH.
OH...LAST NIGHT I GOT DRENCHED IN WATER... AND THEN I WENT OUT IN THE COLD.
AND WHEN I WOKE UP, I WAS TIED TO A CHAIR.
AND I WAS LEFT LIKE THAT.
MAYBE I SHOULD TAKE SOME MEDICINE.
LET'S SEE... SOME COLD MEDICINE?
WHAT'S THIS?
MOTHER'S PILLS?

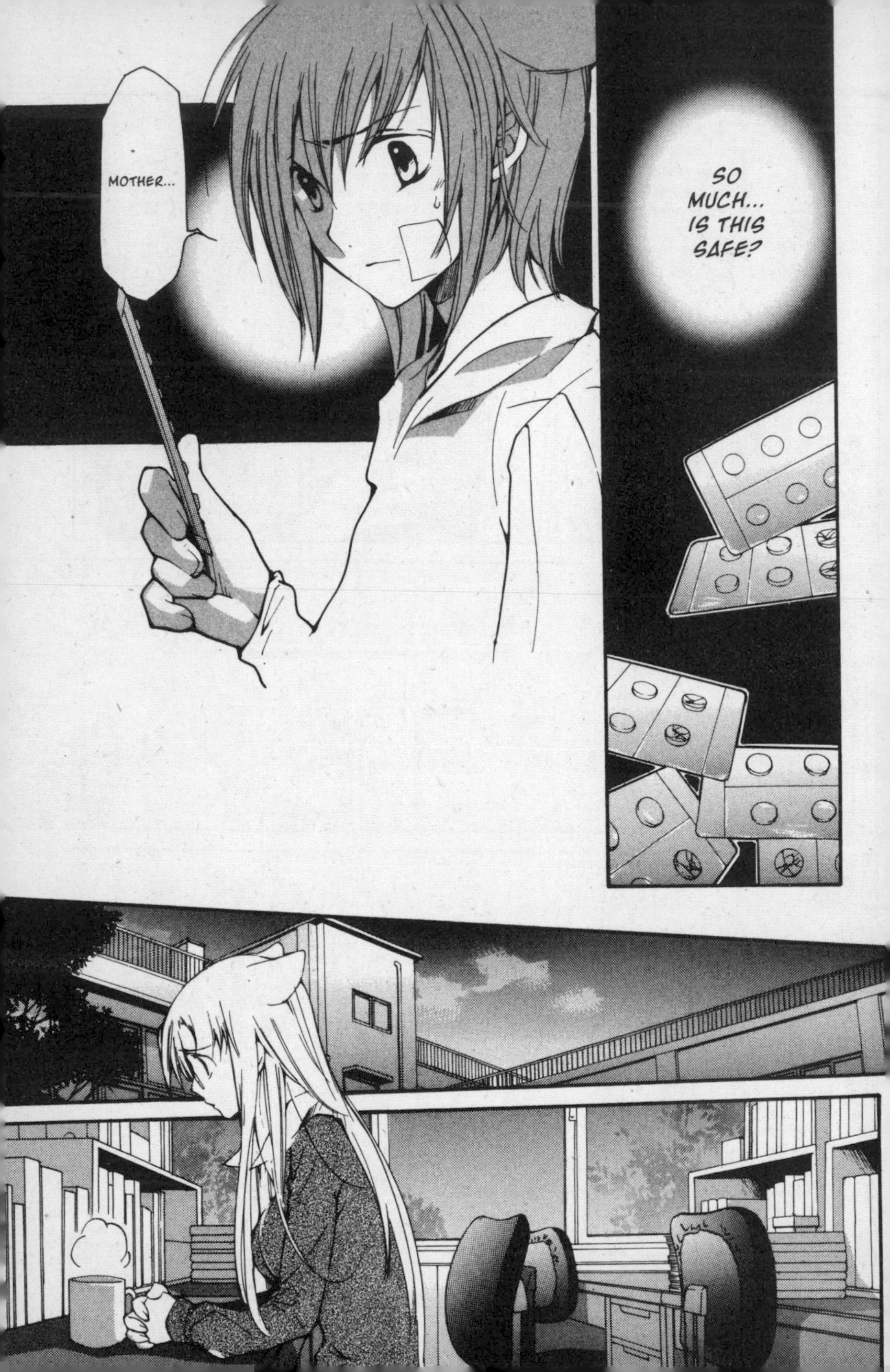
SO MUCH... IS THIS SAFE?
MOTHER...

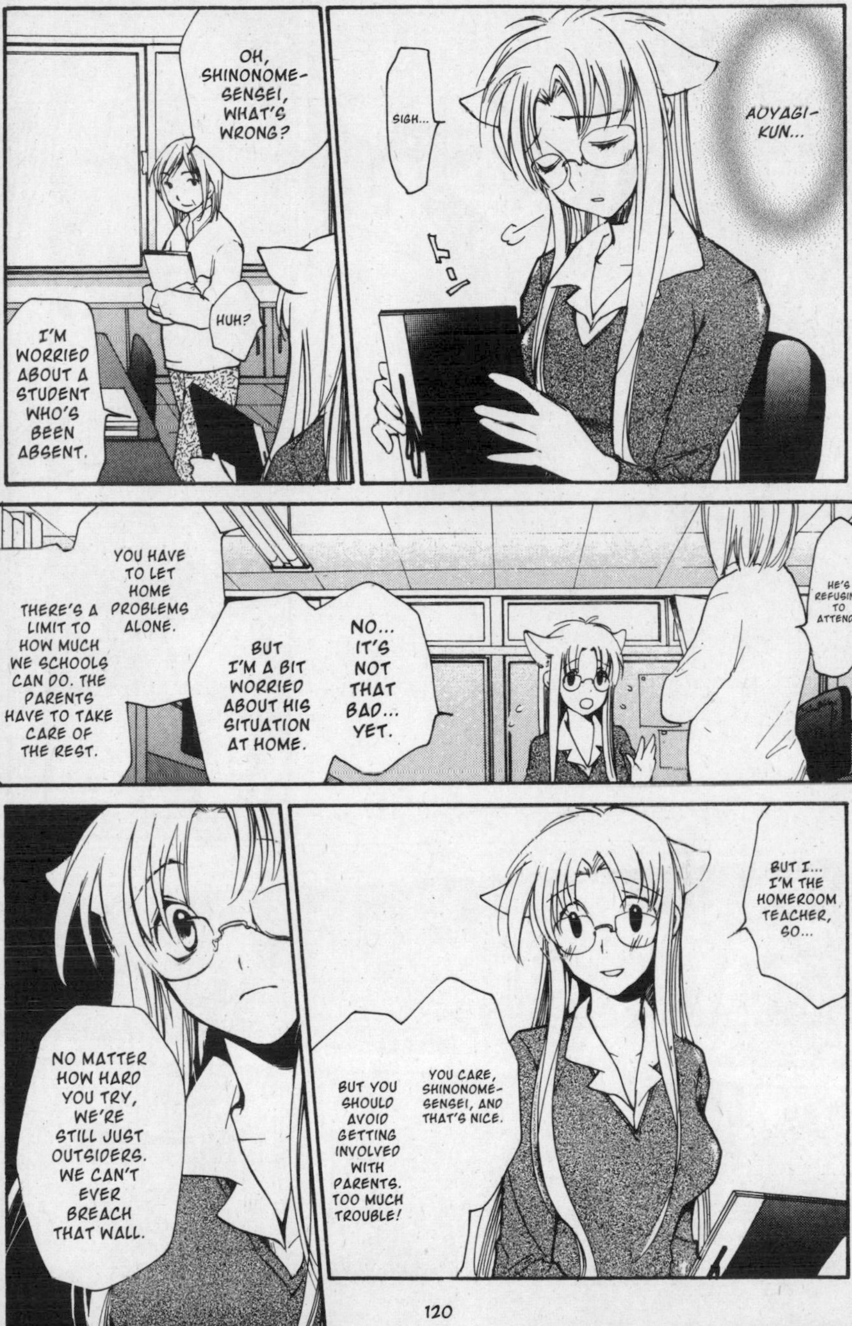
AOYAGI-KUN...
SIGH...
OH, SHINONOME-SENSEI, WHAT'S WRONG?
HUH?
I'M WORRIED ABOUT A STUDENT WHO'S BEEN ABSENT.
HE'S REFUSING TO ATTEND?
NO... IT'S NOT THAT BAD... YET.
BUT I'M A BIT WORRIED ABOUT HIS SITUATION AT HOME.
YOU HAVE TO LET HOME PROBLEMS ALONE.
THERE'S A LIMIT TO HOW MUCH WE SCHOOLS CAN DO. THE PARENTS HAVE TO TAKE CARE OF THE REST.
BUT I... I'M THE HOMEROOM TEACHER, SO...
YOU CARE, SHINONOME-SENSEI, AND THAT'S NICE.
BUT YOU SHOULD AVOID GETTING INVOLVED WITH PARENTS. TOO MUCH TROUBLE!
NO MATTER HOW HARD YOU TRY, WE'RE STILL JUST OUTSIDERS. WE CAN'T EVER BREACH THAT WALL.

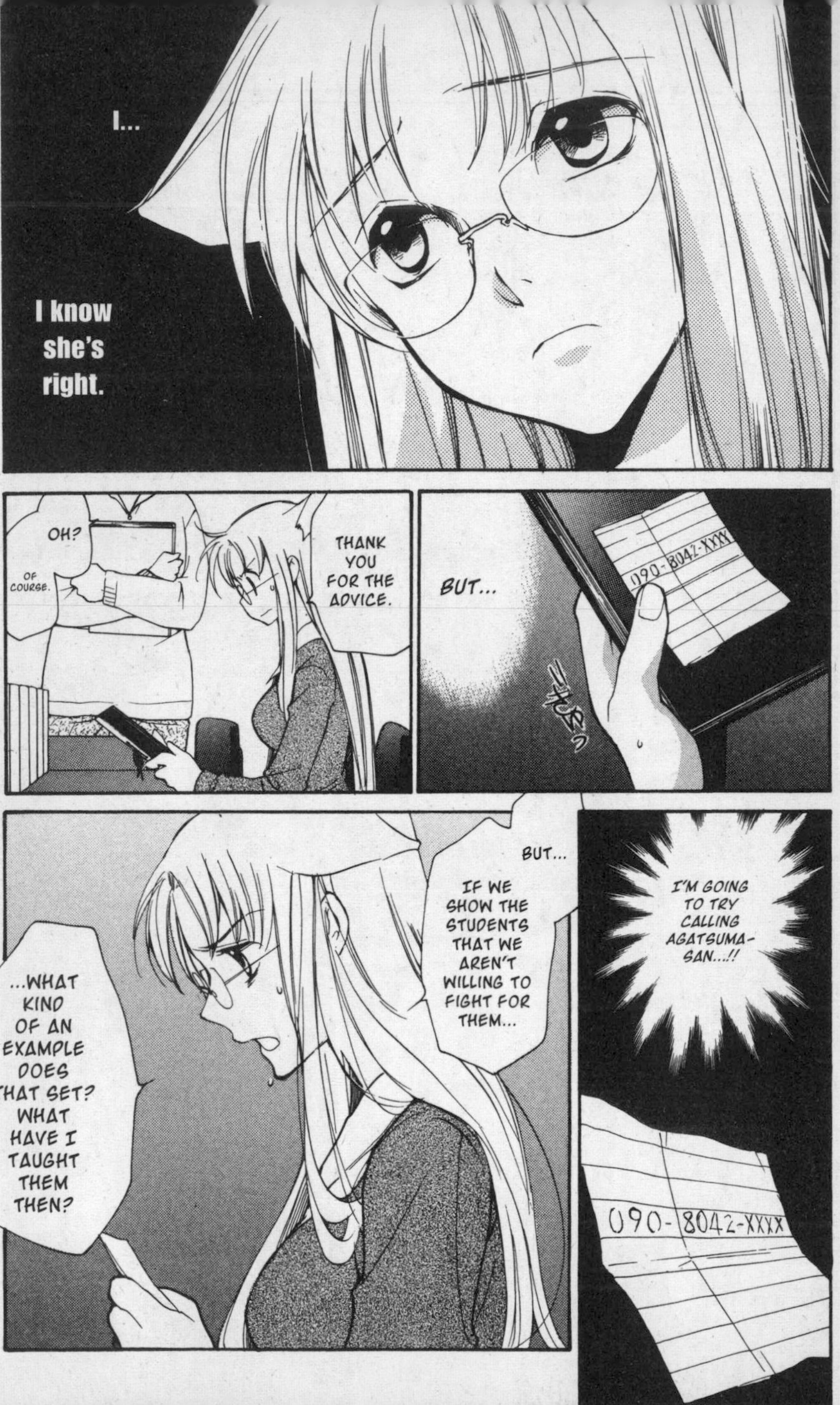
I...
I know she's right.
BUT...
090-8042-XXXX
THANK YOU FOR THE ADVICE.
OH?
OF COURSE.
I'M GOING TO TRY CALLING AGATSUMA-SAN...!!
090-8042-XXXX
BUT...
IF WE SHOW THE STUDENTS THAT WE AREN'T WILLING TO FIGHT FOR THEM...
...WHAT KIND OF AN EXAMPLE DOES THAT SET? WHAT HAVE I TAUGHT THEM THEN?

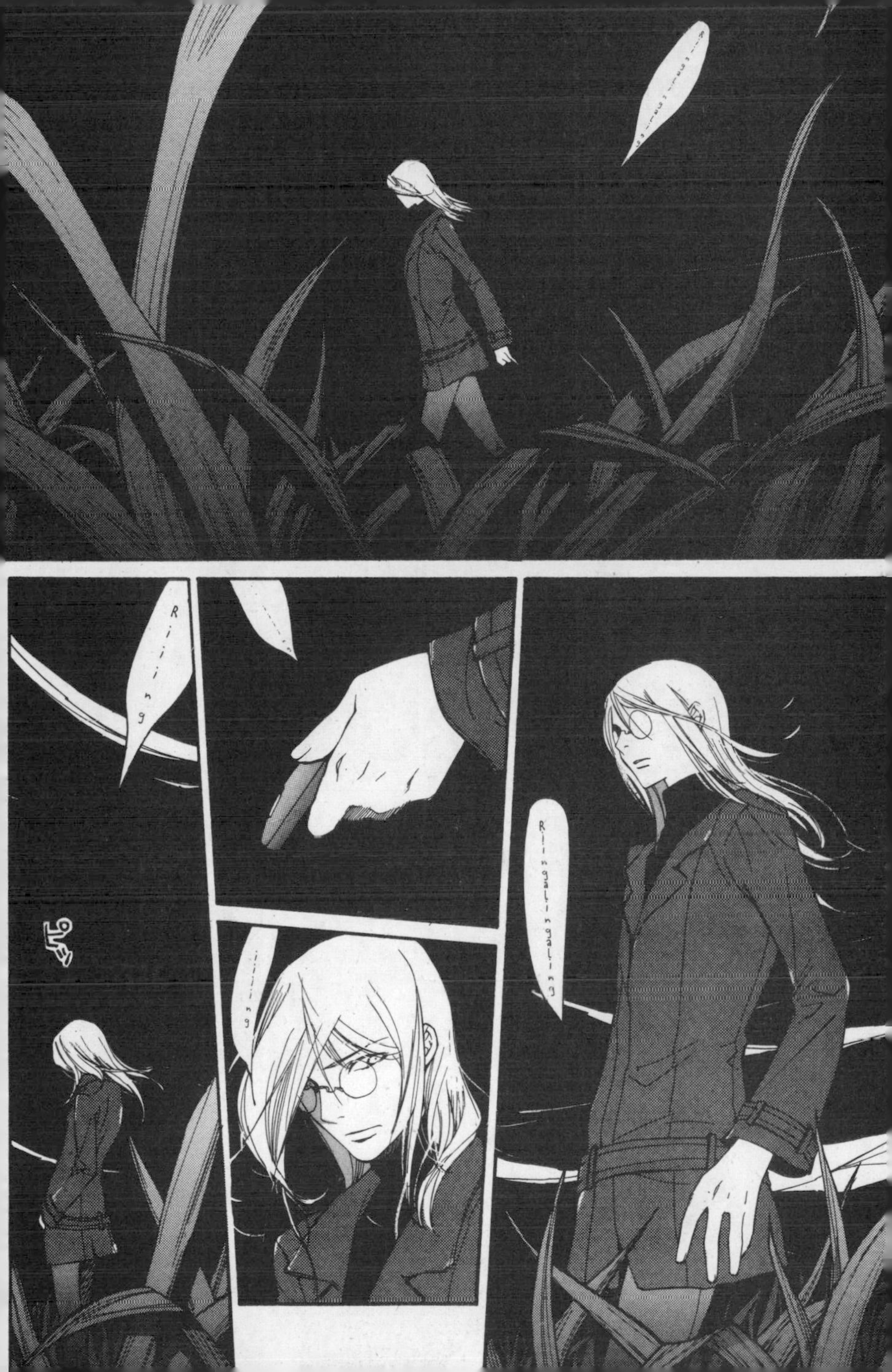
Riingalingaling
iiing
Riiing

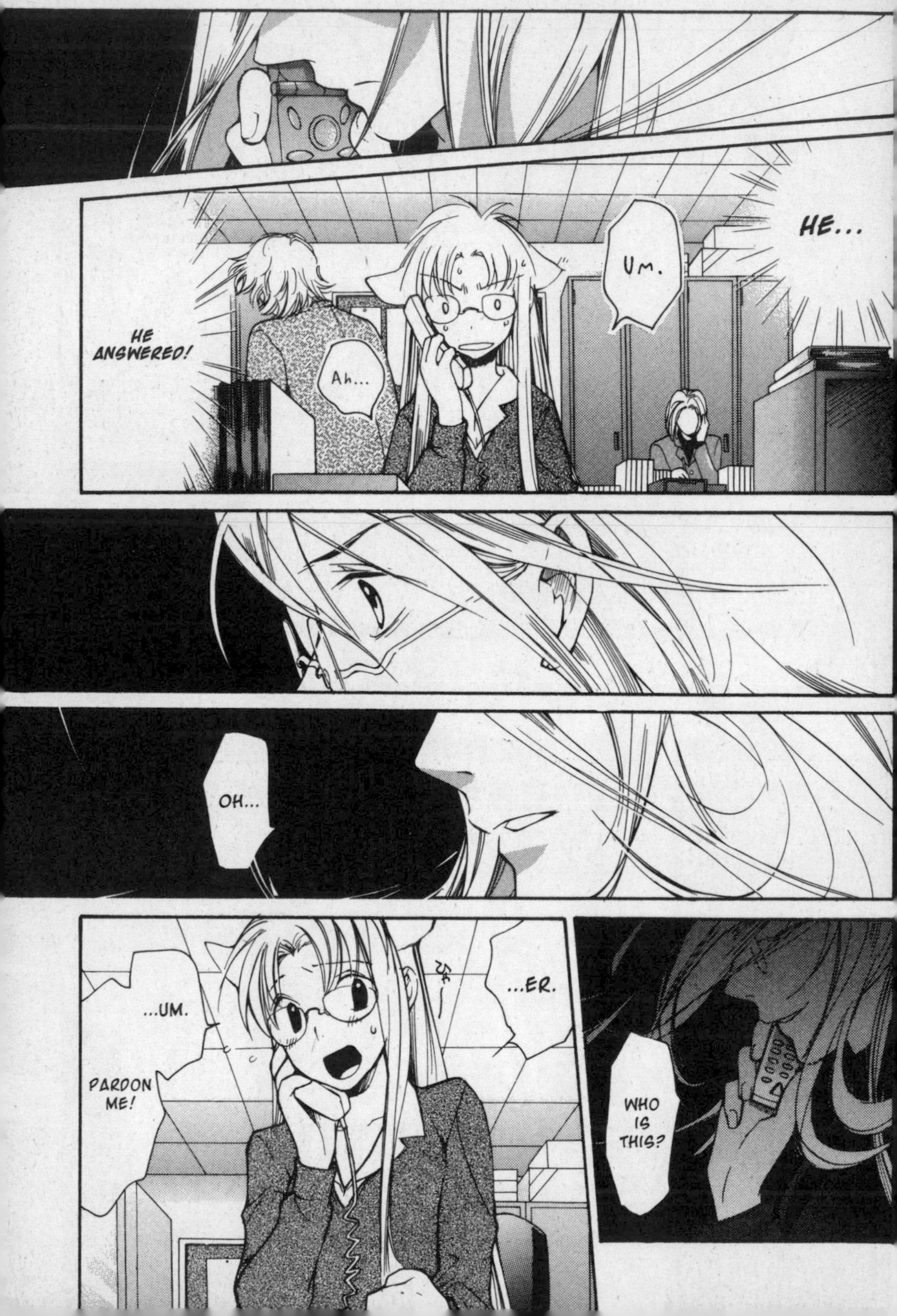
HE...
UM.
Ah...
HE ANSWERED!
OH...
WHO IS THIS?
...ER.
...UM.
PARDON ME!

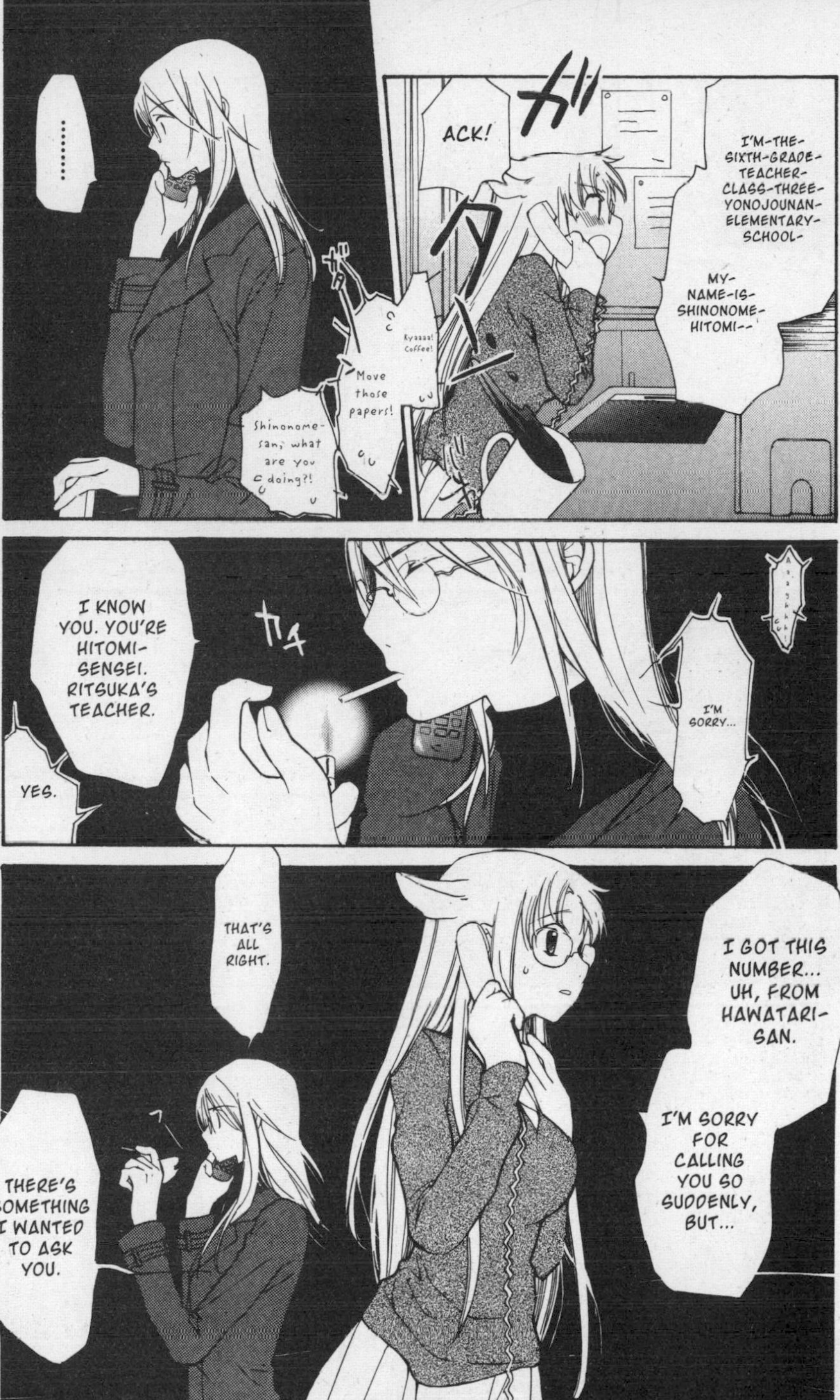
I'M-THE-SIXTH-GRADE-TEACHER-CLASS-THREE-YONOJOUNAN-ELEMENTARY-SCHOOL-
MY-NAME-IS-SHINONOME-HITOMI--
ACK!
Kyaaaa! Coffee!
Move those papers!
Shinonome-san, what are you doing?!
......
Aaashhh!
I'M SORRY...
I KNOW YOU. YOU'RE HITOMI-SENSEI. RITSUKA'S TEACHER.
YES.
I GOT THIS NUMBER... UH, FROM HAWATARI-SAN.
I'M SORRY FOR CALLING YOU SO SUDDENLY, BUT...
THAT'S ALL RIGHT.
THERE'S SOMETHING I WANTED TO ASK YOU.

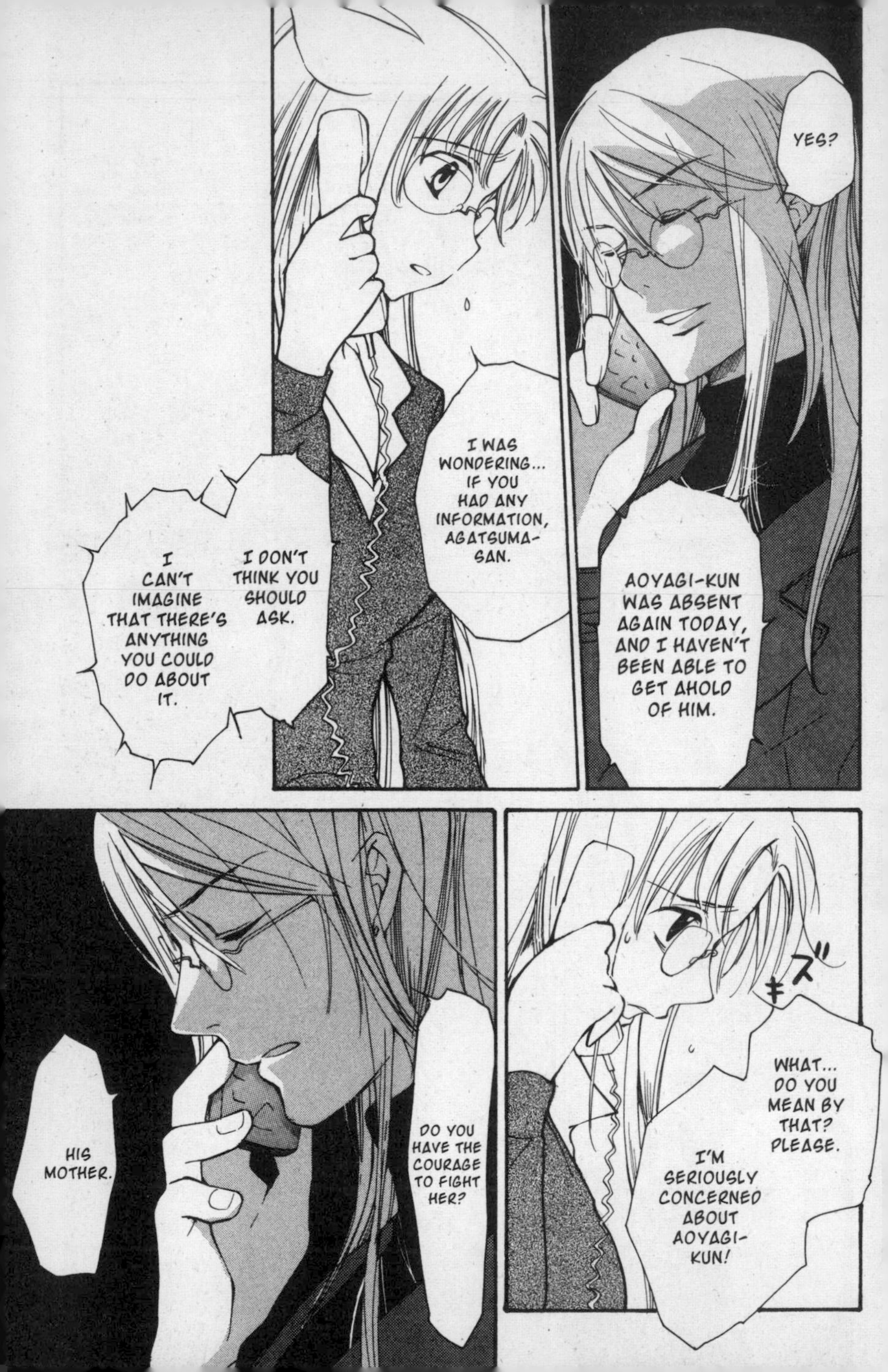
YES?
AOYAGI-KUN WAS ABSENT AGAIN TODAY, AND I HAVEN'T BEEN ABLE TO GET AHOLD OF HIM.
I WAS WONDERING... IF YOU HAD ANY INFORMATION, AGATSUMA-SAN.
I DON'T THINK YOU SHOULD ASK.
I CAN'T IMAGINE THAT THERE'S ANYTHING YOU COULD DO ABOUT IT.
ズキ
WHAT... DO YOU MEAN BY THAT? PLEASE.
I'M SERIOUSLY CONCERNED ABOUT AOYAGI-KUN!
HIS MOTHER.
DO YOU HAVE THE COURAGE TO FIGHT HER?

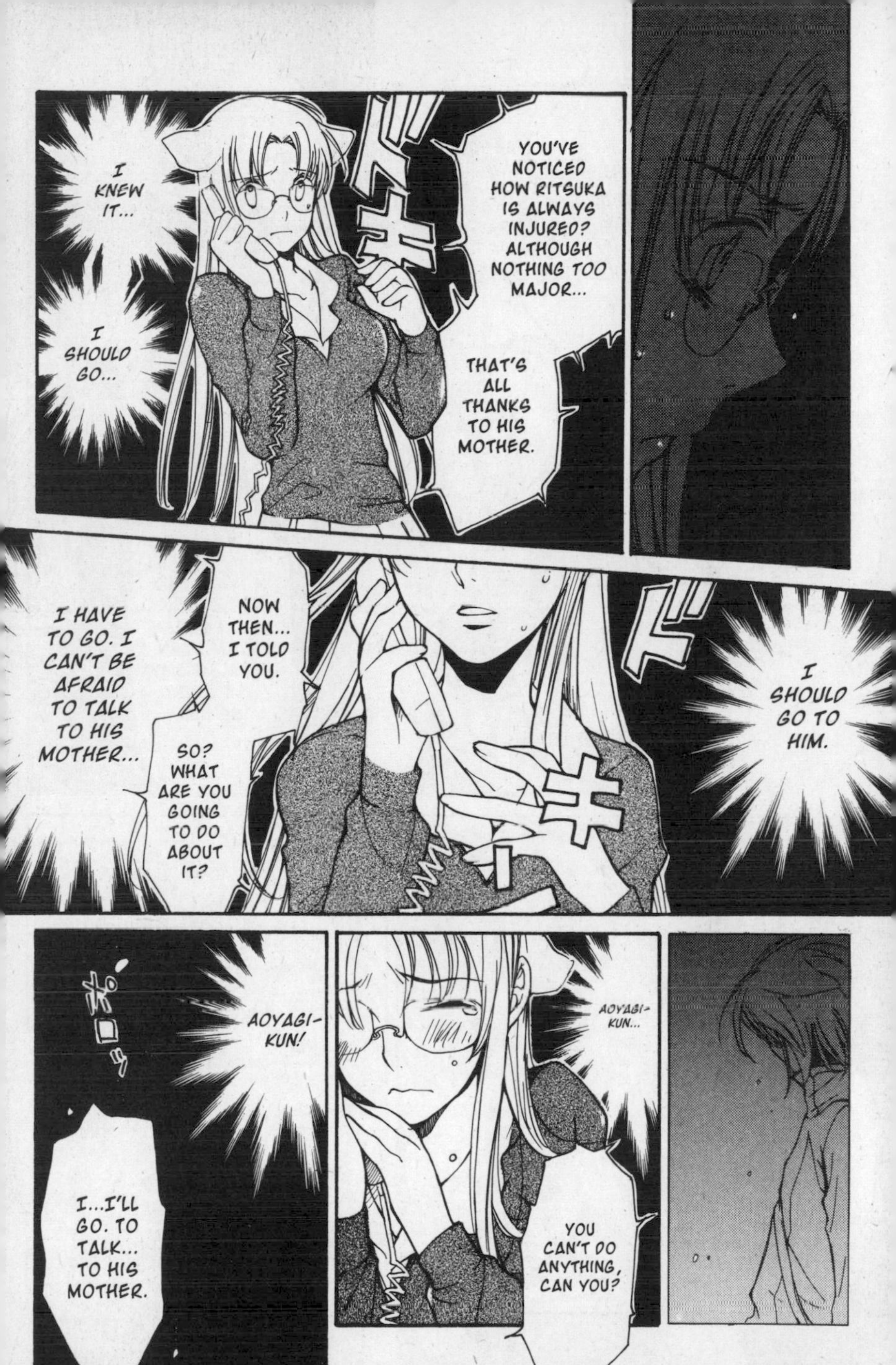

YOU'VE NOTICED HOW RITSUKA IS ALWAYS INJURED? ALTHOUGH NOTHING TOO MAJOR...
ドキ
THAT'S ALL THANKS TO HIS MOTHER.
I KNEW IT...
I SHOULD GO...
I SHOULD GO TO HIM.
ドキ
NOW THEN... I TOLD YOU.
SO? WHAT ARE YOU GOING TO DO ABOUT IT?
I HAVE TO GO. I CAN'T BE AFRAID TO TALK TO HIS MOTHER...
AOYAGI-KUN...
YOU CAN'T DO ANYTHING, CAN YOU?
AOYAGI-KUN!
ポロッ
I...I'LL GO. TO TALK... TO HIS MOTHER.

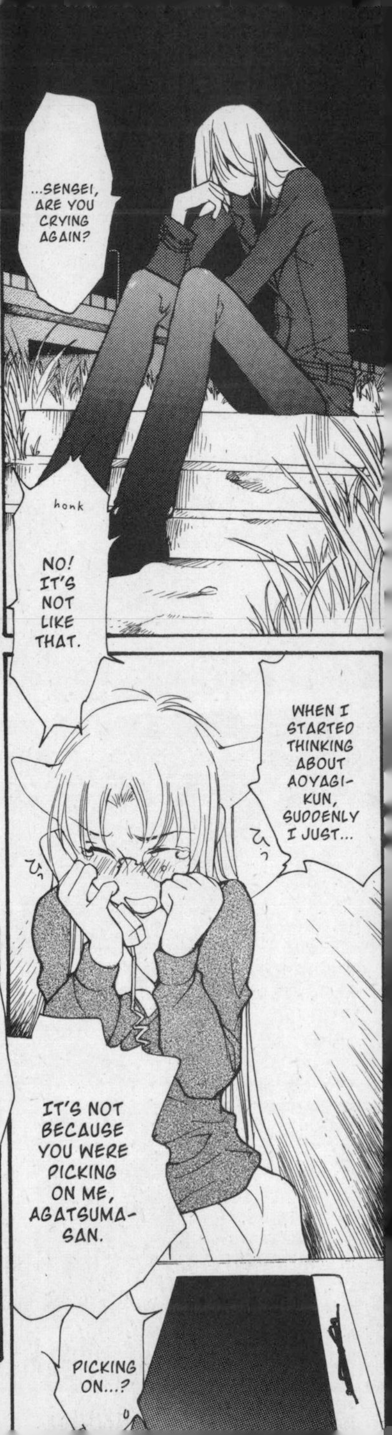
...SENSEI, ARE YOU CRYING AGAIN?
honk
NO! IT'S NOT LIKE THAT.
WHEN I STARTED THINKING ABOUT AOYAGI-KUN, SUDDENLY I JUST...
IT'S NOT BECAUSE YOU WERE PICKING ON ME, AGATSUMA-SAN.
PICKING ON...?
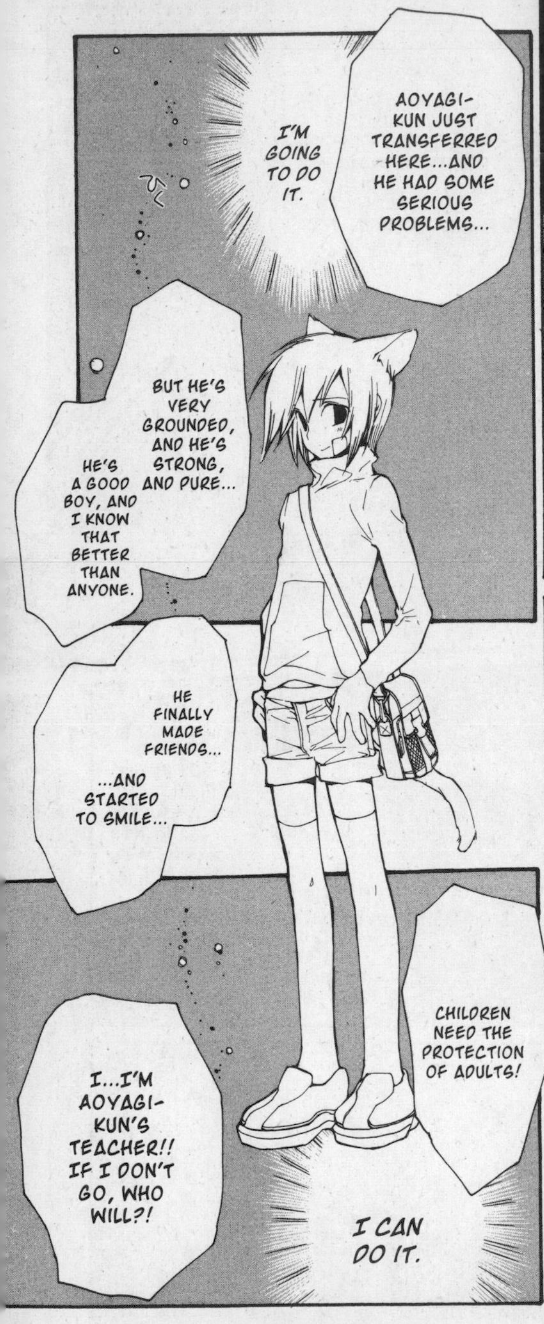
AOYAGI-KUN JUST TRANSFERRED HERE...AND HE HAD SOME SERIOUS PROBLEMS...
I'M GOING TO DO IT.
BUT HE'S VERY GROUNDED, AND HE'S STRONG, AND PURE...
HE'S A GOOD BOY, AND I KNOW THAT BETTER THAN ANYONE.
HE FINALLY MADE FRIENDS...
...AND STARTED TO SMILE...
CHILDREN NEED THE PROTECTION OF ADULTS!
I...I'M AOYAGI-KUN'S TEACHER!! IF I DON'T GO, WHO WILL?!
I CAN DO IT.

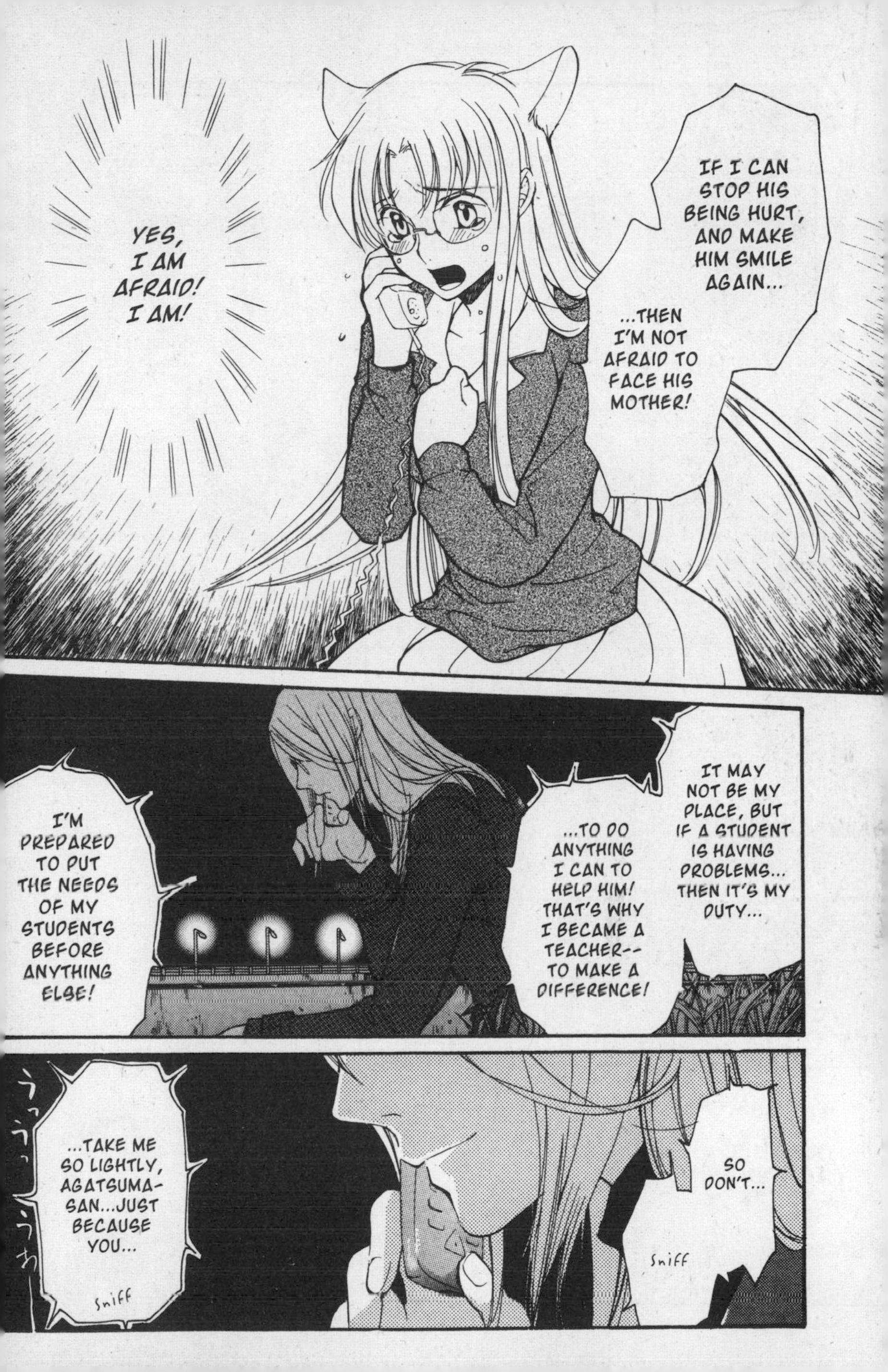
IF I CAN STOP HIS BEING HURT, AND MAKE HIM SMILE AGAIN...
...THEN I'M NOT AFRAID TO FACE HIS MOTHER!
YES, I AM AFRAID! I AM!
IT MAY NOT BE MY PLACE, BUT IF A STUDENT IS HAVING PROBLEMS... THEN IT'S MY DUTY...
...TO DO ANYTHING I CAN TO HELP HIM! THAT'S WHY I BECAME A TEACHER--TO MAKE A DIFFERENCE!
I'M PREPARED TO PUT THE NEEDS OF MY STUDENTS BEFORE ANYTHING ELSE!
SO DON'T...
Sniff
...TAKE ME SO LIGHTLY, AGATSUMA-SAN...JUST BECAUSE YOU...
Sniff

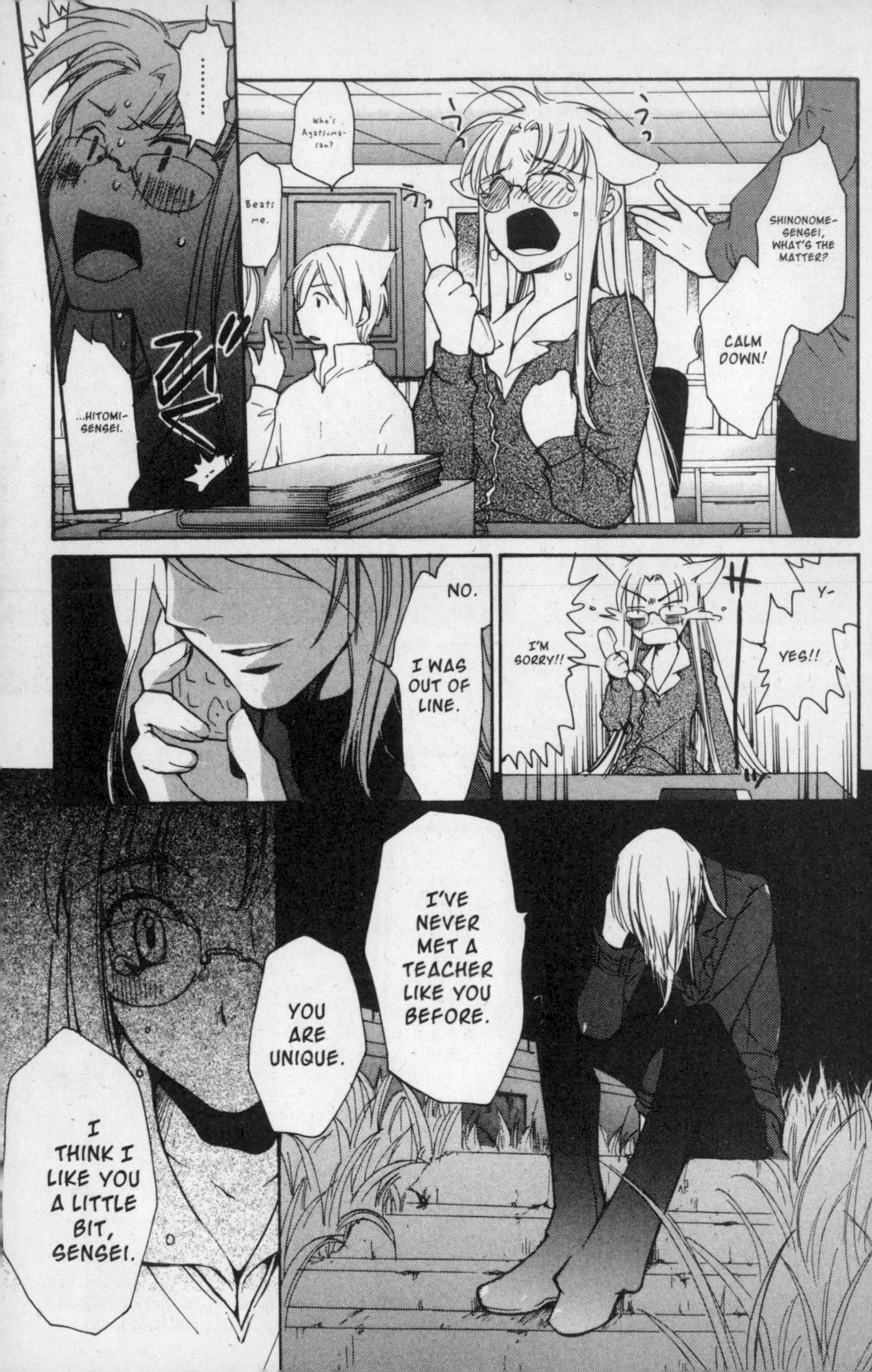
SHINONOME-SENSEI, WHAT'S THE MATTER?
CALM DOWN!
Who's Agatsuma-san?
Beats me.
......
...HITOMI-SENSEI.
Y-
YES!!
I'M SORRY!!
NO.
I WAS OUT OF LINE.
I'VE NEVER MET A TEACHER LIKE YOU BEFORE.
YOU ARE UNIQUE.
I THINK I LIKE YOU A LITTLE BIT, SENSEI.

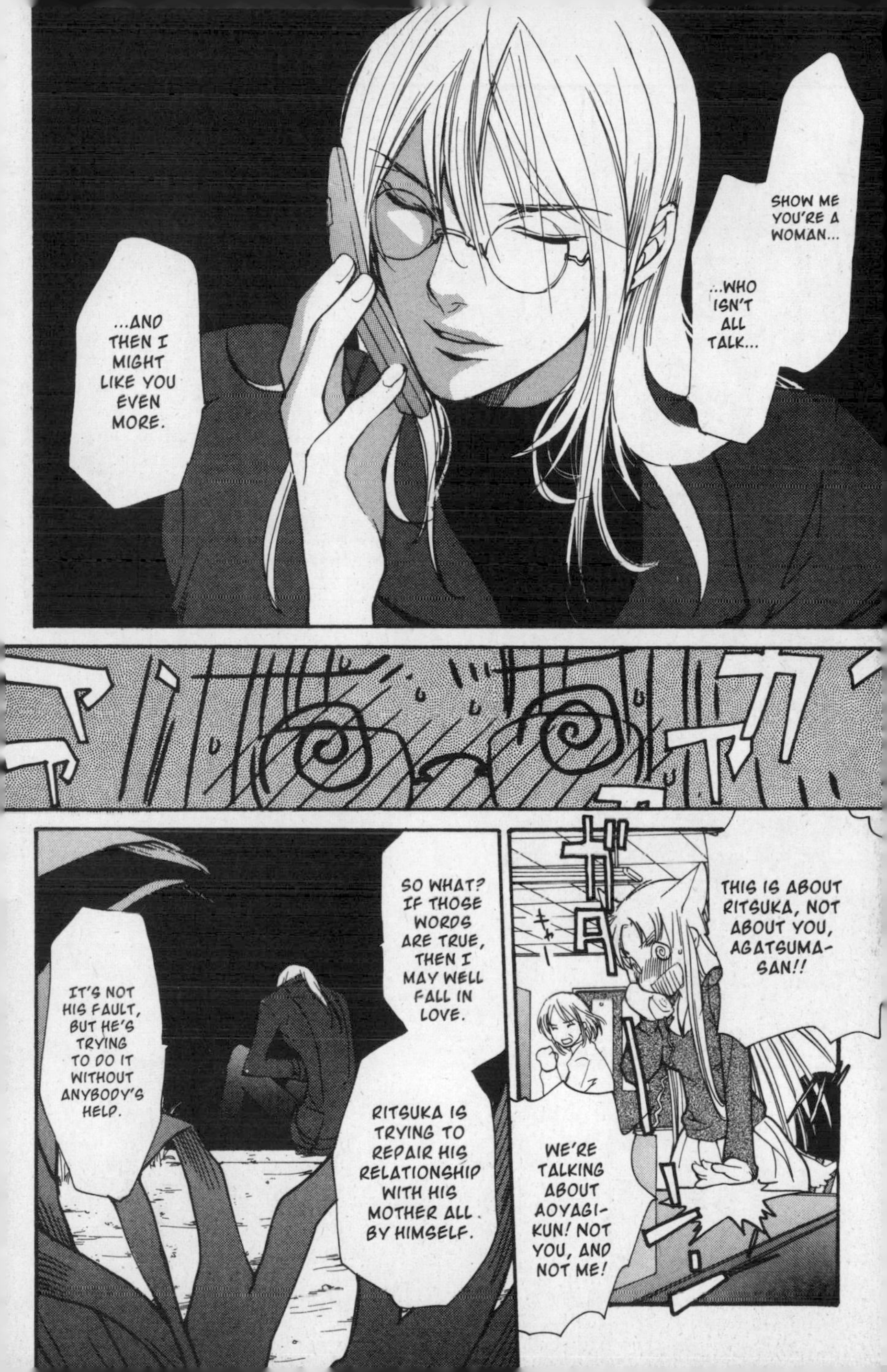
SHOW ME YOU'RE A WOMAN...
...WHO ISN'T ALL TALK...
...AND THEN I MIGHT LIKE YOU EVEN MORE.
THIS IS ABOUT RITSUKA, NOT ABOUT YOU, AGATSUMA-SAN!!
WE'RE TALKING ABOUT AOYAGI-KUN! NOT YOU, AND NOT ME!
SO WHAT? IF THOSE WORDS ARE TRUE, THEN I MAY WELL FALL IN LOVE.
IT'S NOT HIS FAULT, BUT HE'S TRYING TO DO IT WITHOUT ANYBODY'S HELP.
RITSUKA IS TRYING TO REPAIR HIS RELATIONSHIP WITH HIS MOTHER ALL BY HIMSELF.

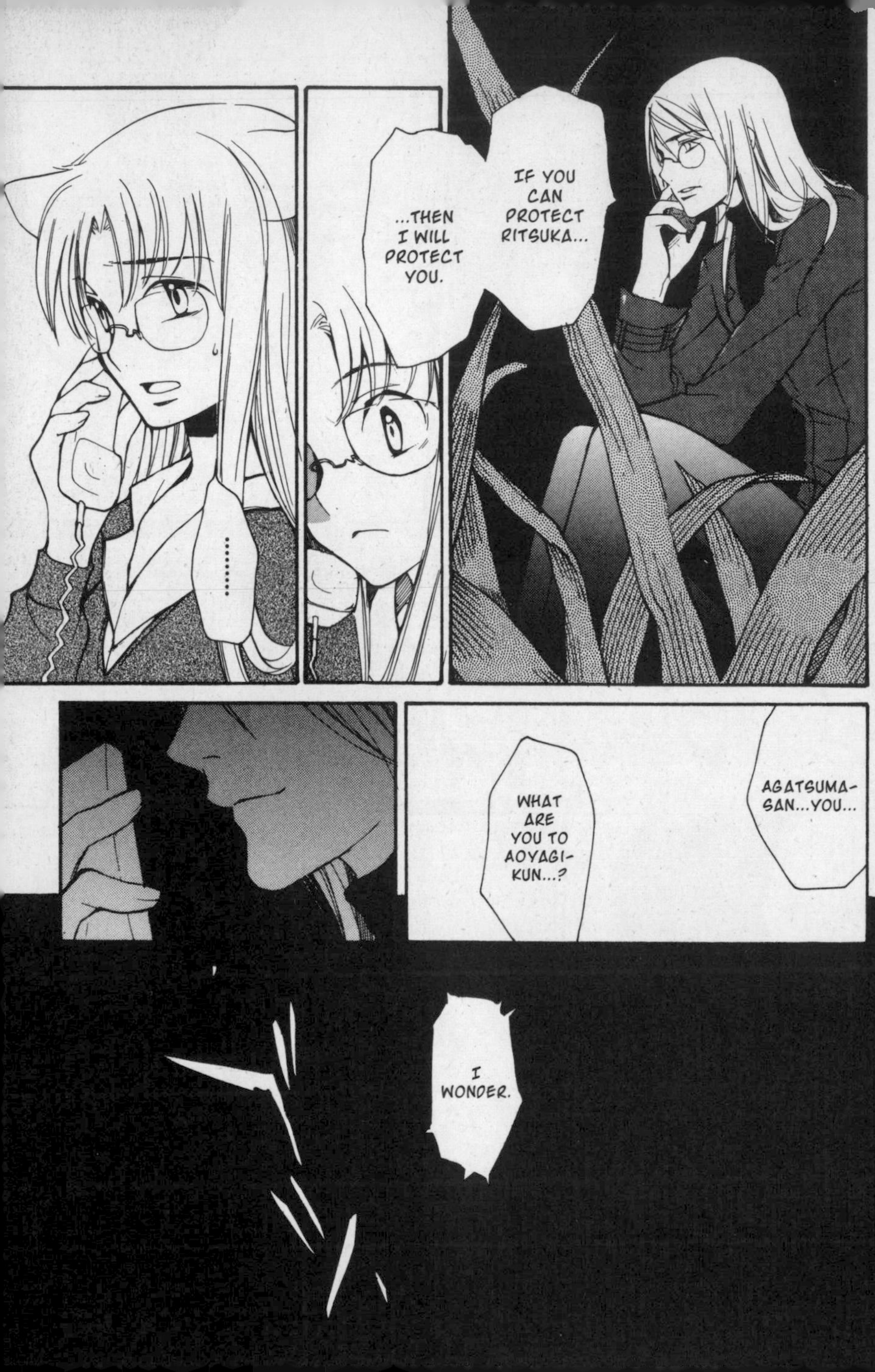
IF YOU CAN PROTECT RITSUKA...
...THEN I WILL PROTECT YOU.
....
AGATSUMA-SAN...YOU...
WHAT ARE YOU TO AOYAGI-KUN...?
I WONDER.

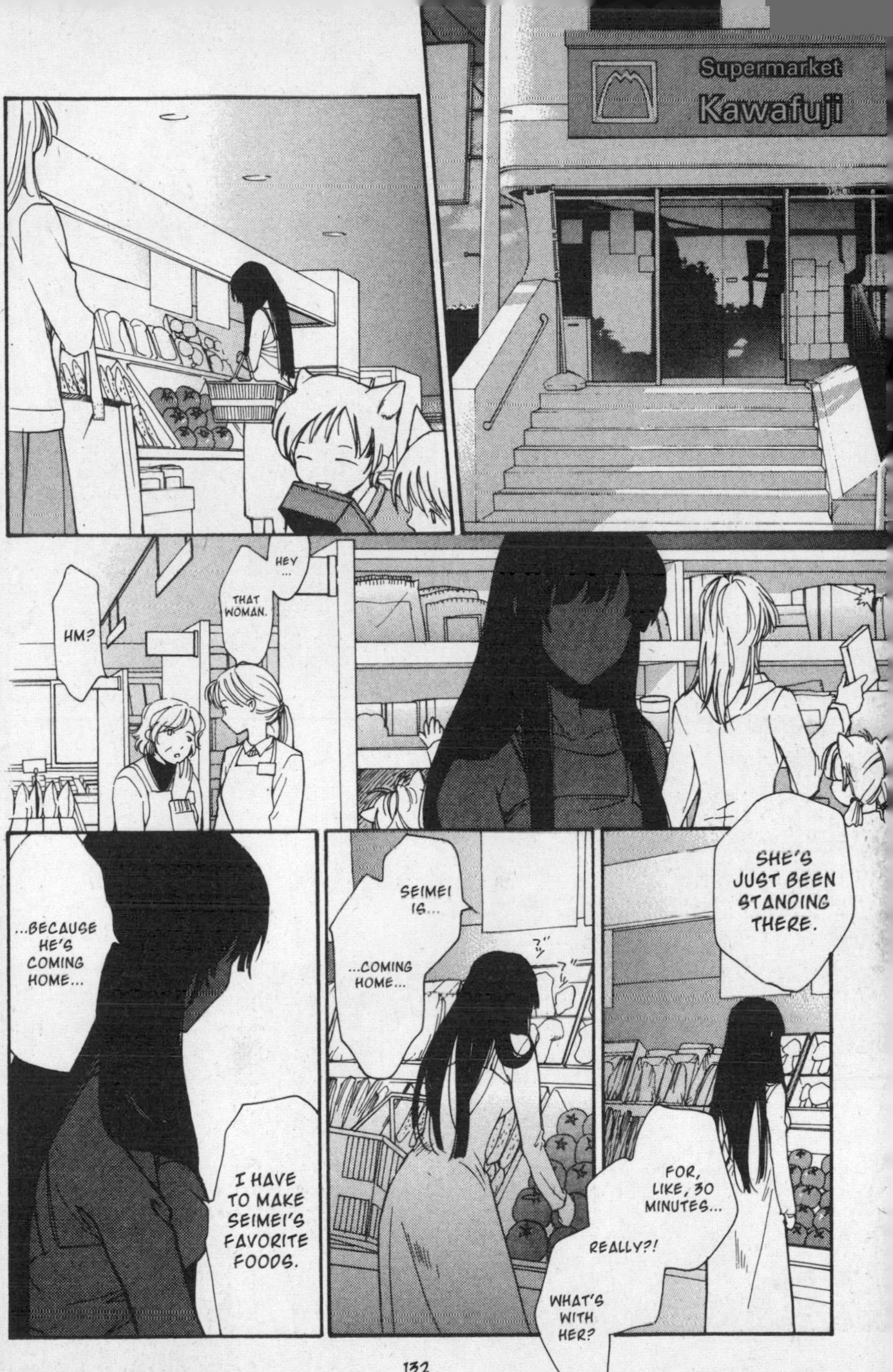
Supermarket
Kawafuji
HEY ...
THAT WOMAN.
HM?
SHE'S JUST BEEN STANDING THERE.
FOR, LIKE, 30 MINUTES...
REALLY?!
WHAT'S WITH HER?
SEIMEI IS...
...COMING HOME...
...BECAUSE HE'S COMING HOME...
I HAVE TO MAKE SEIMEI'S FAVORITE FOODS.

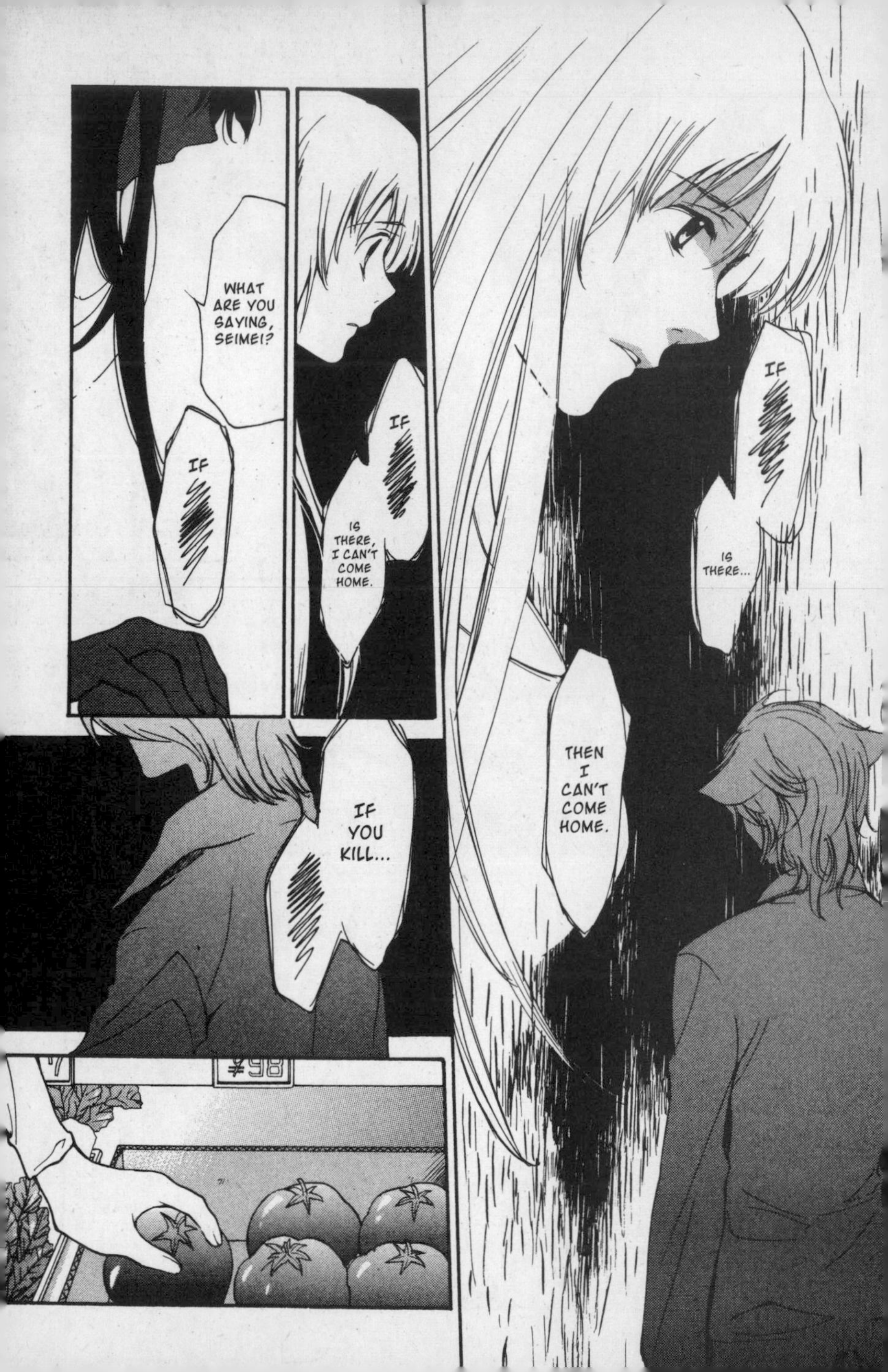
IF
IS THERE...
THEN I CAN'T COME HOME.
IF
IS THERE, I CAN'T COME HOME.
WHAT ARE YOU SAYING, SEIMEI!?
IF
IF YOU KILL...
¥98

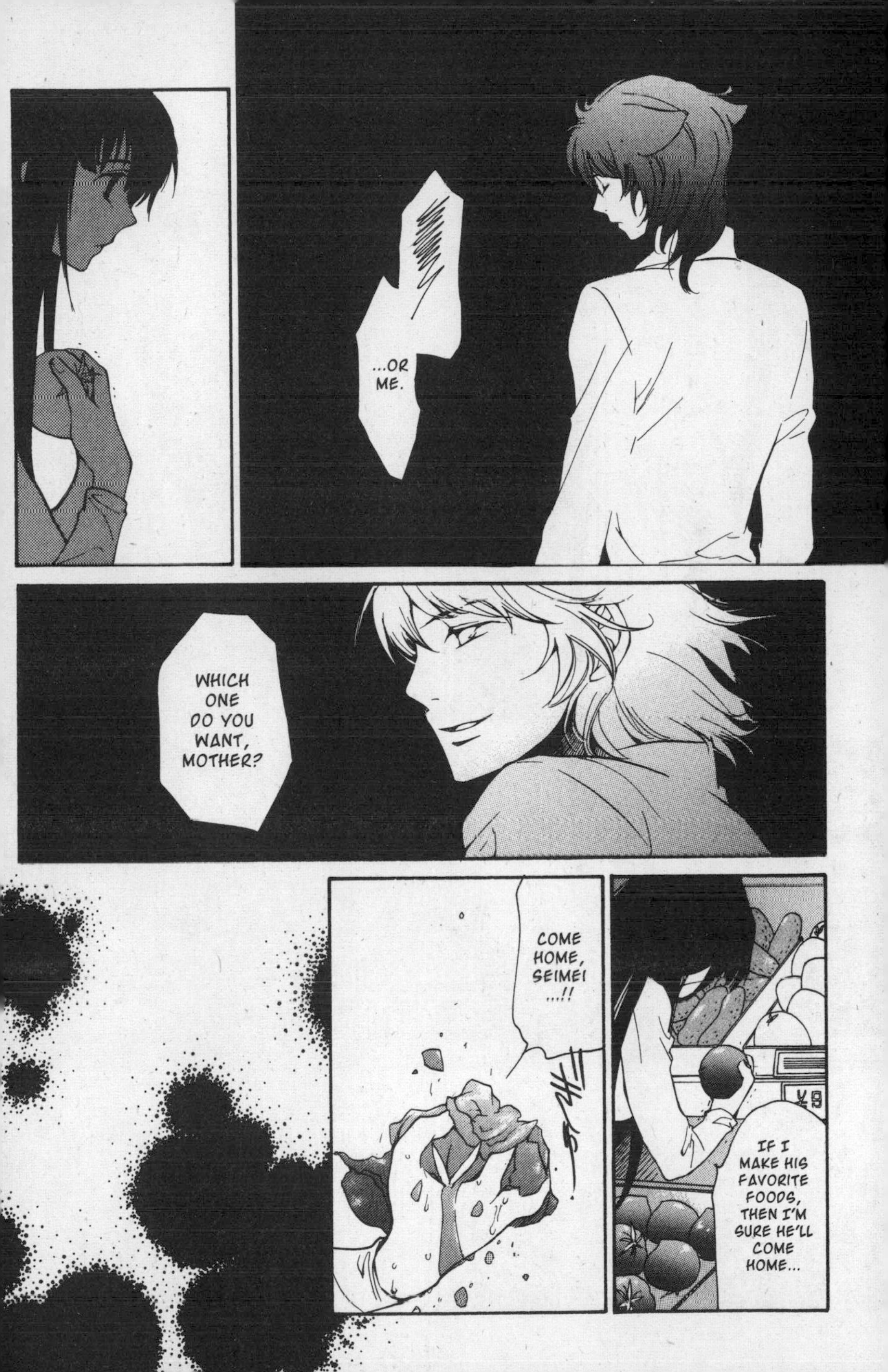
...OR ME.
WHICH ONE DO YOU WANT, MOTHER?
IF I MAKE HIS FAVORITE FOODS, THEN I'M SURE HE'LL COME HOME...
COME HOME, SEIMEI ...!!

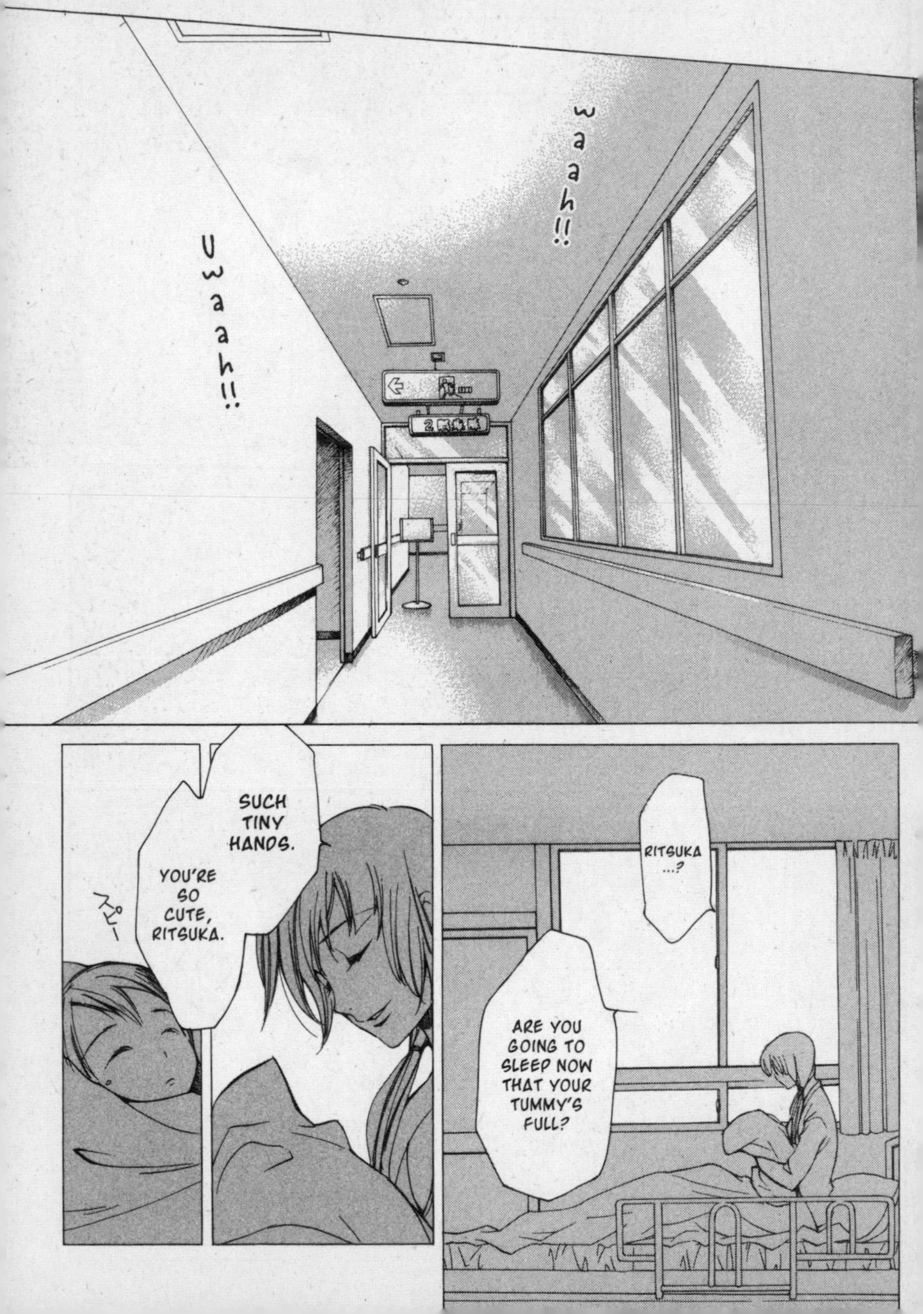
waah!!
Uwaah!!
RITSUKA ...?
ARE YOU GOING TO SLEEP NOW THAT YOUR TUMMY'S FULL?
SUCH TINY HANDS.
YOU'RE SO CUTE, RITSUKA.
スピー

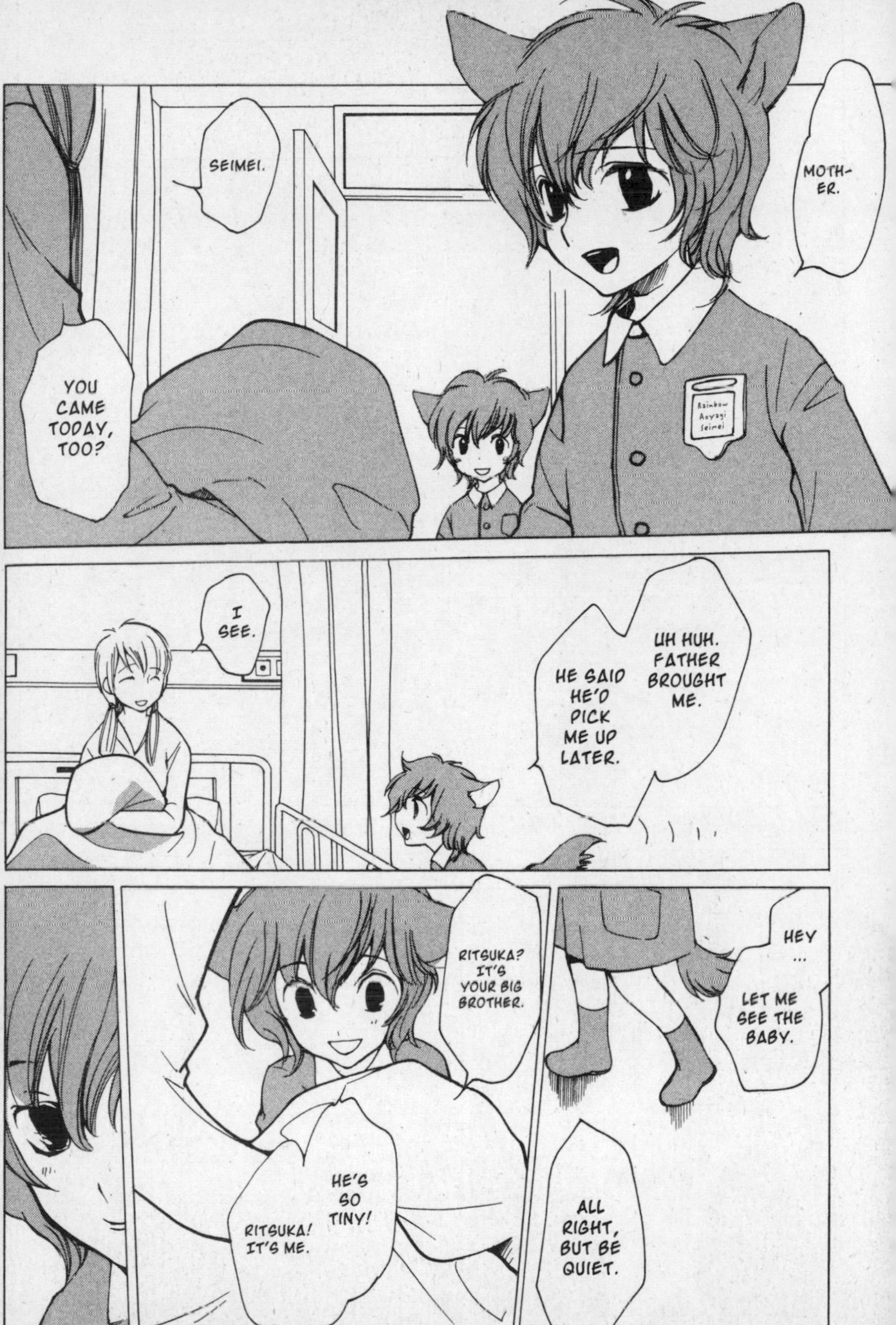
MOTH-ER.
SEIMEI.
Rainbow Aoyagi Seimei
YOU CAME TODAY, TOO?
UH HUH. FATHER BROUGHT ME.
HE SAID HE'D PICK ME UP LATER.
I SEE.
HEY ...
LET ME SEE THE BABY.
ALL RIGHT, BUT BE QUIET.
RITSUKA? IT'S YOUR BIG BROTHER.
HE'S SO TINY!
RITSUKA! IT'S ME.

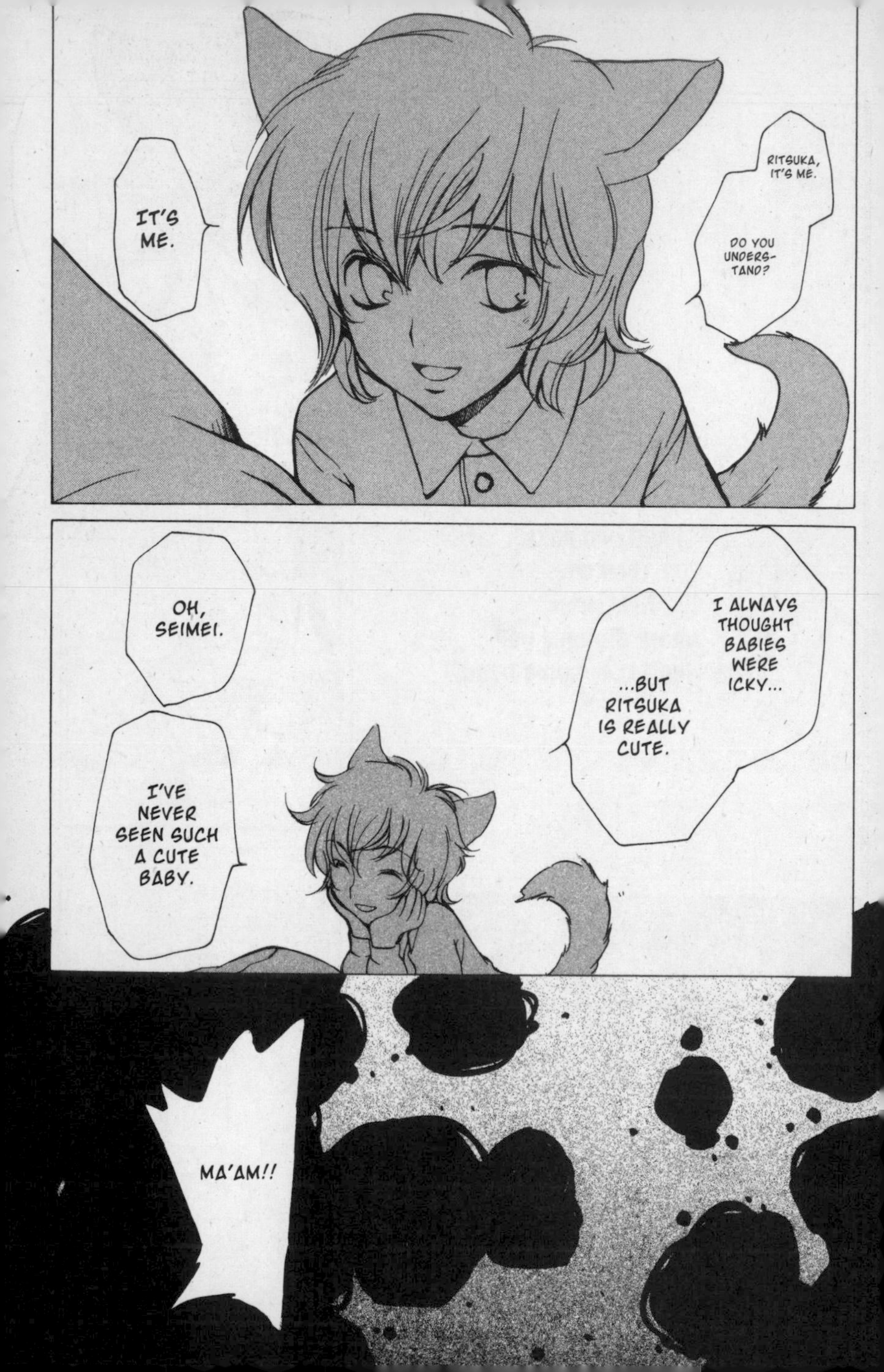
RITSUKA, IT'S ME.
DO YOU UNDERS-TAND?
IT'S ME.
I ALWAYS THOUGHT BABIES WERE ICKY...
...BUT RITSUKA IS REALLY CUTE.
OH, SEIMEI.
I'VE NEVER SEEN SUCH A CUTE BABY.
MA'AM!!

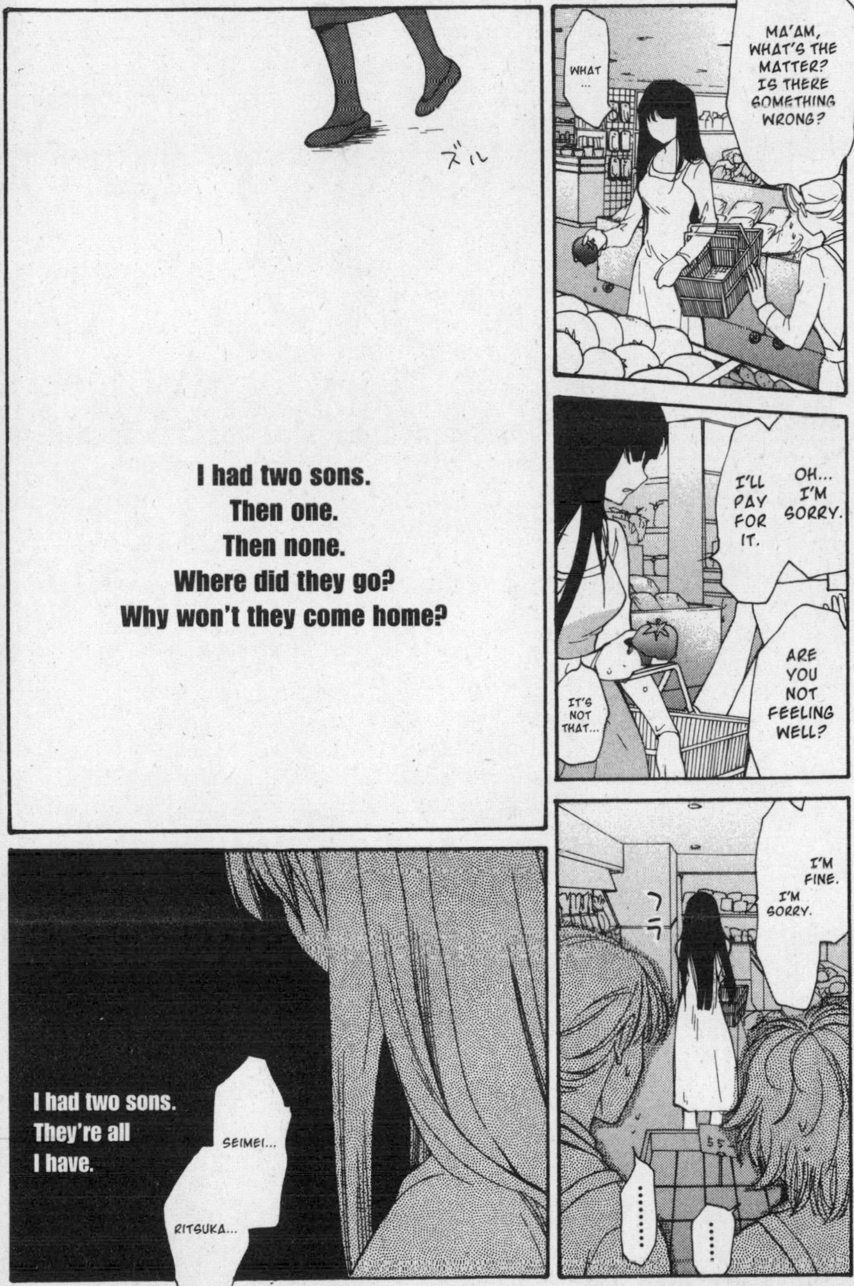
MA'AM, WHAT'S THE MATTER? IS THERE SOMETHING WRONG?
WHAT ...
OH... I'M SORRY.
I'LL PAY FOR IT.
ARE YOU NOT FEELING WELL?
IT'S NOT THAT...
I'M FINE.
I'M SORRY.
フラ
....
....
ズル
I had two sons.
Then one.
Then none.
Where did they go?
Why won't they come home?
I had two sons.
They're all
I have.
SEIMEI...
RITSUKA...

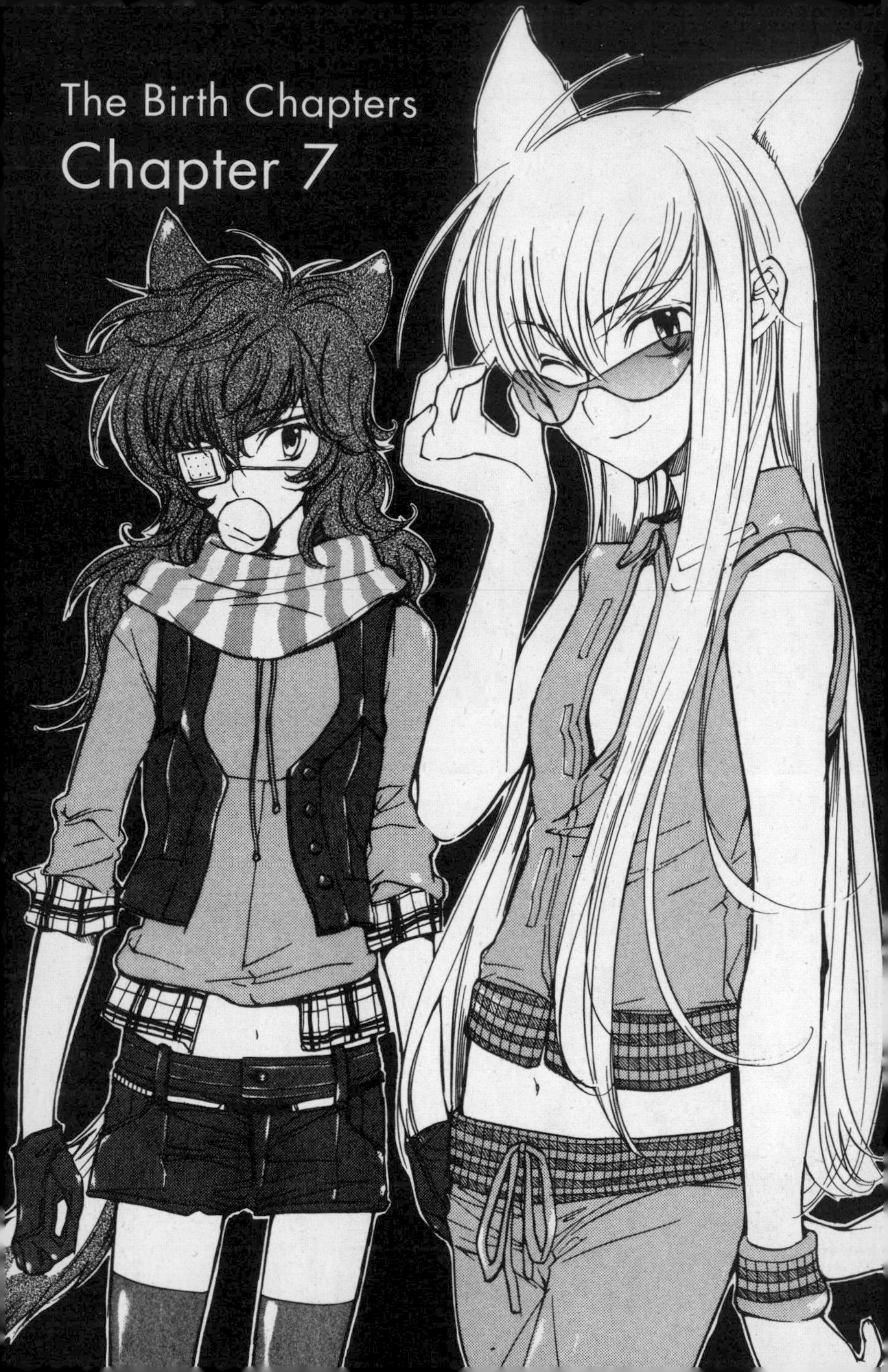
The Birth Chapters
Chapter 7

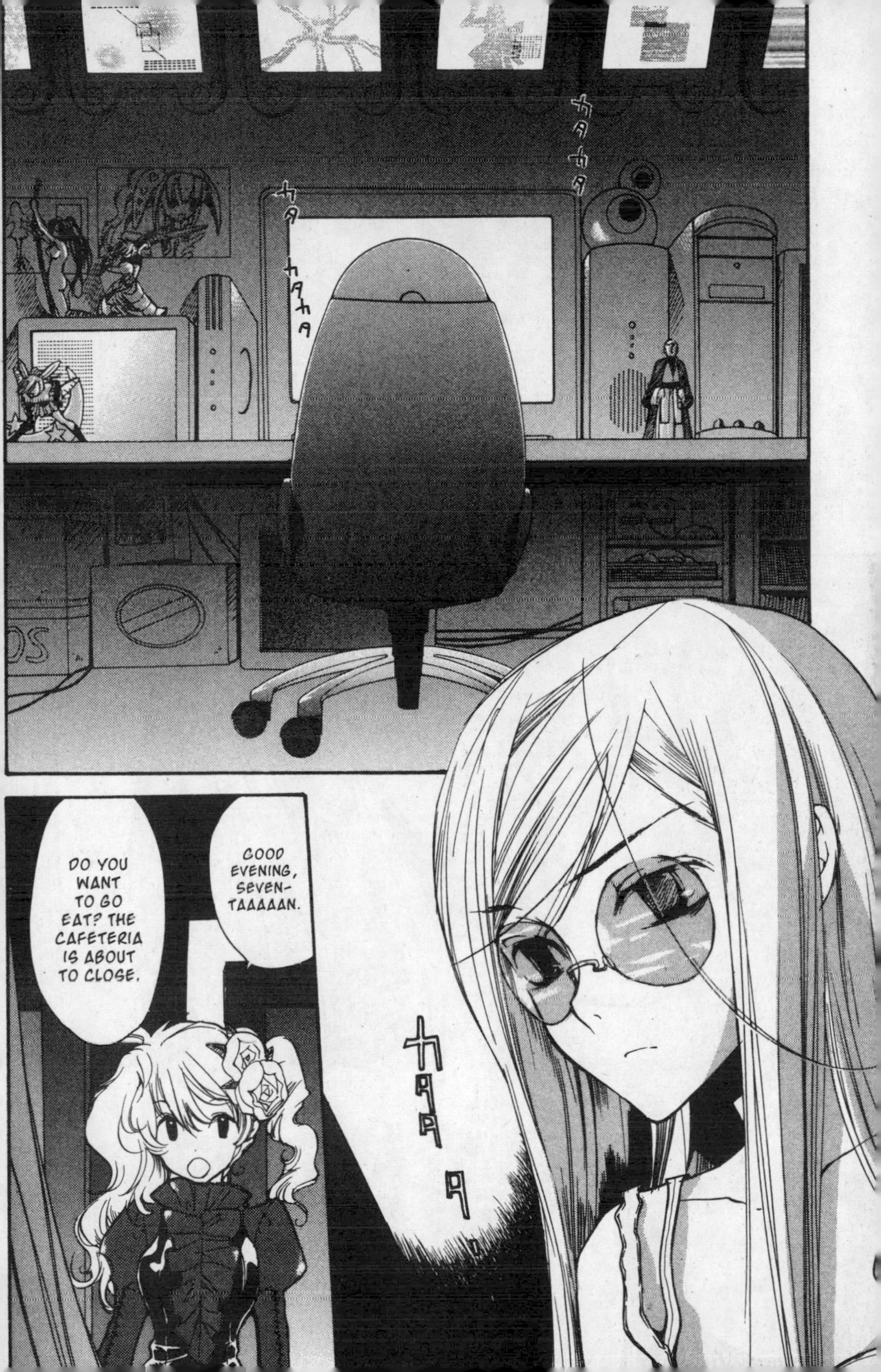
カタカタ
カタ
カタカタ
GOOD EVENING, SEVEN-TAAAAAN.
DO YOU WANT TO GO EAT? THE CAFETERIA IS ABOUT TO CLOSE.
カタタタ
タ

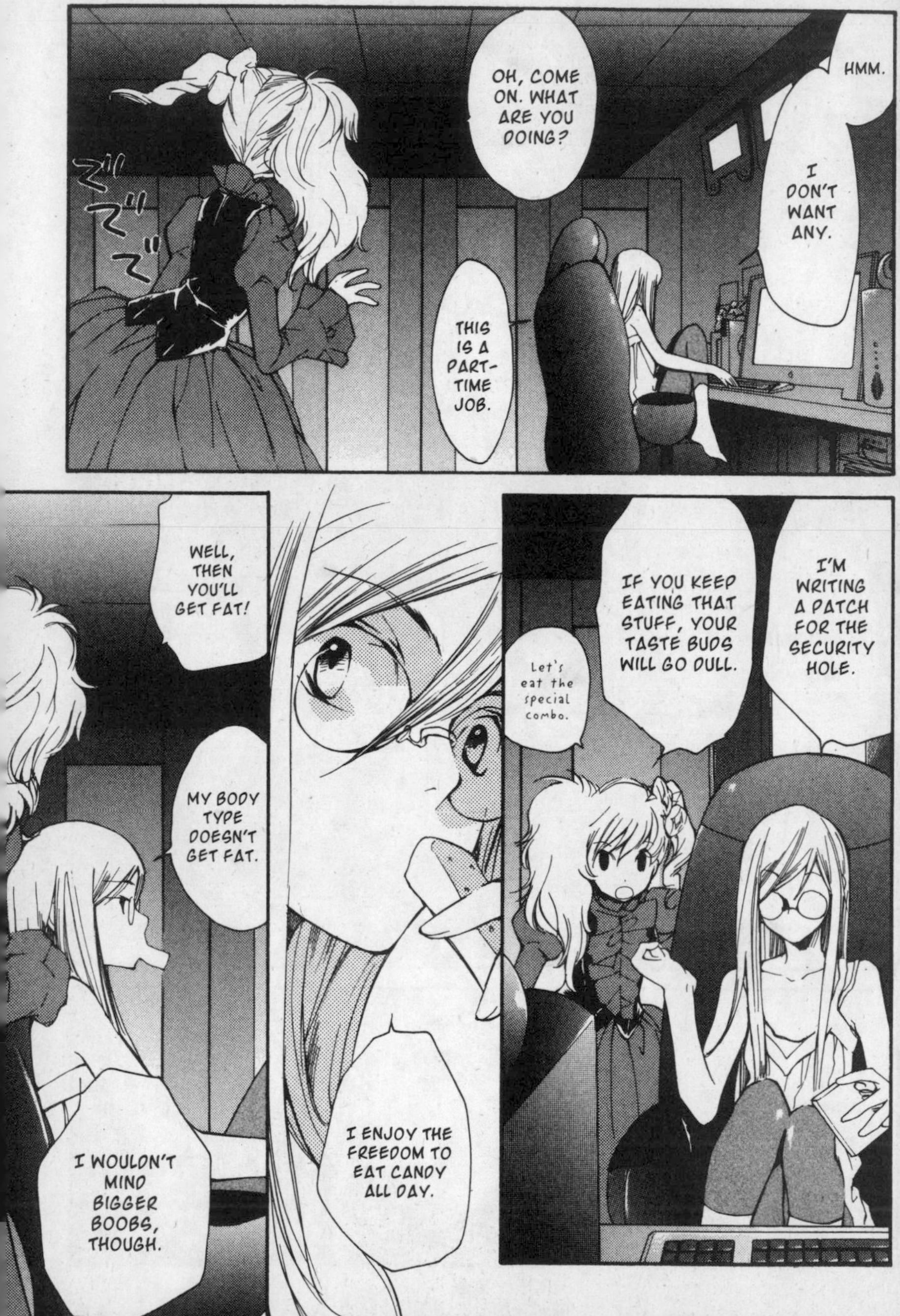
HMM.
I DON'T WANT ANY.
OH, COME ON. WHAT ARE YOU DOING?
THIS IS A PART-TIME JOB.
ずずず
I'M WRITING A PATCH FOR THE SECURITY HOLE.
IF YOU KEEP EATING THAT STUFF, YOUR TASTE BUDS WILL GO DULL.
Let's eat the special combo.
I ENJOY THE FREEDOM TO EAT CANDY ALL DAY.
WELL, THEN YOU'LL GET FAT!
MY BODY TYPE DOESN'T GET FAT.
I WOULDN'T MIND BIGGER BOOBS, THOUGH.

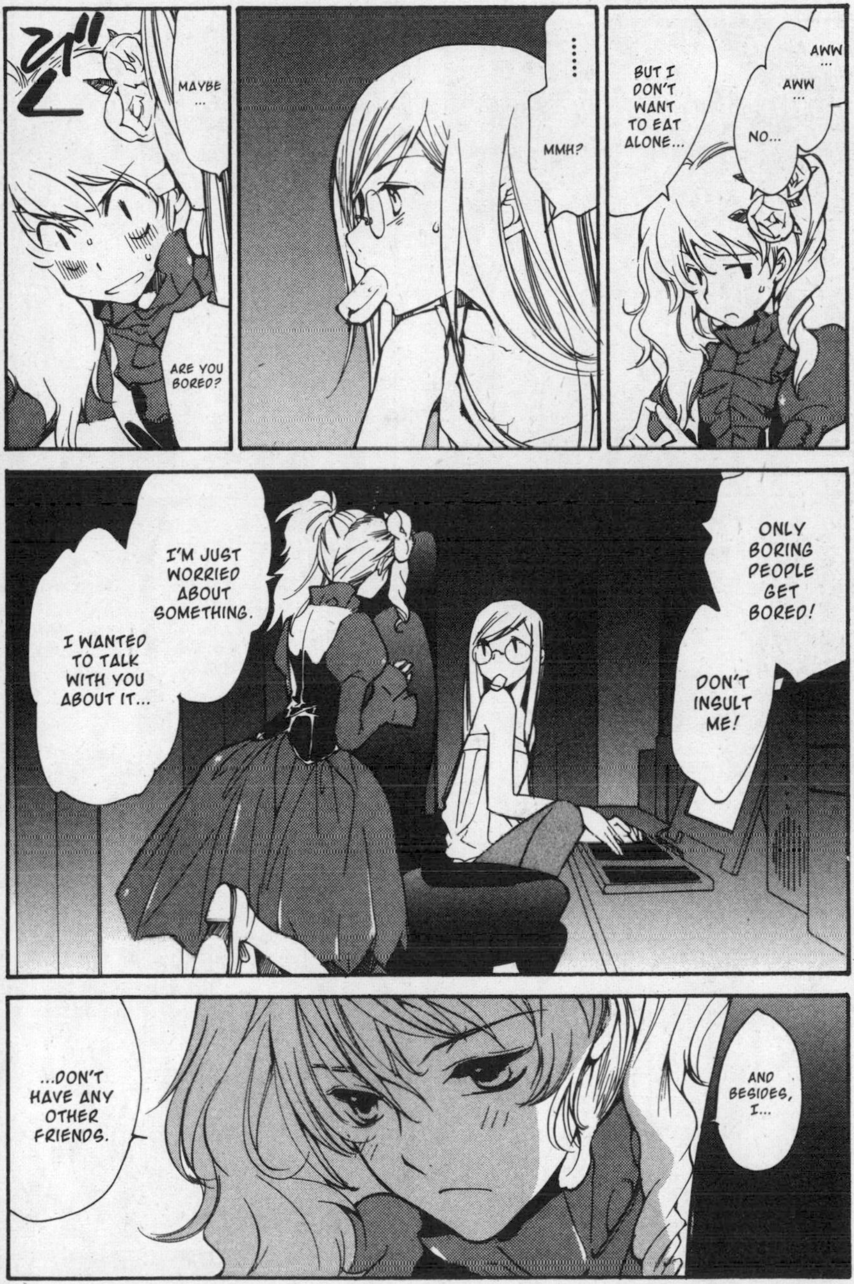
AWW...
AWW...
NO...
BUT I DON'T WANT TO EAT ALONE...
......
MMH?
MAYBE ...
ARE YOU BORED?
ONLY BORING PEOPLE GET BORED!
DON'T INSULT ME!
I'M JUST WORRIED ABOUT SOMETHING.
I WANTED TO TALK WITH YOU ABOUT IT...
AND BESIDES, I...
...DON'T HAVE ANY OTHER FRIENDS.

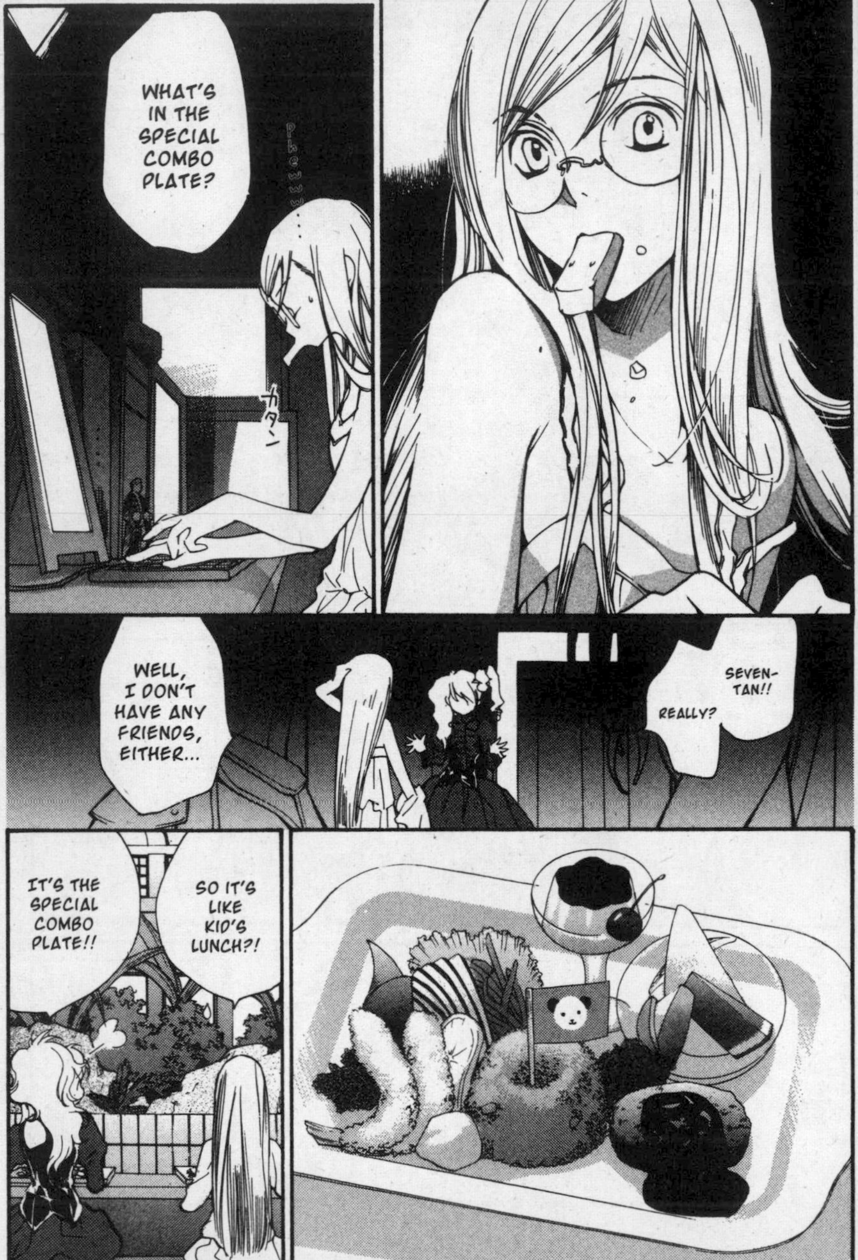
WHAT'S IN THE SPECIAL COMBO PLATE?
Phewww
カタン
SEVEN-TAN!!
REALLY?
WELL, I DON'T HAVE ANY FRIENDS, EITHER...
SO IT'S LIKE KID'S LUNCH?!
IT'S THE SPECIAL COMBO PLATE!!

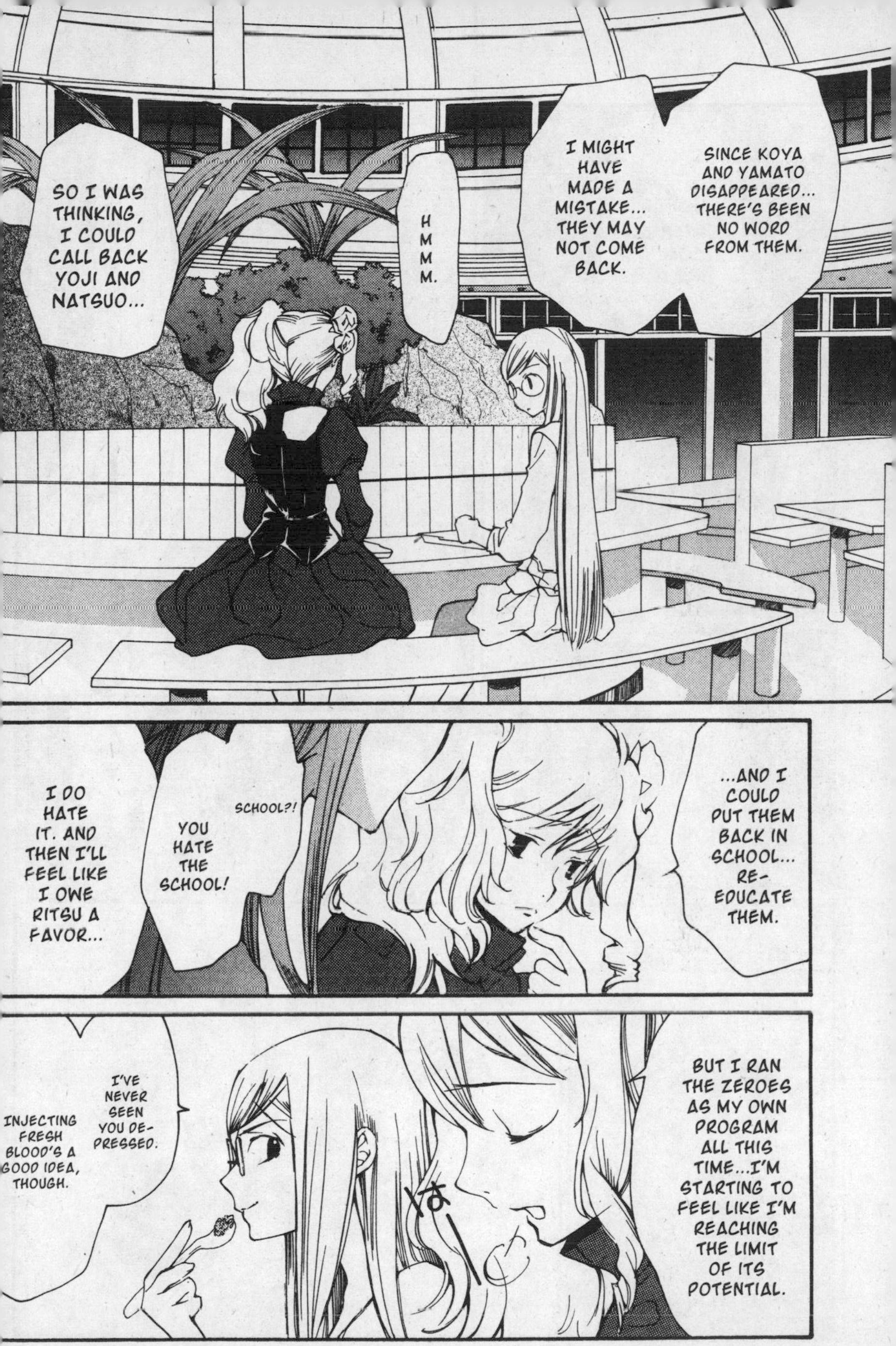
SINCE KOYA AND YAMATO DISAPPEARED... THERE'S BEEN NO WORD FROM THEM.
I MIGHT HAVE MADE A MISTAKE... THEY MAY NOT COME BACK.
HMMM.
SO I WAS THINKING, I COULD CALL BACK YOJI AND NATSUO...
...AND I COULD PUT THEM BACK IN SCHOOL... RE-EDUCATE THEM.
SCHOOL?!
YOU HATE THE SCHOOL!
I DO HATE IT. AND THEN I'LL FEEL LIKE I OWE RITSU A FAVOR...
BUT I RAN THE ZEROES AS MY OWN PROGRAM ALL THIS TIME...I'M STARTING TO FEEL LIKE I'M REACHING THE LIMIT OF ITS POTENTIAL.
は
I'VE NEVER SEEN YOU DEPRESSED.
INJECTING FRESH BLOOD'S A GOOD IDEA, THOUGH.

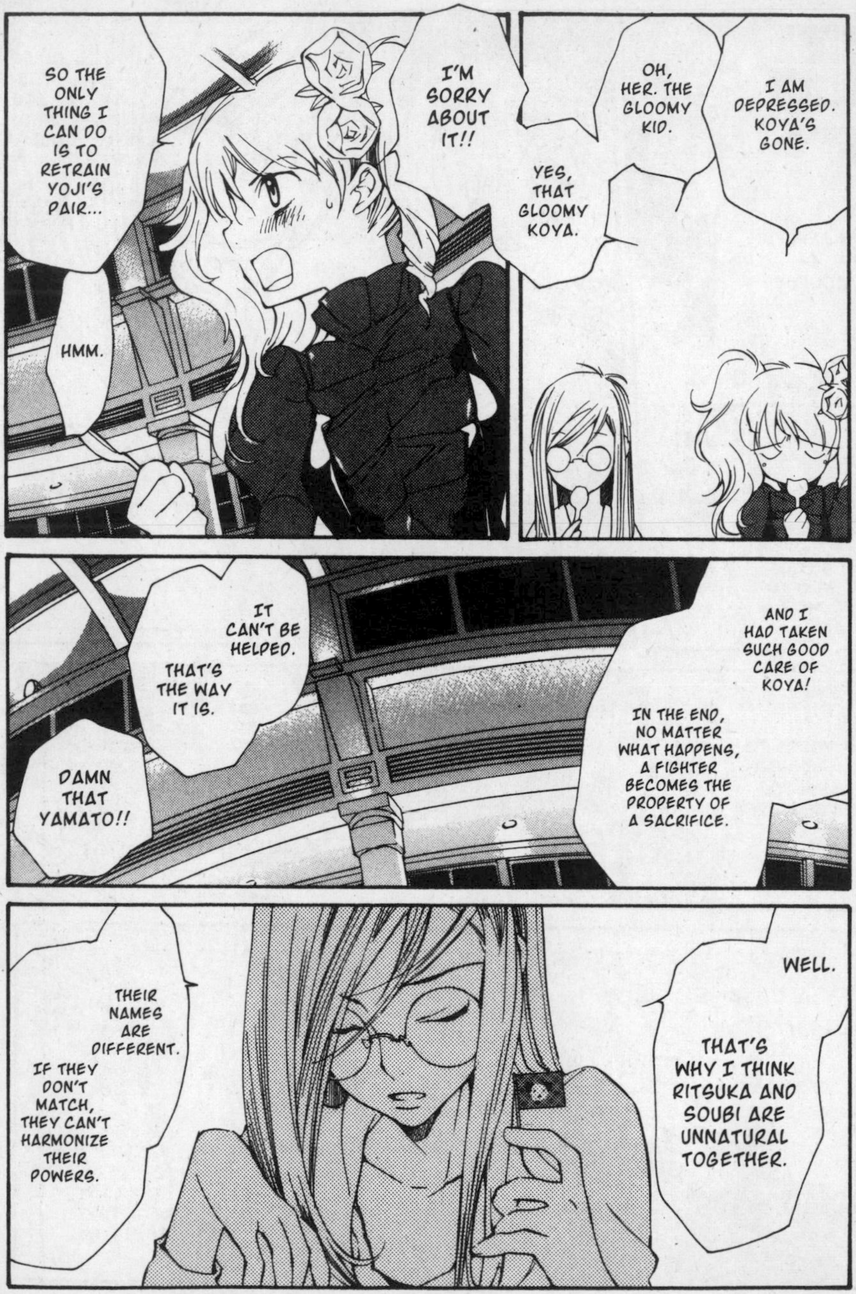
I AM DEPRESSED. KOYA'S GONE.
OH, HER. THE GLOOMY KID.
YES, THAT GLOOMY KOYA.
I'M SORRY ABOUT IT!!
SO THE ONLY THING I CAN DO IS TO RETRAIN YOJI'S PAIR...
HMM.
AND I HAD TAKEN SUCH GOOD CARE OF KOYA!
IN THE END, NO MATTER WHAT HAPPENS, A FIGHTER BECOMES THE PROPERTY OF A SACRIFICE.
IT CAN'T BE HELPED.
THAT'S THE WAY IT IS.
DAMN THAT YAMATO!!
WELL.
THAT'S WHY I THINK RITSUKA AND SOUBI ARE UNNATURAL TOGETHER.
THEIR NAMES ARE DIFFERENT.
IF THEY DON'T MATCH, THEY CAN'T HARMONIZE THEIR POWERS.

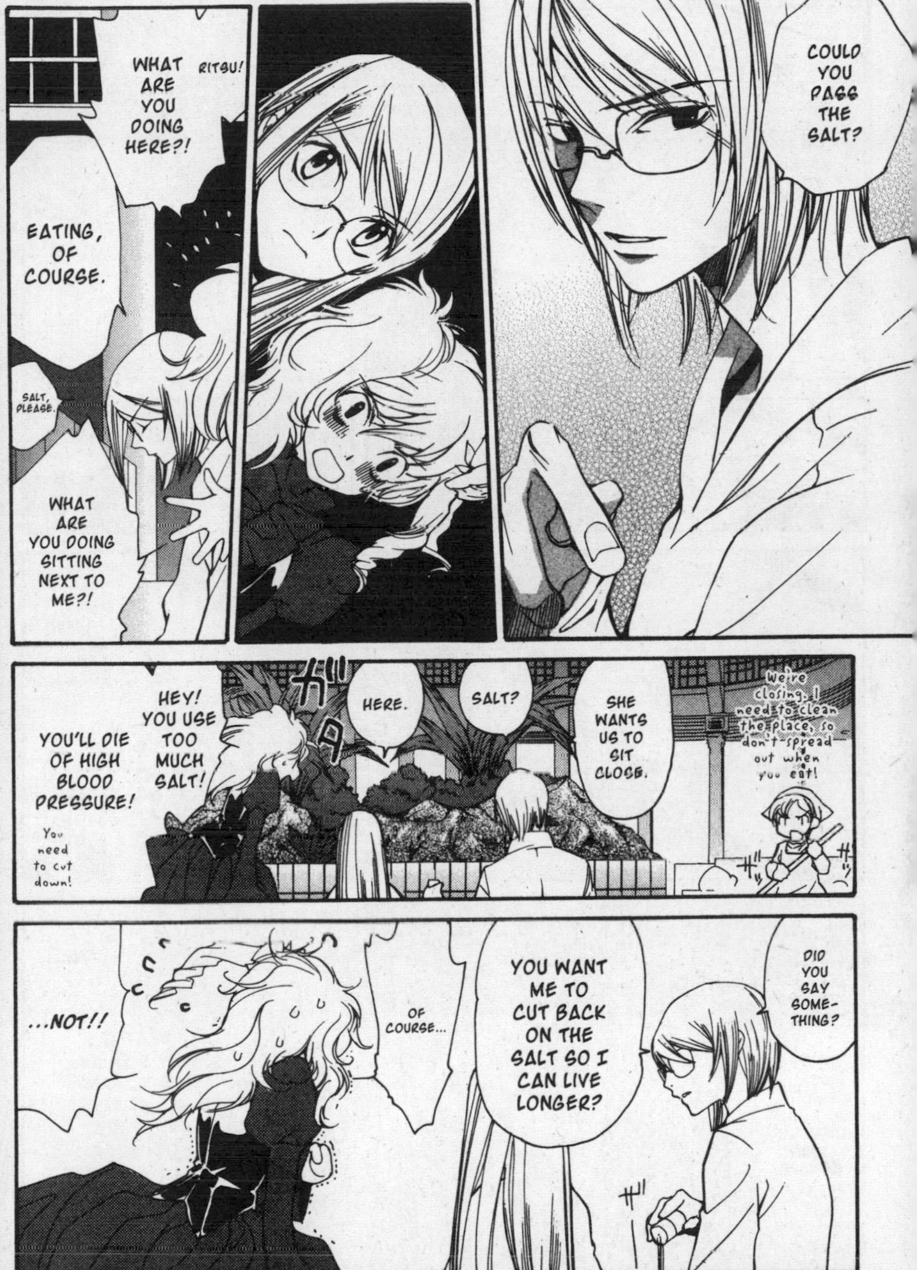
COULD YOU PASS THE SALT?
RITSU!
WHAT ARE YOU DOING HERE?!
EATING, OF COURSE.
SALT, PLEASE.
WHAT ARE YOU DOING SITTING NEXT TO ME?!
We're closing. I need to clean the place, so don't spread out when you eat!
SHE WANTS US TO SIT CLOSE.
SALT?
HERE.
HEY! YOU USE TOO MUCH SALT!
YOU'LL DIE OF HIGH BLOOD PRESSURE!
You need to cut down!
DID YOU SAY SOME-THING?
YOU WANT ME TO CUT BACK ON THE SALT SO I CAN LIVE LONGER?
OF COURSE...
...NOT!!

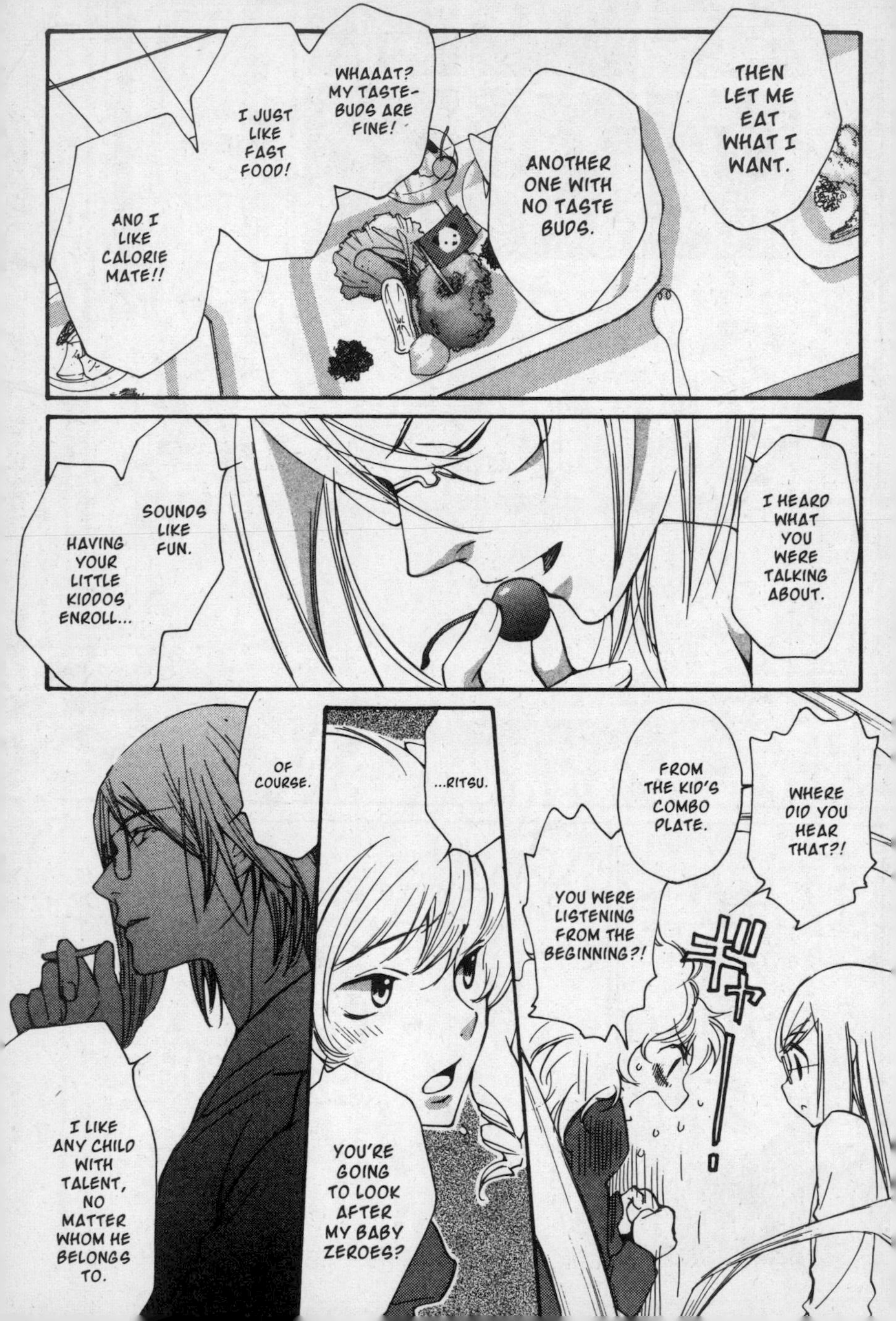
THEN LET ME EAT WHAT I WANT.
ANOTHER ONE WITH NO TASTE BUDS.
WHAAAT? MY TASTE-BUDS ARE FINE!
I JUST LIKE FAST FOOD!
AND I LIKE CALORIE MATE!!
I HEARD WHAT YOU WERE TALKING ABOUT.
SOUNDS LIKE FUN.
HAVING YOUR LITTLE KIDDOS ENROLL...
WHERE DID YOU HEAR THAT?!
FROM THE KID'S COMBO PLATE.
YOU WERE LISTENING FROM THE BEGINNING?!
...RITSU.
YOU'RE GOING TO LOOK AFTER MY BABY ZEROES?
OF COURSE.
I LIKE ANY CHILD WITH TALENT, NO MATTER WHOM HE BELONGS TO.

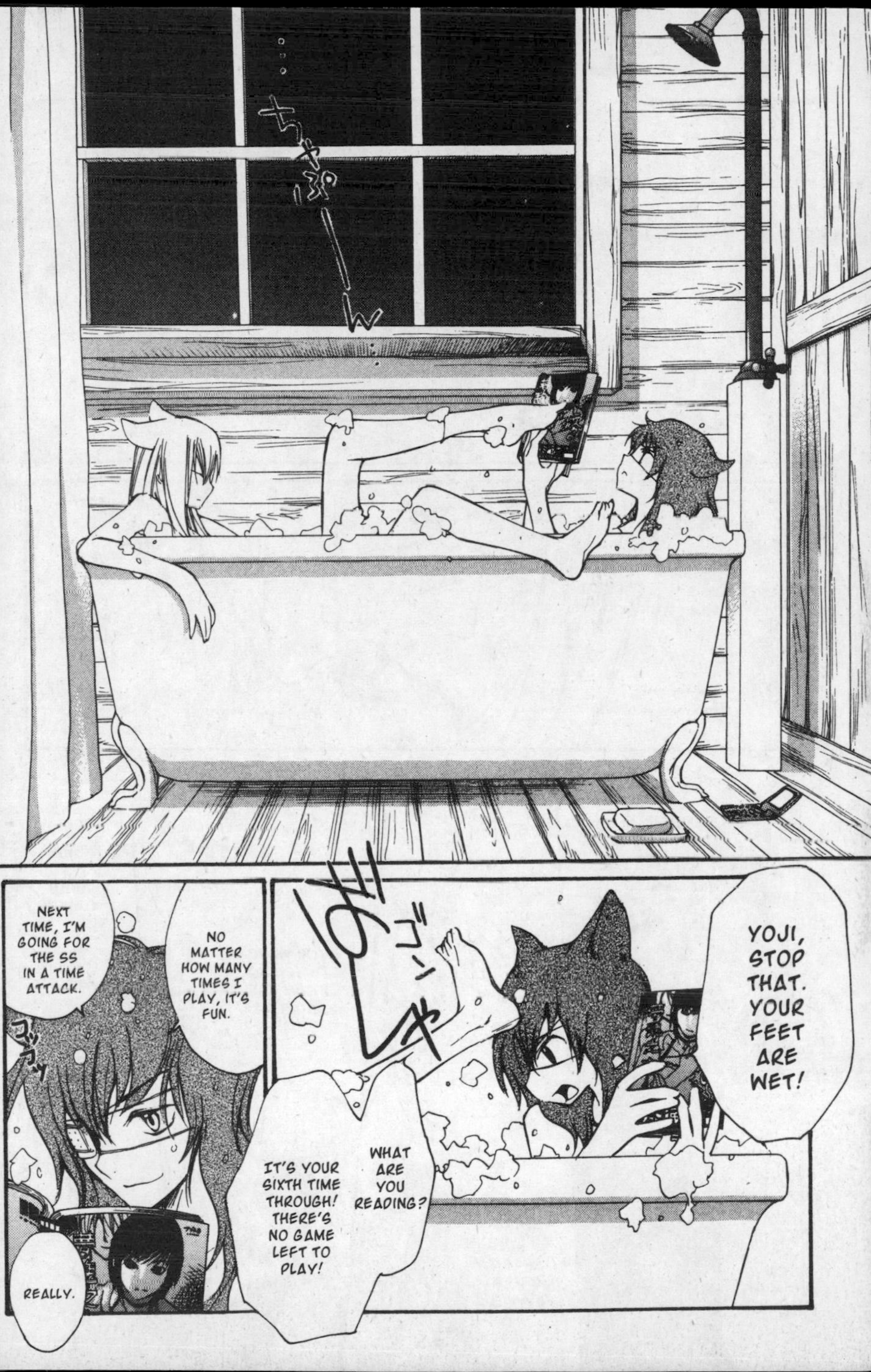
ちゃぷーーん
ばしゃ
YOJI, STOP THAT. YOUR FEET ARE WET!
WHAT ARE YOU READING?
IT'S YOUR SIXTH TIME THROUGH! THERE'S NO GAME LEFT TO PLAY!
NO MATTER HOW MANY TIMES I PLAY, IT'S FUN.
NEXT TIME, I'M GOING FOR THE SS IN A TIME ATTACK.
REALLY.

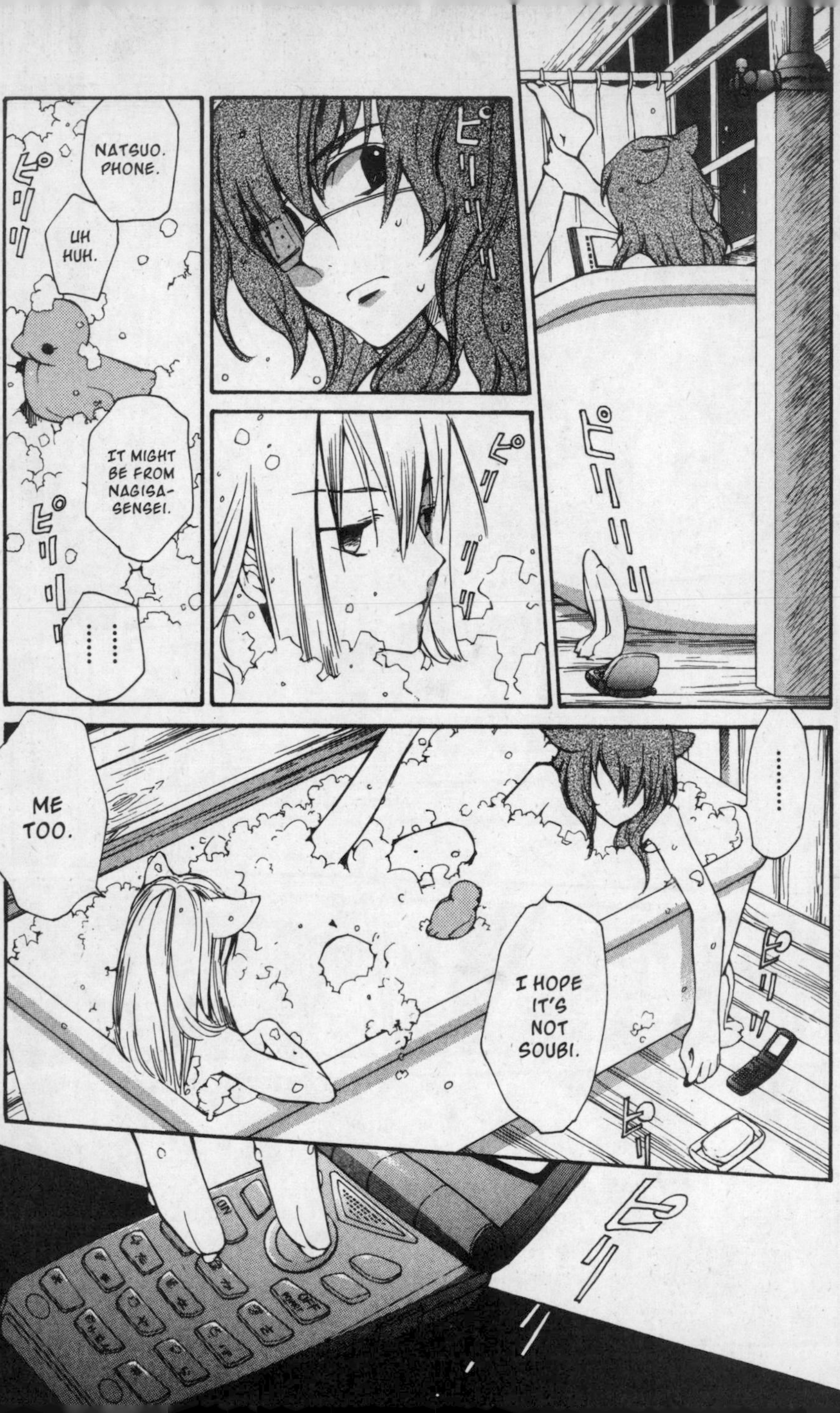
NATSUO. PHONE.
UH HUH.
IT MIGHT BE FROM NAGISA-SENSEI.
......
......
I HOPE IT'S NOT SOUBI.
ME TOO.

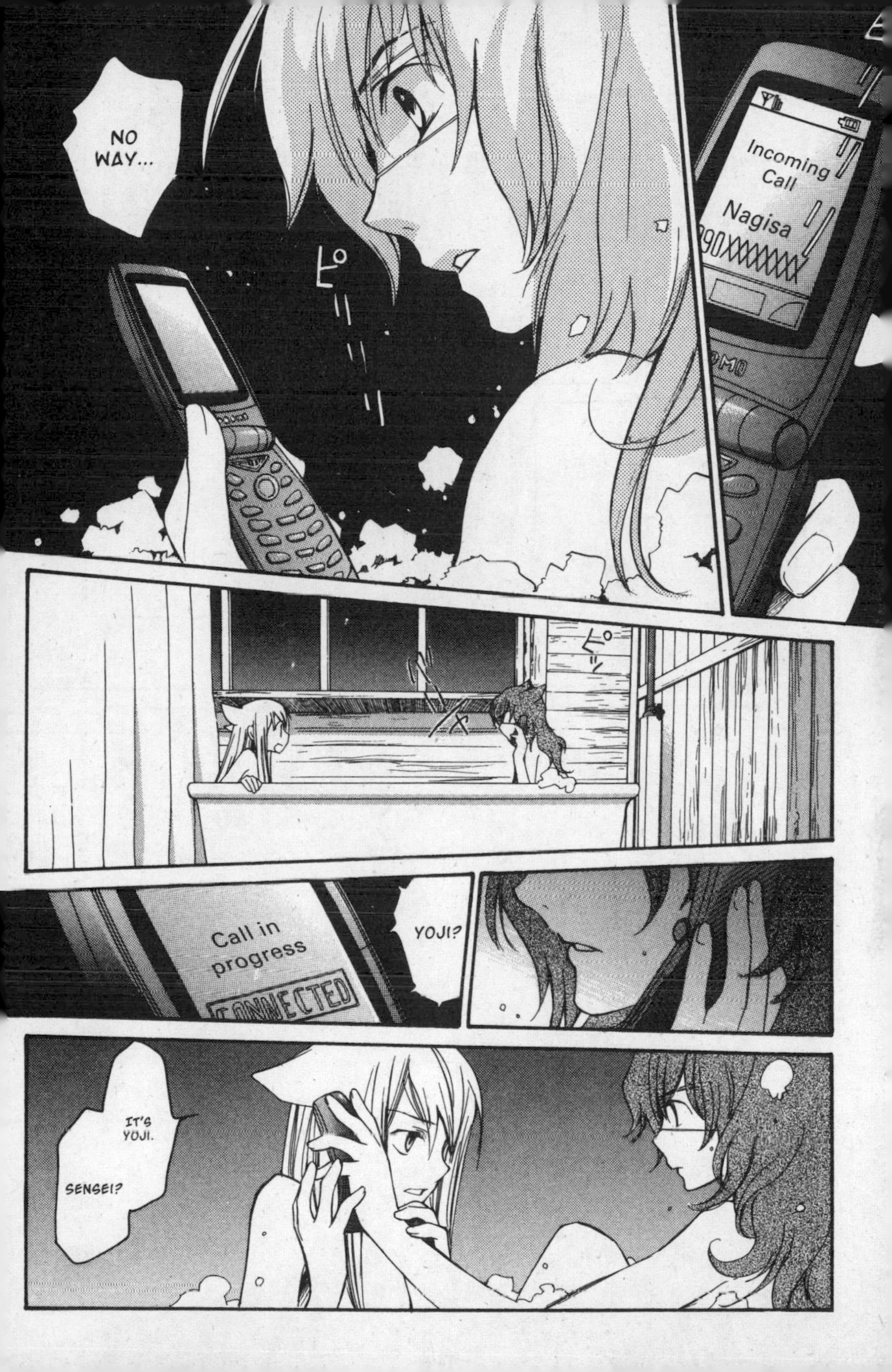
Incoming Call
Nagisa
NO WAY...
ピ
ピ
YOJI?
Call in progress
CONNECTED
IT'S YOJI.
SENSEI?

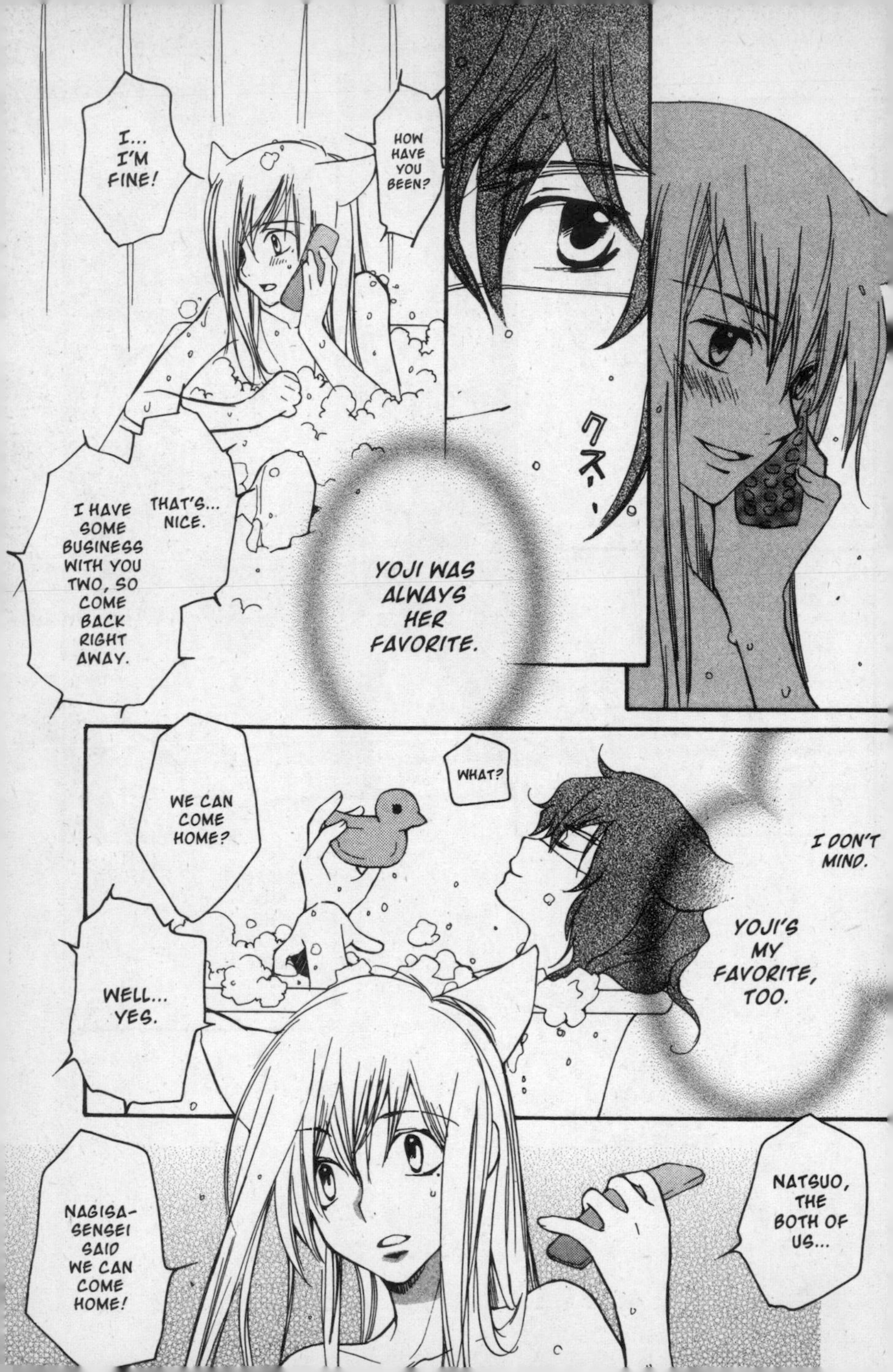
クス・
HOW HAVE YOU BEEN?
I... I'M FINE!
THAT'S... NICE.
I HAVE SOME BUSINESS WITH YOU TWO, SO COME BACK RIGHT AWAY.
YOJI WAS ALWAYS HER FAVORITE.
I DON'T MIND.
YOJI'S MY FAVORITE, TOO.
WHAT?
WE CAN COME HOME?
WELL... YES.
NATSUO, THE BOTH OF US...
NAGISA-SENSEI SAID WE CAN COME HOME!

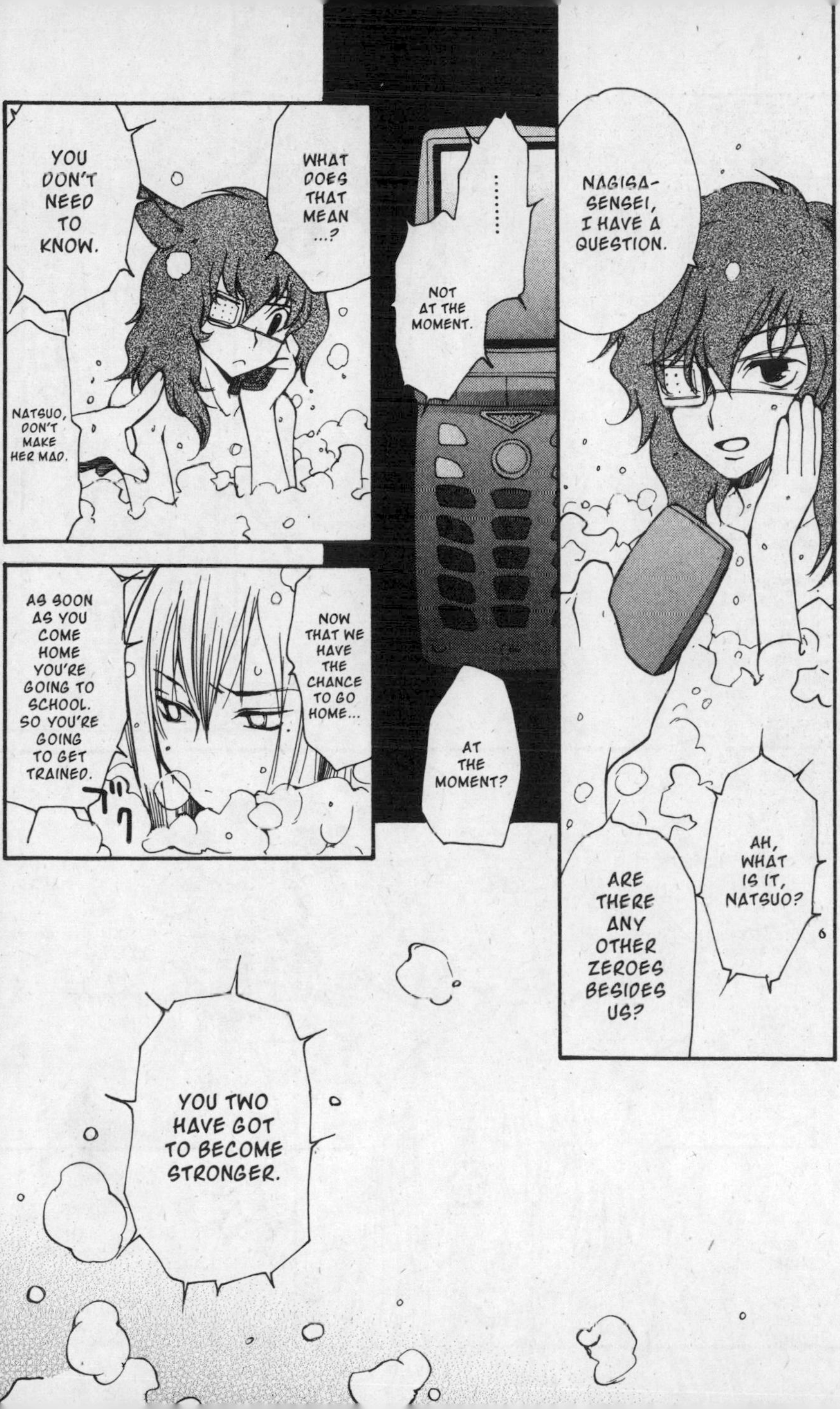
NAGISA-SENSEI, I HAVE A QUESTION.
AH, WHAT IS IT, NATSUO?
ARE THERE ANY OTHER ZEROES BESIDES US?
......
NOT AT THE MOMENT.
AT THE MOMENT?
WHAT DOES THAT MEAN ...?
YOU DON'T NEED TO KNOW.
NATSUO, DON'T MAKE HER MAD.
NOW THAT WE HAVE THE CHANCE TO GO HOME...
AS SOON AS YOU COME HOME YOU'RE GOING TO SCHOOL. SO YOU'RE GOING TO GET TRAINED.
YOU TWO HAVE GOT TO BECOME STRONGER.

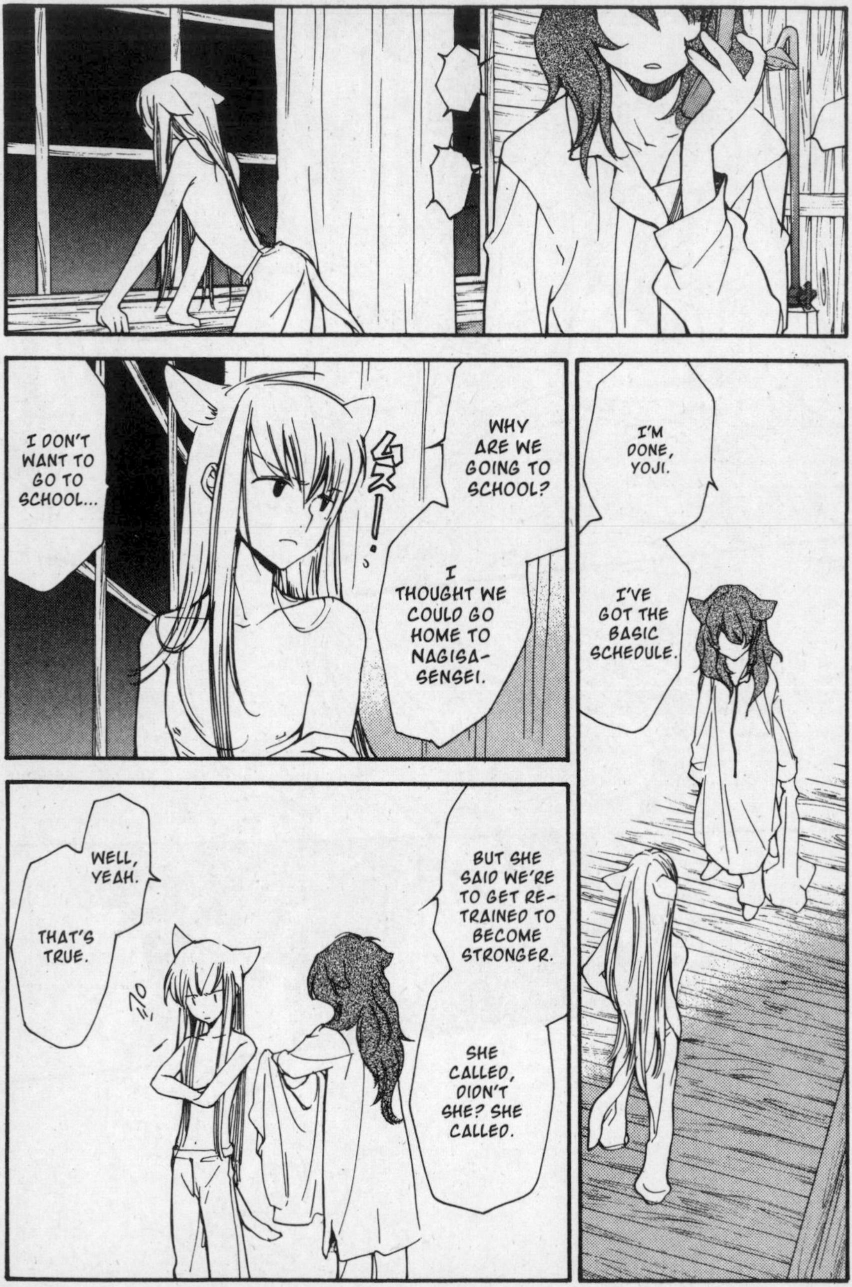
I'M DONE, YOJI.
I'VE GOT THE BASIC SCHEDULE.
WHY ARE WE GOING TO SCHOOL?
I THOUGHT WE COULD GO HOME TO NAGISA-SENSEI.
ムスー!
I DON'T WANT TO GO TO SCHOOL...
BUT SHE SAID WE'RE TO GET RE-TRAINED TO BECOME STRONGER.
SHE CALLED, DIDN'T SHE? SHE CALLED.
WELL, YEAH.
THAT'S TRUE.

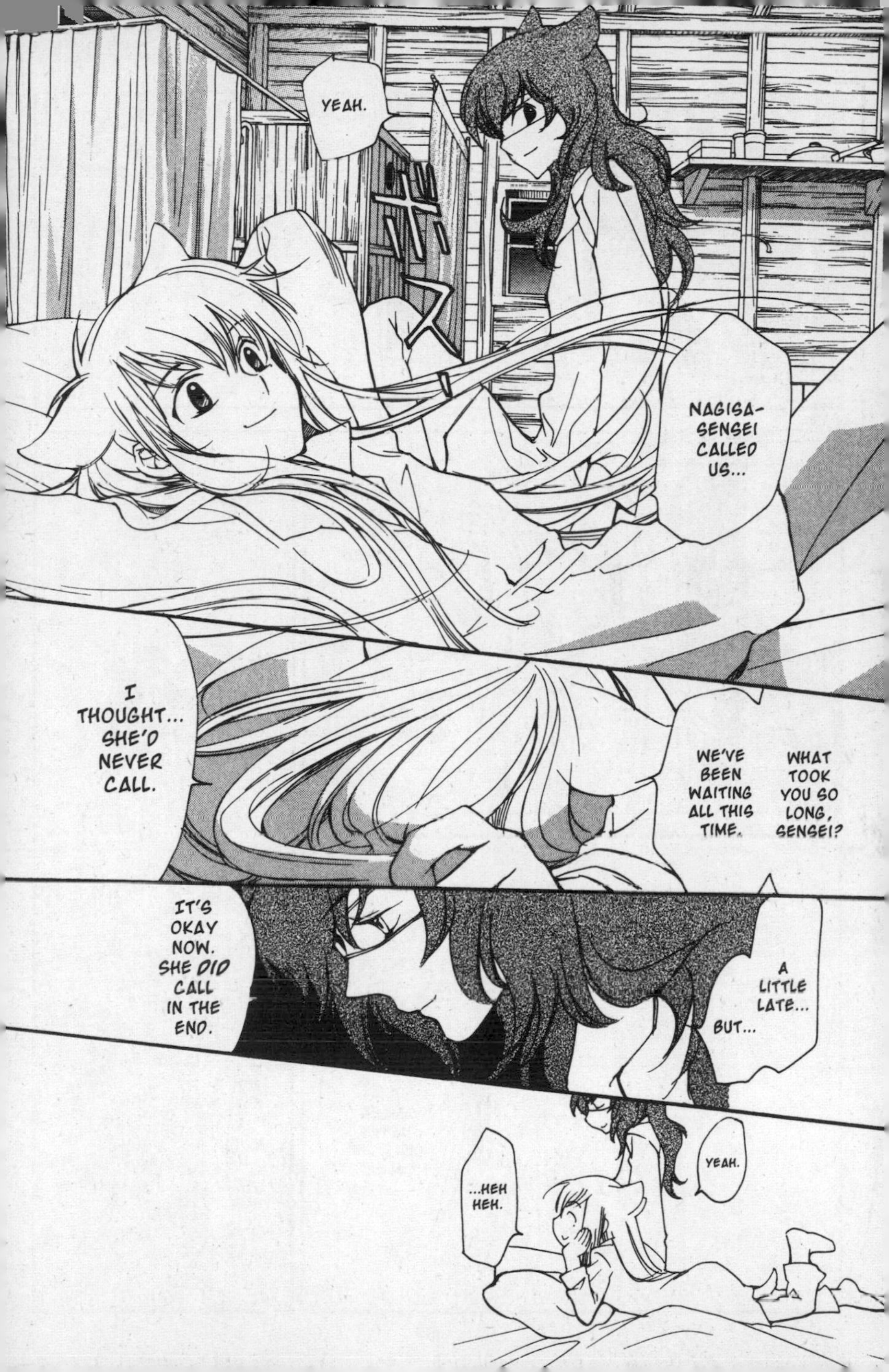
NAGISA-SENSEI CALLED US...
YEAH.
WHAT TOOK YOU SO LONG, SENSEI?
WE'VE BEEN WAITING ALL THIS TIME.
I THOUGHT... SHE'D NEVER CALL.
A LITTLE LATE... BUT...
IT'S OKAY NOW. SHE *DID* CALL IN THE END.
YEAH.
...HEH HEH.

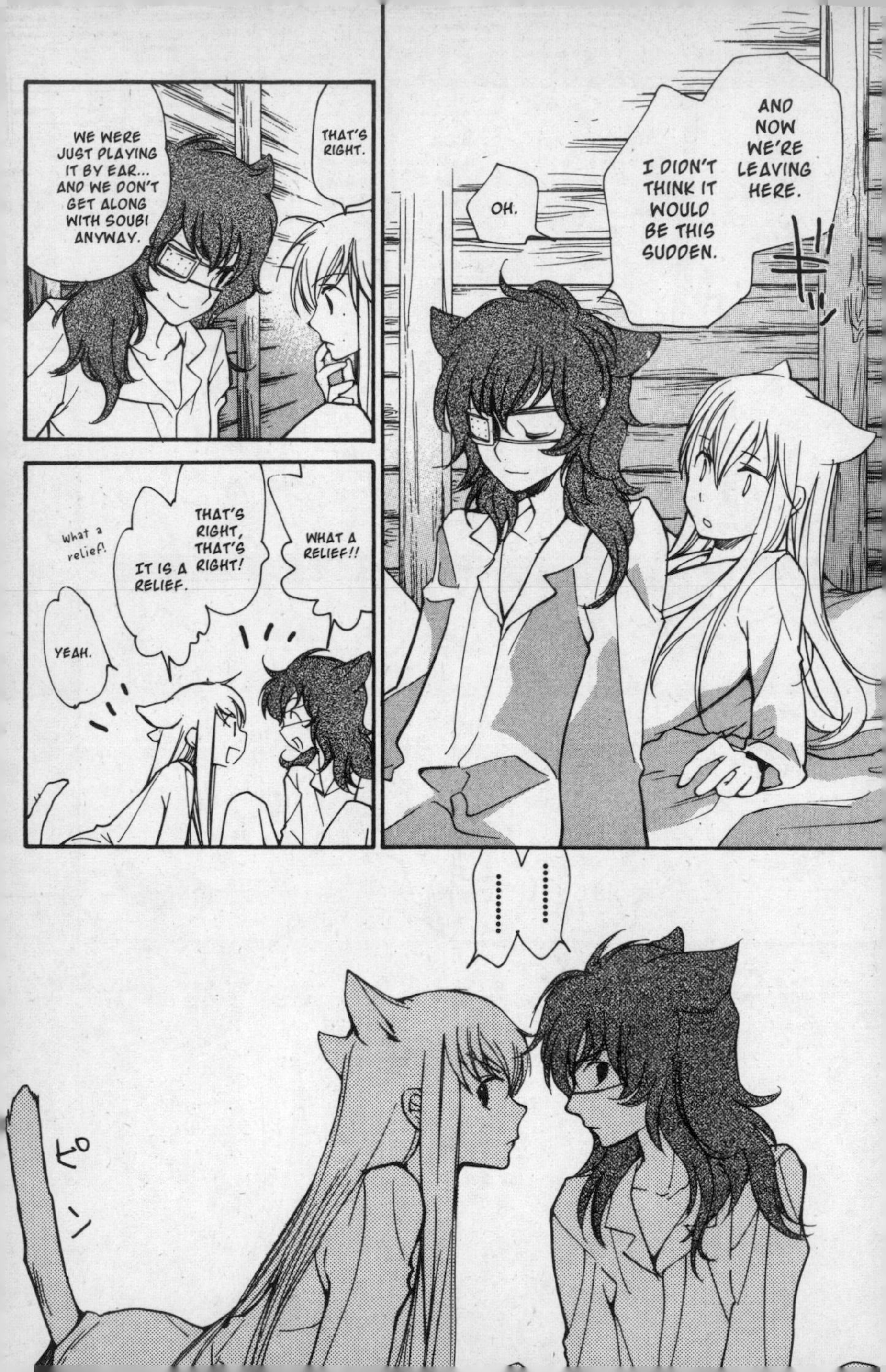
AND NOW WE'RE LEAVING HERE.
I DIDN'T THINK IT WOULD BE THIS SUDDEN.
OH.
THAT'S RIGHT.
WE WERE JUST PLAYING IT BY EAR... AND WE DON'T GET ALONG WITH SOUBI ANYWAY.
WHAT A RELIEF!!
THAT'S RIGHT, THAT'S RIGHT!
IT IS A RELIEF.
What a relief!
YEAH.
......
......

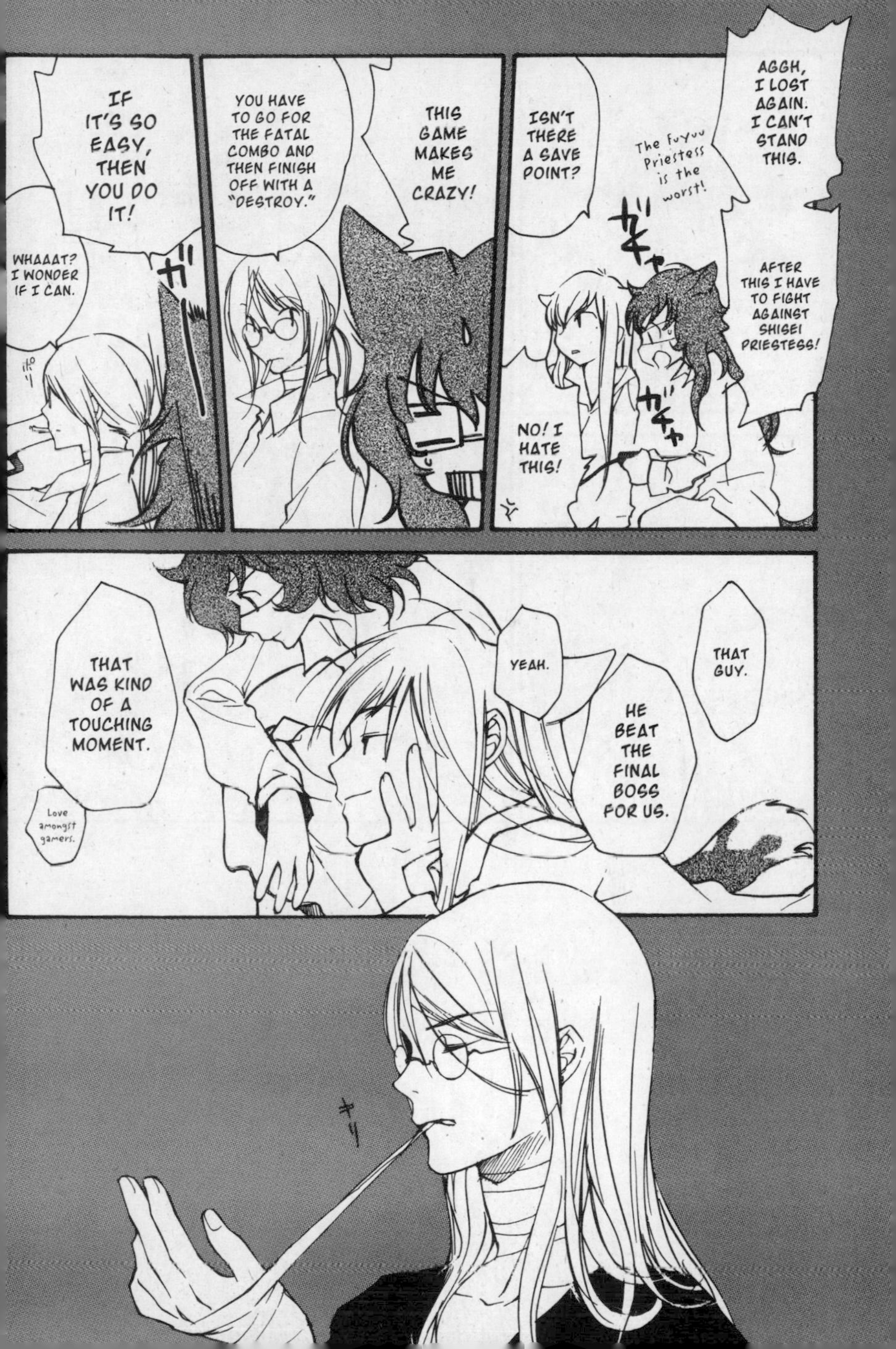
AGGH, I LOST AGAIN. I CAN'T STAND THIS.
The Fuyuu Priestess is the worst!
ISN'T THERE A SAVE POINT?
AFTER THIS I HAVE TO FIGHT AGAINST SHISEI PRIESTESS!
NO! I HATE THIS!
THIS GAME MAKES ME CRAZY!
YOU HAVE TO GO FOR THE FATAL COMBO AND THEN FINISH OFF WITH A "DESTROY."
IF IT'S SO EASY, THEN YOU DO IT!
WHAAAT? I WONDER IF I CAN.
THAT GUY.
YEAH.
HE BEAT THE FINAL BOSS FOR US.
THAT WAS KIND OF A TOUCHING MOMENT.
Love amongst gamers.

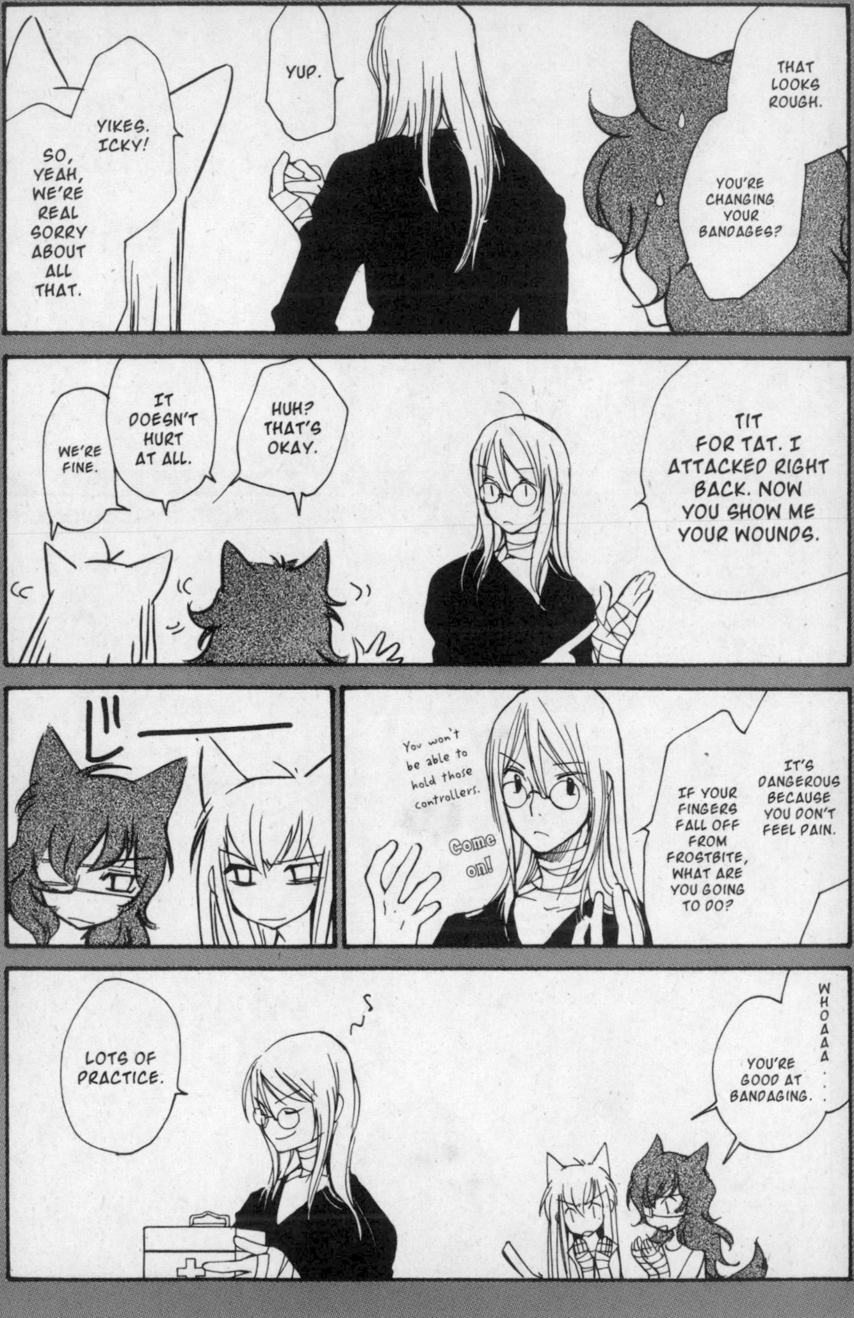

THAT LOOKS ROUGH.
YOU'RE CHANGING YOUR BANDAGES?
YUP.
YIKES. ICKY!
SO, YEAH, WE'RE REAL SORRY ABOUT ALL THAT.
TIT FOR TAT. I ATTACKED RIGHT BACK. NOW YOU SHOW ME YOUR WOUNDS.
HUH? THAT'S OKAY.
IT DOESN'T HURT AT ALL.
WE'RE FINE.
IT'S DANGEROUS BECAUSE YOU DON'T FEEL PAIN.
IF YOUR FINGERS FALL OFF FROM FROSTBITE, WHAT ARE YOU GOING TO DO?
You won't be able to hold those controllers.
Come on!
ジー
WHOAAA...
YOU'RE GOOD AT BANDAGING.
LOTS OF PRACTICE.

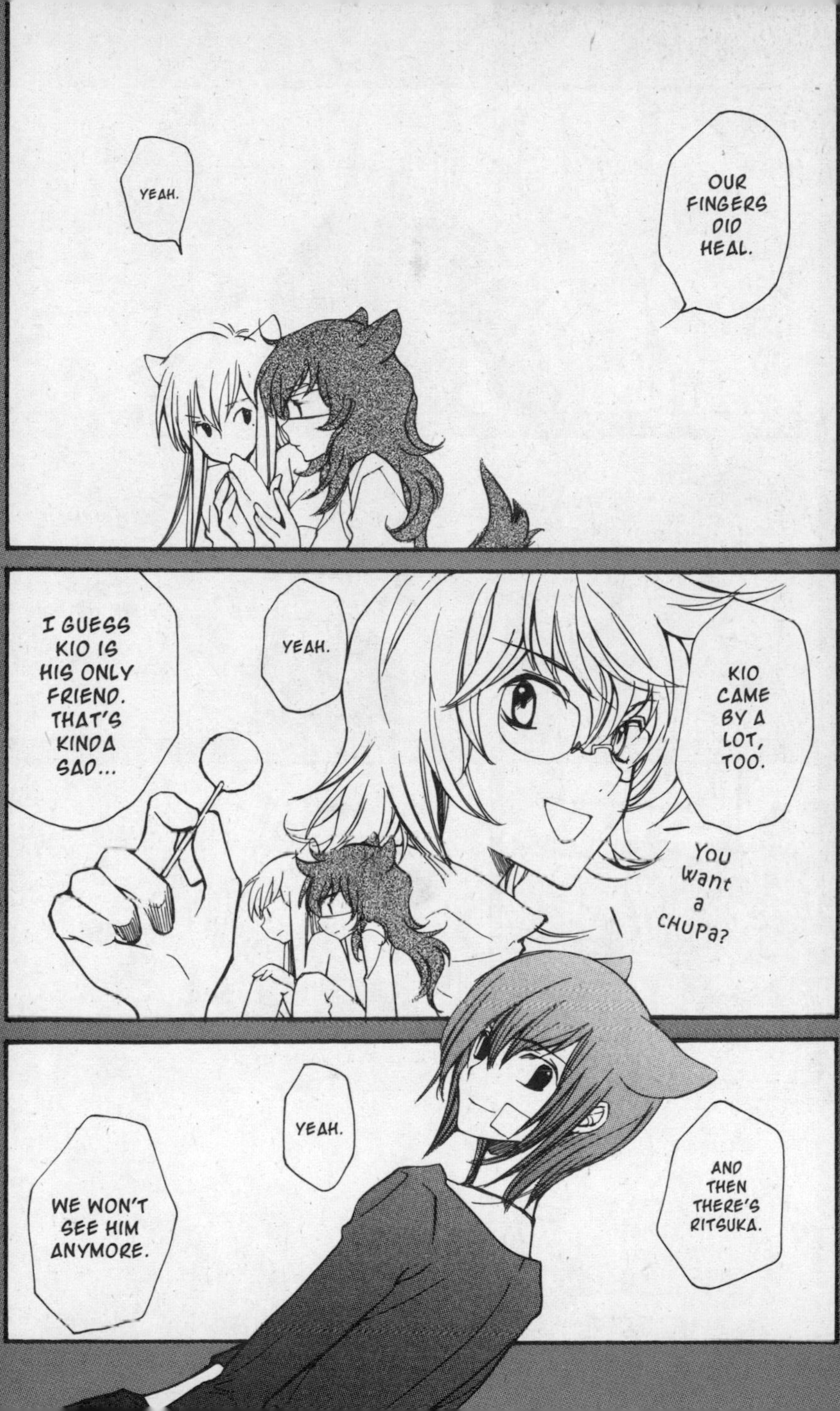
OUR FINGERS DID HEAL.
YEAH.
KIO CAME BY A LOT, TOO.
You want a CHUPa?
YEAH.
I GUESS KIO IS HIS ONLY FRIEND. THAT'S KINDA SAD...
AND THEN THERE'S RITSUKA.
YEAH.
WE WON'T SEE HIM ANYMORE.

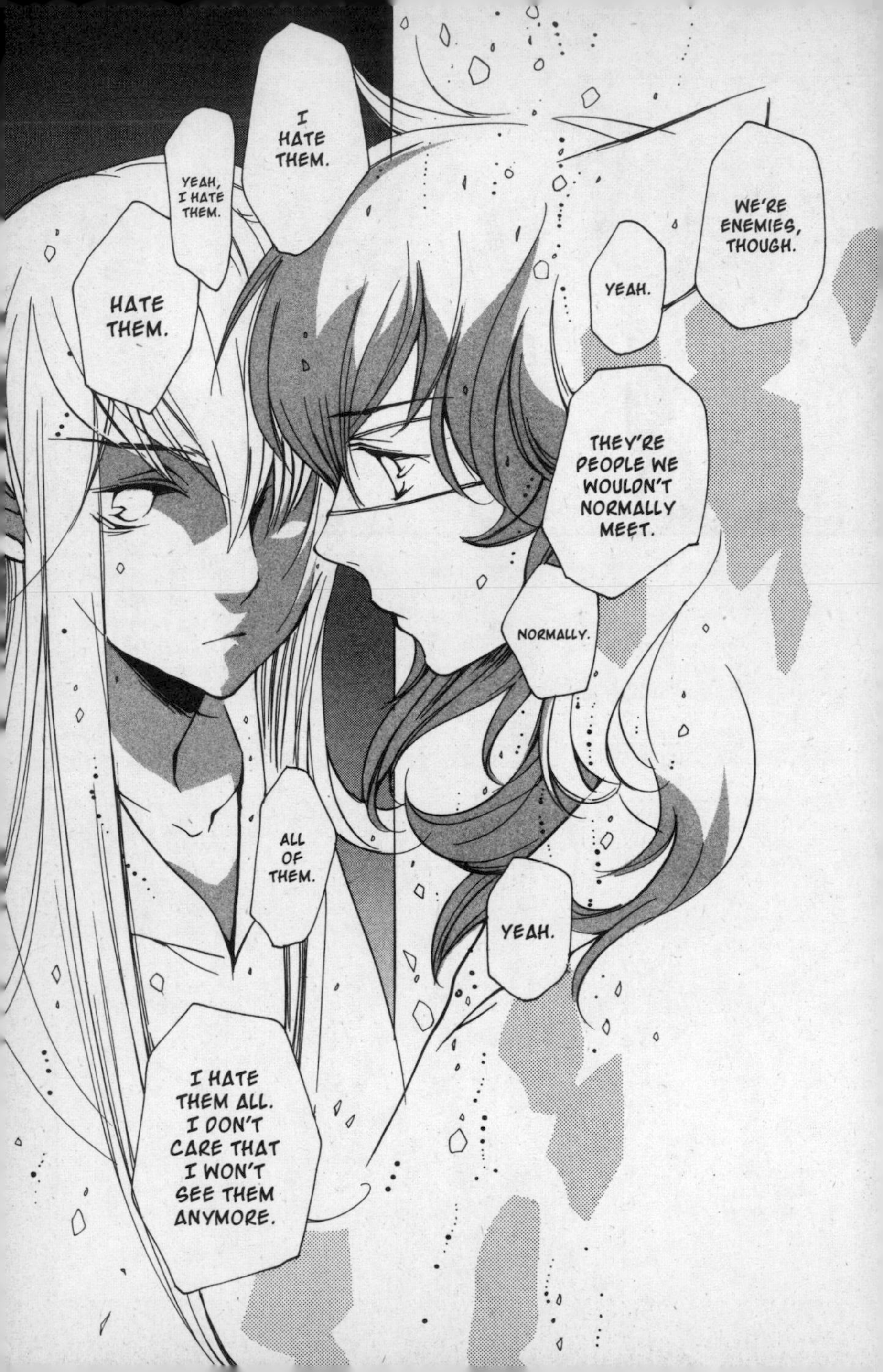
WE'RE ENEMIES, THOUGH.
YEAH.
THEY'RE PEOPLE WE WOULDN'T NORMALLY MEET.
NORMALLY.
YEAH.
I HATE THEM.
YEAH, I HATE THEM.
HATE THEM.
ALL OF THEM.
I HATE THEM ALL. I DON'T CARE THAT I WON'T SEE THEM ANYMORE.

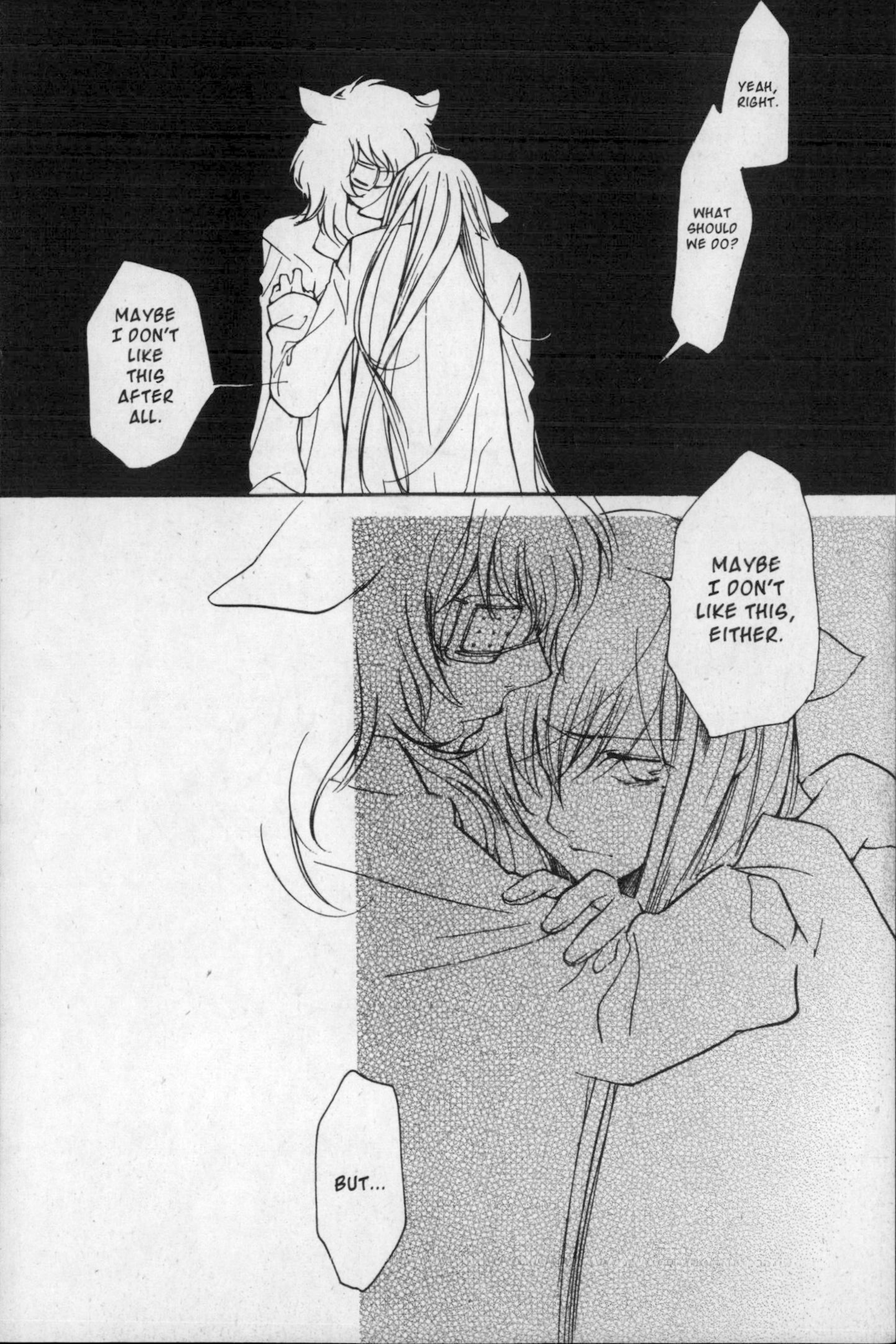
YEAH, RIGHT.
WHAT SHOULD WE DO?
MAYBE I DON'T LIKE THIS AFTER ALL.
MAYBE I DON'T LIKE THIS, EITHER.
BUT...

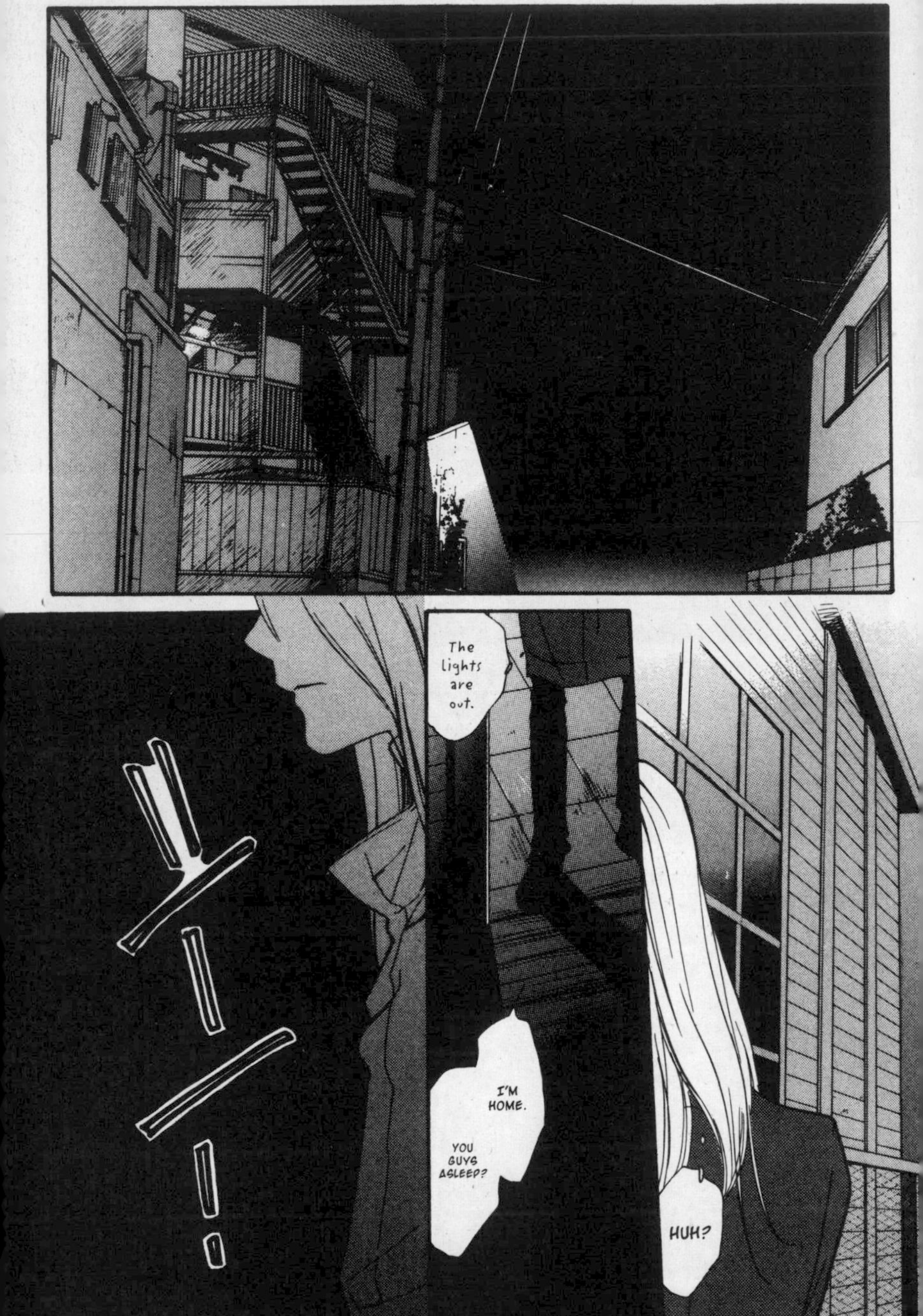
The lights are out.
I'M HOME.
YOU GUYS ASLEEP?
HUH?

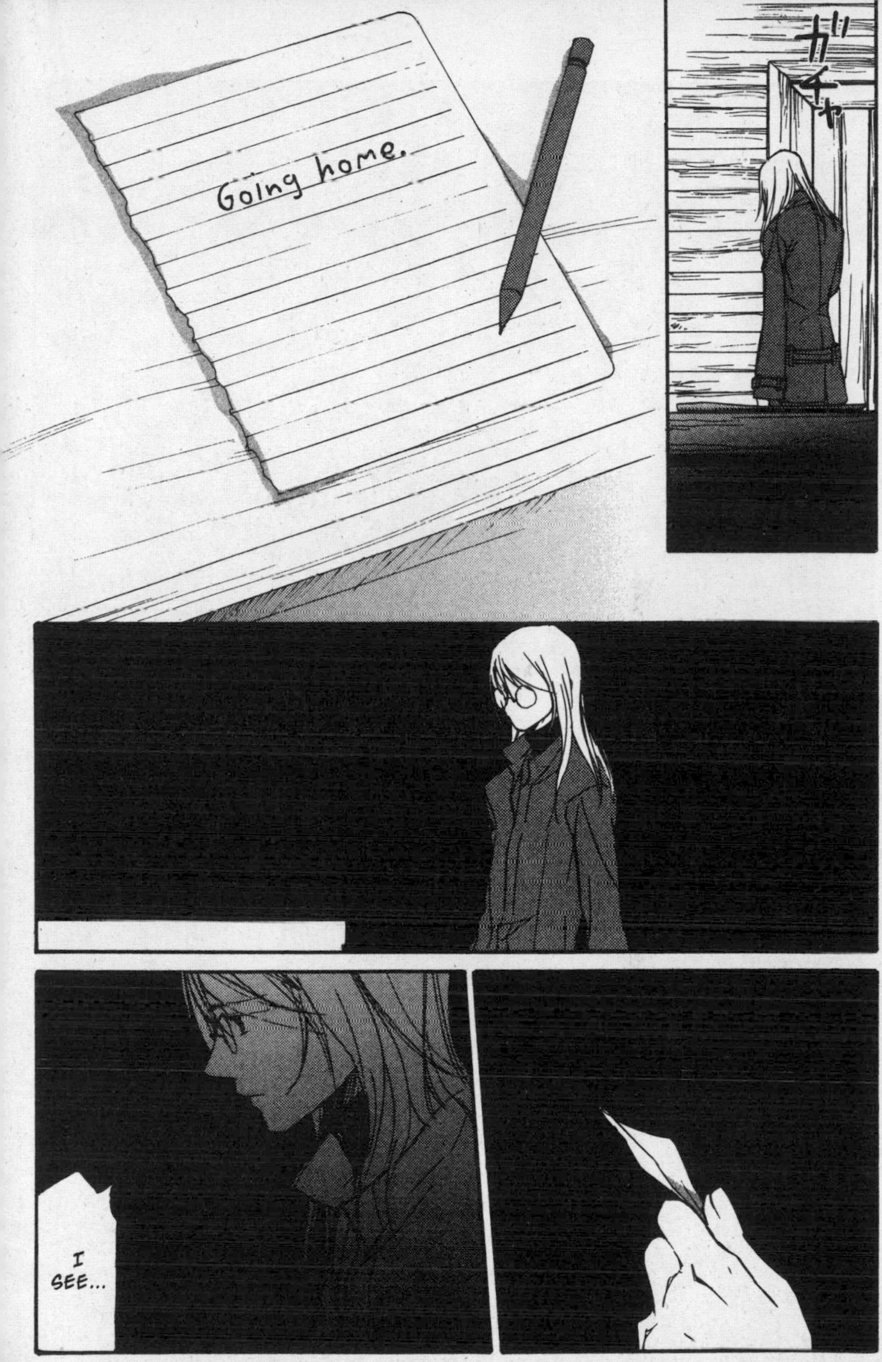
ガチャ
Going home.
I SEE...

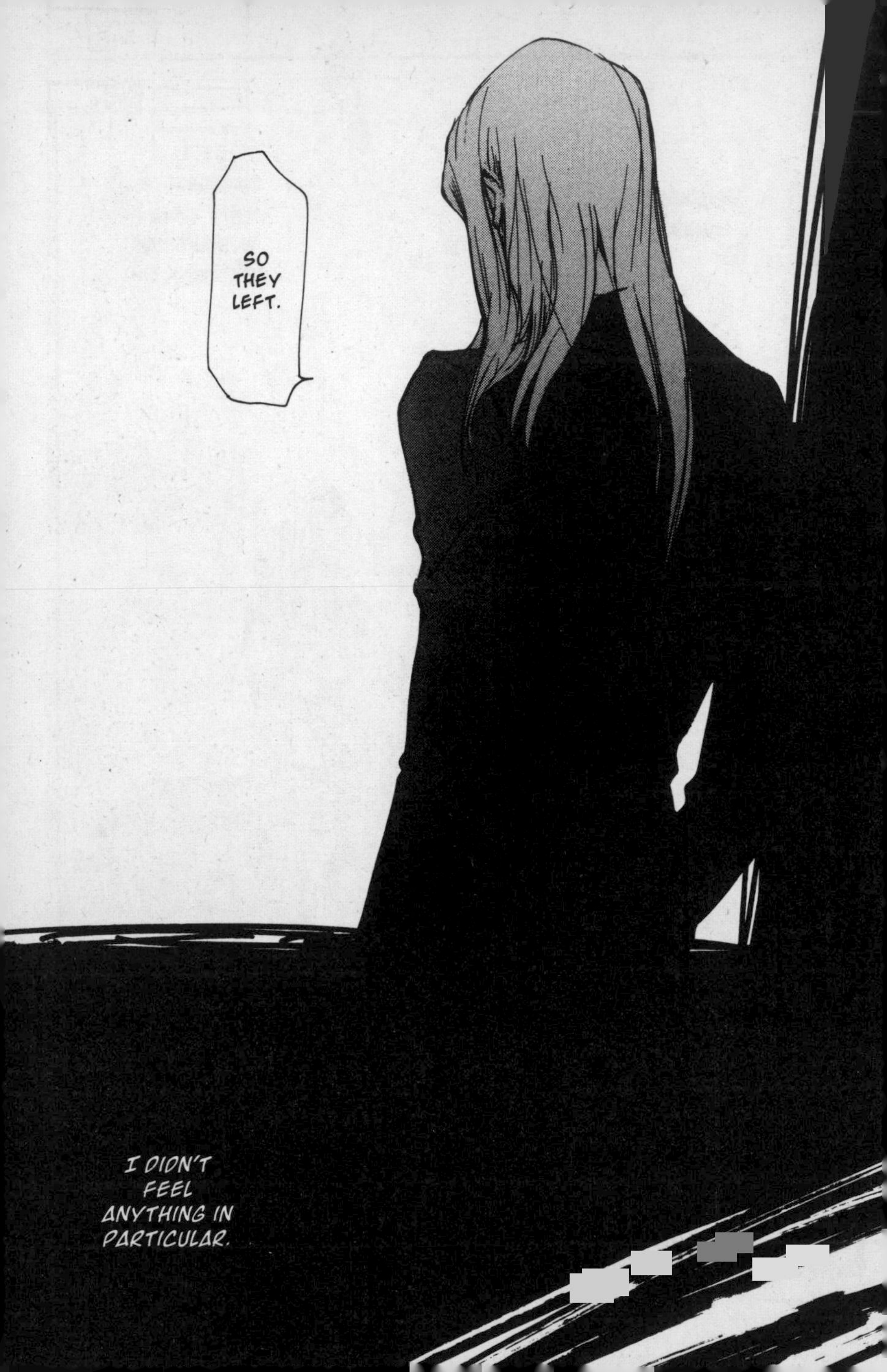
SO THEY LEFT.
I DIDN'T FEEL ANYTHING IN PARTICULAR.

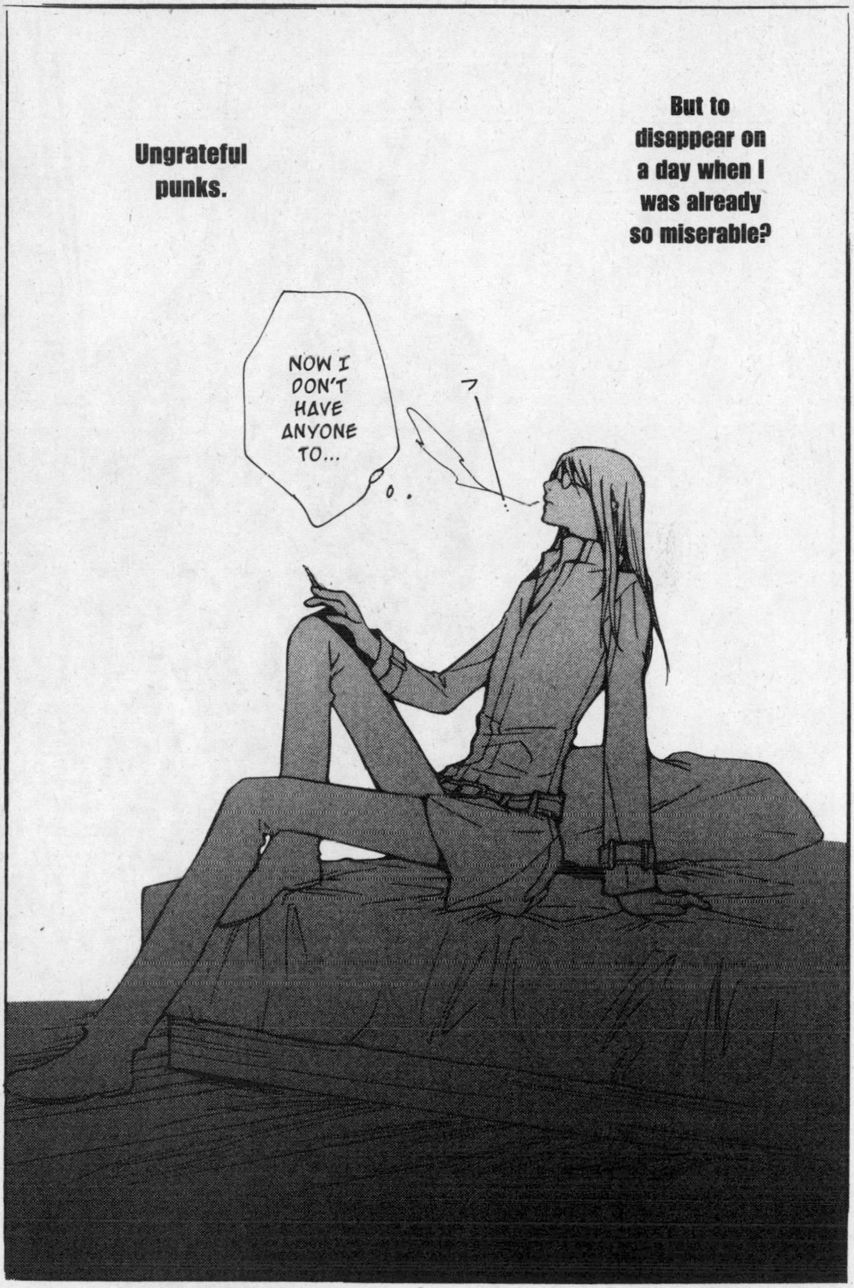
But to disappear on a day when I was already so miserable?
Ungrateful punks.
NOW I DON'T HAVE ANYONE TO...

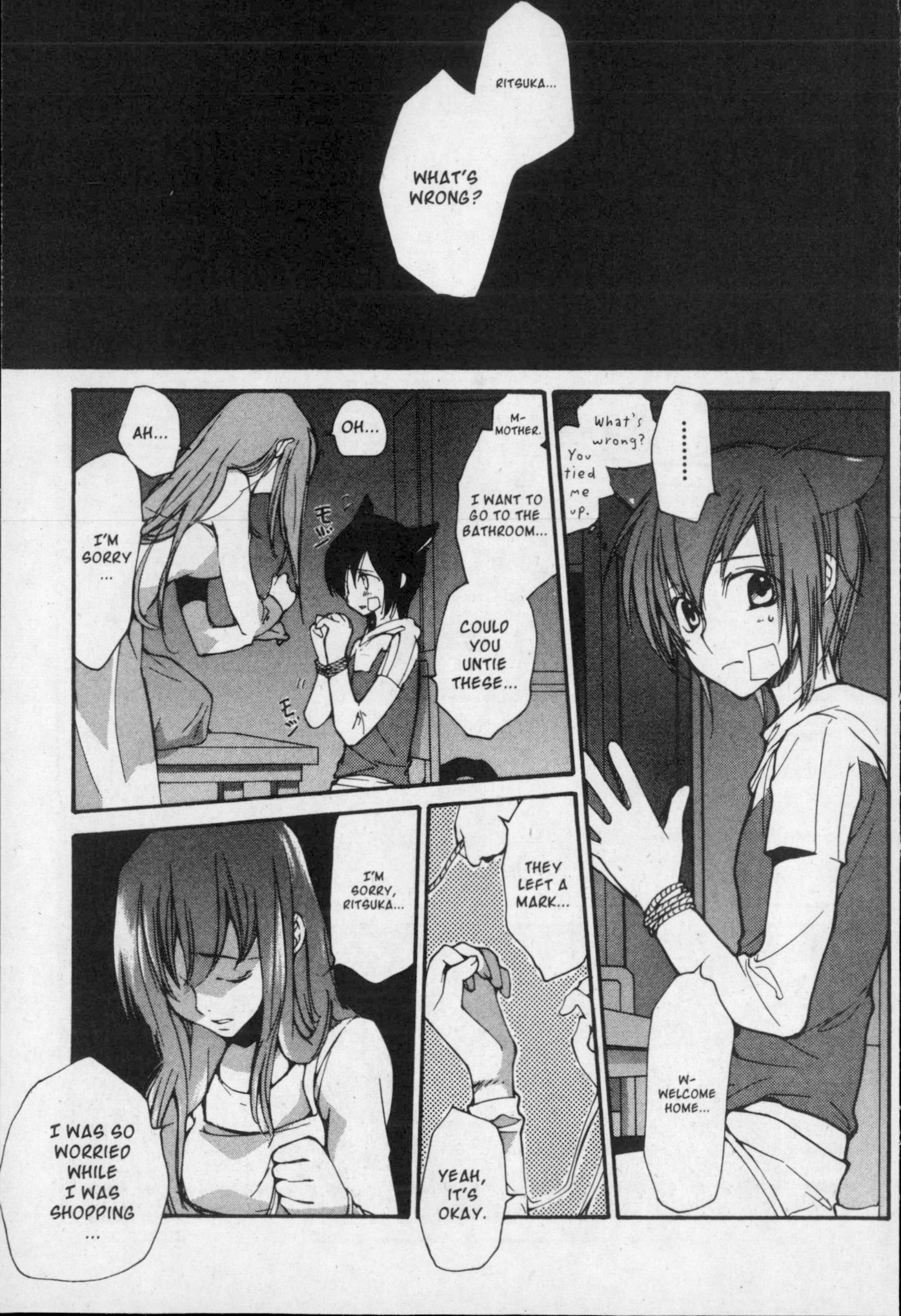
RITSUKA...
WHAT'S WRONG?
......
What's wrong? You tied me up.
W-WELCOME HOME...
M-MOTHER.
I WANT TO GO TO THE BATHROOM...
COULD YOU UNTIE THESE...
OH...
AH...
I'M SORRY ...
THEY LEFT A MARK...
YEAH, IT'S OKAY.
I'M SORRY, RITSUKA...
I WAS SO WORRIED WHILE I WAS SHOPPING ...

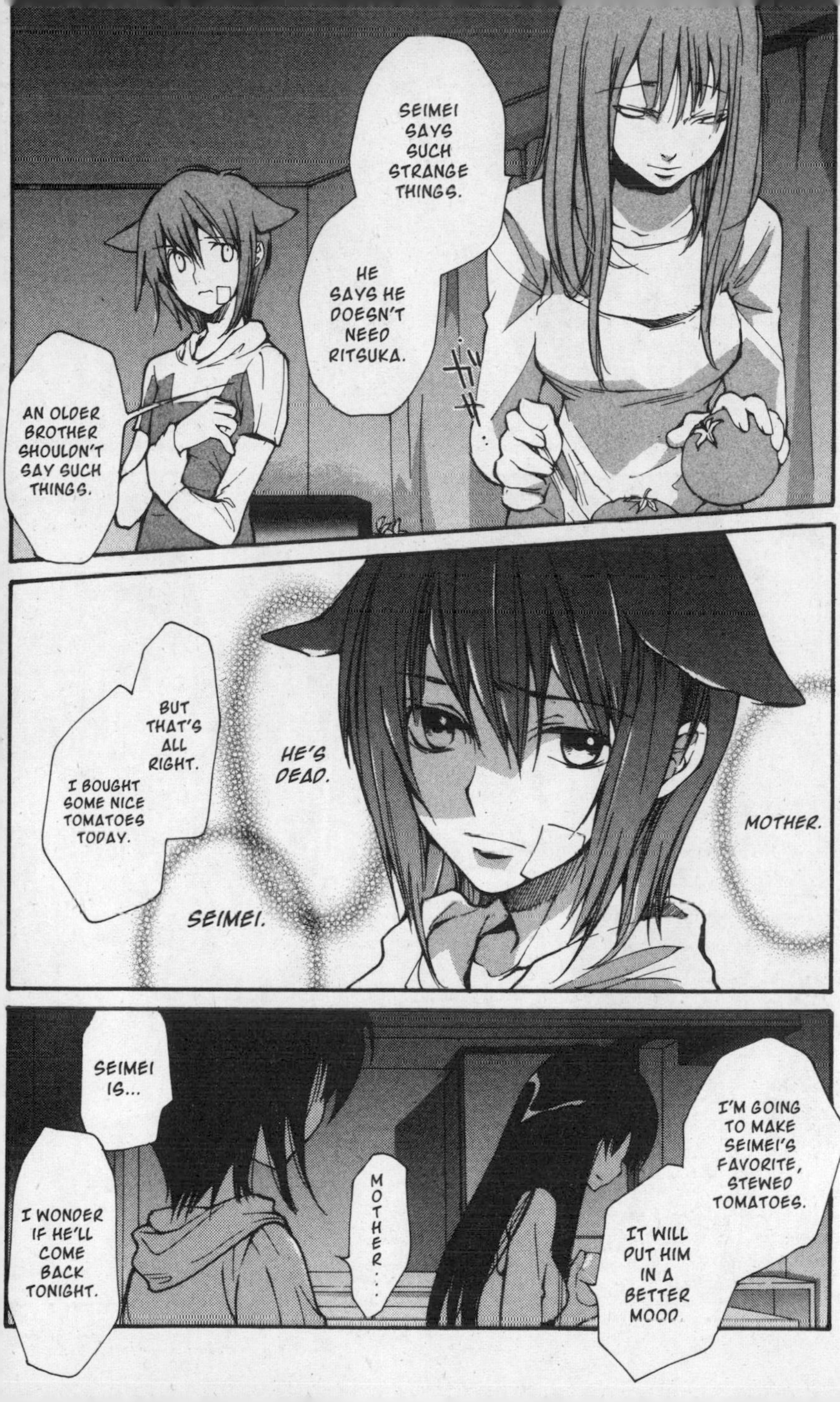
SEIMEI SAYS SUCH STRANGE THINGS.
HE SAYS HE DOESN'T NEED RITSUKA.
AN OLDER BROTHER SHOULDN'T SAY SUCH THINGS.
MOTHER.
HE'S DEAD.
BUT THAT'S ALL RIGHT.
I BOUGHT SOME NICE TOMATOES TODAY.
SEIMEI.
I'M GOING TO MAKE SEIMEI'S FAVORITE, STEWED TOMATOES.
IT WILL PUT HIM IN A BETTER MOOD.
MOTHER...
SEIMEI IS...
I WONDER IF HE'LL COME BACK TONIGHT.

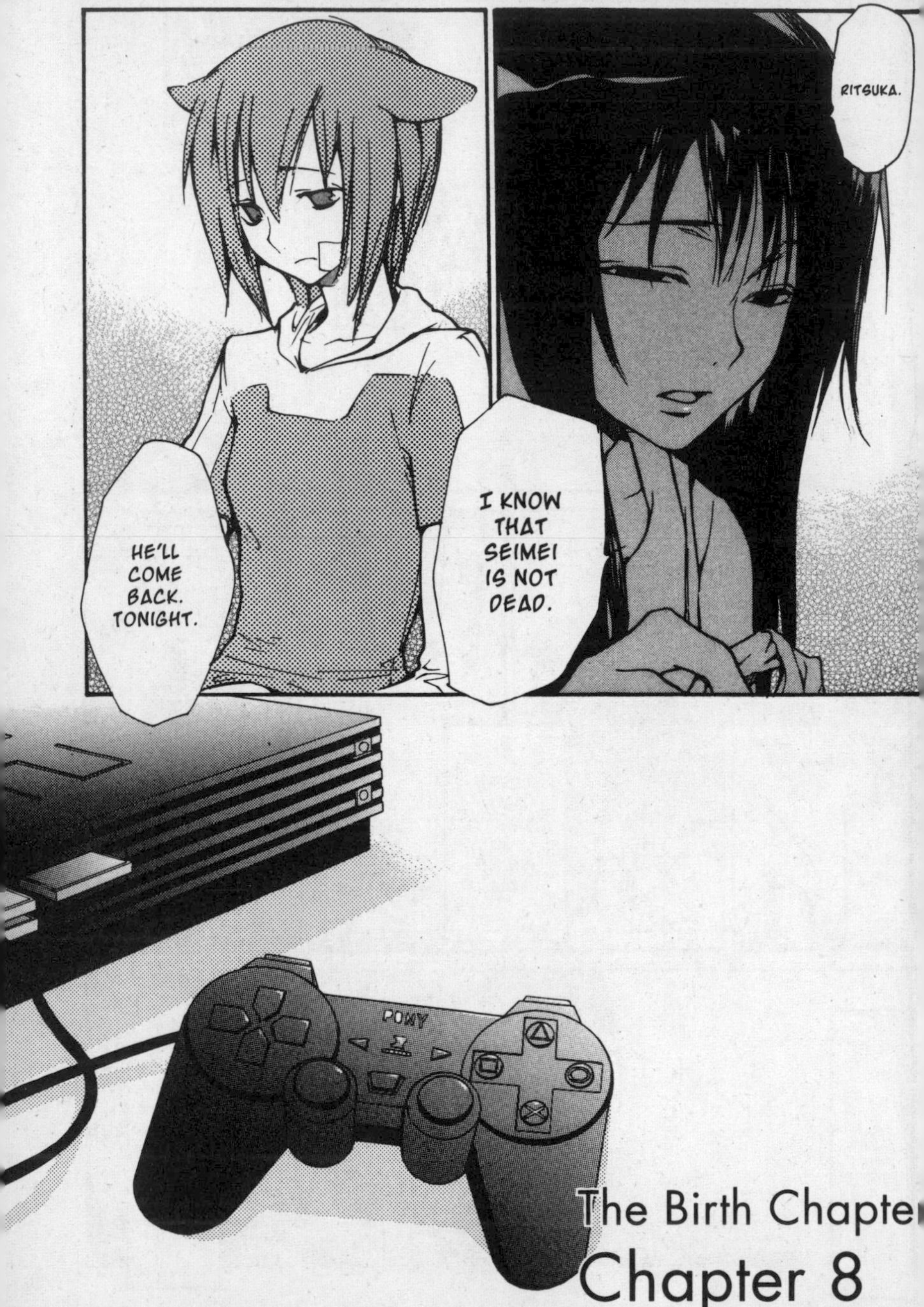
RITSUKA.
I KNOW THAT SEIMEI IS NOT DEAD.
HE'LL COME BACK. TONIGHT.
PONY

The Birth Chapte
Chapter 8

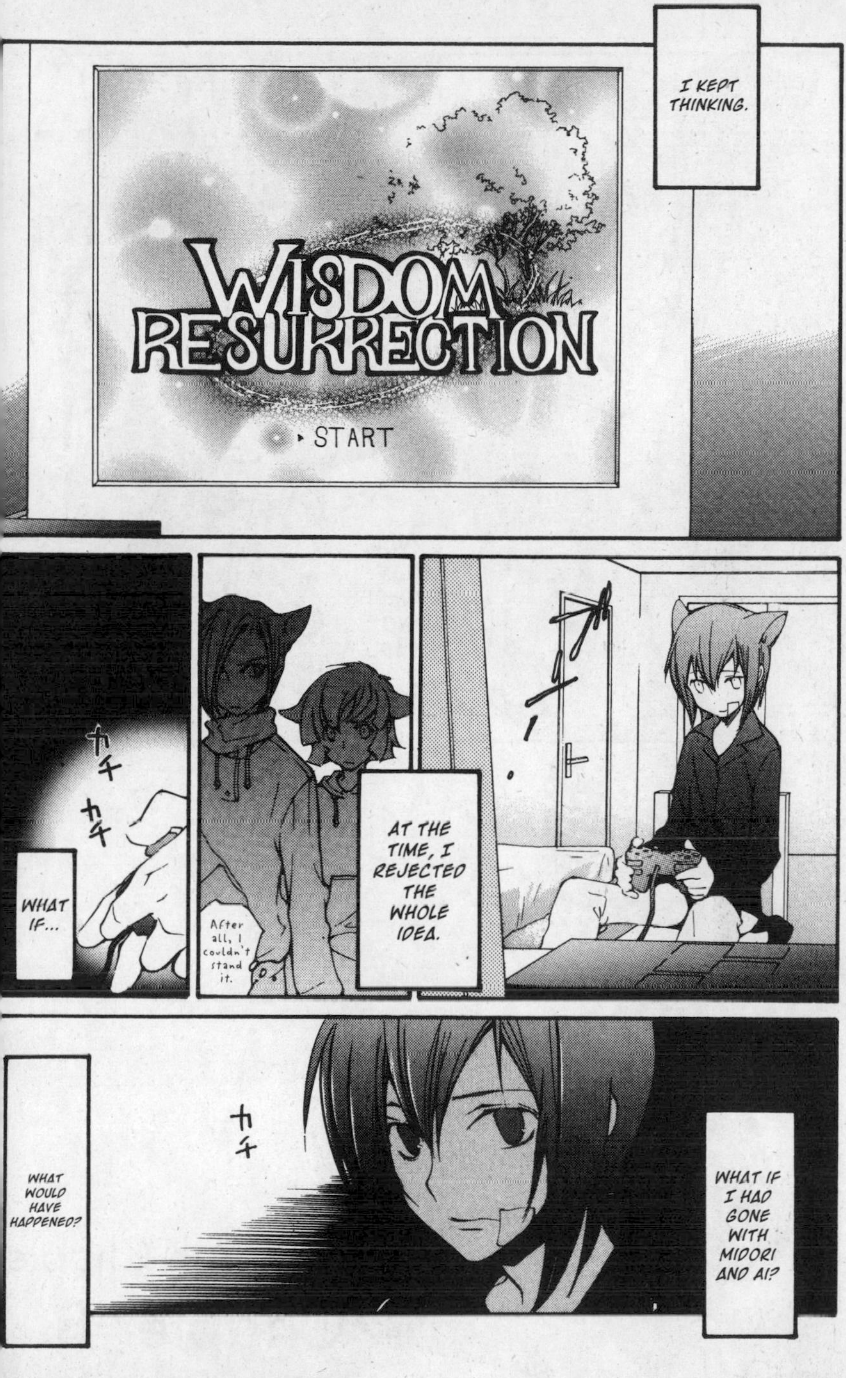
I KEPT THINKING.
WISDOM RESURRECTION
START
AT THE TIME, I REJECTED THE WHOLE IDEA.
After all, I couldn't stand it.
カチ
カチ
WHAT IF...
WHAT IF I HAD GONE WITH MIDORI AND AI?
カチ
WHAT WOULD HAVE HAPPENED?

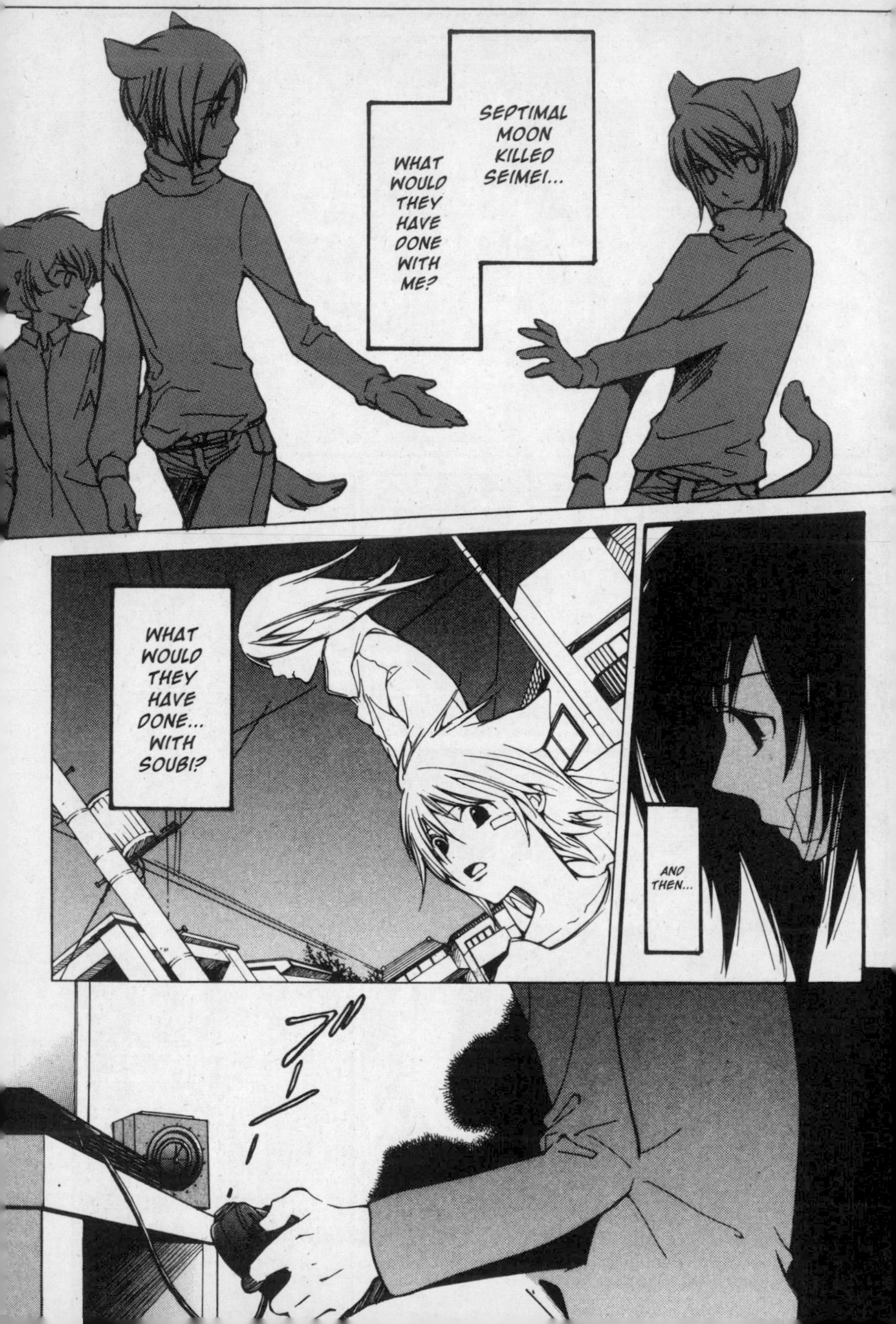
SEPTIMAL MOON KILLED SEIMEI...
WHAT WOULD THEY HAVE DONE WITH ME?
AND THEN...
WHAT WOULD THEY HAVE DONE... WITH SOUBI?

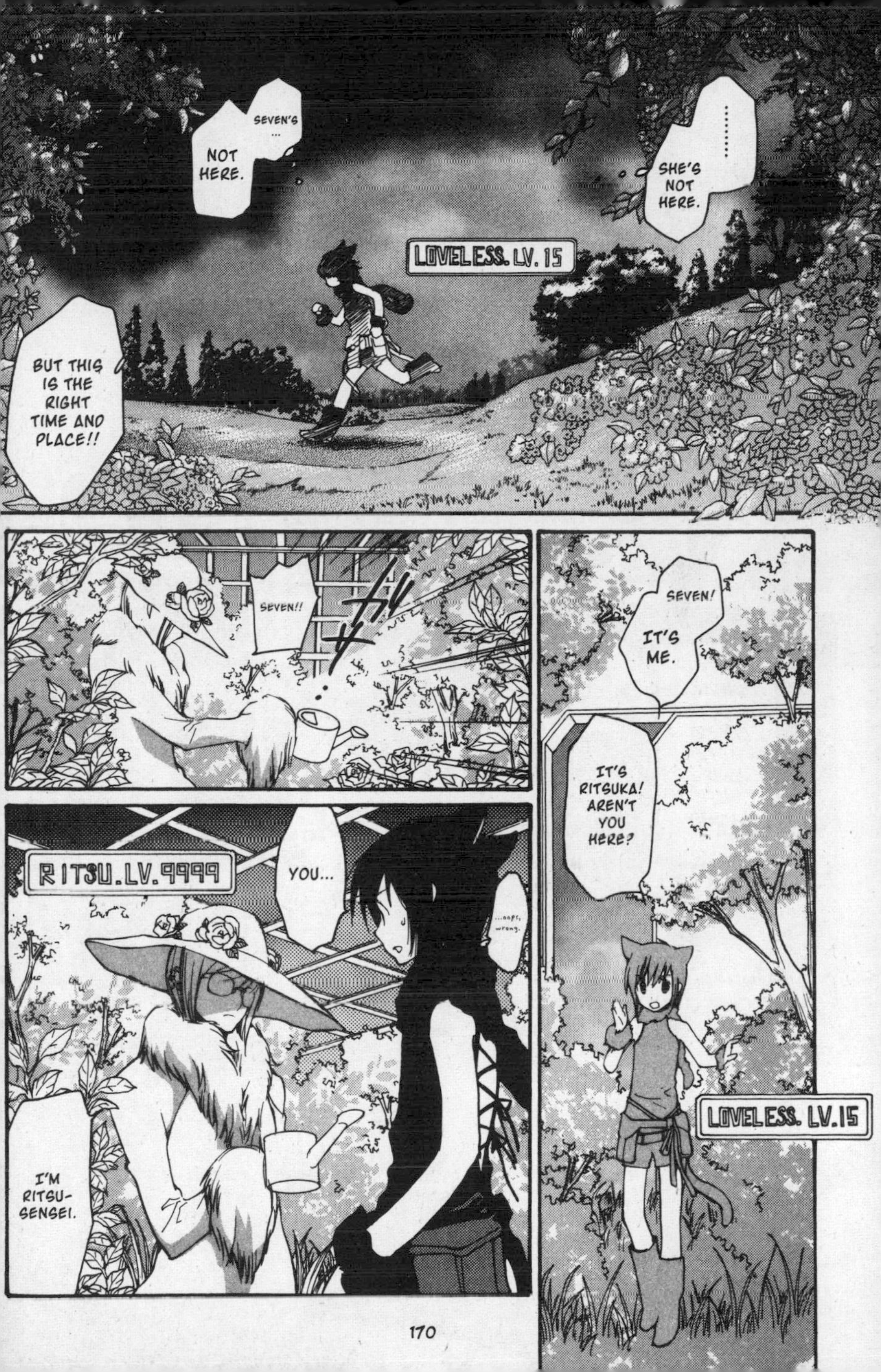

......
SHE'S NOT HERE.
SEVEN'S ...
NOT HERE.
LOVELESS. LV. 15
BUT THIS IS THE RIGHT TIME AND PLACE!!
SEVEN!
IT'S ME.
IT'S RITSUKA! AREN'T YOU HERE?
LOVELESS. LV.15
SEVEN!!
YOU...
...oops, wrong.
RITSU.LV.9999
I'M RITSU-SENSEI.

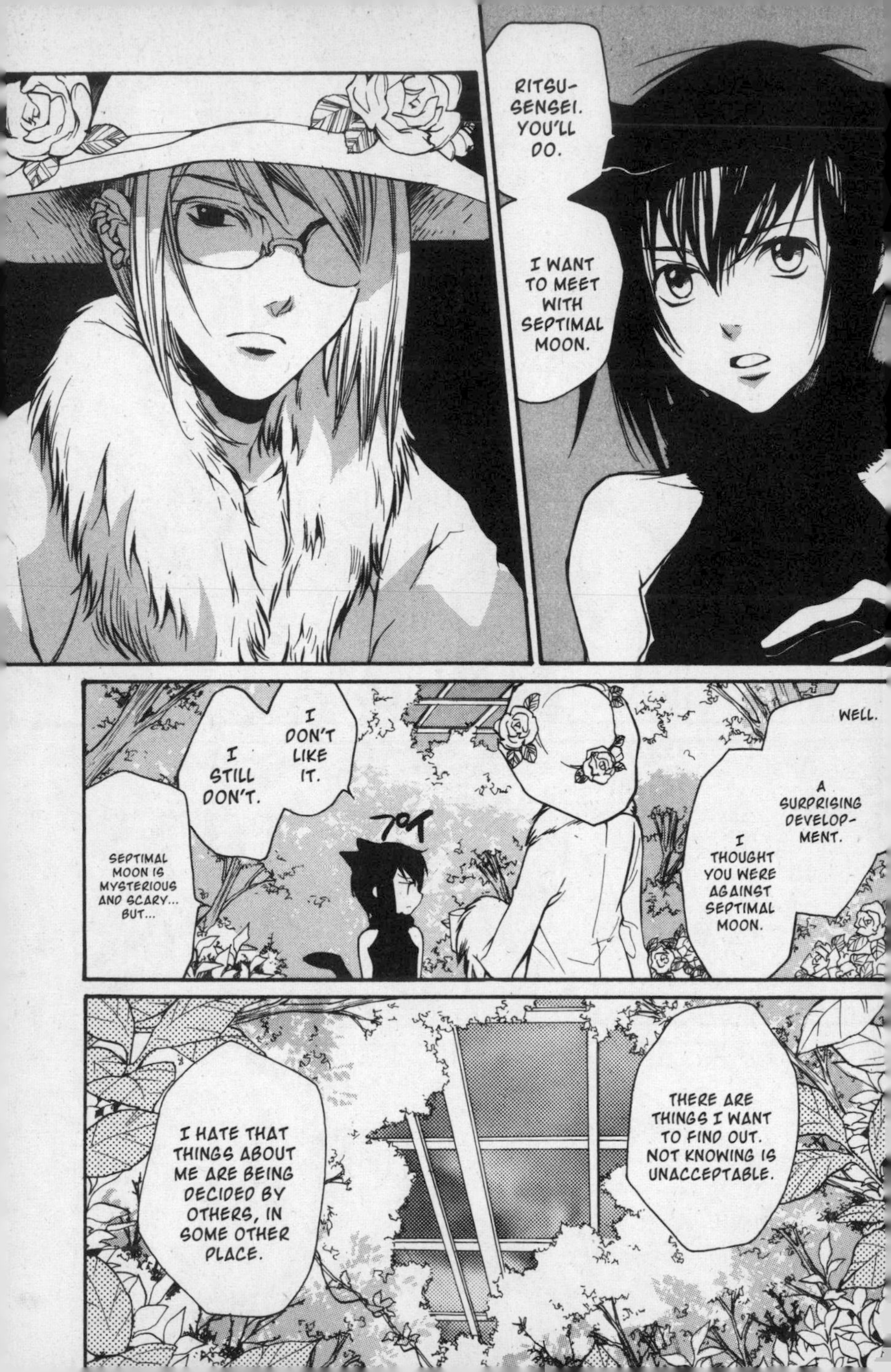
RITSU-SENSEI. YOU'LL DO.
I WANT TO MEET WITH SEPTIMAL MOON.
WELL.
A SURPRISING DEVELOPMENT.
I THOUGHT YOU WERE AGAINST SEPTIMAL MOON.
I DON'T LIKE IT.
I STILL DON'T.
SEPTIMAL MOON IS MYSTERIOUS AND SCARY... BUT...
THERE ARE THINGS I WANT TO FIND OUT. NOT KNOWING IS UNACCEPTABLE.
I HATE THAT THINGS ABOUT ME ARE BEING DECIDED BY OTHERS, IN SOME OTHER PLACE.

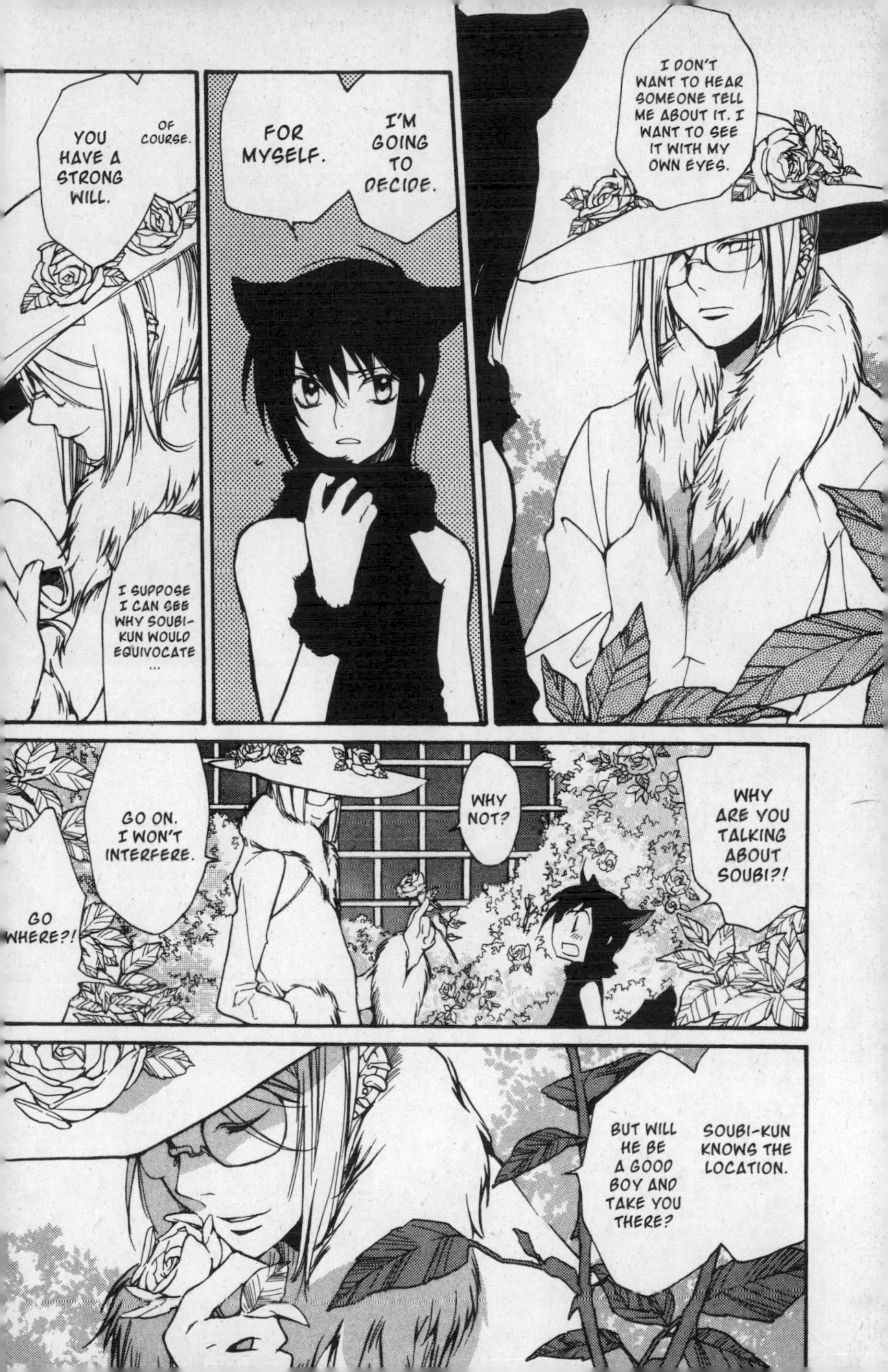

I DON'T WANT TO HEAR SOMEONE TELL ME ABOUT IT. I WANT TO SEE IT WITH MY OWN EYES.
I'M GOING TO DECIDE.
FOR MYSELF.
OF COURSE.
YOU HAVE A STRONG WILL.
I SUPPOSE I CAN SEE WHY SOUBI-KUN WOULD EQUIVOCATE ...
WHY ARE YOU TALKING ABOUT SOUBI?!
WHY NOT?
GO ON. I WON'T INTERFERE.
GO WHERE?!
SOUBI-KUN KNOWS THE LOCATION.
BUT WILL HE BE A GOOD BOY AND TAKE YOU THERE?

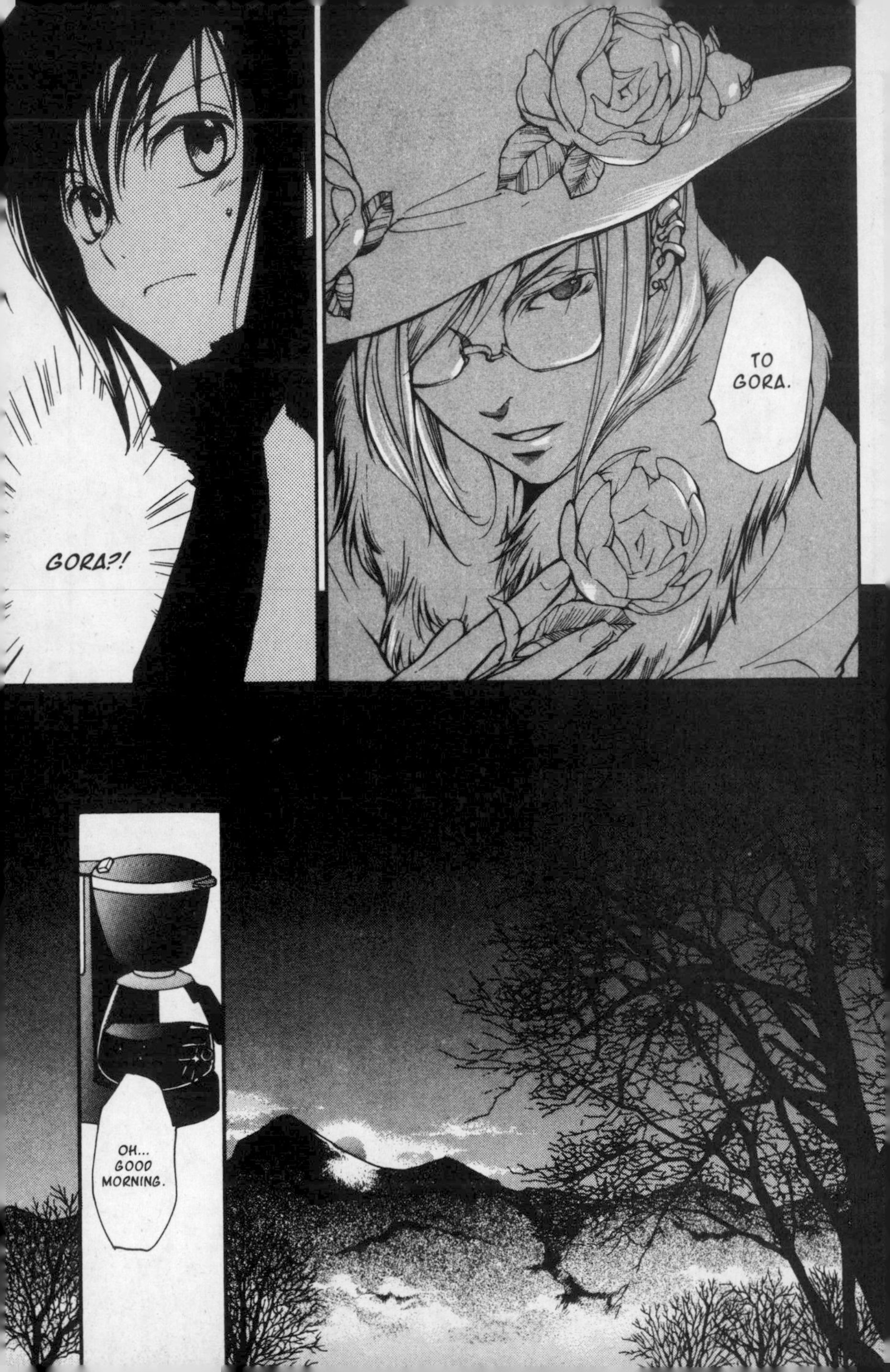
TO GORA.
GORA?!
OH... GOOD MORNING.

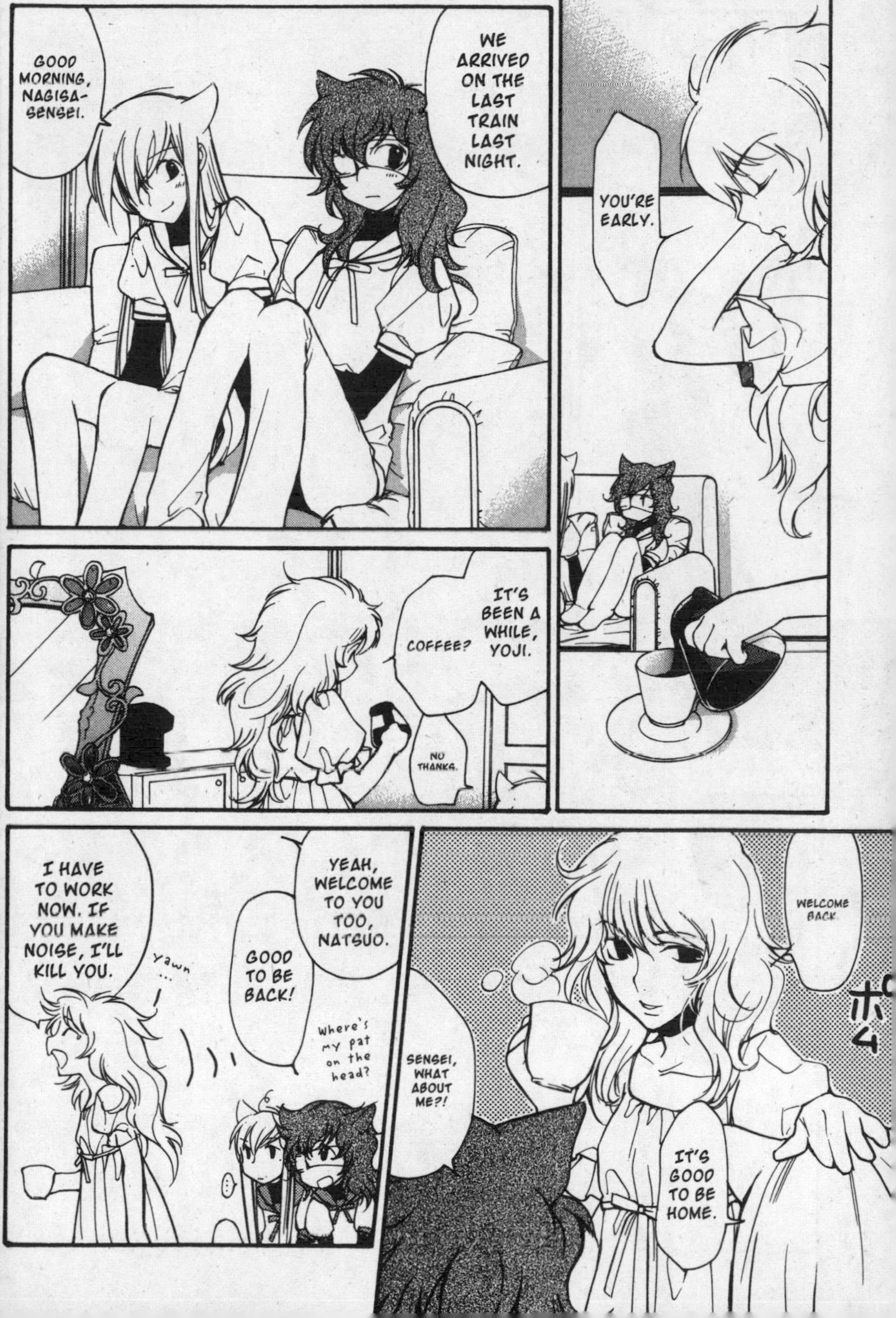
YOU'RE EARLY.
WE ARRIVED ON THE LAST TRAIN LAST NIGHT.
GOOD MORNING, NAGISA-SENSEI.
IT'S BEEN A WHILE, YOJI.
COFFEE?
NO THANKS.
WELCOME BACK.
ポム
SENSEI, WHAT ABOUT ME?!
IT'S GOOD TO BE HOME.
YEAH, WELCOME TO YOU TOO, NATSUO.
GOOD TO BE BACK!
Where's my pat on the head?
I HAVE TO WORK NOW. IF YOU MAKE NOISE, I'LL KILL YOU.
Yawn...

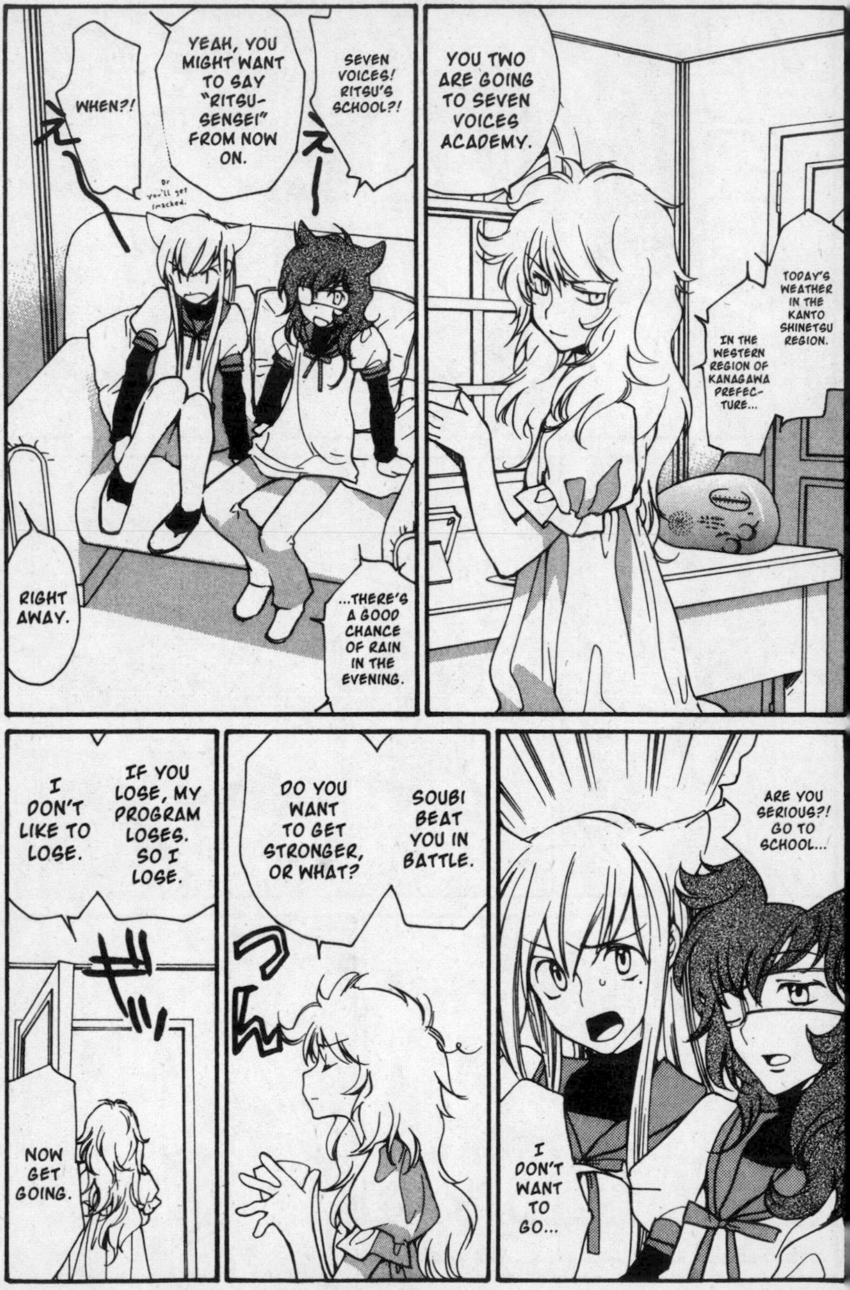
YOU TWO ARE GOING TO SEVEN VOICES ACADEMY.
TODAY'S WEATHER IN THE KANTO SHINETSU REGION.
IN THE WESTERN REGION OF KANAGAWA PREFECTURE...
SEVEN VOICES! RITSU'S SCHOOL?!
YEAH, YOU MIGHT WANT TO SAY "RITSU-SENSEI" FROM NOW ON.
WHEN?!
Or you'll get smacked.
RIGHT AWAY.
...THERE'S A GOOD CHANCE OF RAIN IN THE EVENING.
ARE YOU SERIOUS?! GO TO SCHOOL...
I DON'T WANT TO GO...
SOUBI BEAT YOU IN BATTLE.
DO YOU WANT TO GET STRONGER, OR WHAT?
IF YOU LOSE, MY PROGRAM LOSES. SO I LOSE.
I DON'T LIKE TO LOSE.
NOW GET GOING.

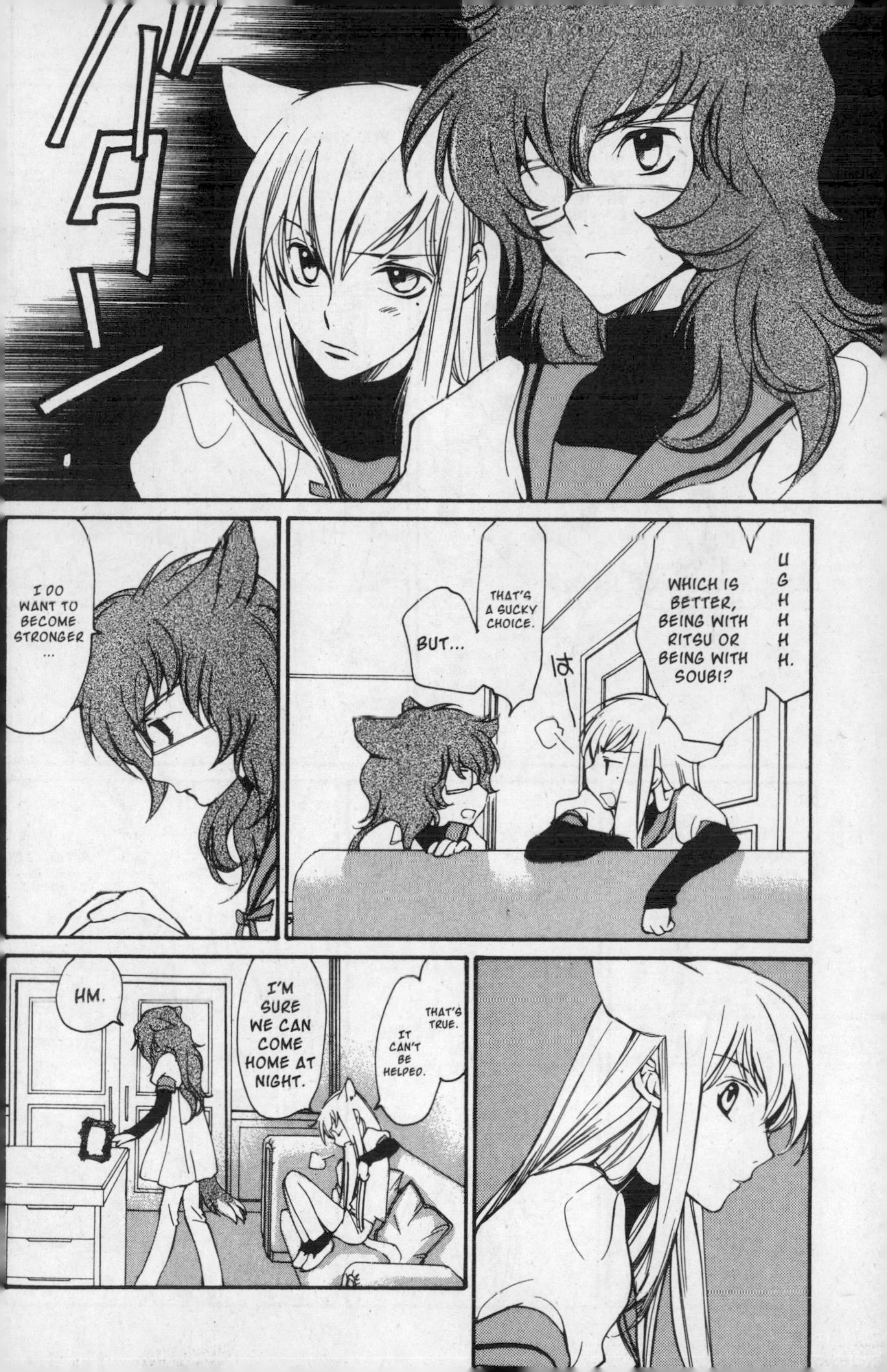
UGHHHHH.
WHICH IS BETTER, BEING WITH RITSU OR BEING WITH SOUBI?
は
THAT'S A SUCKY CHOICE.
BUT...
I DO WANT TO BECOME STRONGER ...
THAT'S TRUE.
IT CAN'T BE HELPED.
I'M SURE WE CAN COME HOME AT NIGHT.
HM.

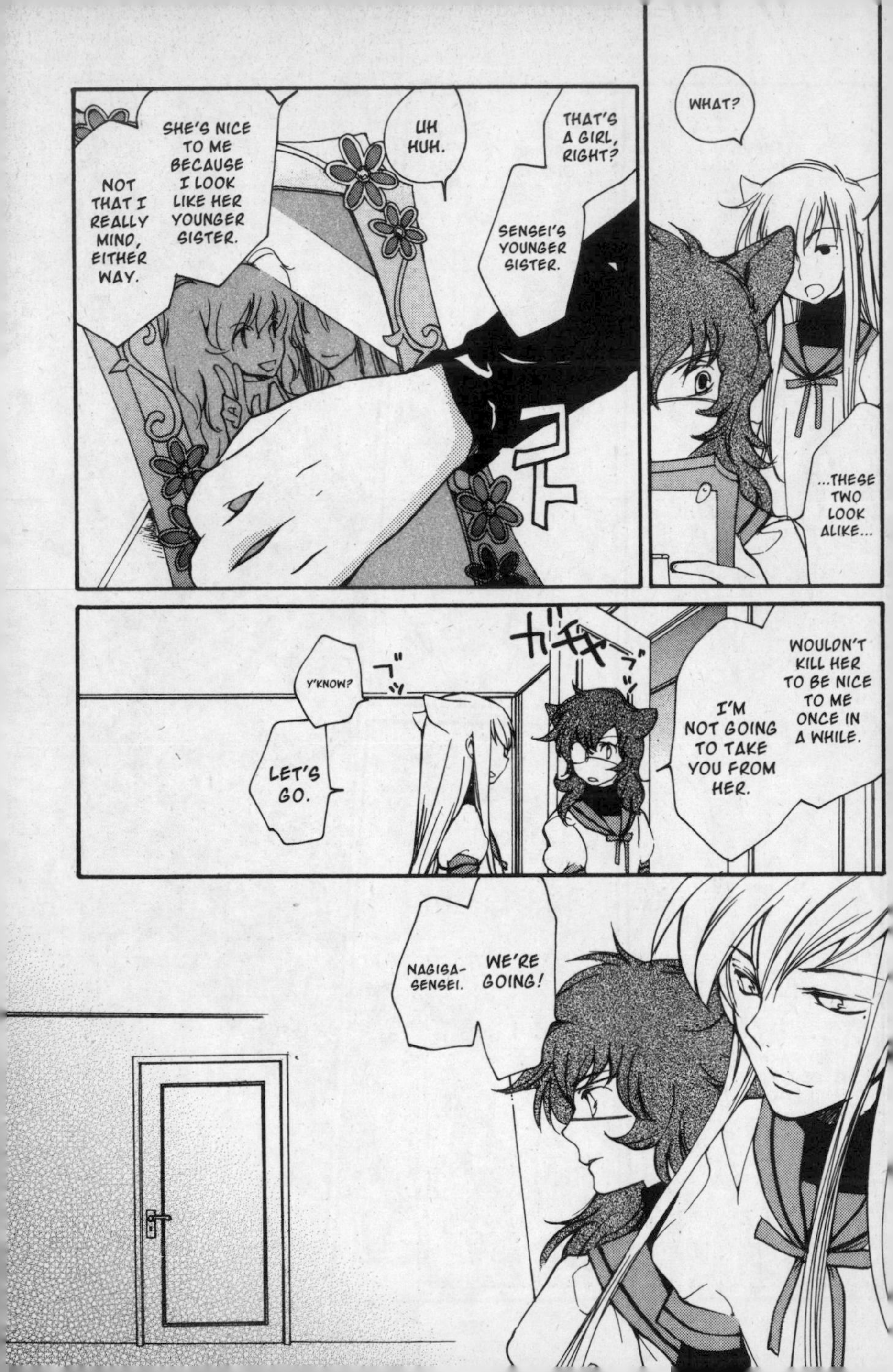

WHAT?
...THESE TWO LOOK ALIKE...
THAT'S A GIRL, RIGHT?
SENSEI'S YOUNGER SISTER.
UH HUH.
SHE'S NICE TO ME BECAUSE I LOOK LIKE HER YOUNGER SISTER.
NOT THAT I REALLY MIND, EITHER WAY.
WOULDN'T KILL HER TO BE NICE TO ME ONCE IN A WHILE.
I'M NOT GOING TO TAKE YOU FROM HER.
Y'KNOW?
LET'S GO.
WE'RE GOING!
NAGISA-SENSEI.

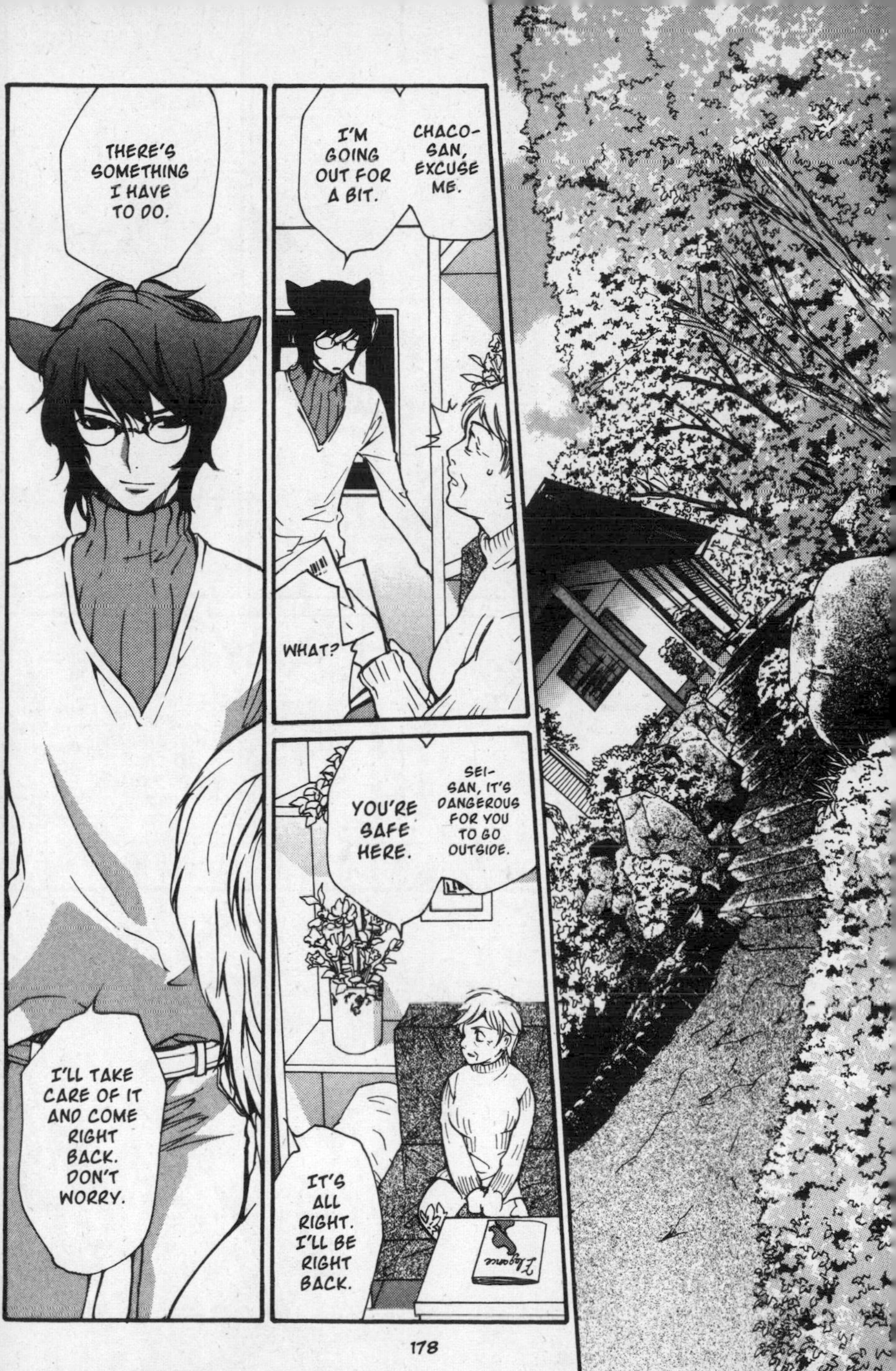
CHACO-SAN, EXCUSE ME.
I'M GOING OUT FOR A BIT.
WHAT?
SEI-SAN, IT'S DANGEROUS FOR YOU TO GO OUTSIDE.
YOU'RE SAFE HERE.
IT'S ALL RIGHT. I'LL BE RIGHT BACK.
THERE'S SOMETHING I HAVE TO DO.
I'LL TAKE CARE OF IT AND COME RIGHT BACK. DON'T WORRY.

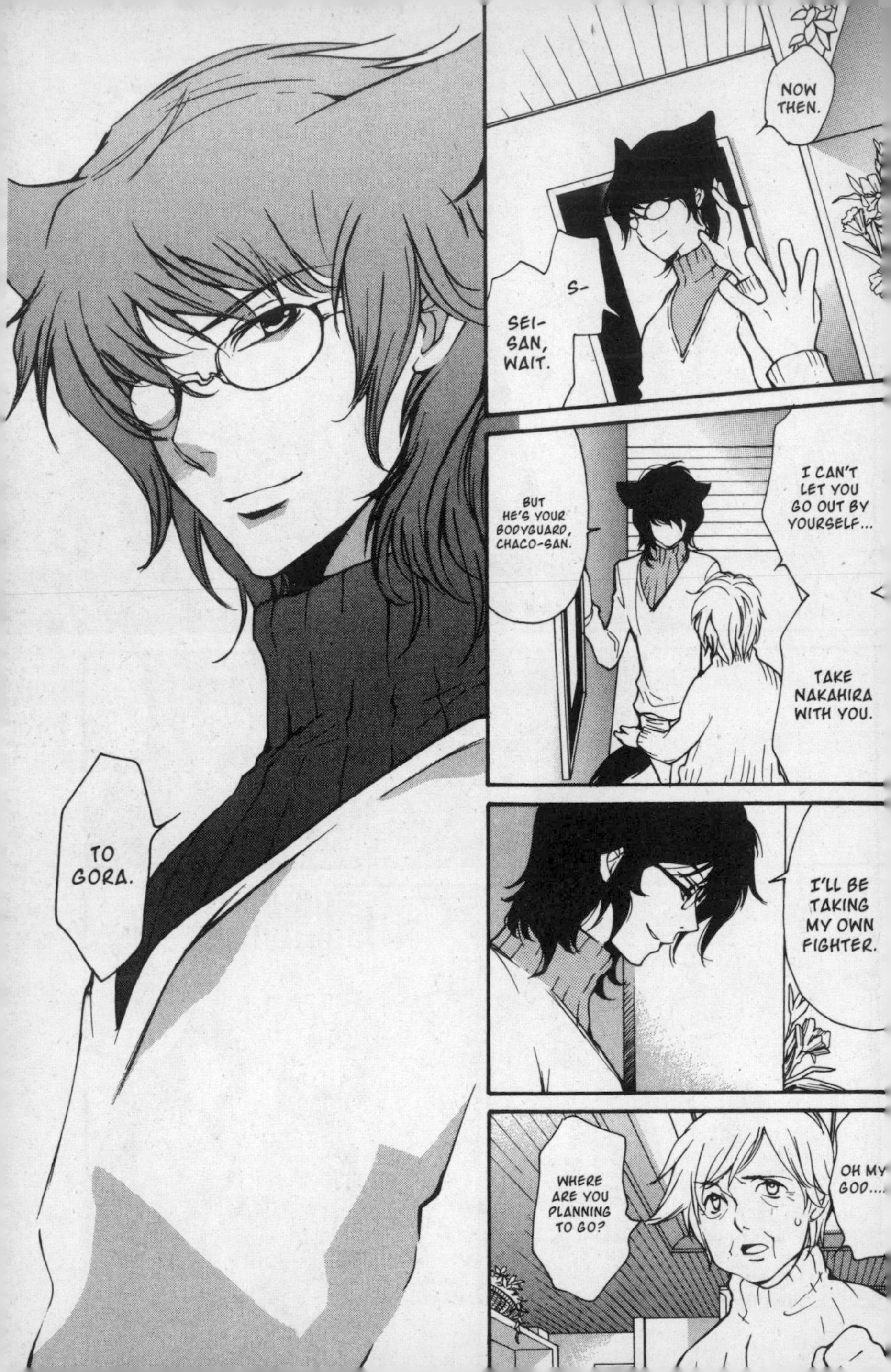

NOW THEN.
S-
SEI-SAN, WAIT.
I CAN'T LET YOU GO OUT BY YOURSELF...
TAKE NAKAHIRA WITH YOU.
BUT HE'S YOUR BODYGUARD, CHACO-SAN.
I'LL BE TAKING MY OWN FIGHTER.
OH MY GOD....
WHERE ARE YOU PLANNING TO GO?
TO GORA.

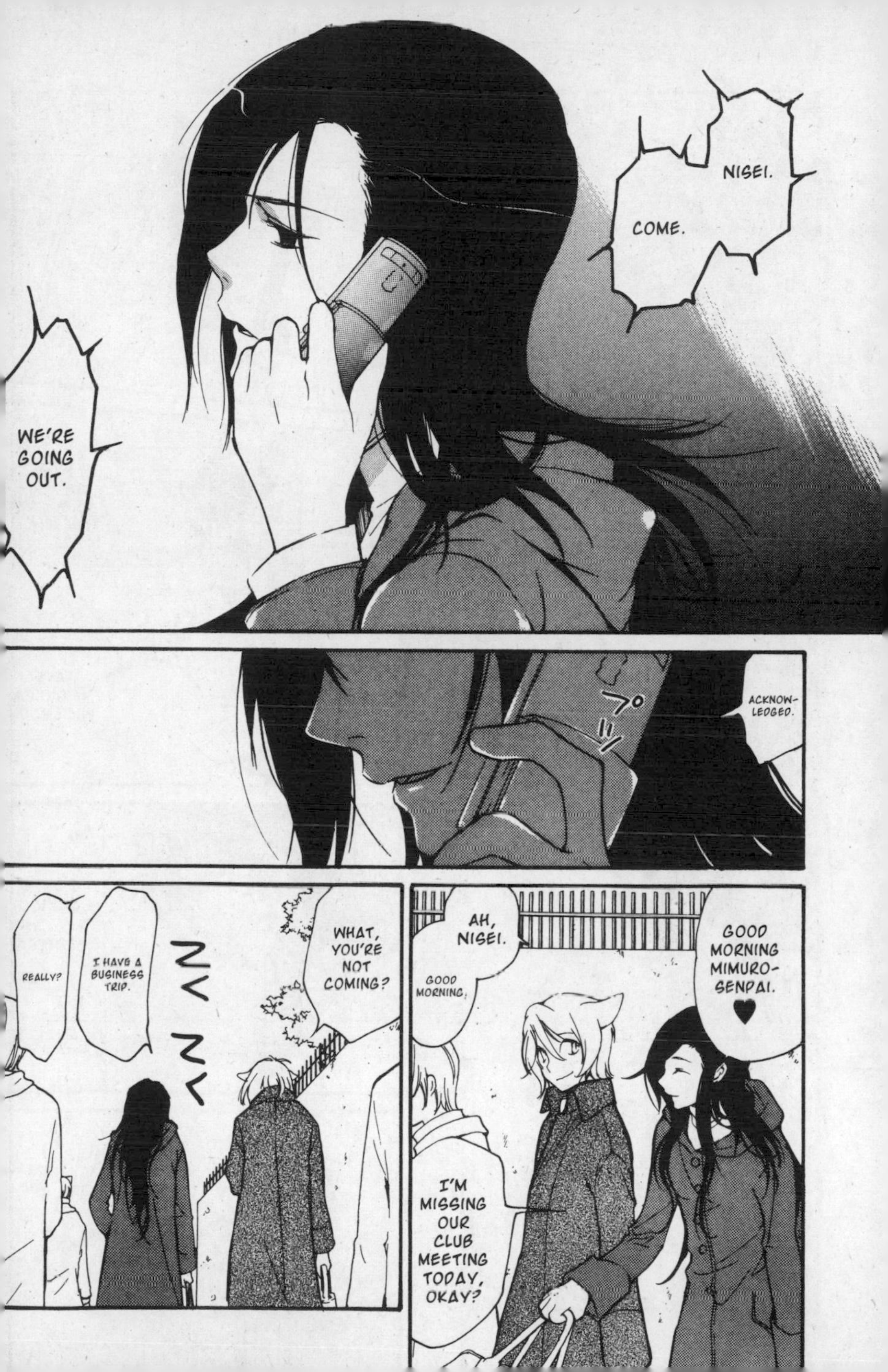
NISEI.
COME.
WE'RE GOING OUT.
ACKNOW-LEDGED.
プツ
GOOD MORNING MIMURO-SENPAI. ♥
AH, NISEI.
GOOD MORNING.
I'M MISSING OUR CLUB MEETING TODAY, OKAY?
WHAT, YOU'RE NOT COMING?
I HAVE A BUSINESS TRIP.
REALLY?

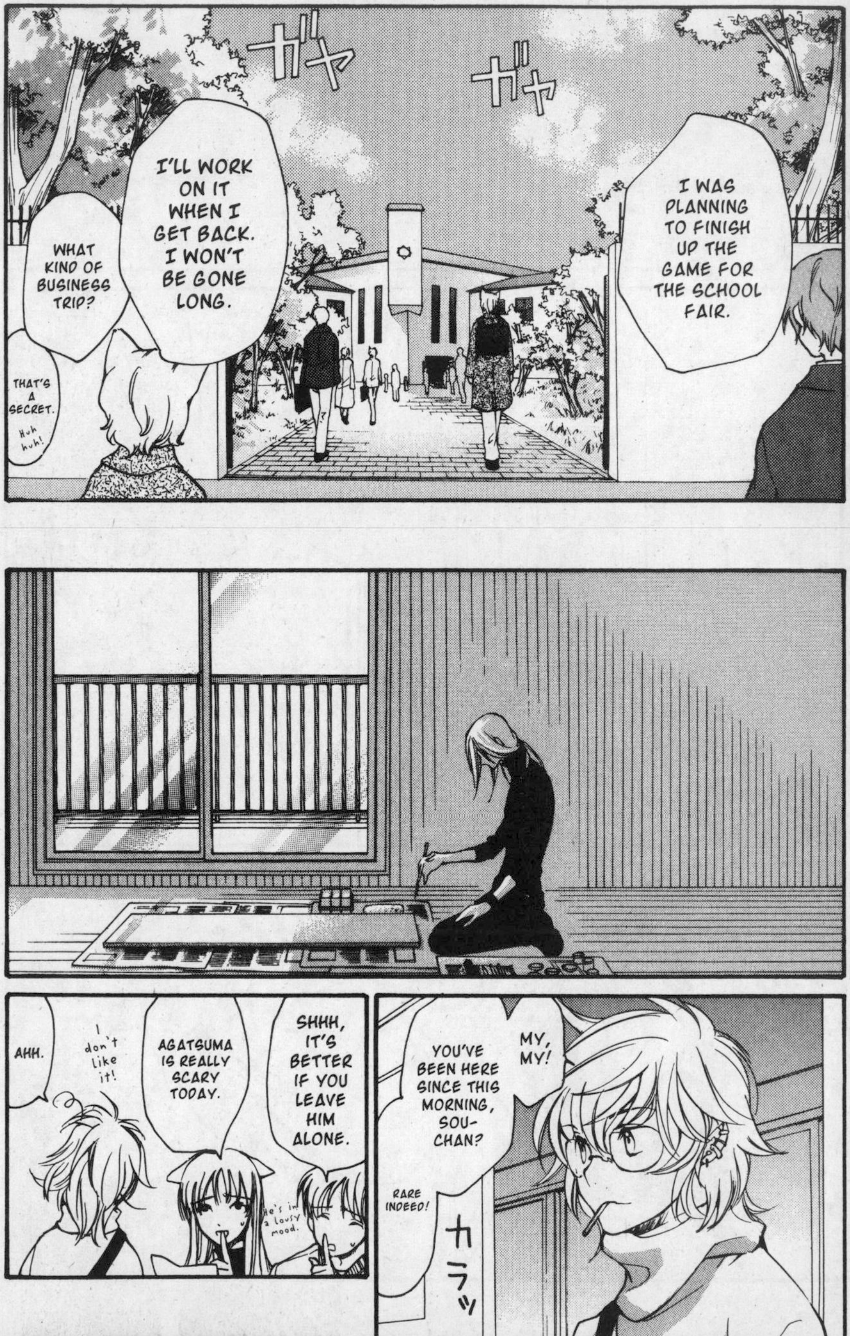
I WAS PLANNING TO FINISH UP THE GAME FOR THE SCHOOL FAIR.
ガヤ
ガヤ
I'LL WORK ON IT WHEN I GET BACK. I WON'T BE GONE LONG.
WHAT KIND OF BUSINESS TRIP?
THAT'S A SECRET.
Huh huh!
MY, MY!
YOU'VE BEEN HERE SINCE THIS MORNING, SOU-CHAN?
RARE INDEED!
カラッ
SHHH, IT'S BETTER IF YOU LEAVE HIM ALONE.
AGATSUMA IS REALLY SCARY TODAY.
I don't like it!
AHH.
He's in a lousy mood.

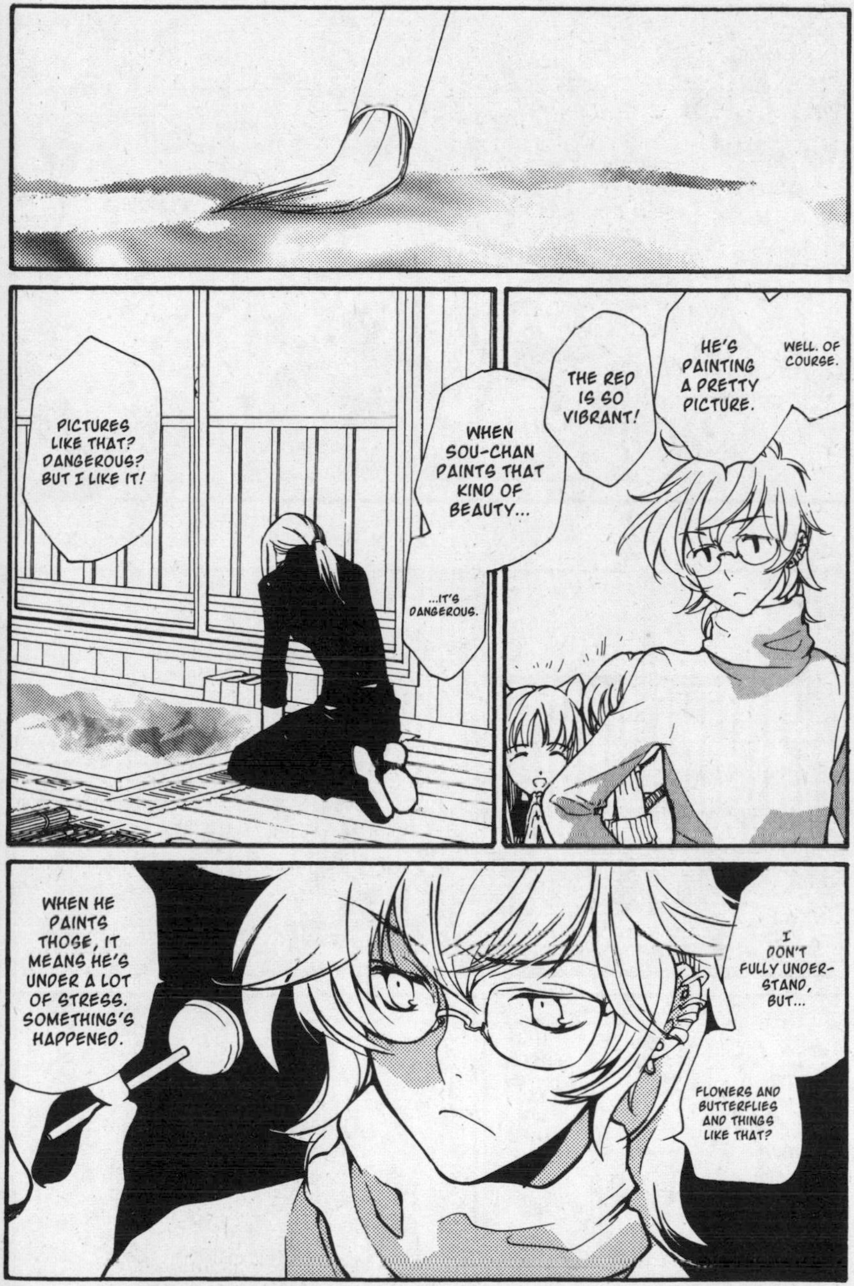
WELL. OF COURSE.
HE'S PAINTING A PRETTY PICTURE.
THE RED IS SO VIBRANT!
WHEN SOU-CHAN PAINTS THAT KIND OF BEAUTY...
...IT'S DANGEROUS.
PICTURES LIKE THAT? DANGEROUS? BUT I LIKE IT!
I DON'T FULLY UNDER-STAND, BUT...
FLOWERS AND BUTTERFLIES AND THINGS LIKE THAT?
WHEN HE PAINTS THOSE, IT MEANS HE'S UNDER A LOT OF STRESS. SOMETHING'S HAPPENED.

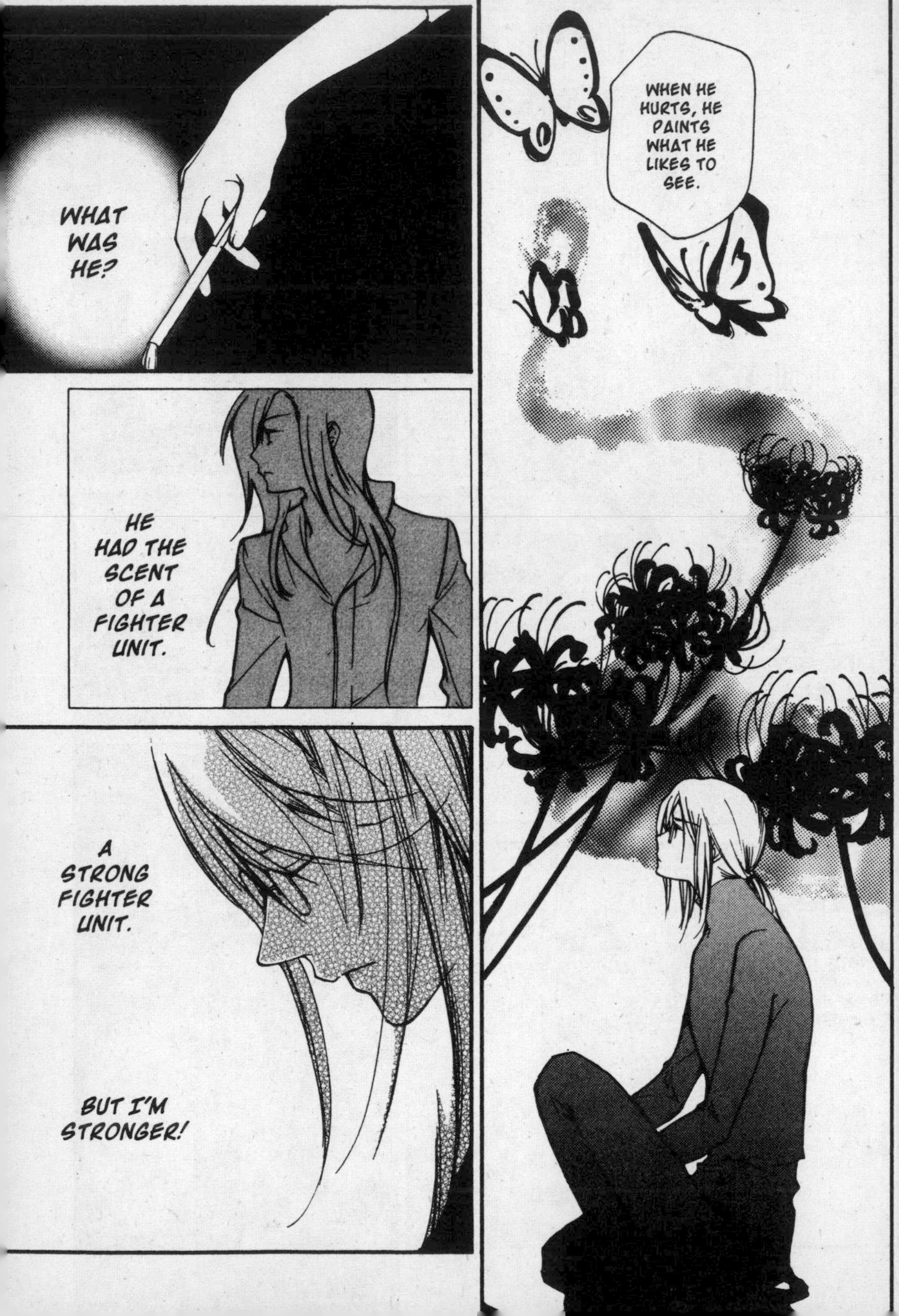
WHEN HE HURTS, HE PAINTS WHAT HE LIKES TO SEE.
WHAT WAS HE?
HE HAD THE SCENT OF A FIGHTER UNIT.
A STRONG FIGHTER UNIT.
BUT I'M STRONGER!

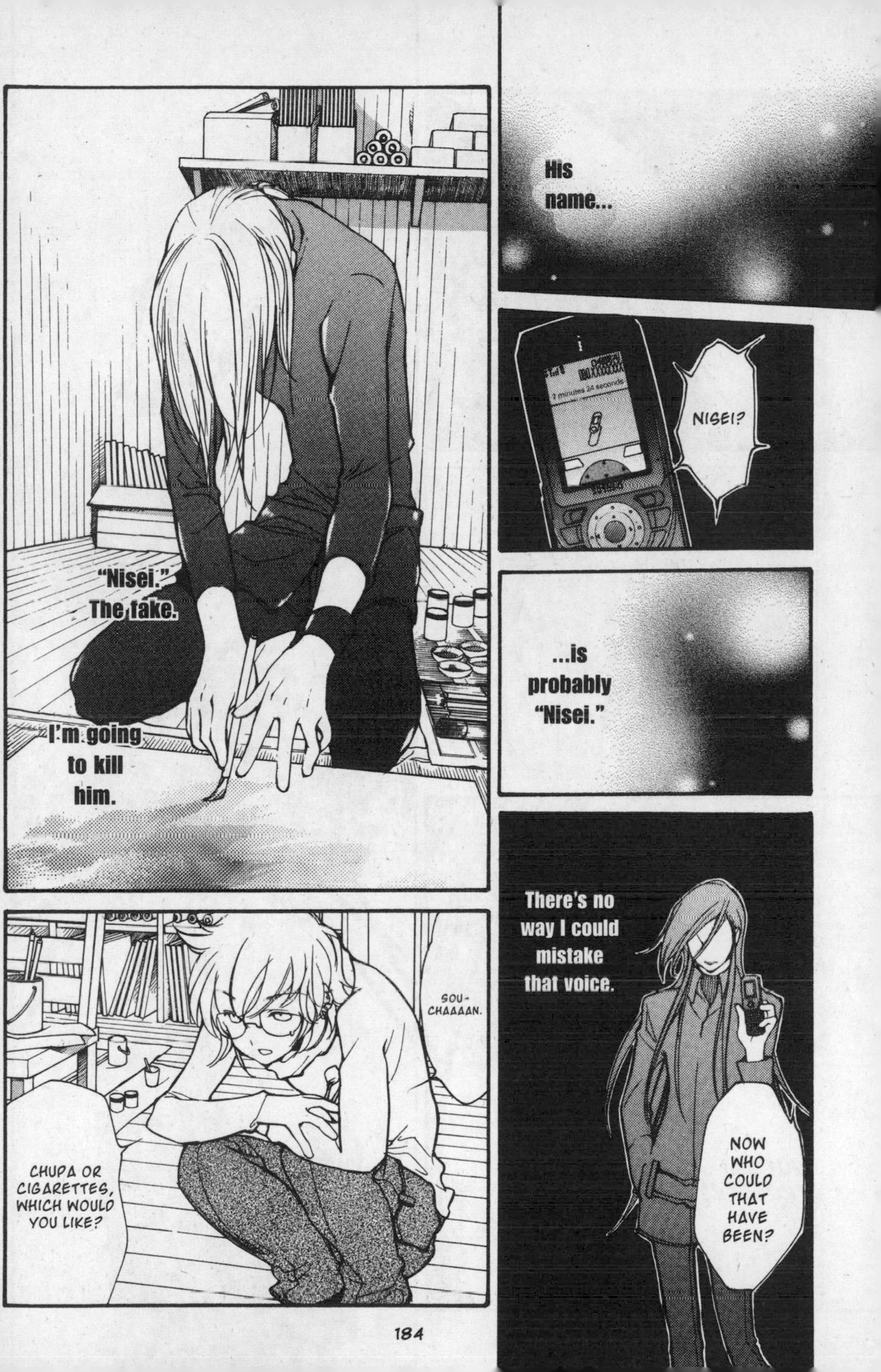
His name...
NISEI?
...is probably "Nisei."
There's no way I could mistake that voice.
NOW WHO COULD THAT HAVE BEEN?
"Nisei." The fake.
I'm going to kill him.
SOU-CHAAAAN.
CHUPA OR CIGARETTES, WHICH WOULD YOU LIKE?

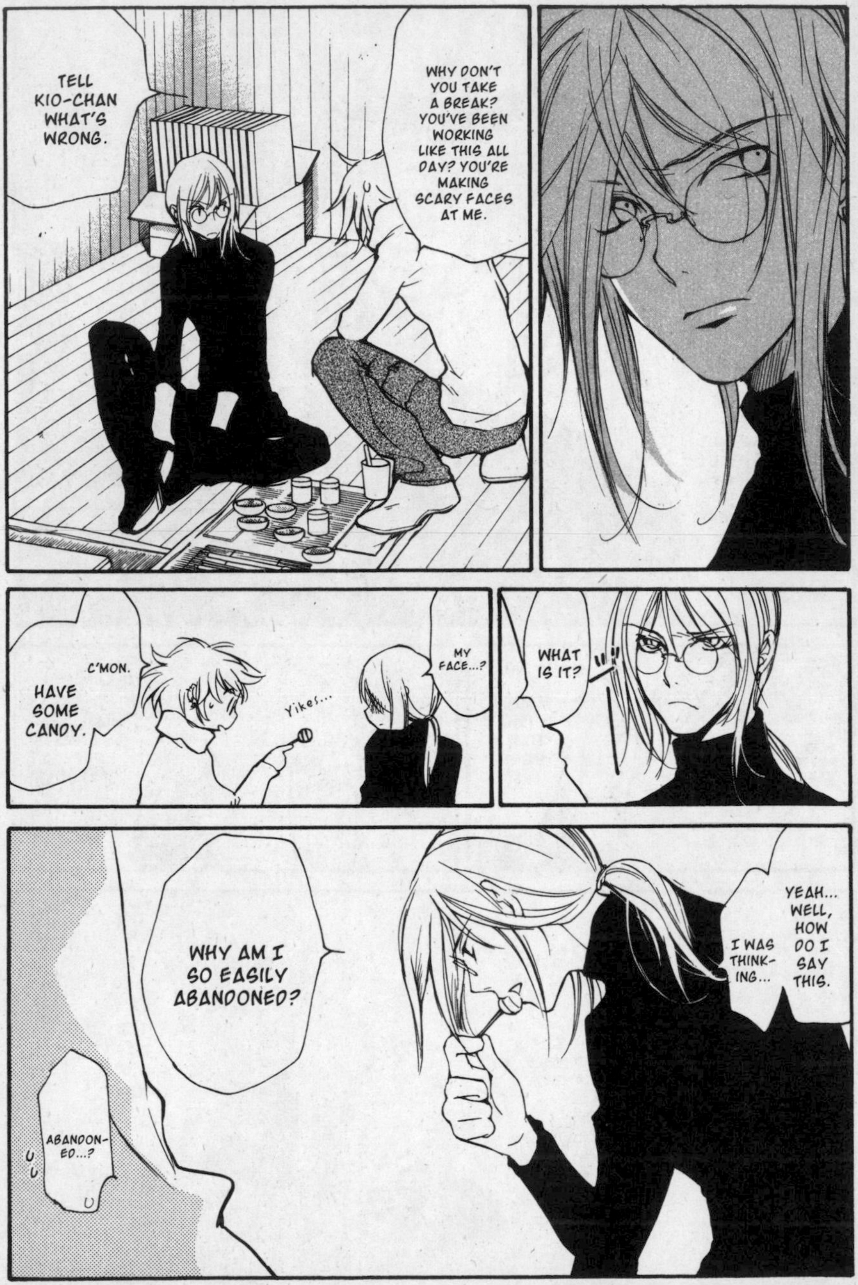
WHY DON'T YOU TAKE A BREAK? YOU'VE BEEN WORKING LIKE THIS ALL DAY? YOU'RE MAKING SCARY FACES AT ME.
TELL KIO-CHAN WHAT'S WRONG.
WHAT IS IT?
MY FACE...?
Yikes...
C'MON.
HAVE SOME CANDY.
YEAH... WELL, HOW DO I SAY THIS.
I WAS THINKING...
WHY AM I SO EASILY ABANDONED?
ABANDONED...?

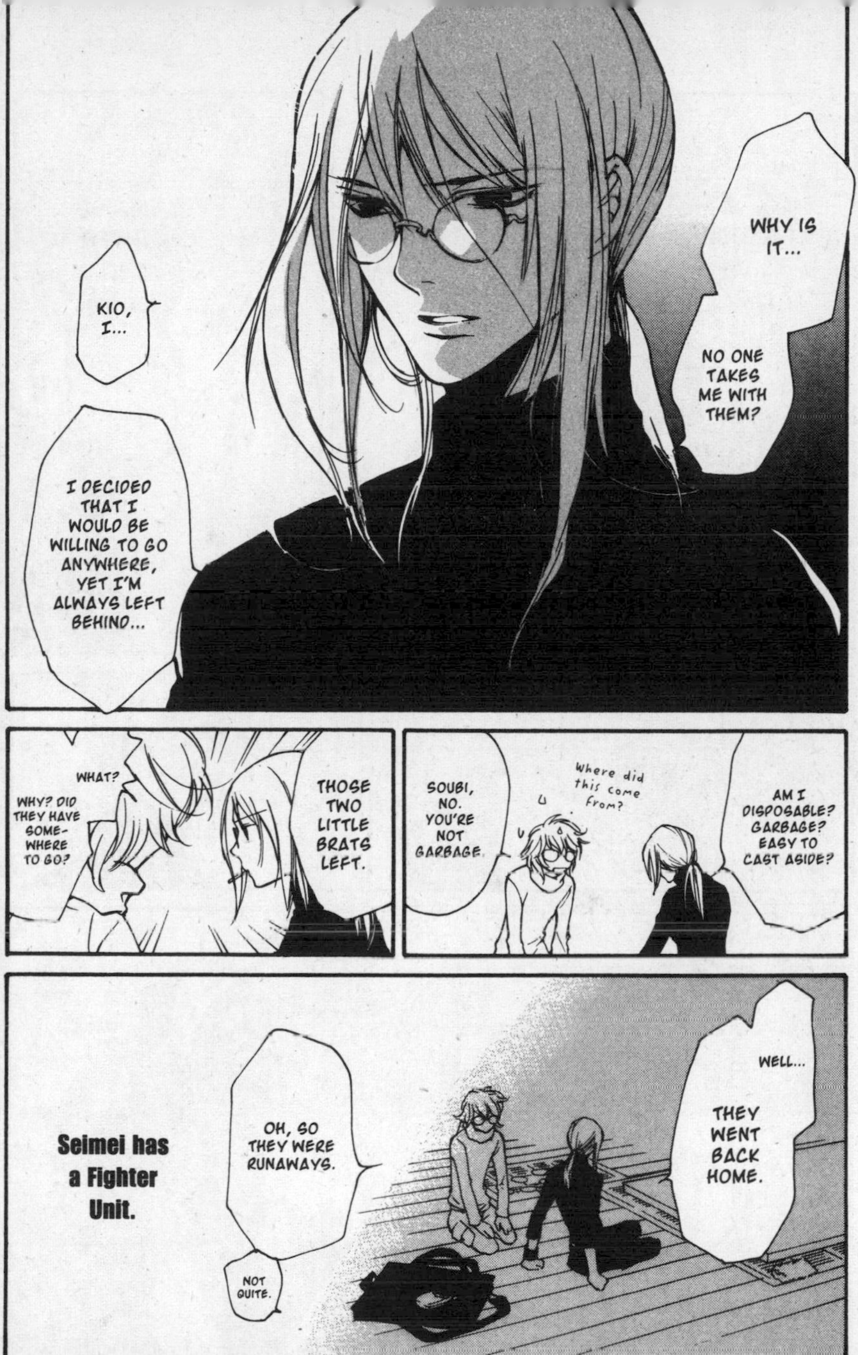
WHY IS IT...
NO ONE TAKES ME WITH THEM?
KIO, I...
I DECIDED THAT I WOULD BE WILLING TO GO ANYWHERE, YET I'M ALWAYS LEFT BEHIND...
AM I DISPOSABLE? GARBAGE? EASY TO CAST ASIDE?
Where did this come from?
SOUBI, NO. YOU'RE NOT GARBAGE.
THOSE TWO LITTLE BRATS LEFT.
WHAT?
WHY? DID THEY HAVE SOME-WHERE TO GO?
WELL...
THEY WENT BACK HOME.
OH, SO THEY WERE RUNAWAYS.
NOT QUITE.
Seimei has a Fighter Unit.

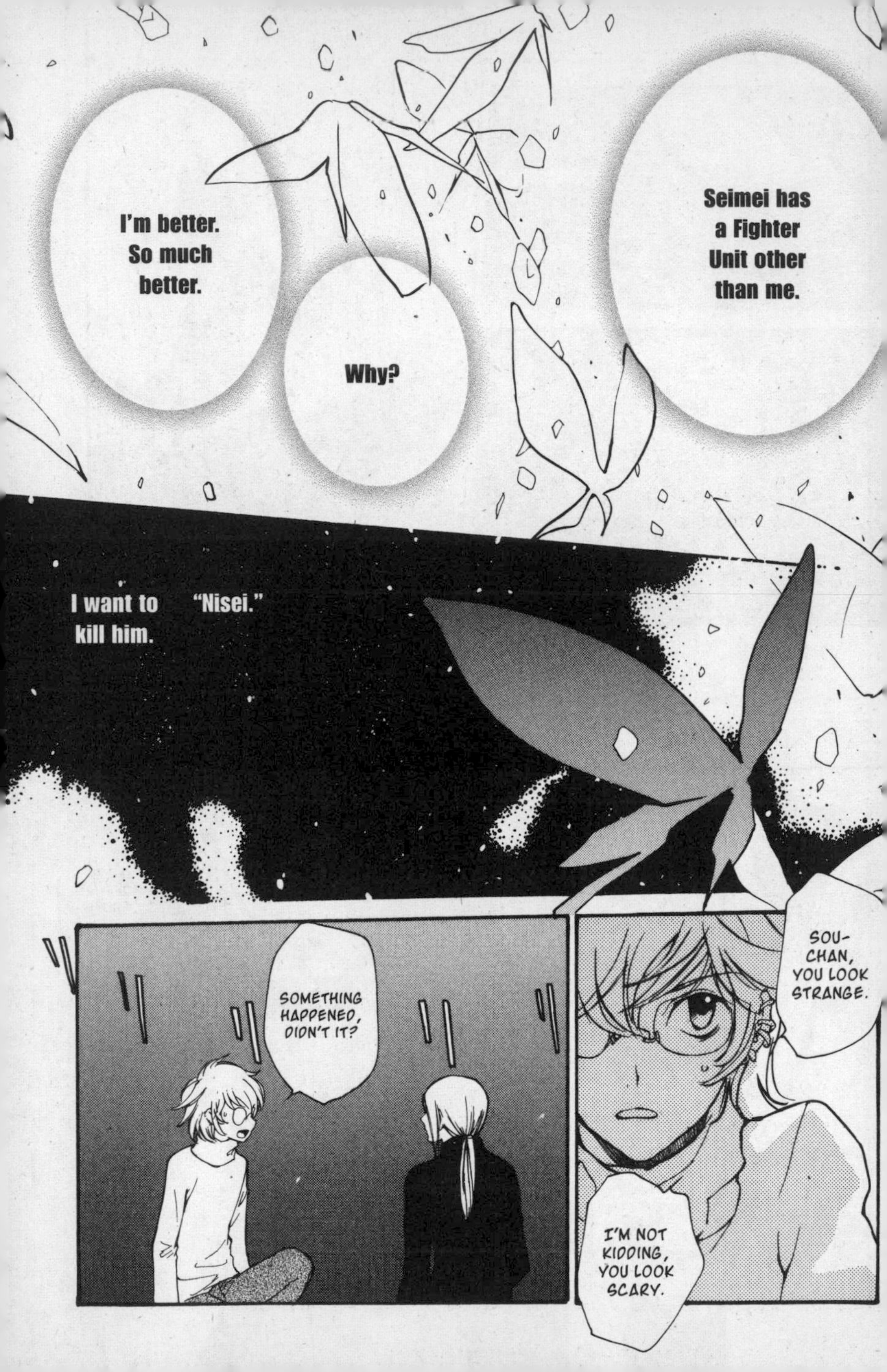
Seimei has a Fighter Unit other than me.
Why?
I'm better. So much better.
"Nisei."
I want to kill him.
SOU-CHAN, YOU LOOK STRANGE.
I'M NOT KIDDING, YOU LOOK SCARY.
SOMETHING HAPPENED, DIDN'T IT?

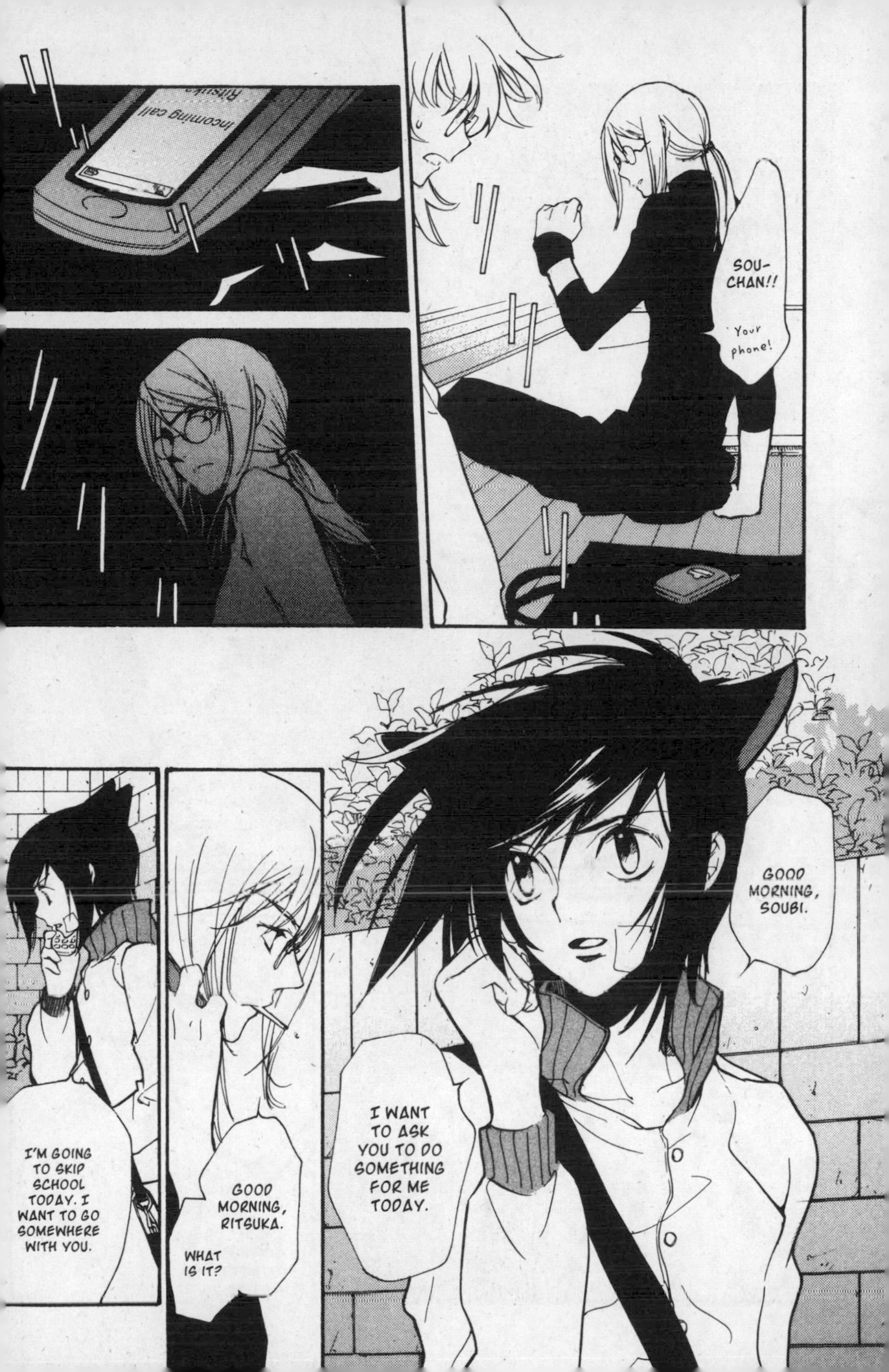
SOU-CHAN!!
Your phone!
Incoming call
Ritsuka
GOOD MORNING, SOUBI.
I WANT TO ASK YOU TO DO SOMETHING FOR ME TODAY.
GOOD MORNING, RITSUKA.
WHAT IS IT?
I'M GOING TO SKIP SCHOOL TODAY. I WANT TO GO SOMEWHERE WITH YOU.

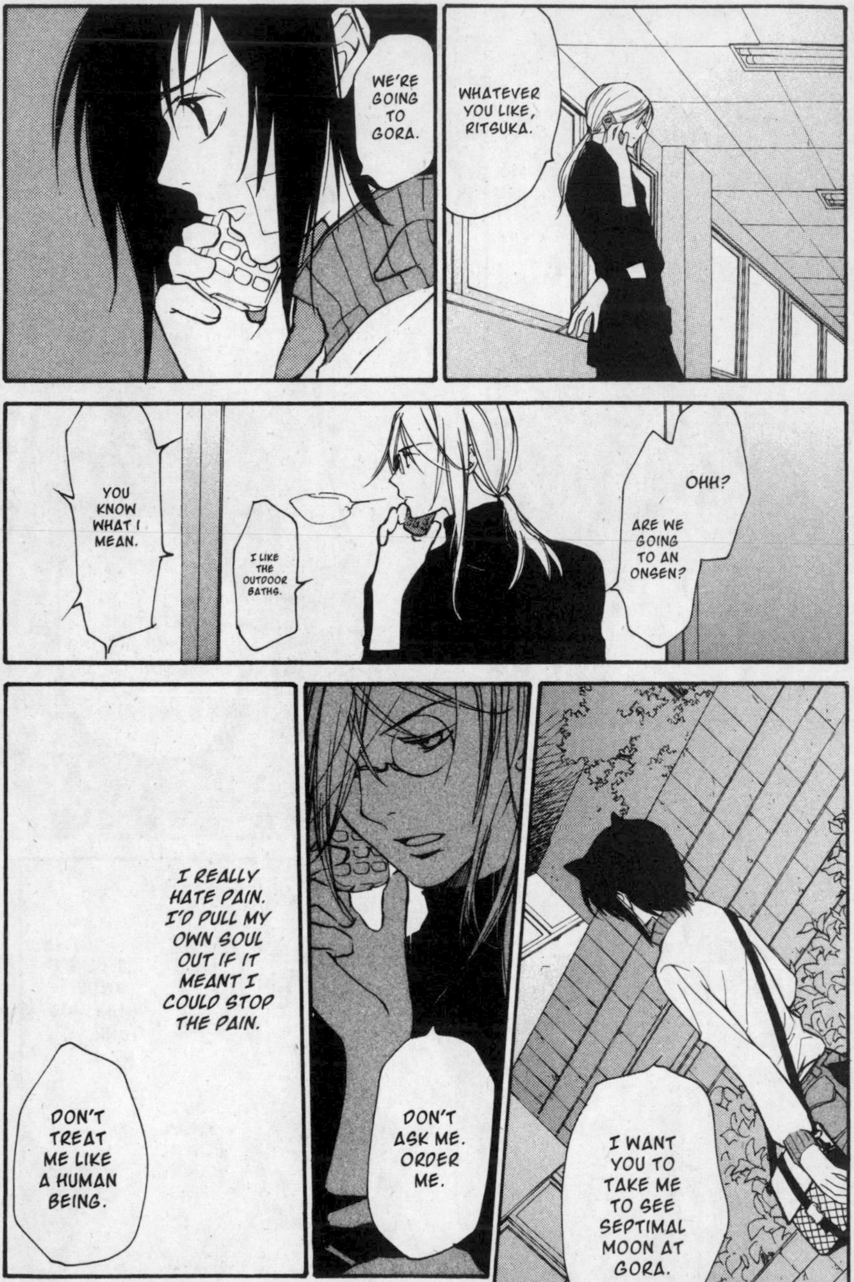
WHATEVER YOU LIKE, RITSUKA.
WE'RE GOING TO GORA.
OHH?
ARE WE GOING TO AN ONSEN?
I LIKE THE OUTDOOR BATHS.
YOU KNOW WHAT I MEAN.
I WANT YOU TO TAKE ME TO SEE SEPTIMAL MOON AT GORA.
DON'T ASK ME. ORDER ME.
I REALLY HATE PAIN. I'D PULL MY OWN SOUL OUT IF IT MEANT I COULD STOP THE PAIN.
DON'T TREAT ME LIKE A HUMAN BEING.

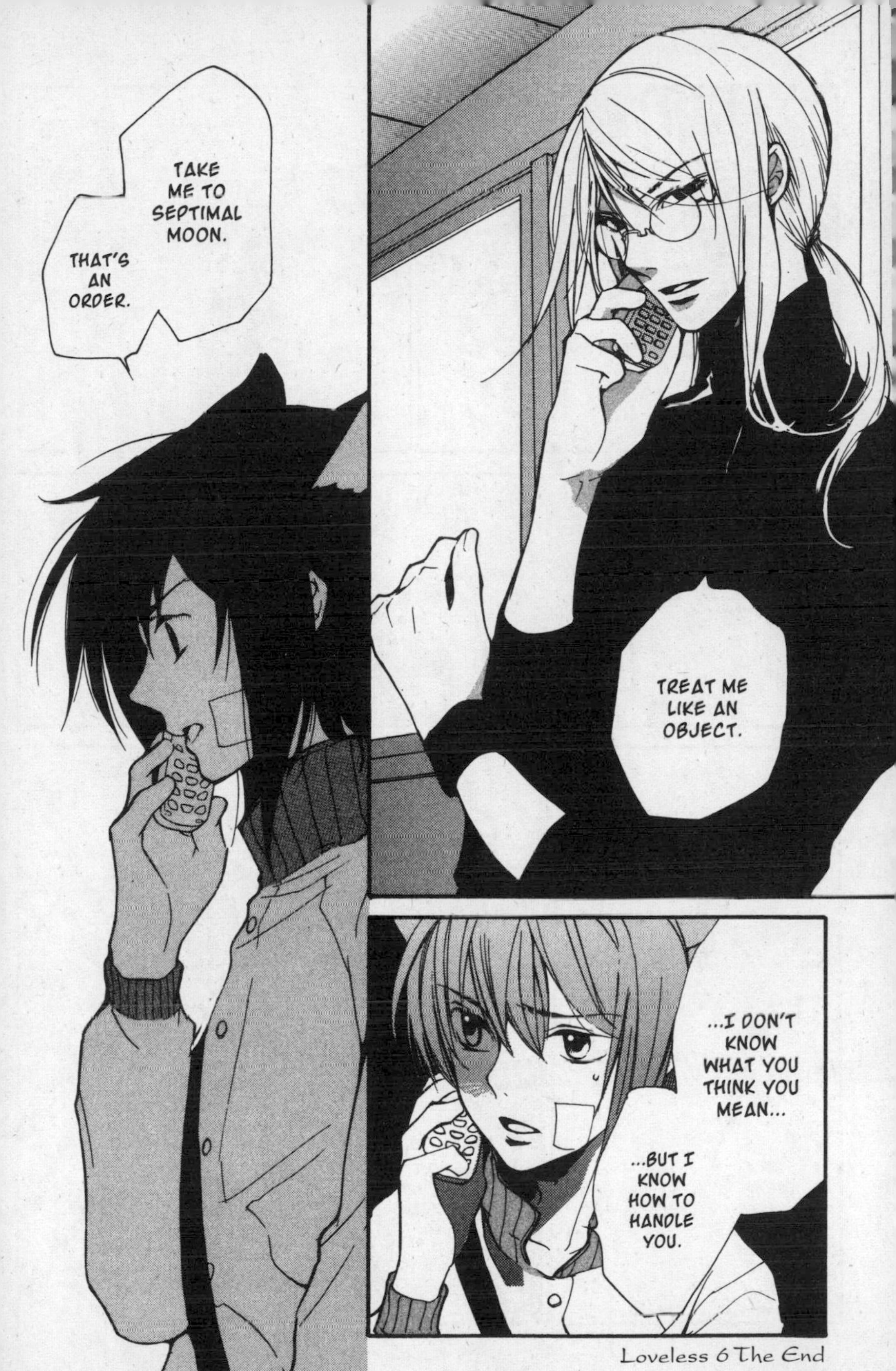
TREAT ME LIKE AN OBJECT.
...I DON'T KNOW WHAT YOU THINK YOU MEAN...
...BUT I KNOW HOW TO HANDLE YOU.
TAKE ME TO SEPTIMAL MOON.
THAT'S AN ORDER.

Loveless 6 The End

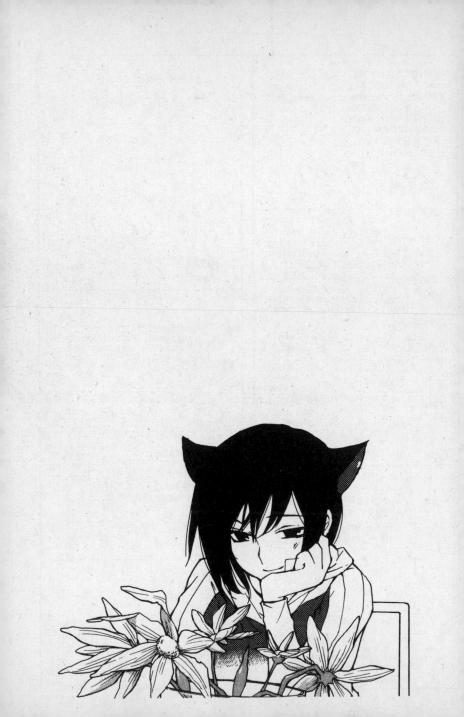

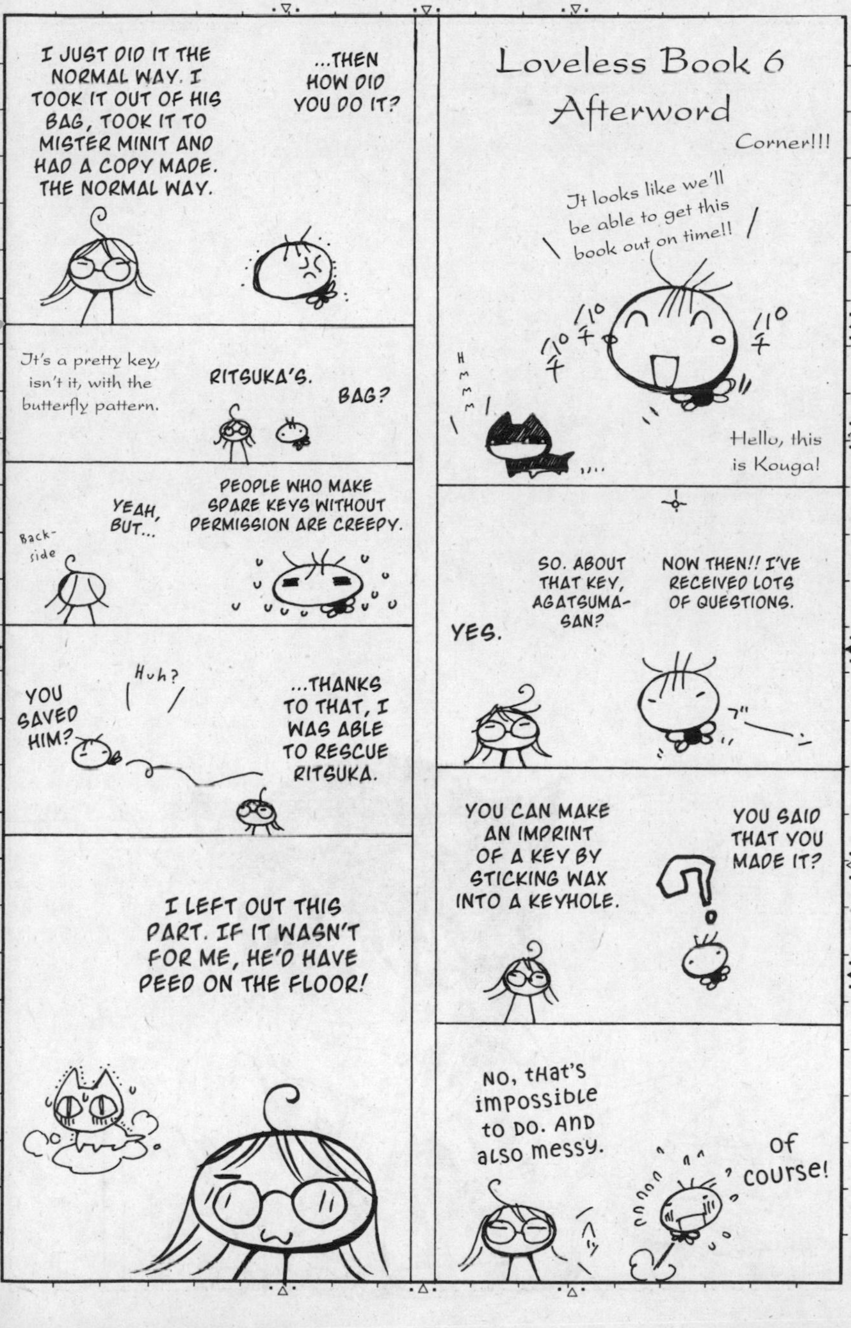
Loveless Book 6 Afterword
Corner!!!
It looks like we'll be able to get this book out on time!!
Hello, this is Kouga!
HMMM
NOW THEN!! I'VE RECEIVED LOTS OF QUESTIONS.
SO. ABOUT THAT KEY, AGATSUMA-SAN?
YES.
YOU SAID THAT YOU MADE IT?
YOU CAN MAKE AN IMPRINT OF A KEY BY STICKING WAX INTO A KEYHOLE.
Of course!
No, that's impossible to do. And also messy.
...THEN HOW DID YOU DO IT?
I JUST DID IT THE NORMAL WAY. I TOOK IT OUT OF HIS BAG, TOOK IT TO MISTER MINIT AND HAD A COPY MADE. THE NORMAL WAY.
BAG?
RITSUKA'S.
It's a pretty key, isn't it, with the butterfly pattern.
PEOPLE WHO MAKE SPARE KEYS WITHOUT PERMISSION ARE CREEPY.
YEAH, BUT...
Back-side
...THANKS TO THAT, I WAS ABLE TO RESCUE RITSUKA.
Huh?
YOU SAVED HIM?
I LEFT OUT THIS PART. IF IT WASN'T FOR ME, HE'D HAVE PEED ON THE FLOOR!

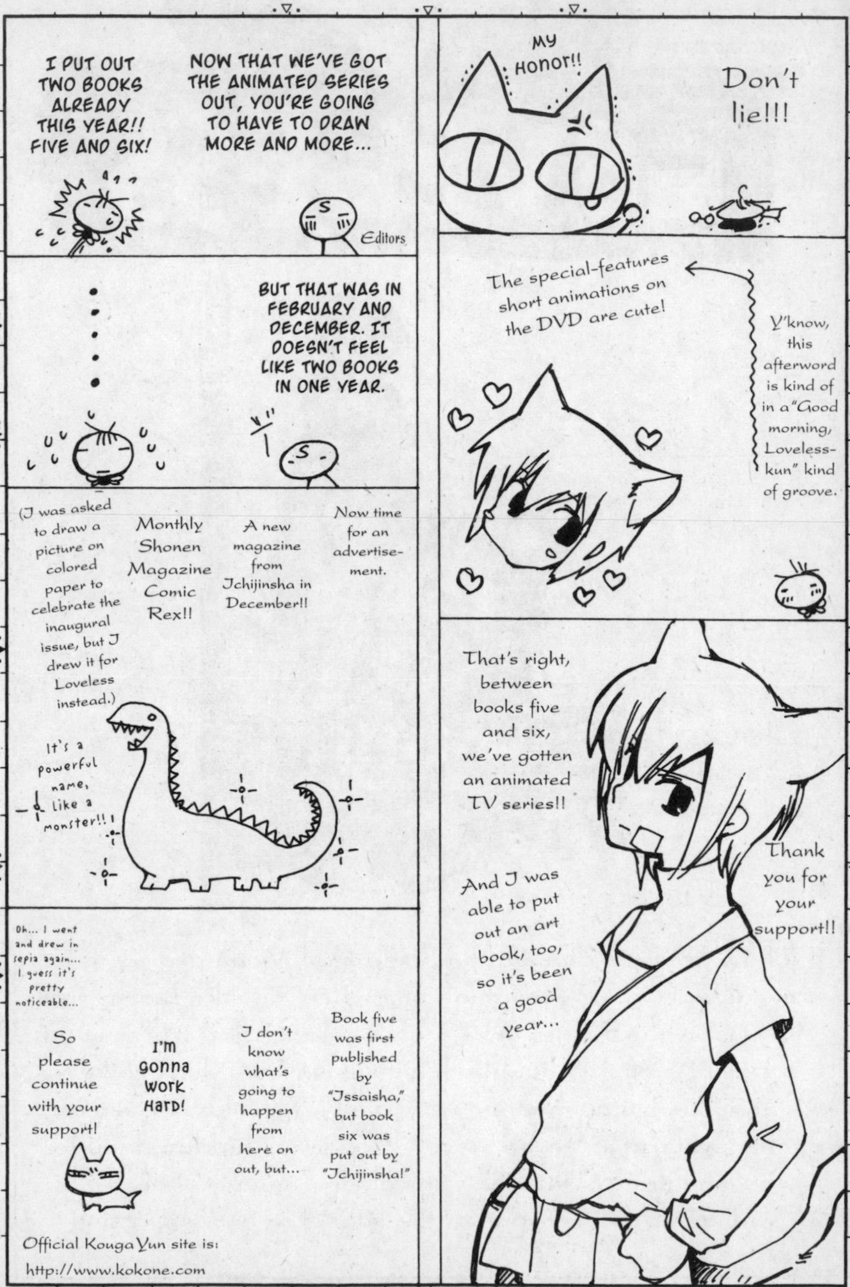
My Honor!!
Don't lie!!!
Y'know, this afterword is kind of in a "Good morning, Loveless-kun" kind of groove.
The special-features short animations on the DVD are cute!
That's right, between books five and six, we've gotten an animated TV series!!
And I was able to put out an art book, too, so it's been a good year...
Thank you for your support!!
I PUT OUT TWO BOOKS ALREADY THIS YEAR!! FIVE AND SIX!
NOW THAT WE'VE GOT THE ANIMATED SERIES OUT, YOU'RE GOING TO HAVE TO DRAW MORE AND MORE...
Editors
BUT THAT WAS IN FEBRUARY AND DECEMBER. IT DOESN'T FEEL LIKE TWO BOOKS IN ONE YEAR.
Now time for an advertisement.
A new magazine from Ichijinsha in December!!
Monthly Shonen Magazine Comic Rex!!
(I was asked to draw a picture on colored paper to celebrate the inaugural issue, but I drew it for Loveless instead.)
It's a powerful name, like a monster!!
Book five was first published by "Issaisha," but book six was put out by "Ichijinsha!"
I don't know what's going to happen from here on out, but...
I'M GONNA WORK HARD!
So please continue with your support!
Oh... I went and drew in sepia again... I guess it's pretty noticeable...
Official Kouga Yun site is:
http://www.kokone.com

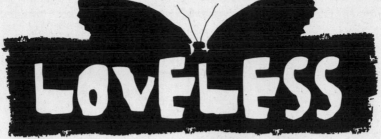

In The Next Volume of

LOVELESS

TOKYOPOP
LOVELESS
by Yun Kouga
6

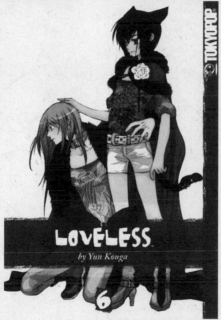

The journey to Gora to find Septimal Moon proves to be revealing in more ways than one when Ritsuka learns from Kio just what Seimei and Soubi's relationship truly meant. Full of anxiety about both his memories of his brother and his own connection with Soubi, Ritsuka arrives at the mysterious Seven Voices Academy, hidden deep in the mountains. But when unwelcome guests show up, it will be up to everyone at the school to try and resist!

Loveless Vol. 7 Available November 2007

The dissonance (or not) between high and low art:

I recently had the pleasure of consulting with a local high-school student writing a paper on manga. She came into the office for the day (lucky girl, right?), and she and I found a quiet corner where we could discuss different artistic styles used in shojo manga and how different techniques create different atmospheres-everything from ink weight and spot blacks, to tones, to how the panels of the page fit together help to define what sort of manga you are reading. A manga artist chooses his or her techniques carefully in order to convey both emotion and action. It might seem simple and easy, but visual storytelling is a sophisticated process, worthy of artistic recognition in its own right.

The juncture between popular culture and art has always been far more fluid than many believe. Literature that is now touted as "classic" often started off as popular serialized novels—"junk" that was intended for the entertainment of the masses (and, in the case of a certain famous Dickens story, caused mass hysteria when new installments were released). But the passage of a decade or ten can put a new perspective on what once seemed like trash. And comics, whether in the United States or Japan, have followed a similar trajectory. From their roots in the dime stores of the early 20th century, through two world wars and into the modern period, the parallel development of the two industries has started to reach a point where the mainstream sees value and merit in the stories told and the worlds rendered so carefully. Comics are no long automatically considered a disposable medium, good only for light entertainment and warping young minds.

Loveless, as an example of a medium currently considered by most to be "low art," still achieves a very "high art" level of complexity of storytelling and characterization, but the book itself occasionally toys with these cultural boundaries internally, as well. Soubi is both a practitioner of fine art, as we see in his college classes with Kio, and he is a very accomplished one. He is a graceful and expressive artist whose talent and ease impress his classmates, and who can capture his own emotional turmoil in his work. But he is a master of low culture, as well, as demonstrated in his video-game prowess, which impresses even the Zero boys. Similarly, Seven, who is clearly a bit of an otaku, with her cartoon key chains and plastic figurines, lives very much in a virtual world, but the skills that she has gained there will prove to be essential as our story progresses. She is an artist who creates magic through computer code and can protect her friends and the school through her creative prowess. In a particularly charming but poignant scene, Yuiko misconstrues Yayoi's wish to be a novelist with being a manga creator, but, either way, Ritsuka volunteers to help contribute to the artistic effort (and hopes that "this Ritsuka" will be around to remember his promise).

The story that unfolds through the medium of Wisdom Resurrection is also a crucial part of the revelation about Seimei, and the game continues to be a communication device and gathering place over the course of several volumes. There are volumes to be learned through the digital worlds of current popular culture, and perhaps a new form of storytelling is already evolving through those worlds that will one day yield the new classics of a new kind of literature.

~Lillian Diaz-Przybyl

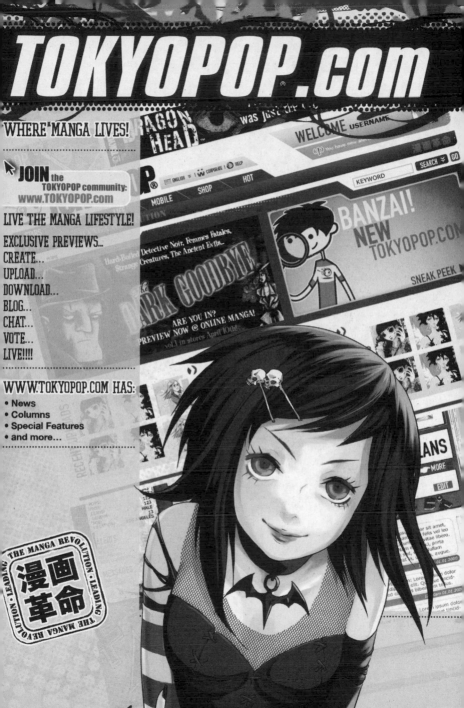

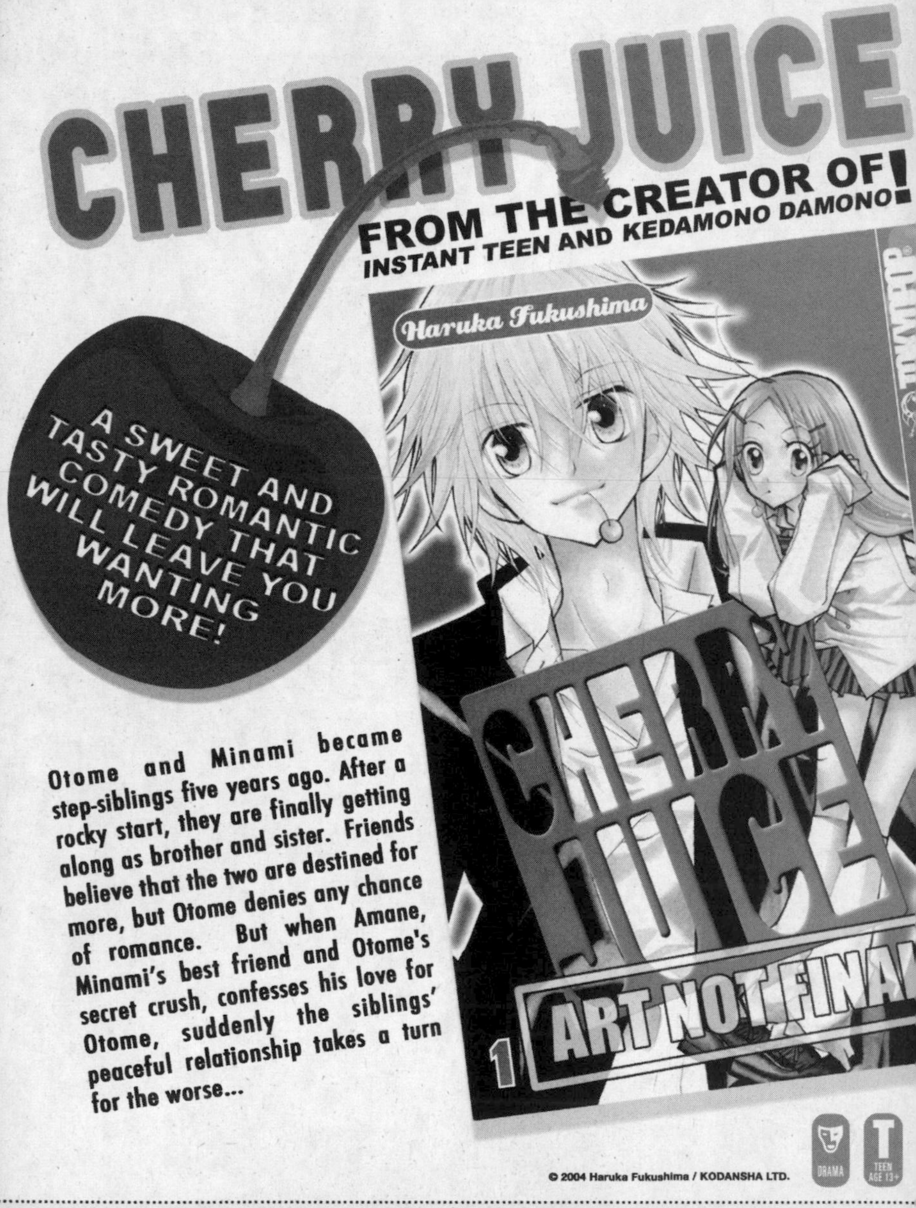
CHERRY JUICE
FROM THE CREATOR OF INSTANT TEEN AND KEDAMONO DAMONO!
A SWEET AND TASTY ROMANTIC COMEDY THAT WILL LEAVE YOU WANTING MORE!
Haruka Fukushima
TOKYOPOP
CHERRY JUICE
1 ART NOT FINAL
Otome and Minami became step-siblings five years ago. After a rocky start, they are finally getting along as brother and sister. Friends believe that the two are destined for more, but Otome denies any chance of romance. But when Amane, Minami's best friend and Otome's secret crush, confesses his love for Otome, suddenly the siblings' peaceful relationship takes a turn for the worse...
© 2004 Haruka Fukushima / KODANSHA LTD.
DRAMA
T
TEEN AGE 13+

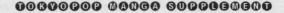

TOKYOPOP MANG

DARK MOON DIARY™

After losing her parents in a tragic accident, Priscilla goes to live in a new town with her aunt's family. As if adjusting to a new family wouldn't be tough enough, her relatives turn out to be vampires who live in the ghoul-filled town of Nachtwald! Priscilla tries hard to assimilate, but with a ghost for a teacher, a witch as a friend, and food that winks at you, can she ever adapt to life in her new town? Or will she pack her garlic and head back to normal-ville?

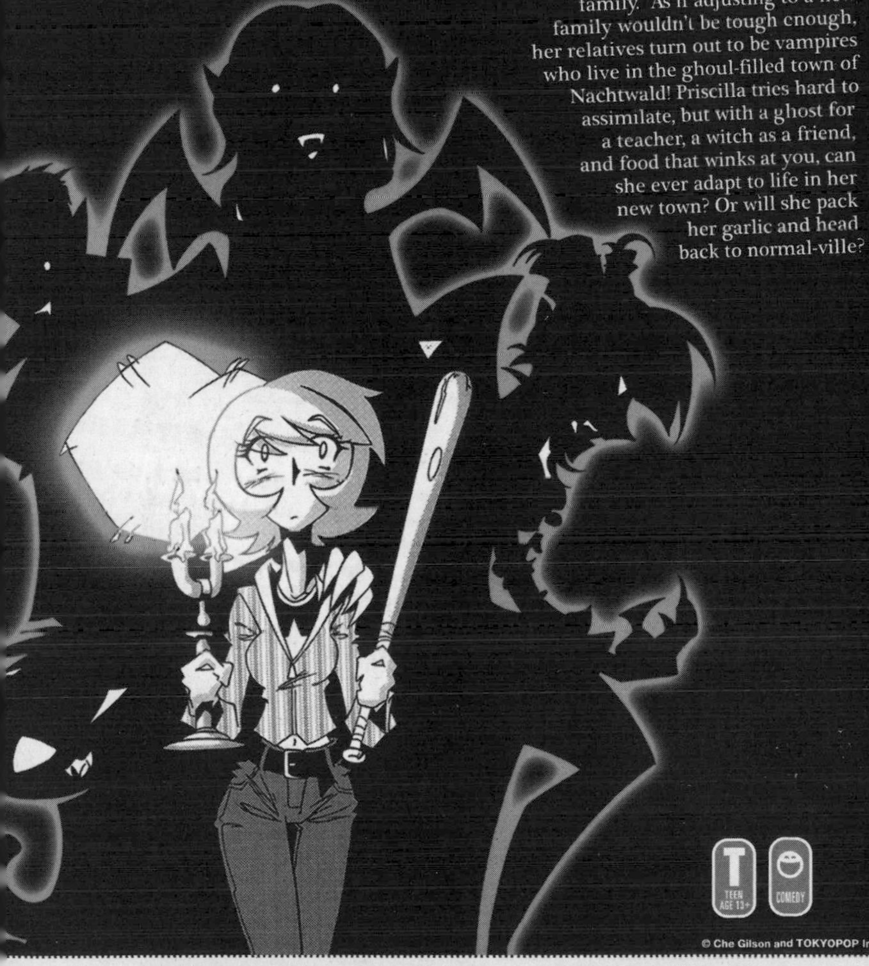

T TEEN AGE 13+

COMEDY

FOR MORE INFORMATION VISIT: WWW.TOKYOPOP.COM